A Concise History
of the
Second World War

Its Origin, Battles
and Consequences

Richard Z. Freemann, Jr.

HOOSICK FALLS, NEW YORK
2019

First published in 2016 by the Merriam Press

Second Edition (2019)

ISBN 978-0-359-75407-6
Library of Congress Control Number: 2016906035

This work was designed, produced, and published in
the United States of America by the

Merriam Press
489 South Street
Hoosick Falls NY 12090

E-mail: ray@merriam-press.com
Web site: merriam-press.com

The Merriam Press publishes new manuscripts on historical subjects, especially military history and with an emphasis on World War II, as well as reprinting previously published works, including reports, documents, manuals, articles and other materials on historical topics.

Dedication

This book is dedicated to my father, my uncle and my father-in-law, each of whom faced danger while serving honorably in the United States military during World War II.

Contents

Introduction 9

Photographs 11

Maps 29

Part 1: The Seeds of War 45

    Germany 45

    The Soviet Union 55

    The British Empire 61

    Japan 63

    The United States 68

    Italy 72

    France 75

Part 2: The Conflict in Europe and North Africa 79

    The Hostilities Begin (1939) 79

    Axis Aggression in Europe (1940) 84

    War Waged in Europe and North Africa (1941) 102

    The European Battles Intensify (1942) 121

    The Tide Begins to Turn in Europe (1943) 135

    Germany in Retreat (1944) 163

    The Final Year of Combat in Europe (1945) 207

Part 3: War in the Pacific 223

    Japan Starts A War Against China (1937) 223

    The Sino-Japanese War Expands (1938) 225

    The Conflicts in Asia Continue (1939) 226

Japanese Territorial Expansion (1940) 227

Japan Attacks Across the Far East (1941) 230

The First Full Year of Total War in Asia (1942) 246

The Tide Begins to Turn in the Pacific (1943) 270

Japan in Retreat (1944)..276

The Final Year of Combat in the Pacific (1945) 288

Part 4: World War II's Human and Economic Toll 305

Military and Civilian Deaths 305

Psychiatric Damage...309

Physical Damage 310

Military Misconduct 310

Blacks..311

Women 311

Hunger and Homelessness..312

Prisoners of War and Forced Labor 312

Hostage Executions...313

Biological and Chemical Warfare and Medical Experiments 314

German Plunder..314

Troop Levels 315

Submarine Warfare 316

United States War Production and Economic Aid.................316

Part 5: Reflections on World War II 319

Criminal Prosecutions 319

Intended and Unintended Consequences..............................323

Ethical Questions..332

Sources...335

Maps 27

Europe after the Treaty of Versailles 27

Europe before World War II (1939) 28

North Africa 1942 29

Operation Barbarossa: the German invasion of the Soviet Union, 21 June 1941 to 5 December 1941 30

The Soviet winter counter-offensive, 5 December 1941 to 7 May 1942 ...31

Operation Blue: German advances from 7 May 1942 to 18 November 1942 32

Operations Uranus, Saturn and Mars: Soviet advances on the Eastern Front, 18 November 1942 to March 1943 33

German advances at Kharkov and Kursk, 19 February 1943 to 1 August 1943 34

Soviet advances from 1 August 1943 to 31 December 1944 35

Soviet advances from 1 January 1945 to 11 May 1945 36

Operation Husky, Invasion of Sicily, 1943 37

Italian Campaign, 1943-45 38

Allied invasion plans and German positions in Normandy, 1944 39

Wacht am Rhein: Battle of the Bulge 40

China, Korea, Manchuria, 1930s 41

Pacific Theater, 1941-45 42

Introduction

IN the history of human existence, no conflict has cratered the earth, its people and their ways of living like World War II. The battles that blazed across the globe from the late 1930s until 1945 caused more than sixty million deaths. Almost every corner of society heard gunfire. Nations were destroyed, others founded, and some re-configured. Philosophies of government were tested and frequently found lacking. Reputations were won and lost. Tyranny was commonplace. Some, but not all tyrants were toppled. For many decades now, civilization has shuddered at the brutal impact of this war.

This writing aspires to present the tale of World War II in a concise yet digestible fashion, and to stimulate the reader to delve further into its history. Consider questions such as these:

- When, where and how did the combatants face the challenges of this brutal conflict?
- Who sided with whom, why, and what help did each participant furnish?
- Who evidenced courage and when did cowardice prevail?
- Where were the military successes and blunders?
- Were the techniques of war ethically appropriate?
- How, why and when did the fighting end?
- What were the intended and unintended consequences of World War II?
- Where did the loss of life strike hardest?
- What were the economic and social tolls and achievements?
- What of lasting value has civilization gleaned from the conflict?

In addition to the "What, Where and When" of war, it is appropriate to consider what forces and flaws contributed to the war's emergence. The following may be found in almost any war, but all were abundant in World War II:

- Ambition for increased food supplies and natural resources.
- Hunger for territorial gains.
- Retribution for perceived wrongs.
- Expressions of nationalism.
- Critical alliances and failed compacts.
- Troubled economies.
- Expanding and contracting political power.
- Isolationism.
- A contest between theories of government, *e.g.*, Communism versus capitalism.
- Efforts to eradicate ethnic groups.
- Totalitarian regimes.

This book begins with a review of the events and circumstances that gave birth to the conflict. Then comes a discussion of the war's action in every significant theater of combat — North Africa, Europe, the Soviet Union, Southeast Asia, the Pacific islands and Japan. The history is presented not in conventional prose, but in nuggets of information designed to provide substance without extended length.

In any book on World War II, the author faces a challenge. Should all events be presented in pure chronological order, or is the material more comprehensible if divided in some logical way? I have elected to separate the events of the war into two parts — the European/North African battlegrounds and the conflicts in the Pacific theater. While this approach has the disadvantage of bifurcating the time line of events, hopefully it offers the advantage of an improved understanding of action in each major war locale.

The writing closes with a discussion of the human and economic costs of the conflict, an evaluation of the intended and unintended consequences of World War II, and ethical questions the war has brought to the surface.

Adolf Hitler.

Winston Churchill.

A CONCISE HISTORY OF THE SECOND WORLD WAR

Franklin D. Roosevelt.

Joseph Stalin.

A CONCISE HISTORY OF THE SECOND WORLD WAR

Benito Mussolini.

Hirohito.

A CONCISE HISTORY OF THE SECOND WORLD WAR

Chiang Kai-shek.

George Marshall.

A Concise History of the Second World War

Alan Brooke.

Dwight Eisenhower.

A CONCISE HISTORY OF THE SECOND WORLD WAR

George S. Patton.

Bernard Montgomery.

A CONCISE HISTORY OF THE SECOND WORLD WAR

Omar Bradley.

Douglas MacArthur.

A CONCISE HISTORY OF THE SECOND WORLD WAR

Ernest King.

Chester Nimitz.

A CONCISE HISTORY OF THE SECOND WORLD WAR

Isoroku Yamamoto.

Erwin Rommel.

A Concise History of the Second World War

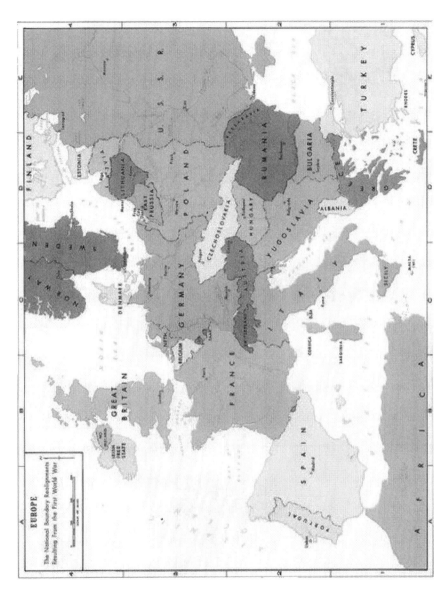

This is a map of Europe after the Treaty of Versailles. Germany got smaller, Austria-Hungary was split into Austria and Hungary, and the Ottoman Empire was disbanded and became Turkey.

Europe before World War II (1939).

A CONCISE HISTORY OF THE SECOND WORLD WAR

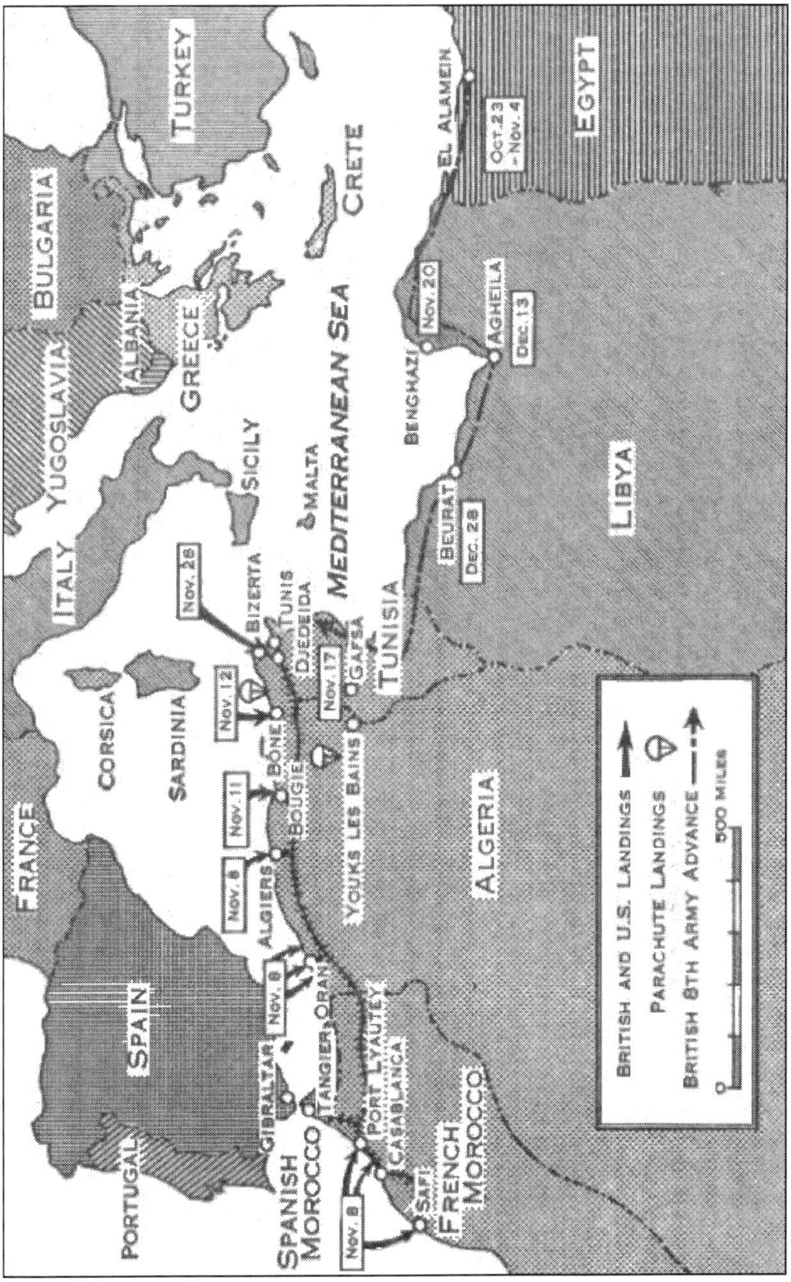

FRANCE
SPAIN
PORTUGAL
ITALY
YUGOSLAVIA
BULGARIA
ALBANIA
GREECE
TURKEY
CORSICA
SARDINIA
SICILY
MALTA
CRETE
MEDITERRANEAN SEA
SPANISH MOROCCO
FRENCH MOROCCO
ALGERIA
TUNISIA
LIBYA
EGYPT
GIBRALTAR
TANGIER
PORT LYAUTEY
CASABLANCA
SAFI
ORAN
ALGIERS
BOUGIE
BONE
BIZERTA
TUNIS
DJEDEIDA
GAFSA
YOUKS LES BAINS
BEURAT
BENGHAZI
AGHEILA
EL ALAMEIN
Nov. 8
Nov. 8
Nov. 8
Nov. 11
Nov. 12
Nov. 17
Nov. 28
Dec. 28
Dec. 13
Nov. 20
Oct. 23 – Nov. 4
BRITISH AND U.S. LANDINGS
PARACHUTE LANDINGS
BRITISH 8TH ARMY ADVANCE
0
500 MILES

North Africa 1942.

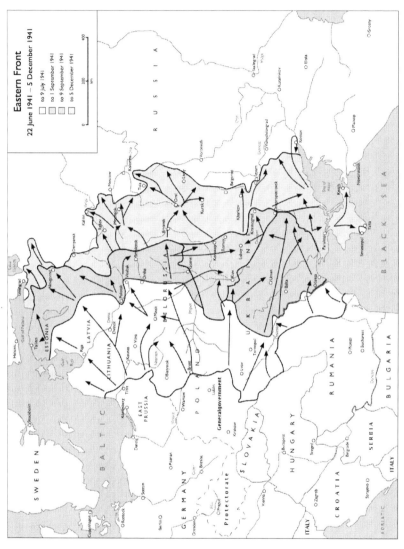

Operation Barbarossa: the German invasion of the Soviet Union, 21 June 1941 to 5 December 1941.

A CONCISE HISTORY OF THE SECOND WORLD WAR

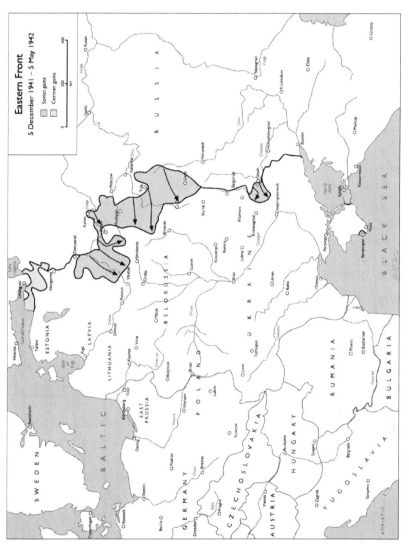

The Soviet winter counter-offensive, 5 December 1941 to 7 May 1942.

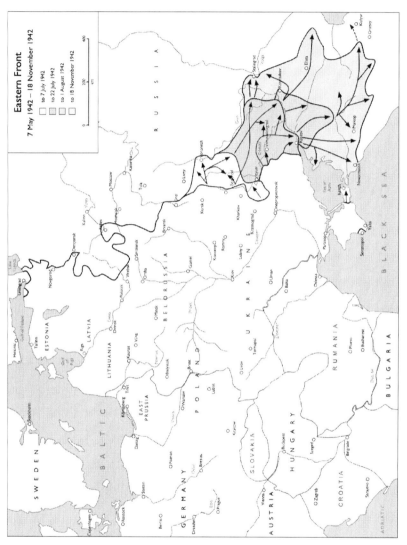

Operation Blue: German advances from 7 May 1942 to 18 November 1942.

A CONCISE HISTORY OF THE SECOND WORLD WAR

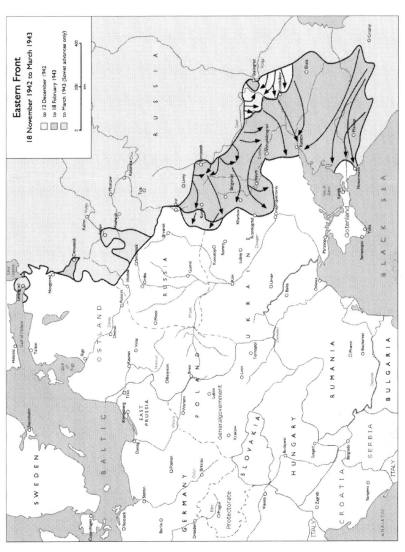

Operations Uranus, Saturn and Mars: Soviet advances on the Eastern Front, 18 November 1942 to March 1943.

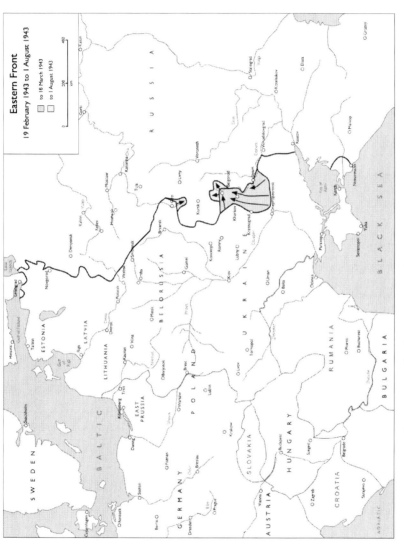

German advances at Kharkov and Kursk, 19 February 1943 to 1 August 1943.

A CONCISE HISTORY OF THE SECOND WORLD WAR

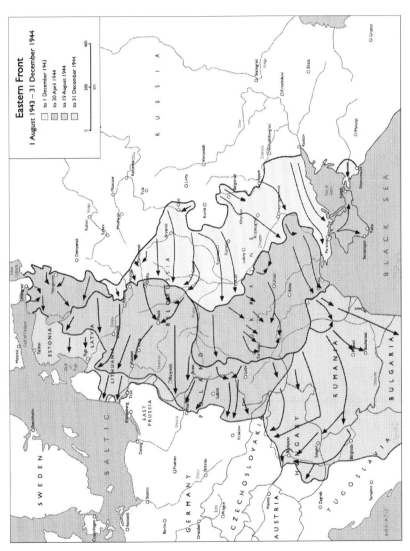

Soviet advances from 1 August 1943 to 31 December 1944.

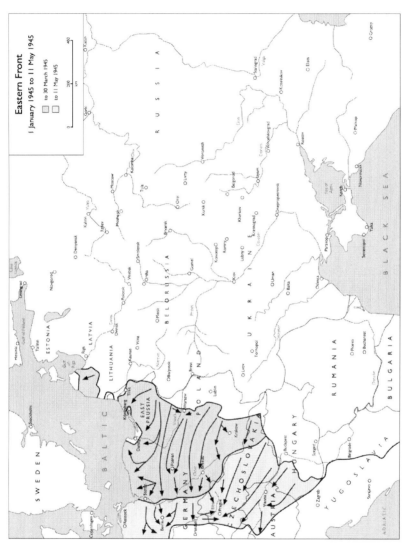

Soviet advances from 1 January 1945 to 11 May 1945.

A CONCISE HISTORY OF THE SECOND WORLD WAR

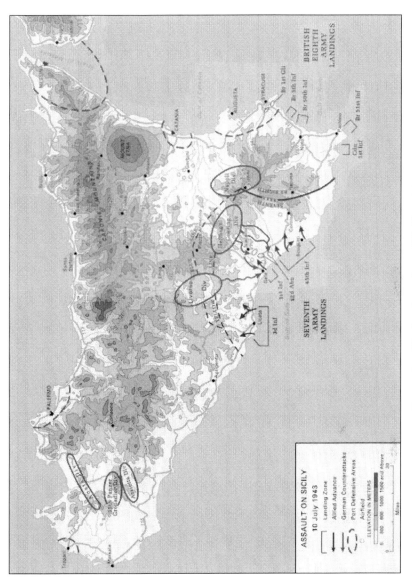

Operation Husky, Invasion of Sicily, 1943.

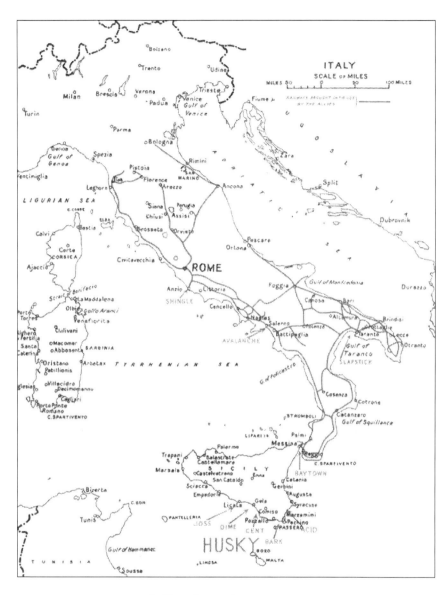

Italian Campaign, 1943-45.

A Concise History of the Second World War

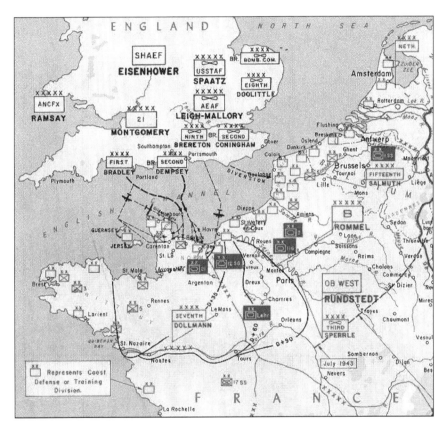

Allied invasion plans and German positions in Normandy, 1944.

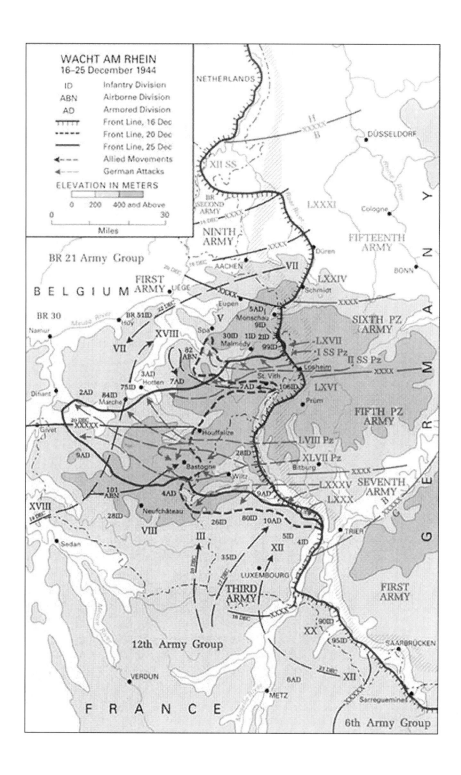

A CONCISE HISTORY OF THE SECOND WORLD WAR

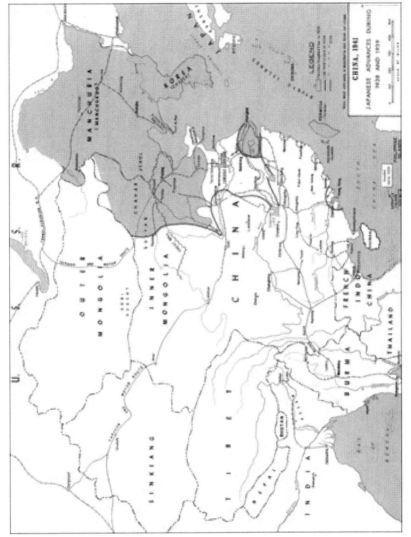

China, Korea, Manchuria, 1930s.

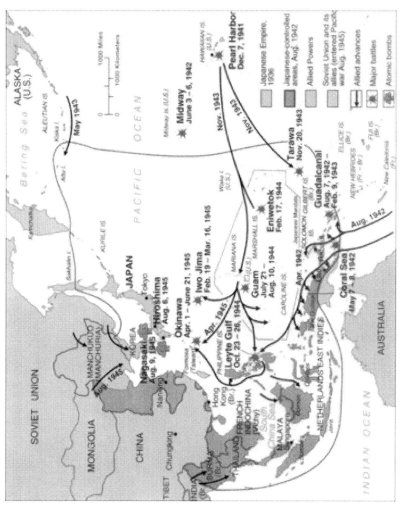

Pacific Theater, 1941-45.

Part 1

The Seeds of War

TO make sense of World War II, it is of value to identify each significant participant's pre-war circumstances and the forces, internal and external, that drove it to become mired in the conflict. In a number of cases, the seeds of war were planted roughly a generation earlier and were linked to aspects of the Great War (1914-1918). In a few cases, the ingredients had been simmering even longer. Seldom did a single factor indelibly mark a nation's path to war, but several forces played leading roles. Included among them were the competition among nations for territory and resources, the staggering impact of the Great Depression, Communism's announced goal of dominating the world, the human losses suffered by the victors in World War I, the burdens losers were forced to shoulder after that conflict ended, the ambition and ruthlessness of individuals who maneuvered themselves to head repressive regimes, the weakness of other governments and their chosen leaders, the conviction in some cultures that its members were racially superior, and the preference in other lands for isolation.

What follows is a review of many coalescing circumstances, discussed country by country, that contributed to the emergence of World War II.

GERMANY

The June 1914 assassination of Austrian Archduke Franz Ferdinand triggered, in a fractious and unstable Europe, the Great War. The conflict eventually pitted Germany, the Habsburg monarchy, the Ottoman Empire and Bulgaria against Great Britain, France, the Russian Empire, Italy, Serbia and the United States.[1]

Germany's World War I invasion and occupation of parts of Poland, the Baltic coast, Belarus and Ukraine whetted its appetite to retain

---

[1] *A Peace to End All Peace* (*"Peace"*), David Fromkin, Henry Holt and Company, LLC (1989), 45, 49, 55, *Bloodlands: Europe between Hitler and Stalin* (*"Bloodlands"*), Timothy Snyder, Basic Books (2010), 1.

those lands as its own. In March 1918, Germany forced the new Russian Bolshevik regime to sign the harsh Treaty of Brest-Litovsk, which ended the fighting between Germany and Russia and freed up German troops to move west to join the battle against France and Britain. The pact also confirmed Germany's influence over Poland, Finland, Latvia, Lithuania, Estonia, Belarus and Ukraine — all lands Russia once dominated.[2]

The German Weimar Republic was established on November 9, 1918 as part of the armistice a quelled Germany signed in France that ended World War I. The Republic replaced the monarchy of the abdicated Kaiser.[3]

Many in Germany later argued that the 1918 armistice was a product of political weakness at home and had no meaning because the German army had not been defeated in the field and the armistice papers had been signed in France.[4]

By 1919, the Communist doctrine that had recently prevailed in Russian affairs of state was having an impact on German politics. Some citizens feared Communism while others, influenced by the Bolsheviks, worked to implant it in Germany. To that end, German Communists, a number of whom were Jewish, incited rebellions in Berlin and Munich in 1919. At their peak, German Communists represented about ten percent of those voting in national elections.[5]

After Germany and its allies were subdued in World War I, the warring nations signed the June 1919 Treaty of Versailles (which Germany had no role in negotiating). The treaty eliminated Germany's territorial gains from the Brest-Litovsk Treaty, reconstituted Poland, imposed staggering war debts on Germany, restricted the size of the German army to 100,000, and barred the German navy from building submarines and large ships. As a result, Germans viewed themselves as a "have-not nation." Germany continued to aspire to the political and

---

[2] *Fateful Choices- Ten Decisions that Changed the World 1940-1941 ("Fateful Choices")*, Ian Kershaw, Penguin Group (USA) (2007), 55, *IKE: An American Hero ("Ike")*, Michael Korda, Harper Perennial (2007), 139.

[3] *The Rise and Fall of the Third Reich ("Reich")*, William L. Shirer, Simon and Schuster (1960), 52, 59, *Fateful Choices*, 441.

[4] *Reich*, 31, *The Ardennes: The Battle of the Bulge ("Bulge")*, Hugh Cole, Konecky & Konecky, 6.

[5] *Stalin's Curse ("Curse")*, Robert Gellately, Alfred A. Knopf (2013), 290, *Ike*, 203, *Bloodlands*, 4, 9, *Reich*, 33, 54-55, 185, *Iron Curtain: The Crushing of Eastern Europe 1944-1956 ("Iron Curtain")*, Anne Applebaum, Doubleday (2012), 40, 53, *1944: FDR and the Year That Changed History ("1944")*, Jay Winik, Simon and Schuster (2015), 365.

economic powers held by Great Britain, France and the United States, but realized that those countries would not willingly give up their might.[6]

On April 1, 1920, the National Socialist German Workers' Party (abbreviated as "Nazi") was established. After causing an uprising in Bavaria in 1923, the Nazi Party was banned in Germany until 1925.[7]

In April 1921, the victorious Allies demanded that Germany pay in gold the equivalent of $33,000,000,000 in World War I reparations. In the fall of 1922, the impoverished Germans asked for relief from the reparations debt. Their request was denied. After the Germans defaulted, the French marched troops into the Ruhr and occupied Germany's industrial center. This paralyzed the German economy. Between 1921 and 1922, the German Mark depreciated in value from four to the dollar to four hundred. By January 1923, when the Ruhr was taken, the mark had fallen to 18,000 to the dollar. By August, the exchange rate was 1,000,000 marks to the dollar. In November, the German currency was worthless. People's life savings had been erased and their faith in the German economy destroyed. The nation was in political turmoil.[8]

In 1926, the nation of Germany emerged somewhat from the international isolation caused by World War I, signed a neutrality treaty with the Soviet Union, and joined the League of Nations.[9]

Adolf Hitler, serving as a German corporal, was wounded twice during World War I and decorated twice for bravery.[10]

In 1926, Hitler, as a private citizen, published *Mein Kampf ("My Struggle")*, his treatise asserting that to achieve great power Germans need to acquire more "living space." Whereas Britain had gained territory by overseas conquest, Germany could acquire hers by expanding to the east. Because no nation would voluntarily yield territory, it would have to be taken in battle from the Soviet Union, a Bolshevik nation he considered controlled by Jews. Hitler's aspirations for Germany also included the defeat of Communism. *Mein Kampf* was translated into sixteen languages and sold over ten million copies.[11]

---

[6]   *Fateful Choices*, 14, *Ike*, 178, 186, *Bloodlands*, 7, *Reich*, 57-58.

[7]   *Reich*, 50, *1944*, 367-68.

[8]   *Reich*, 51, 61-68.

[9]   *Fateful Choices*, 253.

[10] *Reich*, 30, *The War Between The Generals ("Generals' War")*, David Irving, Congdon & Lattes, Inc. (1981), 346-47, *1944*, 364.

[11] *Fateful Choices*, 56-57, 254, *Curse*, 53, *Stalin's Folly ("Folly")*, Constantine Pleshakov, Houghton Mifflin Company (2005), 20, *Reich*, 80-90, *1944*, 367-68.

The Nazi Party was slow to grow. In 1928, it claimed only 108,000 members and in that year's elections received only 810,000 votes out of some 31,000,000 cast.[12]

The Depression and the debts imposed on Germany by the Treaty of Versailles staggered the German people. Hitler argued persuasively that his National Socialism offered Germans a new start and a stronger Germany. His popularity grew as the 1930s unfolded.[13]

In the 1930 German elections, 6,409,600 votes were cast in support of the Nazi Party; 4,592,000 in support of the Communists. The Nazis' success in the election attracted further support for them from business and military leaders.[14]

By 1931, as the Depression deepened, 5,000,000 Germans were out of work, farmers and the middle class were struggling, and the government of Reich President Paul von Hindenburg was flailing.[15]

In the April 1932 presidential election, Hindenburg received some 19,000,000 votes; Hitler received over 13,000,000. The popularity of the Nazi Party continued to grow.[16]

After the Nazis emerged from a Reichstag (parliament) election in July 1932 with the most seats of any party (but not a majority), Hitler told President Hindenburg that he wanted to be appointed Chancellor with complete power (*i.e.*, not as part of a coalition government).[17]

On January 30, 1933, the octogenarian Hindenburg, pressed by the army and conservatives, appointed forty-three year old Adolf Hitler to serve as Germany's Chancellor. This gave birth to the Third Reich.[18]

On February 27, 1933, a fire broke out in the Reichstag, the home of Germany's parliament. The Nazis blamed the blaze on Communists and persuaded President Hindenburg to sign a decree the next day suspending portions of the German constitution and permitting restrictions on liberty, free speech and rights of assembly, as well as interception of private communications, warrantless searches, and confiscations of property. The decree also authorized death sentences for armed persons who engaged in serious disturbances of the peace.[19]

Shortly after the decree was issued and before the March 1933 elec-

---

[12] *Reich*, 118, *1944*, 368.
[13] *Fateful Choices*, 58, *Reich*, 62-64, 136, *1944*, 368-69.
[14] *Reich*, 138, 141.
[15] *Reich*, 149.
[16] *Reich*, 159, *1944*, 369.
[17] *Reich*, 166-68, *1944*, 369.
[18] *Curse*, 62, *Fateful Choices*, 58, *Ike*, 202, *Reich*, 4-5, 183, 187-88.
[19] *Reich*, 194.

tions, some 4,000 Communists and liberal leaders were arrested and the liberal press was silenced. In the March 5 elections, the Nazis received more than seventeen million votes, some forty-four per cent of all votes cast. This was the last democratic election that took place in Germany during Hitler's life.[20]

Germany's first concentration camp, Dachau, was established on March 20, 1933. Hitler promptly sent Marxists — Communists and social democrats — to this and other camps. During 1933, some 200,000 Germans, mostly left-wing opponents, were incarcerated. Other Communists fled to the Soviet Union. By year end, the Communist party in Germany had been broken.[21]

On March 23, 1933, the German parliament adopted legislation permitting Hitler and his cabinet to govern the nation by personal decree — without approval of the president or parliament and without the restraints of the constitution. Hitler had become the Reich's dictator.[22]

On July 14, 1933, all political parties in Germany other than the Nazi Party were outlawed.[23]

Asserting its new independence, Germany quit the League of Nations in 1933.[24]

In January 1934, Germany surprised many by signing a ten-year non-aggression treaty with Poland. Hitler had never accepted the post-Great War existence of Poland as legitimate, but wanted to weaken Poland's ties with its historic ally, France, before taking hostile action against the Poles. The treaty with Poland also signaled a downgrade in Germany's previously solid relations with the Soviet Union, and raised fears that Hitler's well-known enmity toward Communism was taking diplomatic form.[25]

On July 25, 1934, 154 Austrian Nazis, dressed up as local soldiers, shot Austria's Chancellor Dollfuss dead in Vienna. Initially, Hitler was delighted, thinking this assassination brought closer his goal of merging Austria into Germany. But after Austrian security forces quickly regained control of the government and captured the rebels, Hitler professed dismay and asserted that Germany had played no role in the

---

[20] *Reich*, 194, *1944*, 371.

[21] *Bloodlands*, 60, 63-64, 88, *Curse*, 290, *Reich*, 194.

[22] *Bloodlands*, 60-61, *Reich*, 198-200.

[23] *Reich*, 201, *Bloodlands*, 63.

[24] *Engineers of Victory* ("*Engineers*"), Paul Kennedy, Random House (2013), 286, *Fateful Choices*, 61, *Reich*, 210-12.

[25] *Fateful Choices*, 253, *Bloodlands*, 64, *Reich*, 212-13.

attempted coup.[26]

Upon the death of President Hindenburg on August 2, 1934, the offices of Chancellor and President were combined and Hitler became the *Fuehrer* and Reich Chancellor — the absolute head of the German state.[27]

To consolidate his power following Hindenburg's death, Hitler downsized the role of the German Cabinet, which altogether ceased to meet after February 1938.[28]

One of Hitler's first goals as Chancellor was to restore Germany's military strength.[29]

On March 16, 1935, in violation of the Treaty of Versailles, Hitler announced that Germany was reinstituting the draft and building its army to a strength of 500,000 men. The British and French complained but took no military action.[30]

On March 7, 1936, Hitler sent troops into the Rhineland and reasserted German sovereignty there in disregard of the Versailles Treaty. Economically struggling Britain and France offered no military response.[31]

Shortly after Germany reoccupied the Rhineland, neighboring Belgium withdrew from an alliance with France and Britain and announced that it would henceforth be a neutral nation.[32]

In 1936, Germany began construction of the Siegfried Line which was intended to serve as the defensive wall on Germany's western border. Composed of some 3,000 pillboxes and bunkers, its path ran from the Dutch border down the western side of the Rhine River to Switzerland.[33]

In 1936, a civil war in Spain pitted General Francisco Franco and the Nationalists — backed by conservative landowners, the Catholic Church and the army — against the newly-elected left-wing Popular Front. Concerned that the Spanish government was fostering Com-

---

[26] *Reich*, 279-80.

[27] *Fateful Choices*, 59, 138, *Bloodlands*, 77, *Reich*, 226, *1944*, 372.

[28] *Fateful Choices*, 59.

[29] *Fateful Choices*, 58.

[30] *1939 - The Alliance that Never Was and the Coming of World War II* ("*1939*"), Michael Jabara Carley, Ivan R. Dee (1999), 17, *Fateful Choices*, 61, *Bloodlands*, 77, *Reich*, 284.

[31] *Fateful Choices*, 17, 190, *Reich*, 211, 291-95.

[32] *Reich*, 302.

[33] *The Guns at Last Light* ("*Guns*"), Rick Atkinson, Henry Holt and Company (2013), 249-50, A *Soldier's Story* ("*Soldier's Story*"), Omar N. Bradley, Henry Holt and Company (1951), 397, *Reich*, 295.

munism, Germany and Italy sent planes, tanks, military aid and tens of thousands of troops to support the Nationalists. The Soviet Union supported the left-wing side. Britain and France, now facing several Fascist threats in Europe, meekly remained neutral. The Nationalists prevailed in 1939 and Franco became Spain's dictator.[34]

By the spring of 1937, unemployment within Germany had fallen from 6,000,000 four years earlier to less than 1,000,000.[35]

Hitler considered Jews, such as Trotsky in the Russian revolution and the Jewish activists in German socialist upheavals, to be fomenters of internal unrest, avoiders of military service and war profiteers.[36]

When Hitler became Chancellor in 1933, less than one per cent of the German population was Jewish. By September 1939, only about half of those Jews were still living in Germany.[37]

In 1933, Germany banned Jews from civil service and established barriers that impeded them from practicing law and medicine.[38]

In 1935, Germany adopted the Nuremberg Laws which cancelled all of the civil rights of German Jews (including citizenship), defined Jewishness according to descent rather than just religious belief, and blocked Jews from political participation.[39]

By 1938, German law under Hitler provided that the cultural property of German Jews was "ownerless."[40]

Because German Jews were no longer allowed to own property, their art collections, estimated at more than 22,000 pieces, were "appropriated" by the German government.[41]

During the 1930s, German physicists discovered that the nucleus of the uranium atom could be split and made to throw off energy far greater than the normal chemical reaction. This discovery of nuclear fission led to the prospect of an atomic explosive device, a goal that Germany pursued.[42]

In March 1938, despite his promise two years earlier to respect

---

[34] *1939*, 20, 32, 144-45, *Fateful Choices*, 63, *The Story of World War II* ("*WW II Story*"), Donald L. Miller, Simon & Schuster (2001), 21, *Folly*, 62, *Bloodlands*, 67-68, *Reich*, 297-99.

[35] *Reich*, 231.

[36] *Fateful Choices*, 434.

[37] *Fateful Choices*, 436, 443, *Bloodlands*, viii-ix, 111, *Reich*, 965.

[38] *Fateful Choices*, 442, *Reich*, 203.

[39] *Fateful Choices*, 442, *Bloodlands*, 110, *Reich*, 233.

[40] *The Monuments Men* ("*Monuments Men*"), Robert M. Edsel, Center Street (2009), 13, 42.

[41] *Monuments Men*, 158.

[42] *Eagle Against the Sun* ("*Eagle*"), Ronald H. Spector, Vintage Books (1985), 550.

Austria's independence, Hitler pressured that nation, his birthplace, into agreeing to become a part of Germany. This action brought to Germany more than 6,000,000 new citizens as well as large reserves of hard currency. Italy's leader, Mussolini, who had previously promised to protect Austria, glumly stood aside, as did France, Britain and the Soviet Union.[43]

The Republic of Czechoslovakia, with a population of about 10,000,000, was created after World War I out of parts of the Habsburg Empire. In September 1938, Hitler demanded that the Sudetenland, a part of Czechoslovakia in which some 3,000,000 ethnic Germans lived, be turned over to Germany. The Sudetenland also contained some of the world's best armament manufacturing facilities. After British Prime Minister Neville Chamberlain, French Premier Daladier, Italy's Mussolini and Hitler met in Germany on September 29, they signed the Munich Agreement, which, in disregard of France's treaty obligations to Czechoslovakia and without permitting the Czechs to negotiate, capitulated to Hitler's demand. The Soviet Union, too, was excluded from the talks. Britain and France then forced Czechoslovakia to cede the Sudetenland to Germany within ten days, but guaranteed that they would protect the newly reduced boundaries of Czechoslovakia against any further unprovoked aggression. Upon his return to Britain, Chamberlain proudly declared that he had achieved "peace with honor. I believe it is peace in our time."[44]

On November 9-10, 1938, Nazis stimulated gangs throughout Germany to loot and destroy Jewish shops, houses and over 100 synagogues, an event that has come to be called *Kristallnacht* — the night of the broken glass. As many as 100 Jews were killed and another 20,000 arrested. These horrors were purportedly triggered when a seventeen year old Jew murdered a German diplomat in Paris. German Jews were forced to pay for their own *Kristallnacht* damage because the German government confiscated all of their insurance payments. In 1938-39, almost as many Jews emigrated from Germany as had departed in the previous four years. Hitler's goal of ridding Germany of Jews was finding success.[45]

Several days after *Kristallnacht*, the Nazis developed a plan for de-

---

[43]   *Fateful Choices*, 135, *WW II Story*, 22, *Bloodlands*, 114, *Reich*, 6, 296, 333-53.
[44]   *1939*, 70, *Fateful Choices*, 12, *WW II Story*, 23, *Bloodlands*, 114, *Reich*, 358-427.
[45]   *Fateful Choices*, 442-43, *Ike*, 225, *Reich*, 430-35, *When Paris Went Dark: The City of Light Under German Occupation, 1940-1944* ("*Paris*"), Ronald C. Rosbottom, Little, Brown and Company (2014), 241-43, *Bloodlands*, 112.

porting European Jews (including those in countries other than Germany) by boat to the island of Madagascar, a French colony off the coast of Africa.[46]

Many nations were appalled by Hitler's mistreatment of Jews. President Roosevelt reacted to *Kristallnacht* by recalling the American ambassador to Berlin. An angry Hitler took the international criticism as further proof of the "Jewish world conspiracy."[47]

On December 6, 1938, France and Germany signed a pact of friendship that guaranteed their borders and called for any disputes between them to be settled by consultation. One of Germany's objectives was to weaken France's ties with Britain, and a nervous France sought to minimize conflict with Hitler.[48]

American/German relations worsened during the 1930s as a result of tariff disputes, German abuse of both Christian churches and Jews (including *Kristallnacht*), Germany's refusal to pay its World War I debts, German efforts to rearm, and its repressive regime.[49]

Hitler viewed the United States as a powerful economic rival, but one dominated by Jewish capital and Jewish control of politics and culture.[50]

In a January 30, 1939 speech to the Reichstag, Hitler brashly predicted that:

> If the international Jewish financiers in and outside Europe should succeed in plunging the nations once more into a world war, then the result will not be the Bolshevizing of the earth, and thus the victory of Jewry, but the annihilation of the Jewish race in Europe.[51]

Hitler understood in the late 1930s that his military strength advantage would disappear as Britain and the United States enhanced their armed forces. Although Germany's economy was under duress due to the high cost of the German rearmament, Hitler reasoned that

---

[46] *Bloodlands*, 112, *Fateful Choices*, 446.
[47] *Reich*, 433-35, 685, *Bloodlands*, 111.
[48] *Reich*, 436, *Hitler's Gamble* ("*Hitler's Gamble*"), Giles MacDonogh, Basic Books (2009), 250.
[49] *Fateful Choices*, 390-94, *Reich*, 234-40, 434-35.
[50] *Fateful Choices*, 387.
[51] *Fateful Choices*, 433-34, *Inferno: The World at War, 1939-1945* ("*Inferno*"), Max Hastings, Alfred A. Knopf (2011), 490, *Bloodlands*, 114, *Reich*, 964.

if Germany were to expand territorially he must strike quickly.[52]

In 1939, the *Fuehrer* assumed that because of America's isolationism and its currently weak military, the United States would not go to war against Germany over a relatively short-lived European dispute. Hitler thought Germany had limited time, perhaps a year or so, to achieve supremacy in Europe before a strengthened United States might interfere with his plans. Thus, he sought to maintain neutrality with the United States while pursuing a rapid victory in Europe.[53]

On March 15, 1939, Czechoslovakia ceased to exist. Slovakia had, at Hitler's insistence, declared its independence the day before. Then the German army marched into Bohemia and Moravia, promptly placing what was left of Czechoslovakia under a German "protectorate" in disregard of the Munich Agreement Hitler had reached with Britain and France the previous September. Despite their earlier guarantees to Czechoslovakia, Britain and France did nothing but lodge a formal protest.[54]

Under the Treaty of Versailles, Poland had after World War I been given a land corridor to the Baltic Sea and control over the city of Danzig. Both came at Germany's expense. In late March 1939, Germany sought to reduce Poland's gains. Hitler pressured Poland to return to Germany the city of Danzig and to permit Germany to construct a highway and rail line through the Polish Corridor to Prussia. The strong-willed Poles refused.[55]

In the spring of 1939, Germany and the Soviet Union initiated secret negotiations aimed at forming a mutual non-aggression pact. Germany's participation in these talks was stimulated in part by Hitler's desire to interrupt the Soviet Union's ongoing efforts to negotiate a mutual assistance pact with Britain and France. Stalin's willingness to negotiate with Hitler was boosted by Britain's decision in late March to guarantee protection of Poland, whose land Stalin, too, coveted.[56]

On May 22, 1939, Germany and Italy signed the Pact of Steel, a military alliance that committed each nation (a) to support the other in the event of war and (b) not to sign a peace treaty without the other's consent.[57]

---

[52] *Fateful Choices*, 62.
[53] *Fateful Choices*, 394-95, *Reich*, 645.
[54] *1939*, 99, *Fateful Choices*, 19, 392, *Bloodlands*, 114, *Reich*, 428-54.
[55] *Reich*, 455-71.
[56] *1939*, 159-62, 211, *Reich*, 476-82, 489-96.
[57] *1939*, 150, *WW II Story*, 23-24, *Reich*, 482-83.

On May 23, 1939, Hitler instructed his military leaders to prepare for war against Poland beginning late that summer, and possibly thereafter war against Britain and France.[58]

During the early summer of 1939, the Soviet Union continued its separate and inconsistent treaty negotiations with Germany on one hand and France and Britain on the other. Concerned that Stalin might make a deal with Britain and France that would expose Germany to aggression from the east once it attacked Poland, Hitler urged Stalin to sign a mutual nonaggression pact. On August 23, Stalin consented, but only after extracting Hitler's agreement to a secret protocol under which (a) the two nations would invade and carve up Poland between them, and (b) Germany would facilitate Stalin's desire to take over Latvia, Estonia, Bessarabia (now Moldova) and parts of Finland.[59]

Germany was about to go to war.

THE SOVIET UNION

Tsarist Russia on the eve of World War I was the poorest of the advanced European nations, suffering from feeble leadership, a weak infrastructure, massive public debt and runaway inflation.[60]

During the second year of World War I (1915), the German army (a) invaded parts of Poland that were ruled by the Russian Empire and (b) occupied considerable territory along the Baltic Sea. Within the next two years, Germany also occupied Belarus and Ukraine at Russia's expense.[61]

On March 15, 1917, following a week of worker strikes, public protests and mutiny by elements of the army, Czar Nicholas II abdicated the Russian throne. After his brother Michael declined to replace Nicholas, the Russian Empire morphed into a shaky republic. Civil war was brewing.[62]

In the mid-1800s, two Germans, Karl Marx and Friedrich Engels, developed the theory that as the disparity in circumstances grew between struggling laborers and better-off factory owners, the workers of the world would unite and their revolutions would lead to the end of capitalism and conflicts spawned by private property. In its place so-

---

[58] *Reich*, 484-89.
[59] *Reich*, 513-44, *Iron Curtain*, xxvii.
[60] *Curse*, 389, *Peace*, 240-41.
[61] *Fateful Choices*, 55.
[62] *Peace*, 245.

cialism would arise.[63]

Vladimir Ilyich Ulyanov, who called himself "Lenin," was a Russian Marxist theorist born in 1870. In 1914, Lenin advocated ousting the Russian royalty and dismembering the Russian Empire. In April 1917, the Germans sent Lenin, then living in exile in Switzerland, to Russia hoping that he would foment a revolution that would end Russia's stance as a World War I foe of Germany.[64]

Lenin recruited to his mission Lev Davidovich Bronstein, a Russian Marxist who went by the name "Trotsky."[65]

By November 1917, Lenin, Trotsky and their Bolshevik comrades had, through a revolution in which 13,000,000 Russians died, toppled the shaky republican Russian government. Lenin anointed himself the new Russian dictator.[66]

Lenin viewed World War I as imperialist capitalism's final chapter. The time to stimulate socialist revolutions throughout Europe had arrived. Thus, once he gained control of Russia, he promptly moved to extricate his nation from the Great War. In March 1918, Russia and Germany entered into the Treaty of Brest-Litovsk, which halted fighting between the two nations and confirmed Germany's influence over the Baltic and other lands it had invaded a few years earlier. Lenin reasoned that Germany would continue to fight France and England and hoped that soon all capitalist systems in western Europe would collapse.[67]

Russia's Communist revolution, followed in 1918 by Russia's nationalization of all private investments and refusal to pay billions it owed in foreign debts, severely rattled the foundations of European capitalism.[68]

Moreover, in 1919, the Bolsheviks formed the Communist International ("Comintern") and announced their determination to bring about a socialist revolution throughout the world. In response to the Bolshevik goal of provoking a global socialist uprising, western European nations blockaded Russia and refused to establish diplomatic relations with its Communist government.[69]

At the time of the Russian revolution, most of the world's Jews

---

[63] *Bloodlands*, 3, *Peace*, 242.
[64] *Peace*, 241-46, 298, *Bloodlands*, 4.
[65] *Bloodlands*, 4, *Peace*, 244.
[66] *Bloodlands*, 4, *Peace*, 245-47.
[67] *Peace*, 246-47, *Fateful Choices*, 55, *Bloodlands*, 4, *Reich*, 57, *Iron Curtain*, 39.
[68] *1939*, 6.
[69] *1939*, 6, *Peace*, 247, 272, *Folly*, 29, *Iron Curtain*, 39-40.

lived in lands controlled by Russia. The fact that the revolution had been led by Bolsheviks, a significant number of whom (including Lenin and Trotsky) were Jewish, persuaded many in Europe that Jews wielded substantial political power.[70]

In 1920, Lenin and Trotsky sought by war to impose Communism on Russia's neighbor, Poland. They hoped that a victory over the Poles would trigger a socialist revolution throughout Europe. By August of that year, however, Poland had driven the Russian Red Army back in a stinging defeat for the Communist leaders. In March 1921, Russia and Poland signed a treaty ending the conflict.[71]

Following their defeat in Poland, Lenin and Trotsky concentrated on securing their absolute power within Russia — then largely a pre-industrial nation of peasant farmers. They banned all other political parties and brutally eliminated those citizens who opposed Communism. Free elections did not take place.[72]

Under Lenin's theory, Russian society was subordinate to the state; the state was controlled by the Communist party; the party was represented by the central committee; and the central committee was ruled by a handful of individuals.[73]

Joseph Dzhughashvili, five feet four inches tall and a native of Georgia in the Caucasus, called himself Stalin, meaning "man of steel." He served as a political officer with the Red Army during the Polish/Russian conflict in 1920, and over the next few years rose up the ladder of Russia's Communist leadership.[74]

Russia officially became the Soviet Union in 1924.[75]

Under the auspices of Moscow, the Chinese Communist Party was founded in 1921. The People's Republic of Mongolia, created in 1924, was a Communist satellite of the Soviet Union.[76]

By the mid-1920s, Soviet foreign relations had two main tenets. First, as the imperialist nations competed for control of the world's resources, war was inevitable among those countries, which would benefit the Soviet Union and advance the socialist revolution. Second, the Soviet Union would itself eventually become a target of war and

---

[70] *Peace*, 247, 272, 292, 298, *Folly*, 53, *Bloodlands*, 11.
[71] *Bloodlands*, 6-10, *Iron Curtain*, 41.
[72] *Bloodlands*, 8-11.
[73] *Bloodlands*, 13.
[74] *Curse*, 3-4, *Masters and Commanders* ("*Masters*"), Andrew Roberts, Harper Collins Publishers (2009), 444, *Bloodlands*, 13.
[75] *Fateful Choices*, 251.
[76] *Curse*, 172, *Bloodlands*, 105.

thus socialism would have to be well-rooted within the Soviet Union to enable the country to resist threats from hostile imperialist nations.[77]

During the 1920s, the Soviet Union worked to emerge from the international isolation that had been imposed upon it following the Bolshevik Revolution of 1917. In 1922, Russia and Germany entered into a treaty. By 1925, the Soviets had established diplomatic relations with thirteen European countries, including France and Great Britain.[78]

Lenin died in January 1924. Shortly thereafter, Trotsky, who had founded the Red Army, lost a battle for power within the Communist party and was exiled to Mexico.[79]

By 1929, Joseph Stalin had become the virtually undisputed head of the Soviet Union, and by 1934 he was its dictator.[80]

Stalin's view was that to be strong the Soviet Union must convert from an agrarian to an industrial economy. To fund the development of heavy industry, he needed currency with which to buy equipment from foreign suppliers. By 1928, he had decided to raise the needed funds by "collectivizing" the farms of millions of peasants (mostly in Ukraine), and forcing them to raise crops as state property which could be sold in the international market even if doing so caused famine in the Soviet Union.[81]

By the end of the 1920s, Germany was the Soviet Union's top commercial trading partner and by 1932, Germany was supplying almost half of the Soviet Union's imports.[82]

In December 1929, Stalin announced that *kulaks*, "better off" peasants who would naturally oppose Communist efforts to collectivize their farms, would be "liquidated as a class." The state took all of their land and property and deported them to slave labor camps in Siberia, Kazakhstan and elsewhere. In the first 120 days of 1930, Stalin forcibly sent 113,637 Ukrainians to such camps. By 1932, there were 1,300,000 *kulak* prisoners, a figure that did not change much over the next decade.[83]

By 1931, Stalin had established *gulags*, labor/concentration camps,

---

[77] *Fateful Choices*, 251, *Folly*, 43-44.
[78] *Fateful Choices*, 252, *1939*, 6-7, *Bloodlands*, 9, 57.
[79] *Bloodlands*, 11-13, *Folly*, 30.
[80] *Curse*, 3, 6-8, *Bloodlands*, 13, *Iron Curtain*, 41-42, *Fateful Choices*, 245.
[81] *Bloodlands*, 10-14, 25.
[82] *Fateful Choices*, 252-53.
[83] *Curse*, 24, 31, *Bloodlands*, 25-27, 78-79.

to which perceived enemies of the state were sent. Some 18,000,000 people were subsequently imprisoned in the camps, of whom between 1,500,000 and 3,000,000 died during incarceration.[84]

The first collectivized Soviet harvest, in 1931, was a failure, causing millions of Soviets to die of starvation. The harvest in 1932 was also weak, achieving only about one-third of the government's target. In response, Stalin imposed even greater penalties on Ukrainian farmers who failed to meet their target. About 3,000,000 Ukrainians died of starvation and hunger-related disease in 1932-33. Cannibalism was widespread.[85]

On November 7, 1932, Stalin's second wife, Nadezhda, committed suicide after he publicly rebuked her.[86]

In the 1930s, Stalin also decided to rid the Soviet Union of "capitalist" influences, internal and foreign (including Poles and Germans), that he felt were impeding the embedding of Communism within the country. Between 1930 and 1938, over 3,800,000 people were arrested for "anti-Soviet agitation" and similar charges. Out of 1,500,000 arrested in the Great Terror of 1937-38, 1,300,000 were sentenced and 681,692 were executed. In addition, from 1933 to 1939, 1,800,000 were expelled from the Communist party.[87]

Soviet diplomatic relations with Germany weakened once Hitler took power in 1933 because of his aspiration that Germany expand east into Soviet territory and his strong anti-Bolshevik views.[88]

By 1934, recognizing that he needed his nation's peasants to survive and produce, Stalin had made Soviet grain growing requirements more attainable and permitted peasants to farm garden-sized plots of land for their own consumption.[89]

The United States finally established diplomatic relations with the Soviet Union in November 1933. In 1934, the Soviet Union joined the League of Nations and urged other nations to establish an "international peace front" that would impede aggressive conduct by Germany, Japan and Italy.[90]

Despite his worries about Hitler's desire for territorial expansion, between 1937 and 1938, Stalin decapitated the Red Army. More than

---

[84]   *Bloodlands*, 27, *Curse*, 31.
[85]   *Bloodlands*, 33-35, 40-46, 51-53.
[86]   *Bloodlands*, 40, *Curse*, 32, *Folly*, 39.
[87]   *Curse*, 35-45, *Fateful Choices*, 246, *Folly*, 40-41, *Bloodlands*, 72-75, 81-109.
[88]   *Fateful Choices*, 254.
[89]   *Bloodlands*, 65.
[90]   *Fateful Choices*, 254.

34,000 officers he considered to be enemies were arrested. Of those, 22,705 were shot or missing. Out of 101 members of the supreme military leadership, ninety-one were arrested and eighty of them were shot. As a result, the Red Army was not deemed fit to fight a war for at least five years. Stalin's purge of his military leadership convinced Hitler that the Red Army was weak and increased his willingness to consider an attack on the Soviet Union.[91]

In 1937, the Japanese sent invasion troops into China, which was in the midst of a civil war. The Communist faction in China was led by Mao Tse-tung. Ironically, the Soviet Union supported the anti-Communist Chiang Kai-shek and his Kuomintang government, hoping that by keeping Japan's military actively engaged in China, Japan would be less likely to attack the Soviet Union.[92]

After the western European nations caved in to Germany on Czechoslovakia and the Sudetenland in 1938, the Soviet Union became more concerned about its isolation and the likelihood of a German attack.[93]

In 1939, Japanese troops crossed the border between Manchuria and Mongolia, leading to a military confrontation between the Soviet Union and Japan. The Red Army succeeded in driving the Japanese back, but Soviet worries about Japanese aggression continued.[94]

By 1939, Stalin was a dictator with complete control over the Soviet Union. The Politburo, the Communist party's decision-making body, which once had convened weekly, met only twice in each of the years 1939 and 1940.[95]

In the spring of 1939, the Soviets, French and British began negotiations to create an anti-German alliance. However, France and Britain proceeded in the talks very slowly. They were hesitant to conclude an agreement with the Soviet Union in large part because of anti-Bolshevik sentiments and their distrust of Stalin.[96]

As France and Britain dithered in their alliance negotiations with the Soviet Union, Stalin concluded the time was ripe to initiate trade and non-aggression discussions with Germany. By mid-August the Soviet/German discussions had yielded a trade agreement. The non-

---

[91] *Fateful Choices*, 246-47, 292, *Folly*, 15-16, *Bloodlands*, 75.
[92] *1939*, 95, *Fateful Choices*, 254, *Bloodlands*, 68-70.
[93] *Fateful Choices*, 255, *1939*, 77.
[94] *1939*, 257.
[95] *Fateful Choices*, 248-49.
[96] *Fateful Choices*, 256, 293, *1939*, 4, *Reich*, 478-79.

aggression talks then picked up speed.[97]

On August 23, 1939, out of frustration with French and British negotiating delays and hoping to avoid (or at least put off) a possible German attack, the Soviet Union signed a non-aggression pact with Germany — even though Hitler was considered the world's most anti-Communist government leader.[98]

The von Ribbentrop-Molotov pact served at least three motivations: (a) the Germans wanted to avoid a two-front war, (b) the Soviet Union wanted additional time to prepare for the feared attack by Germany, and (c) the Soviets wanted to establish a sphere of influence in the Baltic nations, Poland and Bessarabia.[99]

Under a secret component of their 1939 agreement, Germany and Russia agreed to carve up and take control of Eastern Europe. Stalin accepted Hitler's expansionist policies in Europe, gave Germany important material aid, and conceded German claims to Lithuania and the western part of Poland. In return, Hitler conceded Soviet claims to eastern Finland, Estonia, Latvia, Bessarabia and parts of eastern Poland.[100]

Following the 1939 Soviet/German trade agreement, commerce between those nations grew to levels not seen since before Hitler came to power.[101]

Stalin anticipated the coming of World War II and believed that when the capitalist countries fighting each other were weakened by battle, they would be susceptible to Communism. Stalin's theory was that the Soviet Union would do what it could to prolong a war in Western Europe, leading eventually to rebellion by the masses who would then welcome Soviet Communism.[102]

THE BRITISH EMPIRE

At least 750,000 British soldiers were killed in the Great War, leaving the British people with an intense desire to avoid another war.[103]

After World War I ended, the goal of Great Britain, a nation with

---

[97] *1939*, 159-62, *Reich*, 476-82.
[98] *Masters*, 278, 451, *Curse*, 47, *1939*, 209, 212, *Fateful Choices*, 256-57, *Folly*, 43, *Bloodlands*, 116, *Reich*, 513-44.
[99] *Curse*, 46-47, *Fateful Choices*, 258, *Reich*, 513-44.
[100] *Inferno*, 5, *1939*, 206-7, *Bloodlands*, 116, *Reich*, 544.
[101] *Fateful Choices*, 259.
[102] *Curse*, 46-48, *1939*, 229, *Folly*, 44, *Reich*, 185.
[103] *Ike*, 178, *Dawn*, 13.

a powerful navy and colonies spread across the globe, was to preserve its empire during financially challenging times. Britain was confronted by signs of a growing desire for independence within many of its colonies, including Ireland, India, Egypt, Canada, Australia, New Zealand and South Africa.[104]

In the 1930s, as it was squeezed by the Depression, Britain significantly reduced spending on its armed forces.[105]

From the French perspective, Britain was insufficiently concerned in the 1930s about future German aggression because Britain was protected by both the English Channel and those French troops who would be the first forces drawn into a future fight.[106]

When, in March 1935, Hitler announced his establishment of a half-million man German army and an air force, Britain realized that it needed to expand its military power. However, it was stretched thin by its global commitments and the Depression, and many English citizens (particularly in the labor and liberal spheres) were opposed to a buildup in arms. Britain was then unequipped to fight a war against Germany and would not be ready for at least several years.[107]

Britain understood in the mid-1930s that if Hitler was intent on expanding Germany's territory (as *Mein Kampf* predicted), it was better for Britain if Hitler's gaze was aimed toward the east and southeast rather than the west.[108]

Still, Britain worried about Hitler's westward ambitions. In a speech to the hesitant House of Commons in April 1936, Winston Churchill (with uncanny foresight) warned:

> Herr Hitler has torn up treaties and has garrisoned the Rhineland. His troops are there, and there they are going to stay .... The creation of a line of forts opposite the French frontier will enable the German troops to be economized on that line, and will enable the main forces to swing around through Belgium and Holland. That is for us a danger of the most serious kind.[109]

When the Spanish civil war broke out in the summer of 1936, the

---

[104] *Fateful Choices*, 13-14, *Peace*, 282.
[105] *Fateful Choices*, 16.
[106] *1939*, 29-30.
[107] *Fateful Choices*, 16-18, *1939*, 30.
[108] *1939*, 32-33.
[109] *Ike*, 220-21.

British worried that France, with its left-leaning government, might support the socialist side of the Spanish dispute and then "go Bolshevik" internally. Because this could significantly bolster the Soviets and the spread of Communism, the British took steps to influence the French government to stay out of the Spanish conflict.[110]

Neville Chamberlain became Great Britain's Prime Minister in May 1937, inheriting a confused and uncertain foreign policy shaped by British military weakness and the aggression of Europe's dictators. Even as Hitler's move toward war became clearer, Chamberlain limited the military budget and refused to conclude an alliance with the Soviet Union that might prevent war.[111]

In September 1938, Chamberlain (accompanied by the Italians and French) met with Hitler in Munich to discuss Germany's proposed taking of the Sudetenland from Czechoslovakia. Representatives from the government of Czechoslovakia were not invited. On September 30, the parties reached agreement and accepted Germany's aggressive action. Chamberlain apparently believed that once Hitler had taken the Sudetenland, he would be satisfied. Thus, upon returning to London, Chamberlain proclaimed that he had achieved "peace for our time."[112]

In the House of Commons, a frustrated Churchill called the Munich Agreement "a total and unmitigated defeat." He added that "[t]he German dictator, instead of snatching his victuals from the table, has been content to have them served to him course by course."[113]

In late March 1939 (after Hitler had seized the rest of Czechoslovakia), the British and French governments, even though they lacked both the will and the means to live up to such a commitment, promised Poland that in the event of aggression by Hitler against Poland, they would both attack Germany.[114]

During the first half of 1939, the British and French fretted that, standing alone, they would be unable to thwart further aggression by Germany. They knew that to prevent war they needed to ally with the Soviet Union. But their efforts to negotiate an agreement with Stalin dragged on into the summer of 1939, in part because Chamberlain de-

---

[110] *1939*, 20-21, 32.

[111] *1939*, 30, 39-40, *Fateful Choices*, 17.

[112] *1939*, 62, 65, 70-71, *Fateful Choices*, 18, *WWII History*, Vol. 13, No. 3 (*"WWII History"*), Sovereign Media, April 2014, 30.

[113] *Fateful Choices*, 19, *1939*, 71.

[114] *Inferno*, 3-4, *Bloodlands*, 115, *Reich*, 465-66.

tested Communism and mistrusted Stalin.[115]

The fear of Communism that contributed to the failure of British-French-Soviet cooperation against Nazism was driven by the perception in the west that if war occurred, the Nazis could be defeated only with Soviet assistance, but that assistance would increase Soviet prestige and thereby enhance the risk that Communism would become widespread in Europe.[116]

On August 23, 1939, the Soviets struck a stunning deal with Germany. An opportunity to hobble Hitler had been wasted.[117]

Winston Churchill was strongly anti-Communist in the 1930s, but he considered Communism less of a threat to Britain than the Nazis. Consistently, in 1939, he spoke out in favor of a British alliance with the Soviet Union.[118]

But now Britain faced the likelihood of another war with Germany.

JAPAN

The Japanese were raised to believe that they were a unique and superior race of humans. They treasured their closed culture and their divine emperor, who with his ancestors was said to have reigned for more than 2,500 years. The Japanese also revered conformity, discipline and meeting one's obligations.[119]

Beginning in the early 1900s, the Japanese government produced or approved all school books, and students were taught militarism, strict obedience and emperor worship.[120]

Since at least the mid-1800s, Japan had aspired to rule the Far East and believed it had a divine right to do so.[121]

After Commodore Perry forced the Japanese in 1853 to open their ports to trade with America, the emperor declared that Japan must drive the "barbarians" from Japan's sacred soil and "expand overseas"

---

[115] *1939*, 138-44, 158, 177, 256, *Fateful Choices*, 18, *Reich*, 479-82.

[116] *1939*, 14, 27, 256-57.

[117] *1939*, 206-07, *Fateful Choices*, 257-58.

[118] *1939*, 10, 148, *Folly*, 248, *Reich*, 479.

[119] *Shattered Sword: The Untold Story of the Battle of Midway* ("*Sword*"), Jonathan Parshall and Anthony Kim, Potomac Books (2005), 72-73, 76.

[120] *The Ghosts of Iwo Jima* ("*Ghosts*"), Robert S. Burrell, Texas A&M University Press (2006), 43.

[121] *Fateful Choices*, 92, *Pacific Victory* ("*Pacific*"), Derrick Wright, Sutton Publishing Limited (2005), 1.

to create a buffer zone against future western encroachment.[122]

As an island nation, Japan recognized that it must have a strong navy to thwart any foreign attackers and, if it was the aggressor, to convey its troops abroad.[123]

Prior to World War II, Japan had never lost a war. Seeking to establish itself as an Asian power, Japan defeated China in 1894-95, thereby gaining control of Korea, Formosa (Taiwan) and other lands. In 1904-05, Japan defeated Russia on land and at sea, thereby acquiring southern Manchuria. During World War I, Japan sided with the Allies and was rewarded with control of German assets in the Pacific, including the Caroline, Marshall and Mariana island groups.[124]

Following its victory over Russia, Japan wielded considerable influence and power over parts of China, including Manchuria and Formosa. It maintained troops in Peking and other Chinese cities, purportedly to protect Japanese citizens. Japan believed that its control of the state of Manchuria provided economic benefits and strengthened Japan's defenses against Russia.[125]

As Japan industrialized after 1900, it grew to depend on foreign foodstuffs and raw materials like tin, rubber, iron ore, copper, timber and oil. Viewing itself as a world power, Japan recognized that it needed to gain control over the sources of supply of these essential items, either by acquiescence of other world powers or by war.[126]

In the early 1920s, however, Japan was persuaded by international diplomatic pressure and opposition within China to Japanese influence there to be somewhat less aggressive.[127]

At the 1922 Washington Naval Conference, Japan, China, the United States, Britain and other nations with interests in the Pacific negotiated a treaty that recognized China's independence, placed upper limits on the construction of warships, and established battleship and aircraft carrier tonnage ratios among countries. To illustrate, Britain and the United States had parity and, because of their Atlantic and Pacific Ocean responsibilities, received a forty percent warship advantage

---

[122] *Japan's Imperial Conspiracy* (*"Conspiracy"*), David Bergamini, William Morrow and Company (1971), 7, *Sword*, 72-74.

[123] *Pacific Crucible: War at Sea in the Pacific, 1941-1942* (*"Crucible"*), Ian W. Toll, W.W. Norton & Company (2012), xix.

[124] *Engineers*, 284-85, *Fateful Choices*, 92, *Pacific*, 1, *Conspiracy*, 5-6, 149, 167, *Sword*, 72, 420, *Crucible*, xxiv, 82.

[125] *Fateful Choices*, 15, 92, 94, 376, *Eagle*, 35, *Inferno*, 415.

[126] *Engineers*, 284-85, *Sword*, 75.

[127] *Fateful Choices*, 93.

over Japan. (Prior to the conference, the United States had broken the Japanese diplomatic code then in use and was able to read instructions Japan sent to its negotiators). The Conference also forbade further fortifications or military bases in the Pacific island possessions of Britain, France, the United States and Japan.[128]

Like other nations, Japan was concerned about Russia's announced intention to spread Communism throughout the world. This was one reason why some senior members of Japan's government favored an attack on Russia. In May 1923, Japan arrested and imprisoned hundreds of members of Japan's Communist party.[129]

In 1924, the United States enacted legislation that barred immigration from a number of countries, including Japan. This caused diplomatic damage between the two nations.[130]

Emperor Hirohito took the throne in 1926 at the age of 25. Thereafter, he and Japan pursued an ideology based on the concepts of Japanese supremacy and expansion of its territory.[131]

Japan's military was composed largely of persons steeped in rural conservatism. They viewed with skepticism liberal ideas and sought for Japan expanded borders and enhanced strength against the west.[132]

In 1927, Hirohito made a deal with Chiang Kai-shek. Japan would support Chiang in his efforts to (a) unify China south of the Great Wall and (b) eliminate Communists from the Kuomintang army. In return, Chiang would not seriously oppose Japan's efforts to assert influence over Manchuria and Mongolia.[133]

In 1928, Chinese nationalists, under Chiang Kai-shek, established a central government in Nanking. Thereafter, China boycotted certain Japanese goods and sought to reduce the economic benefits Japan was obtaining from Manchuria. These actions created resentment in Japan, particularly because Chiang had once been a student there.[134]

During the Great Depression, Japan's economy collapsed and its seventy million people suffered poverty and near-starvation. Many

---

[128] *Eagle*, 20, *Fateful Choices*, 93, *Pacific*, 1, *Conspiracy*, 500, *Pearl Harbor: Final Judgment ("Judgment")*, Henry C. Clausen and Bruce Lee, Crown Publishers, Inc. (1992), 39, *Sword*, 75, *Stay the Rising Sun ("Rising Sun")*, Phil Keith, Zenith Press (2015), 7-9, *Crucible*, 83.

[129] *Conspiracy*, 436, 997, *Crucible*, 81.

[130] *Pacific*, 4, *Sword*, 75, *Crucible*, 77, 82.

[131] *Fateful Choices*, 105-06.

[132] *Eagle*, 34-35.

[133] *Conspiracy*, 465-68.

[134] *Fateful Choices*, 93-94, *Conspiracy*, 7, 480.

within Japan concluded that overseas expansion was the way out of economic hardship.[135]

The shipbuilding restrictions established at the 1922 Washington Conference were renewed at the 1930 London Naval Conference, except that those applicable to Japan were loosened just a bit. The continuing restrictions led to dissatisfaction within certain Japanese military circles and the forced retirement of several pro-treaty Japanese admirals.[136]

In September 1931, Japanese troops attacked Chinese troops in southern Manchuria. Within several months, Japan had set up a puppet government of the "independent" state of Manchukuo.[137]

Japan's military aggression in Manchuria and its establishment of a puppet government there led to Japan's international isolation, which in turn increased anti-Chinese and anti-western sentiments within Japan. In May 1932, Japan replaced its parliamentary government with a cabinet staffed largely by military leaders and bureaucrats.[138]

After being censored by the League of Nations for its hostile actions in Manchuria, Japan quit that organization in March 1933.[139]

In 1933, Japan expanded the borders of Manchuria to include the Great Wall of China and to come within forty miles of Peking. When Chiang's government withdrew from the Peking area two years later, Japan set up local puppet governments headed by Chinese warlords.[140]

As a matter of custom (and law after 1936), those Japanese cabinet ministers who represented the views of the army and navy were chosen from each military branch's senior officers. By refusing to name a minister, either military branch could thwart the formation of the cabinet. By withdrawing a serving minister, they could force an existing government to dissolve. Moreover, the Japanese army and navy General Staffs were considered to be independent of the government, reporting directly and only to the Emperor on matters of national defense.[141]

By the mid-1930s, the military's influence on Japan's governance

---

[135] *Eagle*, 35, *Pacific*, 1-4, *Crucible*, 89.

[136] *Eagle*, 40-41, *Conspiracy*, 500-06, *Crucible*, 84.

[137] *Fateful Choices*, 15, 92, 94, 376, *Eagle*, 35, *Inferno*, 415, *Crucible*, 85.

[138] *Fateful Choices*, 94-95, *Crucible*, 85.

[139] *Engineers*, 286, *Fateful Choices*, 95, *Eagle*, 36, *Pacific*, 4, *Conspiracy*, 688-89, 697.

[140] *Fateful Choices*, 95.

[141] *Eagle*, 33, *At Dawn We Slept: The Untold Story of Pearl Harbor ("Slept")*, Gordon W. Prange, Penguin Books (1982), 213.

had grown significantly and was approaching veto power.[142]

Seeking to halt the European powers' "aggression" in East Asia, Japan's focus in mid-1936 was on enhancing its defenses and expanding into the South Seas to obtain essential natural resources. In furtherance of these goals, both the Japanese army and navy were strengthened. Anticipating that Japan would walk away from the naval arms limitations imposed by the renewed Washington Conference when they expired in 1936, the Japanese navy secretly planned construction of two huge battleships far larger than any then possessed by the United States. The navy was "to be brought to a level sufficient to secure command of the western Pacific against the U.S. Navy," and the army boosted to "a strength to resist the forces the Soviet Union can employ in the Far East."[143]

In the November 1936 Anti-Comintern Pact, Japan and Germany agreed that if the Soviet Union carried out an unprovoked attack on either nation, they would act in concert to safeguard their common interests.[144]

The fates of Germany and Japan had been joined.

THE UNITED STATES

Its success in the Spanish-American War had left the United States with many wide-spread Pacific territories, including the Philippines, Guam and Hawaii. During his presidency, mindful of the need to protect those territories, Teddy Roosevelt succeeded in having the United States develop a navy larger than any other save Great Britain, and commence digging the Panama Canal, which shortened the fleet's trip from the Atlantic to the Pacific by thousands of miles.[145]

The loss of 50,000 American lives in World War I, a conflict started by other nations on a distant continent, gave rise to a strong sense of isolationism within the United States.[146]

In addition, when the European nations they had supported during the Great War did not pay their war debts, Americans were resentful. Many were determined that the United States would not twice become

---

[142] *Fateful Choices*, 96-97, 103, *Pacific*, 1, *Crucible*, 106, 120.
[143] *Fateful Choices*, 96, *Eagle*, 42, *Crucible*, 102-103.
[144] *Reich*, 299, *Fateful Choices*, 96, *Conspiracy*, 875-76.
[145] *Crucible*, xxi-xxii, xxxi-xxxii.
[146] *Fateful Choices*, 188, *Eagle*, 9.

Europe's patsy.[147]

As a sign of America's isolationism, during the 1920s, Army Chief of Staff Summerall opposed attempts to have American industry prepare for a future war. In 1930, he was replaced by General Douglas MacArthur, who directed then-Major Dwight Eisenhower to prepare a detailed plan under which, if circumstances so warranted, American industry could be converted to address the needs of warfare. Upon completion of this assignment in 1932, Eisenhower became the personal assistant to the talented, ambitious and egocentric MacArthur. Decades later, Eisenhower observed that "I studied dramatics for seven years under General MacArthur."[148]

Franklin Roosevelt became President of the United States on March 4, 1933, in the midst of a banking crisis and with about one quarter of the American workforce, some 13,000,000 people, out of work. The American economy had contracted by forty-five per cent; bread lines operated in every city and many were homeless.[149]

During the Depression, the United States Army was reduced in size and actually smaller than the Greek army. American soldiers were poorly armed, trained, paid and housed.[150]

On November 17, 1933, some fifteen years after the Russian revolution, the United States finally gave diplomatic recognition to the Soviet Union in exchange for Stalin's promises to protect Americans there and to end Soviet control of the American Communist Party.[151]

Despite his commitment to Roosevelt, after 1933 Stalin persisted in guiding the American Communist Party. Although this breach upset the President, he considered Nazi Germany a greater evil than Communism and refrained from lodging an objection.[152]

During the mid-1930s, areas of the world distant from the United States experienced the impact of Japanese and German aggression. Still, most Americans remained focused on events at home.[153]

However, since the early 1900s the United States had recognized that Japan was its only likely adversary in the Pacific. If such a war came, Japan could be expected to attack America's interests in the Phil-

---

[147] *Fateful Choices*, 188.

[148] *Ike*, 187-88, 194.

[149] *Fateful Choices*, 188, *1944*, 42-43.

[150] *Ike*, 195.

[151] *Curse*, 62.

[152] *Curse*, 70-71.

[153] *Fateful Choices*, 189, *Crusade in Europe* ("*Crusade*"), Dwight D. Eisenhower, Doubleday & Company, Inc. (1948), 2

ippines, requiring the U.S. Navy to travel 7,000 miles across the seas to defend those islands. This, in turn, meant that the United States needed bases in the Pacific, like Pearl Harbor and Guam, from which the navy fleet could be refueled, provisioned and repaired.[154]

In 1934, driven by isolationism, the United States enacted the Johnson Act which forbade America from giving credit to nations that had defaulted on their World War I debts.[155]

On August 31, 1935, Roosevelt signed the Neutrality Act. This legislation, further reflecting American isolationism, barred the United States from providing weapons to any belligerent involved in a war between or among foreign nations.[156]

Roosevelt was reelected in 1936 with a huge majority, but was subsequently weakened somewhat by the results of the 1938 Congressional elections.[157]

By late 1937, Roosevelt was increasingly concerned about foreign aggression, including Japan's invasion of China and Hitler's violations of the Versailles Treaty, and his country's hesitancy to stand up to totalitarianism. Roosevelt, who considered Hitler a "wild man" and a "nut," began to search for a way to prepare the United States for war.[158]

By 1938, even many average Americans, troubled by the spreading hostility of Fascism, were awakening a bit from their isolationist mood.[159]

Although during 1938, the United States took in some 40,000 European Jews, Roosevelt and America were not yet prepared to enlarge existing immigration quotas to accommodate a greater number of Jewish refugees.[160]

In mid-1939, Congress rebuffed the Roosevelt administration's vigorous efforts to repeal the arms embargo established by the Neutrality Act.[161]

In an effort to address the troubling circumstances abroad, President Roosevelt appointed General George C. Marshall as U.S. Army Chief of Staff on September 1, 1939, the day Germany invaded Poland.

---

[154] *Eagle*, 54, *Ike*, 215-16.
[155] *Fateful Choices*, 189.
[156] *Fateful Choices*, 189.
[157] *Fateful Choices*, 188.
[158] *Fateful Choices*, 192-93.
[159] *Fateful Choices*, 193.
[160] *Fateful Choices*, 193, *Hitler's Gamble*, 251, *1944*, 215-216.
[161] *Fateful Choices*, 194.

A CONCISE HISTORY OF THE SECOND WORLD WAR

Marshall, who was promoted over thirty-four more senior officers, was considered brilliant, stern, authoritarian and incorruptible.[162]

In 1939, the American army had only 191,000 men, about 50,000 of whom were posted in American possessions abroad. Fewer than 4,000 were black. In world rank, the U.S. Army was seventeenth in size and combat power, one place behind Romania. Immediately upon being appointed Army Chief of Staff, General Marshall prodded Congress to increase the American troop strength to 227,000 in the Army and 235,000 in the National Guard.[163]

Constrained by the Depression and the effects of American isolationism, the United States military was operating with wholly inadequate and outmoded equipment, much of which had been carried over from World War I. Due to shrinking Congressional appropriations, ammunition for troop exercises was severely limited and in 1939 the country built only six medium tanks.[164]

In mid-August 1939, after learning that Stalin and Hitler were discussing a pact, Roosevelt cautioned the Soviet ambassador in Washington that if Stalin got into bed with Hitler, once France was defeated, Germany would attack the Soviet Union.[165]

In November, following the unprovoked invasion of Poland by Germany and the Soviet Union, the American arms embargo act was repealed, but in its place Congress imposed a ban on selling arms to belligerents on credit.[166]

In late 1939, the world-famous physicist, Albert Einstein, wrote a letter to President Roosevelt warning of the possibility that the Germans were already constructing an atomic weapon. Roosevelt promptly established a committee to investigate the subject.[167]

As the 1940s beckoned, the United States was still unprepared for war either militarily or emotionally.

---

[162] *Masters*, 33, *Soldier's Story*, 184, *Curse*, 299, *Generals' War*, 17, *The Admirals* ("Admirals"), Walter R. Borneman, Little, Brown and Company (2012), 237, *Crusade*, 18.

[163] *Soldier's Story*, 184, *Masters*, 32, *Eagle*, 10, *An Army at Dawn* ("Dawn"), Rick Atkinson, Henry Holt and Company (2002), 8, *The Day of Battle* ("Battle"), Rick Atkinson, Henry Holt and Company (2007), 381, *Crusade*, 2.

[164] *Dawn*, 9, *Fateful Choices*, 193, *Crusade*, 7.

[165] *Fateful Choices*, 194.

[166] *Fateful Choices*, 194, 196-97, *Inferno*, 181.

[167] *Eagle*, 550-51.

Benito Mussolini, the son of an Italian blacksmith, was a socialist in his early life. However, after serving in the Great War, he rejected socialism and advanced a doctrine that became known as Fascism: the subordination of individual interests to the wellbeing of a master state headed by a powerful leader, and that state's use of force to acquire needed resources to further its goal of becoming an empire.[168]

In March 1919, at an early Fascist meeting, Mussolini asserted that Italy deserved to have more territory to serve its growing population. Several years later he made clear his goals of reestablishing the Roman Empire and reducing Britain's strength in the Mediterranean.[169]

In 1922, a Fascist Italian General, Giulio Douhet, authored a book advocating the use of massive airpower in war. His thesis was that the main goal of bombers should not be destruction of an enemy's planes. Rather, having bombers attack an enemy's population centers, communications facilities and industrial sites would cause many civilian deaths and much hardship. This, in turn, would destroy civilian morale and force a speedier end to the conflict. In other words, the more terrible the impact of weapons on civilians, the shorter the conflict (and ultimately the fewer lives lost).[170]

But following World War I, Italy was burdened with large debts and a small economic base that limited its capacity to become a world power. Its national income was but a quarter of Britain's and its people were war weary.[171]

In October 1922, Italian King Victor Emmanuel III appointed Mussolini to head the Italian government. During the remaining years of the 1920s, Mussolini, known as *il Duce* ("the Leader"), stabilized the Italian economy, strengthened its armed forces, took Italy into minor military skirmishes with Greece, Yugoslavia and Albania, sought to create an Italian sphere of influence in Hungary and Austria, and proceeded to establish a totalitarian state at home.[172]

Mussolini defined "totalitarian" as "[e]verything within the state, nothing outside the state, nothing against the state." Stated another

---

[168] *Battle*, 137-38, *Fateful Choices*, 131-33, *WW II Story*, 19-20.

[169] *Fateful Choices*, 131-32.

[170] *Masters of the Air: America's Bomber Boys Who Fought the Air War Against Nazi Germany ("Air Masters")*, Donald L. Miller, Simon & Schuster (2006), 33-35.

[171] *Fateful Choices*, 132.

[172] *Fateful Choices*, 132-38, *Battle*, 138, *WW II Story*, 20.

way, a totalitarian state is one that has a single political party, one educational system, one centrally planned economy, one moral code, one artistic policy and a monopoly on the distribution of information.[173]

The relationship between Mussolini and Hitler was tense in the period just after Hitler came to power in 1933, for both leaders sought influence over Austria.[174]

After local Nazis assassinated the Austrian Chancellor in Vienna in July 1934, Mussolini sent four divisions of Italian troops up to the Brenner Pass in a gesture of support for the Austrians.[175]

In the autumn of 1935, seeking to demonstrate the power of Fascism and Italy's strength, Mussolini sent the Italian army into the tribal kingdom of Ethiopia (then Abyssinia), which lay between Italy's North African colonies of Italian Somaliland and Libya. Seeking to halt the Italian aggression, the League of Nations imposed economic sanctions. While the international condemnation briefly impacted Italy's economy, it also angered its citizens and enhanced Mussolini's popularity among his countrymen. By May, 1936, Italy had, after using mustard gas on enemy forces, prevailed in Ethiopia. Mussolini proudly announced the existence of a new Roman Empire. In July, the largely ineffective League of Nations withdrew its economic sanctions. Mussolini's relations with Britain and France had, however, soured.[176]

In 1936, as Hitler aggressively occupied the Rhineland and Franco fought Communists in the Spanish civil war, Mussolini sought to align himself with Europe's other Fascist leaders. He sent tens of thousands of troops plus war supplies to Franco, and in November 1936, cemented Italy's close ties to Germany by signing a "Rome-Berlin Axis" agreement that established a common German/Italian foreign policy.[177]

In 1937, Italy became a party to the Anti-Comintern Pact that Germany and Japan had executed the previous November. The compact barred each member nation from providing assistance to the Soviet Union if any signatory was at war with that Communist country.[178]

By March 1938, Mussolini had gained significant control over Italy's foreign and domestic affairs, and claimed to share equally with

---

[173] *Iron Curtain*, xxi-xxii.
[174] *Fateful Choices*, 133.
[175] *Reich*, 279-80.
[176] *Fateful Choices*, 134, 140, *1939*, 13, *Battle*, 138, *Reich*, 290, 297.
[177] *Fateful Choices*, 134, *Reich*, 298.
[178] *Fateful Choices*, 96, *Reich*, 299.

King Emmanuel command of the Italian military.[179]

In the summer of 1938, Italy banned Jews from serving in the professions and decided to define Jews as a race rather than practitioners of a religion. In September, foreign Jews, including about 6,000 from Austria and Germany, were expelled from Italy and Italian Jews were forced to withdraw from schools and universities.[180]

Throughout the 1930s, despite Mussolini's posturing, Italy's military was still quite weak compared to those of Germany and Britain and was not expected to be ready for a significant war until 1942.[181]

Mussolini and Hitler met in Munich, Germany a few days before their September 30, 1938 meeting with British Prime Minister Chamberlain and French Premier Daladier regarding Hitler's demand to take the Sudetenland territory from Czechoslovakia. A concerned Mussolini sought to slow down Hitler's apparent willingness to drive Europe into a war. Britain and France, however, capitulated to Hitler's demand.[182]

In a February 1939 speech, Mussolini, consistent with his desire for more "living space," said Italy was effectively landlocked by British control of Gibraltar and the Suez Canal, circumstances he planned to alter. *Il Duce* sought free access to the oceans and to expand Italy's sphere of influence to include the Balkans.[183]

On March 29, 1939, Mussolini insisted that the Kingdom of Albania either accept Italian control or face invasion. After Albania refused, the Italian army invaded. The weak Albanian army was defeated within a week.[184]

On May 22, 1939, Italy and Germany entered into a military alliance, the "Pact of Steel," in which each nation pledged that if either became involved in a war, the other would (a) immediately come to its assistance "with all its military forces on land, at sea and in the air," and (b) not conclude a separate peace agreement. Mussolini had unwisely committed the relatively weak Italy to fight with Germany even if Hitler deliberately initiated the conflict.[185]

As Hitler was warming up his war muscles in mid-1939, Italy's military leaders warned Mussolini that their forces were not yet capable of

---

[179] *Fateful Choices*, 144-45.
[180] *Hitler's Gamble*, 117, 197.
[181] *Fateful Choices*, 140, 147, *Reich*, 493.
[182] *Hitler's Gamble*, 193-94.
[183] *Fateful Choices*, 133, 135.
[184] *Curse*, 269, *Fateful Choices*, 4-5, 136, 392, *Reich*, 469.
[185] *Fateful Choices*, 136, *Battle*, 138, *Reich*, 482-83.

fighting a war against Western European countries. And King Emmanuel III made it clear that he was opposed to taking Italy into war. Thus, Mussolini was caught between his desire to be Hitler's militaristic twin, and the trepidation of Italy's monarch and military.[186]

FRANCE

During the Great War, at least 1,300,000 French troops were killed and over 4,000,000 were wounded, leaving the nation of 50,000,000 with little appetite for further combat.[187]

After World War I ended, France began construction of the defensive Maginot Line, a collection of bunkers and guns along its eastern border with Germany. The Line extended from just below the Ardennes Forest in Belgium south to Switzerland. Stung by the devastation it had suffered at home during World War I, France was determined to fight any future war in a foreign country. In theory, the Maginot Line would free up soldiers from the section of France that it defended to fight an enemy abroad.[188]

The Great Depression hit France hard, leading to many bankruptcies, high unemployment and almost nightly riots and demonstrations in Paris.[189]

During the 1930s, France maintained colonies in North Africa, Indochina, Syria, Lebanon and central Africa.[190]

France's policies and politics during the 1920s and 1930s were influenced significantly by Communism. The French Communist Party, founded in 1920, was well organized and supported leftist French governments. Conservatives in France fretted about Communism's policies and the influence Stalin exercised over European Communist parties.[191]

Between 1920 and 1940, the fickle French elected forty-two different weak governments, including a dozen after Hitler took power in 1933.[192]

The French debated during the 1930s whether it was Nazi Germany or the Communist Soviet Union that posed a larger threat to

---

[186] *Fateful Choices*, 145-46.
[187] *Inferno*, 27, *Ike*, 178, *Paris*, 131.
[188] *Inferno*, 53-54, 63, *Masters*, 65, *WW II Story*, 30.
[189] *1939*, 15, *Paris*, 215.
[190] *Inferno*, 395, *Dawn*, 158, *Ike*, 178.
[191] *Paris*, 24, 213, *Inferno*, 10, 27, *1939*, 7, 16.
[192] *Inferno*, 73, *Paris*, 20-21.

France's welfare. Concerned more at the moment about future German hostility than Communism, in 1932 France entered into a nonaggression pact with the Soviet Union.[193]

Hitler boldly announced in March 1935 that Germany had established an air force, reintroduced a draft, and built a 500,000 man army. France, still lacking any plan for or interest in offensive war measures, offered no military response. France was, however, motivated to seek a mutual assistance pact with the Soviet Union.[194]

In May 1935, Premier Laval, the conservative premier of France, put aside his anti-Communist sentiments in favor of tamping down the German threat, and signed a French/Soviet mutual assistance pact which the French Parliament ratified in early 1936.[195]

In March 1936, when Hitler's army took back the demilitarized Rhineland in violation of the Versailles Treaty, France, with the strongest army in the world, did nothing. Britain, too, stood aside.[196]

In the spring of 1936, the left-leaning Popular Front won French national elections and a Jewish socialist, Leon Blum, briefly became premier of France.[197]

When the Spanish Civil War began in mid-1936, Italy and Germany supported the conservative forces and Communist Russia supported the left-wing forces. Now facing three Fascist nations on its borders and internal political divisions between the left and right, France remained neutral.[198]

By 1937, the French were questioning the value of their mutual assistance pact with the Soviet Union. Stalin's internal purges continued and his killing of most of the Red Army generals suggested that the Soviets might not be an effective and reliable ally in a war against Germany.[199]

In 1938, Hitler sought to take the Sudetenland from Czechoslovakia on the theory that ethnic Germans living there needed protection. In the September 1938 Munich Agreement with Germany, Premier Daladier of France and Britain's Chamberlain quickly capitulated to Hitler's plan to strip Czechoslovakia of a significant part of its territory. The French government voted overwhelmingly in favor of the

---

[193] *1939*, 7, 14.
[194] *1939*, 17, 31.
[195] *1939*, 16-18.
[196] *WW II Story*, 21, *Reich*, 290-96.
[197] *1939*, 18, 20, 37, 42, *Paris*, 24, 215.
[198] *WW II Story*, 21, *Reich*, 297.
[199] *1939*, 26-27, 43.

Munich agreement.[200]

In December 1938, a French government fearful of provoking Hitler signed the Franco-German Declaration that confirmed the friendship and borders between the two nations, and committed them to resolving any differences by consultation.[201]

In March 1939, France promised Poland that within thirteen days after any German invasion of Poland, France would attack the German Siegfried Line. France made this promise solely in an effort to persuade Hitler to holster his guns; the French had no intention of honoring their commitment to Poland.[202]

In late spring, after Hitler had taken Czechoslovakia and Mussolini had invaded Albania, France grew more concerned that war was imminent. Perhaps a pact with the Soviet Union aimed at stopping Nazi aggression would be wise. By this time, however, the Soviets had grown mistrustful of the French (and British) and were becoming more comfortable with the notion of a deal with Hitler.[203]

French (and British) efforts to negotiate a treaty with the Soviet Union moved slowly into the summer, impeded by mutual mistrust and the west's fear of the spread of Communism.[204]

As Hitler's appetite for aggression in Europe grew, a timorous and unprepared France essentially crossed its fingers and hoped for peace.

---

[200] *WW II Story*, 23, *1939*, 71-72.
[201] *Reich*, 436, *Hitler's Gamble*, 250, *1939*, 23, 83-84.
[202] *Inferno*, 4, *Bloodlands*, 115.
[203] *1939*, 123-24, 136-62.
[204] *1939*, 164-75.

Part 2

The Conflict in Europe and North Africa

A LTHOUGH by 1939 the Japanese had already been fighting the Chinese for several years (as will be discussed later), historians tend to consider Germany's September 1, 1939 attack on Poland as the beginning of World War II. Perhaps this is because within about two weeks the conflict in Europe had entangled a fistful of nations. The Soviet Union, acting in concert with Germany, quickly invaded Poland from the east, and the French and British declared war on Germany (although they took no immediate action to assist Poland). Because the conflict in Europe involved many participants and began before Japan was fighting with any Asian nation other than China, this writing will first review the events in Europe and North Africa and then address the contemporaneous and often related events that took place in the Far East.

THE HOSTILITIES BEGIN (1939)

Poland Blitzkrieged

Beginning before dawn on September 1, 1939, Germany, encouraged by a secret pact with Stalin and using some 1,500,000 well-armed German troops, carried out a surprise attack — or *blitzkrieg* — against the neighboring Republic of Poland. Hitler's unprovoked act of aggression launched the Second World War.[205]

Poland in 1939 was a poor nation of thirty million people, including about twenty million Poles, one million ethnic Germans, five million Ukrainians, three million Jews and one million Belarusians. Composed of territory taken from Germany and Russia after the Great War, Poland was established in 1919. Poland's borders, set by the victorious Allies in the Treaty of Versailles, were adjusted somewhat after the Polish-Bolshevik War of 1919-20. Germany and Russia, however, never accepted as legitimate Poland's post-World War I boundaries or

---

[205] *Masters*, 28, *Curse*, 48, *Inferno*, 6, *Bloodlands*, 119-20, *Reich*, 597.

indeed its very existence.[206]

Under the 1939 Pact of Steel, when Hitler's forces invaded Poland, Italy was obligated to join Germany in the battle. However, because King Victor Emmanuel III was opposed to doing so and because Italy's military was unprepared, Mussolini asked for and received Hitler's release of Italy's contractual obligation to declare war.[207]

With Germany's invasion of Poland, Hitler had initiated war in Europe. For the time being, the war he wanted most, against the Soviet Union and its "Jewish Bolshevism," would have to wait.[208]

Western Europe's Token Response

On September 3, 1939, as required by their treaty with Poland, France and Britain formally declared war on Germany. Hitler had assumed that Britain and France would sit still for his aggression in Poland, just as they had done at Munich in 1938. Equally misguided, the French and British hoped that their war declaration would encourage German citizens to rise up and overthrow Hitler. They also hoped that Poland, with the fourth largest army in Europe — some 1,300,000 troops — would be able by itself to fend off Germany for a considerable period of time.[209]

Now at war with the British, a German U-boat torpedoed a British liner off the coast of Scotland late on September 3 and sent her to the bottom with 112 dead, including twenty-eight Americans. During the first week of war, the German navy sank a total of eleven British ships.[210]

When Great Britain declared war against Germany, the British dominions of Australia, Canada, Newfoundland, New Zealand and South Africa joined it in the struggle; Ireland did not (causing considerable Allied bitterness). Still, many people subject to British control in countries like Egypt, Canada, Malaya, India and Burma were opposed to Britain's wartime interests. Other countries that remained neutral (at least nominally) during World War II include Portugal, Spain, Sweden, Switzerland and Turkey.[211]

On September 7, the French tepidly moved ten army divisions five

---

[206] *Inferno*, 4, 15, *Bloodlands*, 7-8, 112, *Curse*, 48.
[207] *Fateful Choices*, 137-38, 146, *Reich*, 551-57, 564-68, 603-04.
[208] *Fateful Choices*, 64.
[209] *Curse*, 48, *Inferno*, 6, 10-11, *Fateful Choices*, 63, *Ike*, 227, *Reich*, 597-622.
[210] *Reich*, 622, 635.
[211] *Engineers*, 19, *Inferno*, 387-88, 401-13, *WW II Story*, 25.

miles into the German Saarland and stopped. Despite having the world's largest army, this was the sum of France's military support for Poland. Neither France nor Britain had the stomach for bombing Germany in 1939.[212]

Poland Falls

By mid-September, the Germans with their *blitzkrieg* method of war had made substantial progress in defeating the Poles. Hitler's tanks destroyed brave Polish cavalry fighting from horseback. In repeated bombing attacks on the resistant city of Warsaw, Germany killed about 25,000 Polish citizens.[213]

On September 17, some 500,000 unprovoked Red Army troops invaded Poland from the east, as contemplated in the secret August 1939 pact between Germany and the Soviet Union. Stalin's foreign minister explained to the stunned Polish ambassador that since the Polish Republic no longer existed, the Red Army was invading to protect ethnic Russians in Poland.[214]

On September 29, 1939, Germany and the Soviet Union signed the German-Soviet Boundary and Friendship Treaty. It defined the new common border between them now that they had invaded Poland and were pocketing its territory. Germany was to get the western part of Poland. The Soviet Union was to control Estonia, Latvia, Lithuania, and parts of Poland, Belarus and Ukraine covering some 77,000 square miles of territory and containing 11,000,000 people. This was the first of three times during World War II that the people in these areas would be invaded and subjected to mass killings.[215]

By October 6, 1939, Poland, which never surrendered, was defeated. That independent nation simply ceased to exist. In seeking to defend against Soviet and German aggression, the Polish army suffered at least 70,000 dead, 140,000 wounded, and 700,000 captured. Germany lost 16,000 killed and 30,000 wounded. Despite their treaty promises, the British and French had forsaken the Poles.[216]

The portion of Poland that Germany seized was home to almost twenty million Poles, Germans and Jews. In the process of defeating Poland, Hitler had increased the number of Jews under his control

---

[212] *Inferno*, 13, 18, *Bloodlands*, 120, *Reich*, 633-35.
[213] *Reich*, 625-26, *Bloodlands*, 119, *Inferno*, 7-8.
[214] *Curse*, 48-49, *Inferno*, 16-17, *Bloodlands*, 123, *Reich*, 626-32.
[215] *Bloodlands*, 124-27, *Reich*, 629-32, *Inferno*, 17.
[216] *Inferno*, 17-21, 23, *WW II Story*, 25, *Bloodlands*, 122, 127, *Dawn*, 5.

from about 330,000 to well over 2,000,000.[217]

Eliminating Polish Leaders

After invading Poland, Hitler pursued his plan to destroy the educated classes of Poles who fell under German control. The Germans killed some 50,000 non-combatant Poles and drove hundreds of thousands of Jews and Poles east into territory then controlled by the Soviets.[218]

Shortly after the Red Army invaded Poland, Stalin, in a program of ethnic cleansing, relocated to the Soviet Union up to 1,500,000 Poles, some 350,000 of whom died from starvation. In order to eliminate senior Polish government officials, military officers and intellectuals who were considered enemies of Russia and Communism, Stalin had 25,000 shot dead and buried in mass graves at Katyn (in Minsk) and elsewhere.[219]

Polish Resistance

Poland was the only nation Germany attacked during World War II in which no subjugated citizens collaborated with the occupying forces. Indeed, about 150,000 Poles fled and later fought with the Allies seeking to defeat Germany.[220]

Waging The Phony War

Once Poland fell, there were no land or air battles between Germany and its passive enemies, France and Britain, for more than six months. Pundits called this the "phony war" or "*sitzkreig*."[221]

In an October 6, 1939 speech, Hitler proposed that Germany, France and Britain enter into a peace agreement. France and Britain rejected the proposal as vague and not correcting the damage Germany had already done to Poland and Czechoslovakia.[222]

In the autumn of 1939, France's army was touted as the best in Europe and Britain's navy was deemed to be invulnerable. Still, France and Britain hoped to strengthen their forces before engaging in actual combat with Germany. After defeating Poland, Hitler was eager to

---

[217] *Bloodlands*, 131-32, *Inferno*, 24, *Dawn*, 5.

[218] *Bloodlands*. 126-27, *Reich*, 659-65.

[219] *Curse*, 49-50, *Inferno*, 22-23, 480, *WW II Story*, 28, *Folly*, 44, *Bloodlands*, 125-26, 128-29, 140.

[220] *Inferno*, 23-24.

[221] *Reich*, 633, *Inferno*, 28, *Dawn*, 5.

[222] *Reich*, 641-43.

attack west immediately but his generals persuaded him to wait until winter had ended and the German military was even stronger.[223]

The Allies did impose a naval blockade on Germany, causing some shortages there. However, the Soviets allowed Germany to receive goods through Russian ports. In addition to the blockade, the British Navy sought to destroy German war ships anywhere they were found on the high seas. During the fall of 1939, the German pocket battleship *Graf Spee* sank nine British merchant ships. On December 14, three British cruisers battled the *Graf Spee* in waters 400 miles off the coast of Uruguay. While the British vessels were seriously damaged, the gravely wounded German ship fled to the harbor in Montevideo where the captain scuttled it on December 17.[224]

Assassination Attempt

On November 8, a bomb placed behind the speaker's platform in Munich exploded just twelve minutes after Hitler finished his speech. Seven people were killed, but the *Fuehrer* was unhurt. Hitler attributed the assassination attempt to the British Secret Service.[225]

War in Finland

On November 30, 1939, Stalin attacked Finland with more than 1,000,000 troops. (Finland had been ruled by Russia until 1918, when anti-Bolsheviks, assisted by German troops, prevailed in a Finnish civil war). The four-month Russian/Finnish battle ended in an armistice on March 12, 1940, but the fact that between 127,000 and 250,000 Russian soldiers were killed exposed to Hitler and the world the weakness of the Red Army.[226]

On December 14, 1939, the Soviet Union was expelled from the League of Nations because of its unprovoked attack on Finland.[227]

As 1939 came to a close, Germany and the Soviet Union had erased Poland from the map, and Hitler held the stronger hand against the hesitant French and British.

---

[223] *Inferno*, 26-27, 41, *Fateful Choices*, 64, *Reich*, 643-47, 652, 670-72, *Paris*, 20.
[224] *Inferno*, 39, 41, 265, *Reich*, 666-70, 673.
[225] *Reich*, 652-53.
[226] *Curse*, 52, *Fateful Choices*, 260, *Inferno*, 31-38, *1939*, 247, *WW II Story*, 27-28., *Reich*, 665-66, 683.
[227] *1939*, 238.

Germany's Early Actions

In 1940, Hitler boldly commissioned an inventory of every work of art in the western world that he claimed rightly belonged to Germany, including every work taken from Germany since 1500, every work by an artist of German or Austrian descent, every work done in Germany, and every work done in the Germanic style.[228]

In January 1940, as a method of dealing with what he called the "Jewish problem," Hitler suggested that the 2,000,000 or more Jews under German control be deported to the Soviet Union. Stalin declined the proposal, which revived the notion in Germany of shipping European Jews to Madagascar.[229]

On February 11, 1940, the Soviet Union and Germany entered into another trade agreement calling for the Soviets to furnish during the next eighteen months huge quantities of foodstuffs, raw materials and oil to Germany in exchange for planes, guns, ships and equipment. In addition, the Soviets agreed to purchase for Germany items that the British blockade prevented Germany from buying for itself.[230]

Although Italy had not joined Germany in declaring war in September 1939, Mussolini assured Hitler on March 18, 1940, that Italy's entry into the war on Germany's side was inevitable — in four months or so.[231]

Germany Invades Denmark and Norway

Even though Germany and Denmark had recently signed a nonaggression pact, on April 9, 1940, German forces invaded Denmark, facing little resistance. Germany took the position that it had not conquered Denmark; rather, it was setting up a protectorate.[232]

On April 9, 1940, Germany also invaded Norway, a nation of 3,000,000 citizens. One objective was to obtain additional ports from which the German navy could escape Britain's blockade and through which Germany could receive needed Swedish iron ore. The Norwegians strenuously resisted, but Germany set up a puppet government headed by Vidkun Quisling, a Norwegian who had collaborated with

---

[228] *Monuments Men*, 118, *Paris*, 8.

[229] *Bloodlands*, 144-45, *Hitler's Gamble*, 6, 144.

[230] *Curse*, 56-57, *Reich*, 668.

[231] *Fateful Choices*, 148.

[232] *Fateful Choices*, 20, *Inferno*, 45, *WW II Story*, 29, *Reich*, 694-700.

the Germans before the invasion. Disorganized British and French troops landed in Norway several weeks later in an attempt to stop the Germans, but were poorly led. They withdrew by May, leaving the Germans in control. In several naval battles near Norway during 1940, the Germans lost three of their eight cruisers, ten of their twenty destroyers and six U-boats, while the British lost three cruisers, seven destroyers, a carrier and four submarines. Overall casualties there were: Germany 5,296, Britain 4,500, French and Polish troops 530, Norway 1,800. On June 7, Norway's powerless monarch and government fled to Britain.[233]

Churchill Becomes Prime Minister

Precipitated by Britain's uninspired military performance in Norway, on May 10, 1940, Winston Churchill was appointed to replace Neville Chamberlain as British Prime Minister. In his address to the House of Commons, Churchill soberly remarked, "I would say to the House, as I said to those who have joined this government: 'I have nothing to offer but blood, toil, tears and sweat.'"[234]

Breaking Secret Codes

In April 1940, the British Code and Cyber School at Bletchley Park in England broke the sophisticated German Enigma code, which the British called "Ultra." Poles who had worked at the Enigma factory had delivered a replica of the code machine to the British in 1939. Thereafter, the Allies made concerted efforts to hide from the Axis forces that their secret code had been broken.[235]

The Japanese used complex machines to encrypt and decrypt secret messages sent to and from their diplomats. Aware that the United States had broken an earlier diplomatic code, in 1938 the Japanese began use of a new electronic coding machine. In September 1940, the United States broke this Japanese "Purple" diplomatic code by developing a machine that replicated the equipment Japan used to encode its messages. The Americans referred to all of their decoding of Japanese messages as "Magic" and took special measures to prevent the Japanese from discovering that their code was no longer secure.[236]

---

[233] *Inferno*, 43-52, *1939*, 250, *Curse*, 51, *WW II Story*, 29-30, *Reich*, 673-83, 694-712.

[234] *Masters*, 35, *Fateful Choices*, 12, *Inferno*, 52, *Ike*, 232.

[235] *The Ultra Secret* ("*Ultra Secret*"), F. W. Winterbotham, Harper & Row (1974), 15, *Battle*, 54-55, *Inferno*, 357-58, *WW II Story*, 175-76, *Judgment*, 42.

[236] *Judgment*, 42, *Eagle*, 446, *Conspiracy*, 980-81, *Reich*, 885, *Dawn*, 80-82.

In 1940, the British proposed that they and the United States exchange secret information of a technical nature. After Roosevelt accepted the proposal, the Americans delivered copies of the Magic Japanese diplomatic code-breaking equipment to Britain, expecting Britain to reciprocate by delivering a copy of the Ultra machine. The British reneged on their promise, claiming that it was against British policy to share code secrets with a neutral nation, which America still was at that time.[237]

Despite having broken the Purple code and having many message listening stations, the Americans in 1941 were able to interpret only about half of the coded Japanese diplomatic messages.[238]

By late 1941, Italian military intelligence had broken the United States diplomatic code and was intercepting messages sent from Cairo.[239]

In 1944, the capture of Japanese code books made reading Japan's current codes easier.[240]

In 1944, at Congress's direction, the Army investigated why the Navy and Army at Pearl Harbor had not been adequately prepared for a surprise attack. To protect from possible public disclosure the fact that the United States was reading Japan's secret diplomatic messages, General Marshall ordered Army witnesses to conceal in their testimony the Purple breakthrough. He later explained that his primary responsibility was to help the United States win the war, and that protecting the Purple secret was more important than providing candid testimony.[241]

Germany Attacks West

Early on May 10, 1940, the "phony war" among Germany, France and Britain that had existed since the previous autumn suddenly ended. Some of Hitler's troops invaded the neutral Netherlands and Belgium. To counter these attacks, the French and British sent their main forces northeast from France toward Belgium. This was just what Hitler wanted. At the center of the French defensive line further south, the main German force of 134,000 soldiers and over 1,000 tanks charged toward France through Luxembourg and the Belgian Ardennes Forest.

---

[237] *Judgment*, 42-44.
[238] *Judgment*, 41, 44, *Inferno*, 358.
[239] *Ike*, 253.
[240] *Inferno*, 358.
[241] *Judgment*, 198-200.

Their objective was to cross the Meuse River in France, then drive northwest to the English Channel, snaring the main British and French forces in Belgium. Even farther south, additional German troops were arrayed against France's Maginot Line.[242]

By May 12, the German forces in the center had reached the Meuse. The next morning more than 1,000 *Luftwaffe* planes bombed the poorly led and equipped French forces, many of whom panicked and retreated. By May 14, substantially all French resistance near the Meuse had collapsed, leading to a French sense of defeat.[243]

The German forces that crossed the Meuse then advanced during the next week toward the English Channel.[244]

On May 15, after Germany bombed Rotterdam and killed almost 1,000 civilians, the Netherlands surrendered — just five days after hostilities began. The Dutch queen and her government fled to London.[245]

Also on May 15, a panicked French Premier Reynaud told Churchill by phone: "We are defeated. We have lost the battle."[246]

By May 20, 1940, the main German forces in France had advanced 150 miles and reached the northern French coast. The British, French and Belgian troops in Belgium were cornered.[247]

The Dunkirk Evacuation

Although British and French military leaders agreed to jointly counterattack the German salient on May 21, little came of it. The French lacked leadership and heart to fight. The British actually attacked but by May 23 were being driven back by German troops commanded by Erwin Rommel. As the British retreated, recriminations between the French and British leaders increased because the British failed to honor a promise to have three of their divisions screen a French withdrawal to the south.[248]

By May 25, the British had decided that their forces should retreat to the Channel coast at Dunkirk, Belgium in anticipation of an emergency evacuation to England. The French felt that the British were fleeing, and the British felt that the French lacked the will to fight.[249]

---

[242] *Masters*, 35, *Fateful Choices*, 20, 65, *Inferno*, 52-54, *WW II Story*, 31-32, *Reich*, 713-29.

[243] *Inferno*, 54-58, 61, *Fateful Choices*, 25.

[244] *Inferno*, 59, *Reich*, 723-29.

[245] *Fateful Choices*, 65, *WW II Story*, 31, *Reich*, 720-23, *Air Masters*, 53.

[246] *Paris*, xi, *1944*, 50.

[247] *Fateful Choices*, 20, *Inferno*, 54, *Reich*, 727-29.

[248] *Inferno*, 61-64.

[249] *Fateful Choices*, 27, *Reich*, 731, *Inferno*, 62, *Paris*, 26.

On May 26, President Roosevelt, acting as an intermediary at the urging of France and Britain, asked Mussolini if Italy would agree to stay out of the war in exchange for (a) participating on an equal basis in the peace process and (b) France and Britain's willingness to address Italy's claims to land in the Mediterranean and North Africa. Mussolini rejected the offer the next day.[250]

Against the unanimous counsel of his own government and without first consulting Allies Britain and France, King Leopold III of Belgium unconditionally surrendered his nation to the Germans on May 28. In doing so, he disobeyed his duties under the Belgian constitution.[251]

Between May 28 and June 4, 1940, 224,301 British and 111,172 French and Belgian soldiers were, on almost 900 military and civilian ships, evacuated from Dunkirk to England across the Channel.[252]

Although Britain's troops escaped the Germans at Dunkirk, their weapons did not. Left behind were 64,000 vehicles, seventy-six tons of ammunition and 2,500 guns. Britain's land forces were substantially disarmed.[253]

In a curious strategic move, on May 24 Hitler had ordered his troops and tanks, then only fifteen miles south of Dunkirk, not to advance because he assumed that the German air force would soon destroy the retreating Allied forces. During the evacuation from Dunkirk German planes did attack, sinking six destroyers and damaging twenty-five others, but British planes provided a strong defense.[254]

Britain Refuses to Surrender

On June 4, 1940, a determined Churchill famously told the House of Commons that "We shall fight on the beaches, we shall fight on the landing grounds, we shall fight in the fields and in the streets, we shall fight in the hills; we shall never surrender ...."[255]

Following British War Cabinet debates over whether to try to reach a peace agreement with Hitler, Churchill announced on June 6 that under "no circumstances whatsoever" would Britain participate in

---

[250] *Fateful Choices*, 30-32.
[251] *Masters*, 37, *Fateful Choices*, 34, *Inferno*, 64, *Reich*, 729-31.
[252] *Soldier's Story*, 182, *Masters*, 37, *Fateful Choices*, 45-46, *Inferno*, 65-66, *WW II Story*, 33-34, *Reich*, 731.
[253] *Inferno*, 67.
[254] *Fateful Choices*, 27, *Inferno*, 66, *Reich*, 731-38.
[255] *Fateful Choices*, 46, *WW II Story*, 37, *Reich*, 737-38.

peace or armistice negotiations with the Germans.[256]

France Falls

In early June, what remained of the French army was fighting with more heart. The Germans, driving toward Paris, were suffering some 5,000 casualties each day. The French boldly promised that their troops would defend Paris.[257]

However, on June 10, 1940, as German forces neared, Premier Reynaud and his French government fled to the Loire. Brigadier General Charles de Gaulle, who had just been named undersecretary for war and national defense, escaped to London. Two days later, Paris was declared an "open city" in the hope that it would not be destroyed in battle.[258]

Without firing a shot in Paris, the Germans occupied the undefended city on June 14, 1940.[259]

In mid-June, a worried Churchill and the British cabinet sought to persuade France not to sign an armistice with Germany. They even went to the extraordinary length of offering to form a Franco-British union — a single nation composed of both countries.[260]

But on June 16, 1940, Paul Reynaud resigned as French Premier and was replaced by Marshal Philippe Pétain, an 84 year old hero of World War I. The next day in a radio address, Pétain told the French people that it was time to stop fighting the Germans. He then asked Germany for an armistice.[261]

On June 22, 1940, after about six weeks of battle, France and Pétain agreed to an armistice with Germany which was signed in the same rail car France used to accept Germany's World War I surrender. Hitler's terms were relatively lenient out of concern that the French fleet would otherwise side with Britain and in the hope that Britain, too, would be encouraged to negotiate an end to hostilities.[262]

On June 28, Hitler travelled from a defeated Belgium to proudly tour Paris as a victor.[263]

---

[256] *Fateful Choices*, 47-49.
[257] *Inferno*, 67-68, *Reich*, 738-39, *Paris*, 29.
[258] *Guns*, 179, *Dawn*, 6, *Inferno*, 68-69, *Generals' War*, 131, *Reich*, 738, 744, *Paris*, xi, 27-29, 41.
[259] *Monuments Men*, 126, *WW II Story*, 35, *Reich*, 738, *Paris*, 12.
[260] *Paris*, 43-44.
[261] *Eagle*, 60, *Dawn*, 6, *Inferno*, 70, *Reich*, 738.
[262] *Fateful Choices*, 65, 160, *Curse*, 53, *Eagle*, 60, *WW II Story*, 36, *Reich*, 735, 740-46.
[263] *Paris*, 72-91.

Germany's victory over France, Belgium and the Netherlands came at a cost to it of 43,000 dead and 117,000 wounded. The French lost more than 50,000 dead and over 100,000 wounded. Britain lost 11,000 dead. The Germans captured some 1,500,000 French prisoners and sent them to Germany to serve as slave labor.[264]

Under its armistice with Germany, the southern forty percent of France (excluding Paris) remained under the control of the Pétain Vichy government and unoccupied by Germany. Vichy France also retained her colonies abroad, including Morocco, Algeria and Tunisia, and was permitted to keep her army of 120,000 men and her navy, in exchange for agreeing to fight all invaders, including the English. Admiral Darlan commanded all Vichy military services and was Pétain's designated successor.[265]

General de Gaulle, living in London and dependent upon the British, formed the Free French, an organization that denounced Vichy France. De Gaulle proclaimed himself head of the French government in exile. Despite his calls for the French to join his cause, few did so. He was intensely anti-British and anti-American. While located in London, his Gaullist secret service used brutality on French citizens to obtain pledges of personal allegiance to de Gaulle.[266]

The United States officially recognized the Vichy government, whereas Britain refused to and instead recognized the Free French government of General de Gaulle.[267]

Out of hatred for and fear of the left, most aristocratic, commercial and bourgeois French citizens backed Pétain until German oppression became intolerable and an Allied victory seemed likely.[268]

Prior to June of 1940, German navy ships and U-boats had to travel north from ports in Germany all the way around northern Scotland in order to reach the Atlantic. After the French capitulated, German ships could sail from ports in France.[269]

Although Jews in France had civil rights, the French had a long

---

[264] *Inferno*, 72, *Paris*, 31.

[265] *Paris*, xxvi,, 193, *Dawn*, 6, *Mark Clark — The Last of the Great World War II Commanders* ("*Clark*"), Martin Blumenson, Congdon & Weed (1984), 65-66, 72, *Reich*, 744-46.

[266] *Guns*, 34, *Dawn*, 6, *Generals' War*, 132, *Paris*, 206, *The Supreme Commander* ("*Supreme Commander*"), Stephen E. Ambrose, Doubleday, Garden City, N.Y. (1970), 98.

[267] *Ike*, 255.

[268] *Inferno*, 80.

[269] *Engineers*, 20.

history of anti-Semitism. After Paris fell, the Vichy government cooperated with the Germans in dealing harshly with Jews. In October 1940, Jews were made to register with the police — about 150,000 did so. On July 16-17, 1942, the French police rounded up 13,000 Jews in Paris and imprisoned them.[270]

After defeating the French, Hitler still considered shipping several million European Jews to the French island of Madagascar. The idea was dropped later in 1941 because Britain continued to oppose the Germans and, thus, Germany could not spare the ships required to transport Jews to Madagascar.[271]

Italian Aggression

On June 10, 1940, as German troops neared Paris and a victory over France, Italy's "me too" Mussolini declared war on France and Great Britain, contending that they were restricting Italy's territorial expansion. But thirty-two attacking Italian divisions were stymied by six French divisions on a front running from the Alps to the Riviera. Hitler said of the Italians, "First they were too cowardly to take part. Now they are in a hurry so that they can share in the spoils."[272]

On June 24, 1940, two days after Germany and France formally ended their hostilities, Italy reached a separate armistice with France that did little more than establish a fifty-mile demilitarized zone between France and Italy. Mussolini, humiliated by his army's lack of success, recognized that it was the Germans who had defeated France.[273]

Before siding with Germany, Mussolini never seriously considered supporting France and England because he was afraid that if he did so Germany would invade Italy, and because he was in awe of Hitler. Even though it was militarily unprepared for war, Italy declined to remain neutral because Mussolini thought he would gain power and lands when Germany prevailed.[274]

After signing an armistice with France, Italy was still at war with Britain. Mussolini's goal was to use Italian forces based in Libya to drive the British forces in Egypt out of Africa, thereby giving Italy

---

[270] *Inferno*, 391, 497, *Paris*, 21, 272-86.
[271] *Fateful Choices*, 446-47, *Inferno*, 491, *Bloodlands*, 160-61.
[272] *Engineers*, 20, *Fateful Choices*, 129, 396, *Dawn*, 5-6, *Battle*, 138-39, *Inferno*, 74, *Reich*, 739-41.
[273] *Fateful Choices*, 160, *Reich*, 740, 746, *Paris*, xxvi, 44.
[274] *Fateful Choices*, 157-59.

control of the Suez Canal.[275]

In the summer of 1940, Mussolini also wanted to invade Yugoslavia and Greece, but Hitler made it clear that he preferred that the Balkans remain quiet for the time being.[276]

Soviet Union Actions

Stalin was stunned by Germany's rapid victories in Europe. His strategic plans had assumed a lengthy contest in the west during which both German and Allied forces would be significantly weakened, giving the Soviets time to rearm.[277]

As the French were yielding to Germany, Stalin aggressively pursued his goal of expanding the parts of Eastern Europe under his control. In mid-June 1940, the Soviet Union issued ultimatums to Lithuania, Latvia and Estonia demanding that key government officials there resign and that the Red Army be given "free passage" through those lands. Several days later Red Army troops occupied the main cities in each country. Those Baltic nations were then intimidated into "asking" to become members of the Soviet Union, which request was granted in August 1940. Within the first year of Soviet occupation, some 135,000 "anti-Soviet" Lithuanians, Latvians and Estonians were killed, deported or missing.[278]

On June 26, 1940, Stalin insisted that Romania cede to the Soviet Union two of its segments: Bessarabia and Bucovina. Romania yielded to the demand the next day. Because the ceded lands did not include Romania's precious oil fields, Germany supported the Soviet demand.[279]

Stalin's view in 1940 was that Hitler's desire to seize land in the east was motivated mainly by Germany's desire for additional food sources and natural resources. Thus, Stalin hoped that if the Soviet Union satisfied much of Germany's need for essential goods, the risk of war would be reduced. By the summer of 1940, the Soviet Union was the most important source of Germany's raw materials and continued to be so for the next year.[280]

Distressed by the Red Army's woeful performance against Finland,

---

[275] *Fateful Choices*, 161.

[276] *Fateful Choices*, 166.

[277] *Inferno*, 73-74, *Curse*, 51.

[278] *Curse*, 51-52, *Inferno*, 74, *Reich*, 794.

[279] *Reich*, 794-95, 800.

[280] *Curse*, 56, *Fateful Choices*, 69, *Inferno*, 74, 98, *Reich*, 839-40.

and still anxious about Hitler's ambition, in mid-1940 Stalin ordered a significant buildup of the poorly trained, led and armed Red Army. By 1941, the Soviet Union's military force had swelled to 5,400,000 men, compared to just 1,600,000 in early 1938.[281]

Britain Continues to Fight

Hitler assumed that once France fell, Britain, having been routed in Norway and Belgium, would be eager to make peace. Thus he was prepared to offer lenient terms: Britain would (unlike France or Poland) continue as a free and intact nation so long as it did not interfere with Germany's actions on the Continent. But the British were not interested in a peace that would assure their freedom at the cost of enslaving the nations Hitler had already defeated.[282]

On June 18, Churchill addressed the House of Commons:

> The whole might and fury of the enemy must very soon be turned on us. Hitler knows that he will have to break us in this island or lose war. If we can stand up to him, all Europe may be free.... But if we fail, then the whole world, including the United States, will sink into the abyss of a new Dark Age, made more sinister, and perhaps more protracted, by the lights of a perverted science. Let us, therefore, brace ourselves to our duties and so bear ourselves that, if the British Empire and Commonwealth last for a thousand years, men will still say, "This was their finest hour."[283]

Still, in 1940 the poorly equipped British army was not prepared to fight the Germans in mainland Europe. Most of its soldiers were stationed in England to counter a possible invasion. In order to defend the Suez Canal, about 100,000 British troops were assigned to Egypt. In adjacent Libya and nearby Abyssinia, Mussolini had stationed some 600,000 troops. Starting in the summer of 1940, the two armies scuffled back and forth in Egypt and Libya for months.[284]

Meanwhile, exile governments from Norway, Belgium, Holland, France, Poland and Czechoslovakia operated out of London. Their tattered military forces trained in Britain for the coming battles against

---

[281] *Fateful Choices*, 264-65.
[282] *Reich*, 747, 751.
[283] *Inferno*, 77-78, *Reich*, 747.
[284] *Inferno*, 103-109, *WW II Story*, 50-51.

the Axis powers.[285]

Hitler assumed that the United States would be prepared to enter the war by 1942. Thus, he believed that Germany had to gain complete control of Europe by the end of 1941.[286]

In July, 1940, Hitler sought a way to both obtain a settlement with Britain and keep the United States out of the war in Europe. Doing so would allow him to turn to the war he had wanted to wage for years — against Jewish Bolshevism in the Soviet Union and to acquire more "living space."[287]

In a speech in Germany on July 19, 1940, Hitler criticized British politicians for continuing the war and made a vague peace offer: "I can see no reason why this war must go on." The gritty British promptly rejected his suggestion.[288]

In order to encourage the British to agree to peace terms, Hitler developed a three-pronged approach: (a) intense German bombing of British shipping, factories, air bases and other facilities, (b) terror attacks against British population centers, and (c) an invasion of England once Germany had gained control of the air.[289]

Hitler also reasoned in July 1940 that if Britain did not promptly agree to peace, Germany could invade and defeat the Soviet Union. This would dash Britain's hope for Soviet support in opposing the Nazis, and Britain would then be compelled to seek a treaty.[290]

Britain's Vital Naval Power

The isolated British relied on their navy (a) to serve as an offensive weapon worldwide, and (b) to guard the delivery of essential supplies from and to Gibraltar, Malta, Egypt, India, the Far East and the United States.[291]

Once France and Belgium fell to the Germans, and Italy, with its substantial navy, joined the Axis powers in 1940, the survival of Great Britain depended on keeping the Atlantic's shipping lanes open.[292]

At the outset of World War II, the combined British and French navies were superior to Germany's, but the French collapse imme-

---

[285] *WW II Story*, 38.

[286] *Fateful Choices*, 85, *Reich*, 821.

[287] *Fateful Choices*, 66, *Inferno*, 78.

[288] *Fateful Choices*, 53, 66, *Reich*, 753-57.

[289] *Reich*, 760.

[290] *Fateful Choices*, 54, 67, *Reich*, 752, 796-800, 846.

[291] *WW II Story*, 44.

[292] *Engineers*, 20-21.

diately threatened that advantage. In order to keep Vichy France from augmenting the German navy, on July 3, 1940, the British navy attacked and destroyed much of the French fleet (anchored at Mers el-Kébir, Algeria) with the loss of 1,297 French lives.[293]

Britain's Mediterranean fleet was substantial but in many parts of those waters it was forced to operate without meaningful air cover. The range of Britain's land-based planes flying from Gibraltar, Malta, Egypt and Palestine was limited, whereas Axis forces had air bases throughout the Mediterranean. Presenting an additional risk, Italy's modern fleet included close to one hundred submarines.[294]

Germany relied primarily on its U-boats to disrupt Atlantic shipping lanes. Allied vessel losses were 3.9 million tons in 1940, 4.3 million tons in 1941 and 7.8 million tons in 1942, mostly suffered in the North Atlantic. Still, ninety-nine percent of all ships sailing the Atlantic to Britain during the war arrived safely, many saved by information gleaned from Ultra intercepts.[295]

During the entire war, the causes of Allied shipping losses included: 6.1 percent due to surface raiders, 6.5 percent due to mines, 13.4 percent due to air attacks, and 70 percent due to U-boats.[296]

The Battle of Britain

The Battle of Britain — Germany's massive air attack on London and surrounding areas — began in August 1940 and continued until late that year. Day after day and week after week, German fighters and bombers crossed the English Channel, sometimes more than 1,000 planes a day. But the Royal Air Force, outnumbered four to one, proved to be more than a match for the enemy fighters and bombers, largely because the British were aided by radar (which the Germans had not yet perfected). On September 7, Hitler switched from trying to eradicate Britain's fighters to intense day and night bombing of London. This change of focus was a tactical error that helped the weakened RAF survive.[297]

In three months during the Battle of Britain, pilots flying for Britain and aided by ground-based radar shot down almost 2,500 German planes, killing some 6,000 German airmen and preserving the English-

[293] *Fateful Choices*, 213, *Dawn*, 26, *Inferno*, 79, *WW II Story*, 44, 50.

[294] *Inferno*, 103, 265, *WW II Story*, 44, 49.

[295] *Engineers*, 21-22, *Inferno*, 268-70.

[296] *Inferno*, 268.

[297] *Engineers*, 90, 98-99, *Inferno*, 85, *WW II Story*, 38-41, *Reich*, 769, 774-82.

speaking nation.[298]

Churchill, referring the RAF pilots, told the British House of Commons on August 20, "never in the field of human conflict was so much owed by so many to so few."[299]

Hitler's air attack on the residents of Britain, instead of persuading its citizens to surrender, inspired the British to fight on. Overall during the war, 60,595 British citizens were killed by German air attacks.[300]

In August, Britain for the first time dropped bombs on Berlin, causing anxiety among German civilians but little military damage.[301]

Had the British lost the Battle of Britain in 1940, they intended to continue waging war from Canada.[302]

Ironically, while the German air force waged war over Britain, the German army fired scarcely a shot for a full year after France fell (except for a small force sent to North Africa in April 1941).[303]

Hitler's Failed Plan to Invade England

Frustrated by Britain's unwillingness to discuss peace terms, on July 16, 1940, Hitler ordered that preparations be made for a September German cross-Channel invasion of Britain ("Operation Sea Lion") that would entail landing 260,000 soldiers on a 200 mile stretch of the English coast. Germany expected to gain air control over the Royal Air Force prior to the invasion.[304]

But because Hitler had long assumed Britain would surrender once France fell, Germany had neglected to design and build the kinds of special landing craft Axis soldiers would need to invade England from the European mainland. As a fallback measure, the German navy was told to gather from one place or another 1,722 barges, 1,161 motorboats, 471 tugs and 155 transports for the planned mid-September invasion across the choppy Channel. But it soon became clear that taking such vessels from Germany would stymie its economy. Some believe that Germany's failure to build the needed landing craft was a prime factor in Germany's ultimate defeat.[305]

Germany's planned invasion of England was also hurt by the naval

---

[298] *Dawn*, 6-7, *Inferno*, 80-81.

[299] *Reich*, 782.

[300] *Inferno*, 95-96, 465.

[301] *Inferno*, 460, *Reich*, 778.

[302] *Burma*, 389, *Fateful Choices*, 26, *Inferno*, 89.

[303] *Inferno*, 98.

[304] *Engineers*, 90, *Reich*, 752-53, 761-65.

[305] *Soldier's Story*, 183, *Inferno*, 79, *Bloodlands*, 159, *Reich*, 759-67.

losses Germany had suffered during the sea battles near Norway. Those sunken ships were unavailable to provide either protection or sea transport.[306]

Another significant factor undermining Germany's plan to invade the British Isles was the *Luftwaffe's* ongoing inability to establish air control over Britain and the English Channel. This lack of air control also meant that Britain's navy and air force were able to bombard the invasion vessels Germany was gathering in ports along the French coast.[307]

On September 14, Hitler delayed the planned invasion of England for two weeks, hoping that in the interim Germany's air force would be able to neutralize the Royal Air Force.[308]

Because Britain's air attacks were causing substantial losses to Germany's invasion vessels, on September 19 Hitler ordered his invasion forces in France to disperse to minimize the risk of further damage.[309]

On October 12, 1940, faced with reluctance from both his navy and his army, a frustrated Hitler postponed the planned invasion of Britain until at least 1941. He reluctantly concluded that a Channel crossing would be quite hazardous and worth pursuing only if all other means failed to bring Britain to terms.[310]

Had the Germans succeeded in landing invasion troops in England, as a last resort Churchill considered using mustard gas against the German soldiers who came ashore.[311]

America Begins to Emerge From Isolation

In the spring of 1940, the United States had just 245,000 men in its army, ranking it twentieth in the world, and only 1,350 planes for defense.[312]

As the U.S. Army's mobilization began in 1940, it had just 14,000 professional officers, many of whom were old, tired and inept.[313]

Congress approved President Roosevelt's May 1940 request for a 500 percent increase in defense spending, including almost 50,000

---

[306] *Reich*, 781.

[307] *Bloodlands*, 159, *Reich*, 770-73, 820.

[308] *Reich*, 772.

[309] *Reich*, 773.

[310] *Engineers*, 99, *Fateful Choices*, 67, 75, *WW II Story*, 41, *Reich*, 774.

[311] *Reich*, 785, *1944*, 49.

[312] *Fateful Choices*, 198, *Crusade*, 2.

[313] *Dawn*, 10, *Crusade*, 7.

planes for the Army and a seventy per cent increase in the Navy's fleet.[314]

In June 1940, President Roosevelt strengthened his cabinet (and ability to prepare for war) by appointing Frank Knox as Secretary of the Navy and Henry L. Stimson as Secretary of War. Both were Republicans and hawkish. Stimson, bright and robust at age seventy-three, had served many presidents and was a longtime advocate of strong British-American ties. Knox, who served as one of Teddy Roosevelt's Rough Riders, had been the Republican vice presidential candidate in 1936.[315]

On June 28, 1940, Congress, out of fear that Roosevelt would give United States naval assets to needy Britain, passed a law saying that no American military material could be turned over to a foreign government unless the Army Chief of Staff (General Marshall) or the Chief of Naval Operations certified that the material was useless for American defense.[316]

At about the same time, however, Congress passed and Roosevelt signed two Naval Expansion Acts which authorized construction of eighteen aircraft carriers, seven battleships, twenty-nine cruisers, 115 destroyers and forty-two submarines.[317]

In July 1940, Democrats nominated Roosevelt for a third term as president.[318]

The Selective Service Act of August 1940 authorized the United States Army to draft 900,000 men, but only for one year of service and only for deployment in the western hemisphere. Sixteen million American men registered for the draft that year. To be drafted in 1940, the candidate had to be at minimum five feet tall, weigh at least 105 pounds, have twelve or more of his natural thirty-two teeth, be free of flat feet, venereal disease and hernias, and not be a father, felon or eighteen years old. Initially, more than forty of every one hundred candidates were rejected.[319]

The American World War II draft was egalitarian in application. In 1942, Princeton University graduated 683 men, 84 percent of whom joined the military. Twenty-five of them would die during the war,

---

[314] *Fateful Choices*, 212, *Air Masters*, 45, *Crucible*, 137.

[315] *Fateful Choices*, 203, 205, *Eagle*, 61, *Judgment*, 27, *Slept*, 55-56, *Crucible*, 126.

[316] *Fateful Choices*, 215.

[317] *Admirals*, 202,-03.

[318] *Fateful Choices*, 213-14.

[319] *Fateful Choices*, 314, *Dawn*, 8-9, *Crusade*, 3.

including nineteen killed in combat.[320]

On August 17, 1940, Attorney General Robert Jackson gave Roosevelt a legal opinion that fifty older United States destroyers (which Churchill had requested to use against the anticipated German invasion of England) could be certified as not essential to American national security — a highly questionable conclusion intended to enable Roosevelt to help Britain.[321]

In September 1940, Britain and the United States signed an agreement swapping those fifty American destroyers for access to certain British bases in Bermuda and elsewhere in the Atlantic. This move, which did not require Congressional approval, signaled the end of United States neutrality.[322]

Public opinion polls taken in August and September of 1940 revealed that eighty-three percent of Americans favored staying out of war with Germany and Italy, and less than thirty-five percent favored more United States help for Britain. Mindful of these sentiments, during a presidential campaign speech Roosevelt cunningly assured American mothers and fathers that, "Your boys are not going to be sent into any foreign wars."[323]

Many left-leaning American intellectuals and academics opposed any United States support for Britain and France, arguing that those nations were imperialists engaged in a war with other imperialists.[324]

On November 5, 1940, Roosevelt was reelected to an unprecedented third term as president, receiving fifty-five percent of the vote.[325]

American military leaders recognized that proper preparation for war included not just boosting troop strength, arms and training, but also developing efficient and effective methods of mobilizing American industry to produce the needs of a powerful military.[326]

British weapons purchases from the United States through the end of 1940 totaled some $5,000,000,000, helping arm the British and reduce American unemployment.[327]

As 1940 closed, Britain was running out of money with which to purchase more American arms. But under United States law, Roosevelt

---

[320] *Battle*, 35-36.
[321] *Fateful Choices*, 218.
[322] *Fateful Choices*, 218-20, *Dawn*, 7.
[323] *Fateful Choices*, 184, *Inferno*, 184, *1944*, 46-47.
[324] *Inferno*, 182-83.
[325] *Fateful Choices*, 221, *Inferno*, 185.
[326] *Crusade*, 19.
[327] *Fateful Choices*, 221.

was not permitted to lend money to nations like Britain that still owed World War I debts. Thus he could sell Churchill weapons only for cash.[328]

Hostilities in Romania, Italy, Albania, Greece and Africa

On August 30, 1940, Hitler pressured Romania to agree to terms that assured Germany's continued supply of oil from the valuable Ploesti oil fields there. This unilateral German action angered the Soviets who also coveted control of Romania.[329]

In early October 1940, Hitler quietly (and without first consulting Mussolini) sent 15,000 German troops into Romania to protect the essential Ploesti oil resources. But Italy, which also depended on Romanian oil, considered Romania to be within its sphere of influence.[330]

Irritated by Hitler's incursion into Romania, on October 28, 1940, Mussolini impetuously ordered an Italian army force of 162,000 men to invade Greece from Albania. He gave virtually no prior notice to Hitler. The Greeks vigorously resisted the invasion with a force of 209,000 men and within weeks pushed the ineffective Italians back deep into Albania where the opposing forces remained stalemated for the next six months.[331]

In the Italian/Greek conflict, Italy suffered 150,000 casualties; the Greeks 90,000.[332]

Furious that the Italian foray into Greece had been a disaster, in December Hitler issued orders calling for the German army to invade Greece in the spring and protect his southern flank from a possible British attack.[333]

In November, 1940, British carrier-launched planes torpedoed the anchored Italian fleet in the port of Taranto, destroying or damaging half of Italy's warships and changing the balance of naval power in the Mediterranean.[334]

In December, the Italians responded by torpedoing two British battleships in the harbor at Alexandria, Egypt, knocking them out of action for seven months.[335]

---

[328] *Fateful Choices*, 221.
[329] *Reich*, 800-01.
[330] *Fateful Choices*, 168-69, *Reich*, 815.
[331] *Curse*, 269, *Inferno*, 113-14, *Fateful Choices*, 130, 169, 175-76, *Reich*, 815-18, 826.
[332] *Fateful Choices*, 180.
[333] *Inferno*, 115, *Reich*, 817.
[334] *Fateful Choices*, 176, *Inferno*, 288, *WW II Story*, 50.
[335] *Inferno*, 288.

By mid-December 1940, British and Australian troops had driven an Italian army twice as large out of Egypt, causing 150,000 Italian casualties. The Italians had earlier advanced into Egypt from their colony of Libya.[336]

The Tripartite Pact

On September 27, 1940, Germany, Japan and Italy signed the Tripartite Pact which committed each Axis member to assist the others if attacked by the United States. In addition, in Article 1 Japan recognized "the leadership of Germany and Italy in the establishment of a new order in Europe," and in Article 2 Germany and Italy recognized Japan's leadership in establishing a new order in "Greater East Asia." The main objective of the Tripartite Pact was to discourage the United States from entering the war.[337]

In the autumn of 1940, in order to put more pressure on Britain to negotiate for peace, Germany considered a plan that included capturing Gibraltar and blocking the Suez Canal, thereby depriving Britain of access to the Mediterranean.[338]

In October 1940, Hitler and Spanish leader Francisco Franco met to discuss a secret German/Spanish accord under which (a) Spain would confirm its readiness to join the Tripartite Pact and intervene in the war, and (b) Germany would provide substantial economic aid to Spain and allow Spain to take certain French colonies in Africa. But Hitler wanted to use German troops to seize the British colony at Gibraltar and made that a condition of providing economic aid to Spain. Franco did not want German troops on Spanish soil and the deal broke down at year end. Contributing to Spain's decision to remain neutral were (a) fear of a British naval blockade of Spain, (b) $13 million in bribes Britain paid to Spanish army generals to encourage them to support neutrality, and (c) Britain's advances against Italy in North Africa. Still, neutral Spain remained generally supportive of the Axis countries.[339]

Mussolini was opposed to having Spain become an Axis member because he did not want to share dominance of the Mediterranean, and because he wanted some of the same French colonies Spain was seek-

---

[336] *Fateful Choices*, 176, *Dawn*, 7, *Reich*, 818-19.
[337] *Fateful Choices*, 79-80, 123-25, 168, *Reich*, 802, 884.
[338] *Fateful Choices*, 77-85.
[339] *Inferno*, 109-11, *Dawn*, 7, *Reich*, 814-19.

ing.[340]

Had Spain joined the Axis, Gibraltar would likely have been taken, dooming British control of Malta and jeopardizing its ability to hold the Middle East.[341]

In mid-November 1940, representatives of Germany and the Soviet Union met. Hitler wanted the Soviet Union to join the Tripartite Pact, aligning it with Germany, Italy and Japan. Germany also proposed that Stalin direct his territorial aspirations toward the Middle East. The Soviets, coveting territory to the west, responded with grievances over German actions in Romania and the Balkans and demanded that Germany withdraw its troops from Finland. In the end, the conference yielded no agreement, but persuaded Hitler that conflict between Germany and the Soviet Union was inevitable.[342]

On December 18, 1940, Hitler ordered that secret formal planning begin for a German invasion of the territories Stalin controlled ("Operation Barbarossa"). His goal was to eradicate Bolshevism, gain territory to the east, eliminate the Soviet threat, and permanently acquire the Soviet's natural resources and foodstuffs.[343]

As 1940 came to an end, the Axis forces were hesitant to invade England but hoped to overpower Britain through air attacks on the homeland and by driving the British out of the Mediterranean.

WAR WAGED IN EUROPE AND NORTH AFRICA (1941)

The United States Gears Up for Battle

Roosevelt was inaugurated for his third presidential term on January 20, 1941.[344]

In January 1941, searching for a way to overcome legal limits on selling arms on credit to struggling Britain, Roosevelt sent proposed Lend-Lease legislation to Congress asking permission to lend arms to friendly nations with the understanding that the weapons would be returned at war's end. To illustrate the concept, Roosevelt imagined a neighbor whose house was burning, and said it made sense to lend the neighbor a hose to extinguish the blaze.[345]

---

[340] *Inferno*, 110.
[341] *Inferno*, 111.
[342] *Fateful Choices*, 262, *Reich*, 802-12.
[343] *Curse*, 54, *Fateful Choices*, 70, *Inferno*, 97-98, *Folly*, 121, *Reich*, 810.
[344] *Masters*, 45.
[345] *Fateful Choices*, 226-31.

Roosevelt recognized that supporting Britain's war efforts carried some risk of drawing the United States into the war, but argued that it was better to help Britain defend itself than to acquiesce in its defeat.[346]

On March 11, 1941, the President signed new Lend-Lease legislation giving the United States authority to produce and deliver, without immediate payment, defensive weapons for any nation whose support the President deemed vital to United States defense. Roosevelt declared: "We must be the great arsenal of democracy." Churchill characterized Lend-Lease as "Hitler's death warrant." By the end of World War II, Lend-Lease had delivered over $50 billion in weapons.[347]

On June 20, 1941, the U.S. Army Air Force was officially established. General "Hap" Arnold was designated to serve as its head.[348]

During the first half of 1941, U. S. Army Chief of Staff Marshall was opposed to any United States intervention in the war in Europe because he did not believe the nation's military strength was yet adequate.[349]

Hitler's Discussions with the Soviets and Japan

On January 10, 1941, the Soviet Union and Germany renewed their 1940 trade agreement and the Soviets promised to furnish even greater supplies of fuel, ore, grain and minerals. Stalin continued to believe that by serving as Germany's most important source of raw materials, the Soviets could at least delay being attacked by Hitler. Stalin recognized that the Red Army was not prepared to defend the Soviet Union against an anticipated German attack and would not be ready until at least 1942.[350]

On March 28, 1941, Hitler urged Japan to weaken the British by taking her Far East colony of Singapore. He argued that doing so would deter the United States from sending its navy into Japanese waters. He added that because the isolationist United States was weak militarily, if it sent precious arms to Britain the U.S. Navy in the Pacific would be vulnerable to a Japanese attack. To encourage such aggressive moves, Hitler pledged that if Japan initiated a conflict with the United States, Germany would promptly join in on Japan's side. The Japanese

---

[346] *Fateful Choices*, 229.
[347] *Fateful Choices*, 187, 230-33, *Curse*, 60, *Inferno*, 186, *1944*, 241, 244.
[348] *Air Masters*, 45.
[349] *Fateful Choices*, 205.
[350] *Curse*, 56-57, *Fateful Choices*, 269-70.

were noncommittal.[351]

Germany Versus Britain

In January 1941, Hitler cancelled most German planning for a cross-Channel invasion of Britain.[352]

In the spring of 1941, Germany resumed its bombing of Britain. Several months later the intensity was reduced as German planes were diverted to the Soviet Union and other fronts.[353]

On May 10, Deputy *Füehrer* Rudolph Hess, who was mentally distressed, flew to and parachuted into Scotland in an unauthorized attempt to gain peace between Germany and Britain. The British rejected his efforts, which were quite embarrassing to Hitler, and Hess was held captive. Hitler issued orders to have Hess shot if he returned to Germany.[354]

In May, the German battleship *Bismarck* left its hiding place in a Norwegian fjord and headed to the Atlantic. On May 24, the *Bismarck* sank the British cruiser *Hood* near Greenland. But the British sank the giant German battleship on May 27, 1941, costing almost 2,300 German sailors their lives and reducing Germany's ability to harass Allied Atlantic shipping.[355]

In May 1941, the British captured a copy of the secret German Enigma naval coding machine and quickly broke the U-boat ciphers.[356]

Action in the Mediterranean

By the end of January 1941, the British had driven the weak Italian army out of Egypt and into Libya, and captured 113,000 Italian soldiers. In February, a frustrated Hitler was forced to send Germany's new Afrika Korps, commanded by General Erwin Rommel, to Africa to support the remaining Italian forces.[357]

In late March 1941, the Italians suffered another military setback. In the battle of Cape Matapan, near the island of Crete, the British navy in the Mediterranean inflicted serious damage on a number of Italian warships, further reducing the effectiveness of the Italian

---

[351] *Reich*, 873-76.
[352] *Engineers*, 99.
[353] *Engineers*, 99.
[354] *Inferno*, 141, *Fateful Choices*, 281, *Folly*, 80-81, *Reich*, 834-38.
[355] *Engineers*, 21, *Inferno*, 265, *WW II Story*, 45.
[356] *Fateful Choices*, 241, *Masters*, 92, *Inferno*, 273.
[357] *Fateful Choices*, 176, *Masters*, 62, *Dawn*, 7, *Inferno*, 111, *WW II Story*, 51, *Reich*, 827.

navy.[358]

On March 24, 1941, Rommel's Afrika Korps attacked the British forces in Libya commanded by General Wavell. By May, the British had been driven back east into Egypt.[359]

Bulgaria, Yugoslavia, Greece, Crete, Iraq and Syria

Hitler wanted to protect his southern flank before invading the Soviet Union. Thus, in February 1941, he persuaded Bulgaria to sign the Tripartite Pact and become a member of the Axis.[360]

In March 1941, to (a) secure his southern flank, (b) gain access to Yugoslavia's mineral resources and (c) facilitate Germany's invasion of Greece, Hitler pressured Prince Paul, the dictator of Yugoslavia, to sign the Tripartite Pact. This angered Serb nationalists who sought in a coup to overthrow the government. Hitler took the coup as a personal insult and on April 6 sent the German army into Yugoslavia, killing tens of thousands there. On April 17, a battered Yugoslavia surrendered. In the months and years that followed, in addition to suffering under the Nazis and then the Soviets, Yugoslav Fascists, Communists, Muslims, Serbs, Croats and Ustaše engaged in brutal ethnic cleansing and partisan warfare. By the war's end, some 1,200,000 Yugoslavians had been killed.[361]

On April 6, 1941, Germany also invaded Greece in order to salvage the failed Italian operation there and to counter the British, who had landed more than 50,000 soldiers on the islands. On April 23, 1941, after Britain withdrew 43,000 troops to Crete and another 11,000 were captured, the Greeks surrendered to Germany. Four days later the Germans took control of Athens.[362]

In the two years following the German invasion of Greece, more than 250,000 Greeks out of a population of about 7,000,000 died of starvation.[363]

On May 20, German paratroopers landed on the island of Crete. After ten days of combat, the British evacuated some 15,000 New Zealand soldiers, leaving behind 1,742 dead and 11,370 captured. In the battle for Crete, the British lost three cruisers and six destroyers and

---

[358] *WW II Story*, 50.

[359] *Inferno*, 112-13, *WW II Story*, 52, *Reich*, 827.

[360] *Reich*, 822-23.

[361] *Inferno*, 115, 450-54, *Reich*, 823-25, *1944*, 246.

[362] *Fateful Choices*, 178-80, 270-71, *Inferno*, 117-19, *WW II Story*, 51-52, *Reich*, 826.

[363] *Fateful Choices*, 180, *Curse*, 273.

suffered damage to seventeen other ships, its worst naval defeat in the entire war.[364]

In the spring of 1941, concerned about growing Nazi influence over the government of oil-rich Iraq, the British sent troops into Baghdad and established a friendly government which subsequently declared war on the Axis countries.[365]

In June, 1941, Australian, British and Free French troops fought the Vichy French in Syria, a French colony. After five weeks of combat and the deaths of more than 1,000 of its troops, Vichy France capitulated. Of the captured French soldiers, some 32,000 elected to return to Vichy France while 5,668 joined de Gaulle's Free French forces.[366]

Planning for, and Rumors of, Operation Barbarossa

In March 1941, Hitler instructed his generals that the forthcoming attack on the Soviet Union ("Operation Barbarossa") was a war of ideologies and thus all Soviet commissars must be "liquidated." He added that because the Soviets had not participated in the Hague Convention, they had no rights thereunder to be protected against war crimes; German troops who violate international law "will be excused."[367]

Operation Barbarossa was intended to serve military, political and economic goals. Hitler, in addition to his desire to obliterate "Jewish Bolshevism" and acquire more "living space," wanted to divert the food supplies of the Soviet Union to Germany, even if that meant that millions of Soviets would starve.[368]

Hitler's plan was to defeat the Soviet Union, which he believed would persuade Britain to negotiate for peace. Germany would then attack the United States, which would face the sobering prospect of war on both coasts.[369]

Hitler was convinced that once Stalin's forces had suffered heavy defeats, the Soviet people would rise up and overthrow the Communist government.[370]

Hitler's April invasion of Yugoslavia to tamp down the coup there and protect the southern flank of his planned attack on the Soviet Union necessitated a four week delay in the Barbarossa invasion, until

---

[364] *Inferno*, 119-20, *WW II Story*, 52.
[365] *Inferno*, 121-22, *WW II Story*, 52, *Reich*, 828-29.
[366] *Inferno*, 123-25.
[367] *Reich*, 830, 846.
[368] *Inferno*, 137-40, *WW II Story*, 59, *Folly*, 121, *Bloodlands*, 162, *Reich*, 833.
[369] *Reich*, 871, 879.
[370] *Reich*, 855-56.

June 22. This pause had catastrophic consequences later when the Russian winter stalled the German drive on Moscow.[371]

Hitler gave neither Japan nor Italy meaningful advance notice of his plan to attack the Soviet Union.[372]

During the first half of 1941, Stalin received more than fifty intelligence reports saying that the Germans soon planned to attack the Soviet Union. Stalin chose to disregard the reports, believing that the Nazis would not attack the Soviets until Britain was defeated — a conclusion fostered by Stalin's Communist theory that the capitalists would fight one another to exhaustion, and then become easy prey for the Soviets.[373]

Roosevelt had been aware since early 1941 of German plans to invade the Soviet Union and passed that information on to the Soviets in March. Churchill gave Stalin a similar warning in April.[374]

In April 1941, the Soviet Union signed a non-aggression pact with Japan. This treaty gave Stalin comfort that his eastern flank would not be attacked in the near future and allowed him to concentrate on threats from Europe.[375]

Eager to reduce diplomatic friction between the Soviet Union and Germany which might trigger a German attack, on May 6, 1941, Stalin removed the pedantic Molotov from his position as Soviet Prime Minister and personally assumed that role.[376]

On May 15, after months of study, the Red Army gave Stalin a fifteen page plan for a pre-emptive Soviet strike against Germany, targeted for 1942. Stalin worried about taking steps to implement the plan out of fear of provoking an earlier German attack.[377]

On June 14, the Soviets broadcast a peculiar announcement to the world asserting that rumors of a German attack on the Soviet Union were an "obvious absurdity."[378]

In early June, Stalin carried out another purge of senior Red Army officials, this time arresting almost 300, including twenty-two who had received the nation's highest military honor, Hero of the Soviet Un-

---

[371] *Reich*, 824, 829-30.

[372] *Reich*, 849, 874.

[373] *Curse*, 54-55, *Fateful Choices*, 271-76, 283-85, *Inferno*, 140-41, *Folly*, 60, 70, 86-87, *Bloodlands*, 165, *Reich*, 839.

[374] *Fateful Choices*, 238, *Reich*, 842-44, *1944*, 253.

[375] *Folly*, 13-14, 72-75, *Reich*, 876-77.

[376] *Reich*, 802, 841-42.

[377] *Fateful Choices*, 279-80, *Folly*, 75-97.

[378] *Reich*, 845.

ion.[379]

By June 1941, the Soviet Union had almost 3,000,000 poorly trained and equipped troops assigned to its western border in a defensive posture. In mid-June, Red Army leaders urged Stalin to put those troops on combat alert to strengthen the Soviet Union's defensive capacity. Stalin angrily dismissed the proposal out of fear of provoking an attack by the Germans, saying, "I am certain that Hitler will not risk creating a second front by attacking the Soviet Union."[380]

On June 21, Hitler warned Admiral Raeder, head of the German navy, that he wanted to avoid any incident, such as a U-boat attack, involving the United States at least until the planned attack on the Soviet Union was well under way.[381]

In the evening of June 21, Soviet Foreign Commissar Molotov complained to the German ambassador about violations of the Soviet border by German aircraft, and asked if Germany was "dissatisfied" with the Soviet government. Ribbentrop evasively said he lacked sufficient information to answer.[382]

Operation Barbarossa Launched

At 3:30 a.m. (Moscow time) on June 22, 1941, Hitler's 3,600,000 Axis troops, 2,000 aircraft and 3,350 tanks attacked the Soviet Union on a 900 mile front. Among the invading forces were troops from Germany, Finland, Romania, Hungary, Italy, Slovakia, Spain and Croatia. Rejecting advice from his top generals to drive in a single thrust to Moscow, Hitler ordered multiple attacks: (a) north through the Baltic States toward Leningrad, (b) toward Moscow in the middle, and (c) in the south toward Ukraine, with its valuable resources, the Crimea and the Black Sea. This was the second occasion during World War II that the people living in what had been Poland, Belarus and Ukraine were trampled in an armed invasion.[383]

On the day of the attack, the German ambassador in Moscow told Soviet representative Molotov that among Germany's reasons for invading the Soviet Union were the need to defend Germany and to stop Moscow from "Bolshevizing" Europe.[384]

---

[379] *Folly*, 85-86.
[380] *Fateful Choices*, 282-83, *Folly*, 82-97, *Inferno*, 140-41.
[381] *Fateful Choices*, 400-01, *Reich*, 880-81.
[382] *Reich*, 846-47.
[383] *Soldier's Story*, 184, *Curse*, 58, *Fateful Choices*, 286, *Dawn*, 8, *Inferno*, 137, 141, *WW II Story*, 59-60, *Folly*, 122, 162, *Bloodlands*, 165-66, *Reich*, 849.
[384] *Curse*, 55, *Reich*, 847-49.

When Operation Barbarossa began, seventy-five percent of the Red Army's field officers had held their posts for a year or less and their competence was limited accordingly. The Red Army's most experienced military leaders had been murdered in Stalin's 1937-38 purges.[385]

Stalin's persistent unwillingness before June 22 to direct the Red Army to attack the Germans or to place his forces in a combat-ready defensive stance gave the invading Germans a huge tactical advantage in the invasion.[386]

On the first day of Operation Barbarossa, the Soviets lost one-quarter of their air force — some 1,200 aircraft — compared to only thirty-five German planes destroyed. Within a week, German forces had moved 300 miles into Soviet territory.[387]

Stalin ordered thousands of soldiers, including eight Red Army generals, shot as scapegoats for the German invasion.[388]

Stalin was stunned by the unexpected German invasion and, lacking the courage to do so himself, delegated to Molotov the task of informing the Russian people that they were at war. Stalin had convinced himself that because the Soviet Union was supplying Germany with such large quantities of food, raw materials and oil, Hitler would not attack. As the Red Army retreated and more cities fell, Stalin withdrew to his dacha outside Moscow. On June 30, when a Kremlin delegation arrived, a deflated Stalin apparently believed that they had come to arrest or depose him for his gross misjudgment. But the weak Kremlin representatives merely asked Stalin to lead them. On July 3, a more invigorated Stalin made his first radio address to the nation, but admitted no fault.[389]

Following the German Barbarossa attack in June 1941, the Soviet Union became a key to the Allied strategy to win World War II — the Communist nation had to be sustained as an enemy of Germany because it could significantly bleed Hitler's war machine.[390]

A few days after the German invasion of the Soviet Union, Roosevelt released some $40,000,000 in Soviet funds that had been frozen in the United States, and promised that other aid would be furnished to

---

[385] *Fateful Choices*, 248, *Inferno*, 140, 149.
[386] *Folly*, 95-96.
[387] *Engineers*, 202-03, *Fateful Choices*, 287-88, *Dawn*, 8, *Inferno*, 142, *Reich*, 852.
[388] *Fateful Choices*, 288, *Inferno*, 147.
[389] *Inferno*, 146-47, *Curse*, 56, 59-60, *Folly*, 114, 157-58, 218-20, 258-60.
[390] *Soldier's Story*, 186-87, *Masters*, 121, *Fateful Choices*, 306, *Inferno*, 279.

the Soviet Union.[391]

In late July, 1941, Roosevelt's emissary, Harry Hopkins, flew to Moscow for meetings with Stalin. The objectives were to gauge how long the Soviet Union could hold out against the Germans and to ask what aid Stalin wanted.[392]

American public opinion after Germany's invasion of the Soviet Union was divided, with many isolationists and religious leaders believing that no aid should be provided to the Communist and atheist nation.[393]

The invading Axis troops were surprised to be welcomed as liberators in parts of Ukraine, Belarus, Estonia, Latvia and Lithuania, where the Soviet Union had abused civilians since its 1939 invasion. Many of those citizens then fought with the Germans against the Soviets. As time went on, however, Germany's terrible treatment of Red Army POWs and its taking of Soviet citizens for slave labor turned the population against the invaders.[394]

By July 1, more than 20,000,000 Soviet citizens had fallen under German control. By year end 1941, almost 75,000,000 were enduring German rule.[395]

Shortly after the Germans invaded the Soviet Union, Stalin announced that Soviet soldiers who became German prisoners of war were to be deemed traitors and their families arrested.[396]

On July 15, the Germans took Stalin's son, Iakov, as a prisoner of war. He died as a captive of the Germans. Stalin ordered his son's wife arrested.[397]

The Germans believed that they would defeat the Red Army in a matter of weeks. The United States and Britain thought it would take a few months. Despite their optimism, the Germans asked the Japanese to attack the Soviet Union from the east, a request Japan declined.[398]

Three weeks after the start of Barbarossa, (a) the northern Axis force was moving through the Baltic States toward Leningrad, the city built by Peter the Great, (b) the center force had penetrated 450 miles and was 200 miles from Moscow, and (c) the southern force was ap-

---

[391] *Fateful Choices*, 303.
[392] *Fateful Choices*, 303.
[393] *Fateful Choices*, 304.
[394] *Inferno*, 142-43, *Folly*, 65-66, *Reich*, 939-40.
[395] *Folly*, 232, 267.
[396] *Bloodlands*, 175.
[397] *Fateful Choices*, 455, *Bloodlands*, 176, 340.
[398] *Curse*, 57, *Fateful Choices*, 298, *Inferno*, 145, *Reich*, 877-78.

proaching Kiev in Ukraine.[399]

In August, Hitler's generals advocated concentrating their efforts in the Soviet center to defeat, before winter, the large Red Army forces gathering west of Moscow. Hitler rejected this proposal in favor of gaining control of agriculture, coal-mining, industrial and oil assets in the south as well as defeating Leningrad in the north. The German forces in the center were not to be the primary offensive weapon at that time.[400]

One consequence of Barbarossa was that all supplies of grain sold by the Soviet Union to Germany ceased, meaning that if the Soviet Union was not quickly defeated Germany would have to acquire that food in other ways and from other sources.[401]

Hitler's victories prior to Barbarossa were over democratic nations in the west where moderation and respect for human life were considered values. He did not consider whether it would be more difficult to conquer a brutalized society like the Soviet Union where the people were accustomed to extreme hardship and abuse.[402]

Churchill said the German invasion of the Soviet Union was one of the four most important events of the war, the others being the fall of France, the Battle of Britain and the American enactment of Lend-Lease legislation.[403]

In July and again in October 1941, Stalin considered making gestures for peace with Germany. The evidence is unclear as to whether any such communications with Germany actually occurred.[404]

After invading the Soviet Union, Hitler sent four German Security Police task forces (*Einsatzgruppen*) into the captured territories. Each task force had from 600 to 1,000 men and was directed to kill Jews, Gypsies, saboteurs and Communist functionaries there. By the end of 1941, one of the four task forces had murdered 229,052 Jews. Overall, the task forces are estimated to have killed over 700,000 people.[405]

Defending Iceland

On July 7, 1941, 4,400 United States Marines landed in Iceland in

[399] *Reich*, 853.
[400] *Reich*, 856-59.
[401] *Bloodlands*, 169-70.
[402] *Inferno*, 139, 175, *Folly*, 231, *Reich*, 855, 863.
[403] *Masters*, 51.
[404] *Curse*, 62, *Fateful Choices*, 288-89, *Folly*, 189-90.
[405] *Fateful Choices*, 431, 450, 453, *Inferno*, 152, 492, *WW II Story*, 520, *Folly*, 236, *Bloodlands*, 182-83, *Reich*, 958-63, 966.

response to that nation's request for such an occupation. The objectives were to protect Iceland from a German invasion and to free British troops stationed there for duty elsewhere in Britain's fight against Axis forces.[406]

America's occupation of Iceland increased the chance of incidents near that island between German U-boats and American naval and merchant ships which could draw the United States into the war.[407]

On September 4, 1941, a German U-boat close to Iceland, after being trailed for hours by an American destroyer, the USS *Greer*, fired two torpedoes at the naval ship. Both missed. Citing the German attack, on September 11, President Roosevelt announced that the United States would protect shipping in its defensive waters, including escorting convoys to Britain, and that any German or Italian ships that enter those waters "do so at their own peril." American public opinion was supportive of Roosevelt's stance even though it moved the nation closer to war.[408]

British and American Discussions

Roosevelt and Churchill and their staffs met secretly aboard a ship in Placentia Bay, Newfoundland from August 9-12, 1941 to discuss ways the United States might assist in military matters. The Americans agreed to provide supplies to Russia, protect ship convoys to Britain, deliver bombers to Britain, and take over anti-submarine patrols east of Iceland.[409]

On August 14, 1941, Britain and the United States issued the Atlantic Charter, a noteworthy statement of principles for a postwar world as those two nations saw it — no territorial aggrandizement, the right of all people to choose their form of government, equal access to trade and raw materials, and efforts to foster economic advancement, social security, world peace and disarmament.[410]

Early in the war, the British did not seriously consider crossing the English Channel to invade the European mainland because they had few resources to devote to such a huge and dangerous undertaking. Britain favored a strategy of exhausting the German war machine through a British naval blockade, bombing German cities, resistance

---

[406] *Fateful Choices*, 312.
[407] *Fateful Choices*, 313.
[408] *Fateful Choices*, 319-324, *Reich*, 882.
[409] *Masters*, 52-3, *Curse*, 61, *Fateful Choices*, 315-18.
[410] *Fateful Choices*, 317.

from occupied countries, and ongoing Soviet efforts to fight the Nazis. Britain hoped this strategy would cause Germany to crumble from within, as had happened in World War I.[411]

The Americans understood Britain's lack of enthusiasm for a cross-Channel invasion, but took the position in 1941 that Germany could be defeated only by confronting it in battle on the European mainland. The United States favored a drive from the northwest coast of France straight to Berlin, a distance of only 550 miles over relatively flat terrain with good highways and railroads.[412]

The Continuing War Against Jews

Beginning on September 1, 1941, Germany mandated that all Jews wear yellow stars for identification.[413]

On September 19, 1941, the Germans seized the Ukrainian city of Kiev. The following week dozens of German troops were killed in explosions there. The Germans blamed Kiev Jews and ordered them all rounded up on September 29. The Jews were then marched out of town to a ravine called Babi Yar where, over the next thirty-six hours, 33,761 were shot and killed.[414]

Before invading the Soviet Union, Germany had contemplated deporting all European Jews to the soon-to-be-defeated Soviet Union, where they could be used as slave labor. By the end of 1941, however, Hitler had abandoned consideration of less lethal methods of dealing with the "Jewish problem" and, instead of deportation, decided to exterminate Europe's Jews — the "final solution." The construction of gas chambers began.[415]

While other European nations like Holland and France assisted Germany's war on Jews, Denmark refused to help deport its Jews and almost all of them survived.[416]

Anti-Semitism permeated Vichy France, and many of its governmental agencies seized Jews almost as eagerly as the Germans did.[417]

Vichy France Supports the Defeat of Britain

---

[411] *Soldier's Story*, 185, *Masters*, 69.

[412] *Soldier's Story*, 185, *Masters*, 70, *Dawn*, 11.

[413] *Fateful Choices*, 468.

[414] *Bloodlands*, 202-03, *Curse*, 189, *Fateful Choices*, 309.

[415] *Fateful Choices*, 432, 460, 463-64, *Inferno*, 495-96, *Bloodlands*, 185-194, 216-17, 235, 253, *Reich*, 963-67.

[416] *Inferno*, 391-93.

[417] *Inferno*, 123, 391-92, *Paris*, 272-86.

On October 24, 1941, Vichy France, through Marshal Pétain, entered into a secret agreement with Germany confirming the two nations' "identical interest in seeing the defeat of England accomplished as soon as possible," and France's commitment to "support, within the limits of its ability, the measures which the Axis Powers may take to this end."[418]

Britain and the United States were not then aware of the pact but the King of England and Roosevelt each implored Pétain to remain neutral.[419]

Allied Aid to the Soviet Union

On October 1, 1941, the Soviet Union, Britain and the United States signed the Moscow Protocol describing aid the United States and Britain would provide to Stalin, and Roosevelt extended Lend-Lease to the Soviet Union.[420]

U.S. Secretary of War Stimson and Army Chief of Staff Marshall despised Communism and the Soviet system, and had argued unsuccessfully against extending Lend-Lease to the Soviet Union.[421]

The promise of Allied economic aid helped keep the Soviet Union fighting Germany. The concept was that the Soviets would shed blood to fight the Axis forces and the United States would pay with weapons and material.[422]

Supplies sent by convoy to the Soviet Union had to travel to its Arctic ports of Murmansk and Archangel through rough seas, freezing weather, iced superstructures, and harrowing German attacks, including those from Norway-based planes, the German battleship *Tirpitz* and U-boats.[423]

Due to production and shipping challenges, relatively little United States aid reached the Soviet Union in 1941.[424]

By 1942, the Americans were shipping an average of 212 planes per month to the Soviet Union, as well as gasoline, steel, ammunition, jeeps, boots and other vital supplies.[425]

Between 1941 and 1945, in Atlantic convoys to the Soviet Union,

---

[418] *Reich*, 815.
[419] *Reich*, 815.
[420] *Curse*, 62-63, *Fateful Choices*, 301, 309.
[421] *Curse*, 63, *Inferno*, 279.
[422] *Curse*, 63-64.
[423] *Inferno*, 279-288.
[424] *Fateful Choices*, 309-10, *Inferno*, 280.
[425] *Masters*, 288, *1944*, 61.

the Allies lost eighteen warships, eighty-seven merchant ships, 1,944 naval personnel and 829 merchant seamen.[426]

The German Advance on Leningrad in the North

In September 1941, the northern German forces, aided by the Finnish army which Hitler had reequipped after the 1940 Soviet attack on Finland, surrounded Leningrad (formerly the Tsar's capital of St. Petersburg) and began a siege that lasted two years. Instead of attacking in force, Hitler intended to bomb and starve the city into submission. By year end, an estimated 200,000 residents had died. By February 1942, up to 20,000 Leningrad residents were dying each day.[427]

On October 3, 1941, Hitler prematurely proclaimed in a speech to the German nation: "I declare today, and I declare it without any reservation, that the enemy in the East [the Soviet Union] has been struck down and will never rise again...."[428]

The German Advance in the Soviet South

During the summer, von Rundstedt's army of Germans, Romanians and Hungarians rapidly advanced through Ukraine, taking Kiev on September 19, and then headed south toward the Crimea and east toward Kharkov.[429]

Axis troops seized Kharkov and its 1,000,000 citizens in late October 1941.[430]

The port city of Odessa on the Black Sea, after being under siege for two months, fell to the Germans before year end.[431]

The Germans then moved south in an effort to take the Crimea and its naval base at Sevastopol.[432]

In late November, the Germans approached Rostov on the Don River, but five days later were driven back some fifty miles, the first major setback the German army had suffered in the war against the Soviets.[433]

The German Advance on Moscow in the Middle

---

[426] *Inferno*, 287.
[427] *Inferno*, 164-71, *WW II Story*, 67-70, *Bloodlands*, 173.
[428] *Reich*, 854.
[429] *WW II Story*, 70, *Reich*, 858.
[430] *WW II Story*, 70.
[431] *WW II Story*, 70.
[432] *WW II Story*, 70.
[433] *Reich*, 860-61.

In early October, Hitler returned his focus to the objective of encircling Moscow. He assigned 1,900,000 soldiers to this task. Simultaneously, Stalin, satisfied that Japan would not attack the Soviet Union, moved many Red Army troops toward Moscow from the east.[434]

By mid-October 1941, the Axis troops were nearing Moscow. One fifth of the city's population fled and most of the government moved 400 miles southeast to Kuibyshev on the Volga. Even Stalin contemplated leaving Moscow, but on October 18 decided to stay.[435]

Facing rain and snow in October and below-zero weather in November, the German forces seeking to take Moscow were slowed by mud, frostbite and a lack of supplies.[436]

On December 4, German soldiers were just twenty-five miles from Moscow, but they had suffered 200,000 killed since Barbarossa began.[437]

On December 6, with the temperature at about -30° Fahrenheit, the Red Army counterattacked in a snowy 200-mile front. By year end, Axis forces had been pushed back 60-150 miles, the Soviet capital had been preserved, and Hitler had replaced most of his German generals on the eastern front.[438]

As 1941 closed, Hitler and his senior advisors recognized that their failure to quickly subdue the Soviet Union meant that, due to a lack of sufficient resources, a military victory in World War II was not attainable. However, Hitler did not believe that this meant a German defeat. Rather, he felt that a long war with enough German successes could lead to a negotiated peace.[439]

Major factors in Germany's inability to quickly defeat the Soviet Union were (a) the harsh Russian weather, (b) Japan's decision not to attack from the east, (c) the vast size of the Soviet Union, which allowed Stalin to move factories and people east away from battle lines, (d) the millions of Red Army soldiers who were sacrificed to slow Germany's better trained and equipped forces, and (e) aid from Britain and the United States.[440]

Stalin's Oppressive Tactics

[434] *Inferno*, 157, *Reich*, 859.
[435] *Fateful Choices*, 289, *Inferno*, 150, 159, *WW II Story*, 64, *Reich*, 859-60.
[436] *Inferno*, 158-59, *Reich*, 860-63.
[437] *Inferno*, 163, *Curse*, 67, *Fateful Choices*, 290, *Reich*, 864.
[438] *Inferno*, 163-64, *WW II Story*, 65-66, *Reich*, 864-66, 903.
[439] *Inferno*, 160-61, *Reich*, 870.
[440] *Folly*, 267-70.

During the war-strewn months between July and the end of 1941, Stalin's terror apparatus put 1,339,702 Soviet residents on trial and sent more than two-thirds of them to the *gulag*.[441]

In December 1941 negotiations with Britain over the form of post-war Europe, Stalin was already seeking both to dismember Germany and obtain international approval of recent Soviet conquests in Poland and the Baltic states.[442]

The United States Anticipates War in Europe

By the summer of 1941, the U.S. Army had a strength of about 1,500,000 troops, but still lacked modern equipment.[443]

In mid-August 1941, Congress, over isolationist opposition and by just one vote, amended the Selective Service Act of 1940 to (a) remove the cap on the size of the American army, (b) retain draftees for as long as a national emergency existed, and (c) allow troops to be sent outside of the western hemisphere.[444]

During the second half of 1941, as war seemed likely to soon engulf America, the Army Air Force officially embraced the doctrine of strategic bombing — "to conduct a sustained and unremitting air offensive against Germany and Italy, to destroy their will and capacity to continue the war, and to make an invasion either unnecessary or feasible without excessive cost." However, the United States would lack until late 1943 the personnel and planes needed to carry out sustained strategic bombing in Europe.[445]

In October 1941, German U-boats twice attacked U.S. Navy destroyers in the North Atlantic, killing a total of 126 sailors. Roosevelt used these attacks to gain Congressional amendments to the Neutrality Act of 1939 to permit the arming of merchant ships and allowing them to travel in combat zones, including Britain and the Soviet Union.[446]

On December 6, 1941, President Roosevelt authorized efforts to construct an atomic bomb. Thereafter, over 120,000 people, working in thirty-seven facilities in nineteen states and Canada, engaged in the largest and most costly weapons research and development effort of the war.[447]

---

[441] *Folly*, 270.

[442] *Curse*, 65.

[443] *Ike*, 238, *Crusade*, 10.

[444] *Fateful Choices*, 314, *Judgment*, 159, *Crusade*, 3.

[445] *Air Masters*, 46, 48.

[446] *Fateful Choices*, 324-29, *WW II Story*, 45-48, *Reich*, 883.

[447] *Fateful Choices*, 7, *Eagle*, 551.

By the end of 1941, the American Army had grown to 1,700,000 men, but few of them were ready for combat.[448]

United States defense spending in 1941, as a percentage of gross national product, was almost ten times what it had been in 1939.[449]

Britain's Ongoing War Efforts

In November 1941, Churchill appointed General Sir Alan Brooke to serve as British Chief of the Imperial General Staff ("CIGS") and his top military advisor. Brooke replaced Field Marshall Sir John Dill.[450]

The newly created British Eighth Army in North Africa launched an attack on Rommel's German and Italian forces on November 18, 1941. By year end the Axis troops had been driven west out of Egypt back to El Agheila, Libya, some 500 miles from where the advance began. Axis forces suffered 38,000 casualties; the British 18,000.[451]

Germany and Italy Declare War on the United States

In early December, at Japan's request, Germany, Italy and Japan discussed a new agreement in which (a) all parties promised to go to war if any of them was involved in war with the United States, and (b) none would sign a peace agreement unless all parties consented. Although an agreement in principle was promptly reached, Japan worried, as its planned war against the United States approached, that Hitler would refuse to sign the new agreement unless Japan also promised to attack the Soviet Union from the east. Curiously, Hitler never demanded such a condition and signed the final agreement several days after Japan went to war against the United States.[452]

Japan gave Germany no advance notice of its December 7 surprise attacks at Pearl Harbor and in the Philippines, but Hitler was delighted with the news.[453]

On December 9, 1941, before Germany formally declared war on the United States, Hitler authorized his U-boats to attack American shipping.[454]

On December 11, 1941, following Japan's belligerence in Asia, and claiming to act in accordance with the terms of the Tripartite Pact,

[448] *Soldier's Story*, 185-86, *Ike*, 238.
[449] *Fateful Choices*, 233.
[450] *Soldier's Story*, 7, *Masters*, 56.
[451] *Inferno*, 125-26, *WW II Story*, 52-53.
[452] *Fateful Choices*, 415, 420-21, *Reich*, 886, 888-92, 900.
[453] *Fateful Choices*, 416-17, *Reich*, 885, 892-93.
[454] *Fateful Choices*, 418.

Germany and Italy elected to declare war against the United States. Consistent with his aggressive nature, Hitler wanted to declare war against the United States before it declared war on Germany.[455]

Actually, the 1940 Tripartite Pact committed Germany and Italy to declare war only if Japan was attacked by a third party, which had not happened. Moreover, Roosevelt's December 8 speech in Congress asked only for a declaration of war against Japan. No mention was made of Germany or Italy.[456]

Hitler's declaration of war against the United States was carried out without extensive consultation with Germany's military leaders, who now faced combat with powerful enemies on two fronts.[457]

In just six months, Hitler had voluntarily moved from a war against only struggling Britain to a war that included as enemies the Soviet Union and the United States, two nations with huge populations and vast natural resources.[458]

Faced with difficulty feeding German citizens, Hitler decided in late 1941 that war prisoners who were not working would have to starve. By 1945, of 5,700,000 Soviet POWs under German control, 3,300,000 had died.[459]

Disenchanted by Hitler's conduct and troubled by Germany's military difficulties in the Soviet Union, in late 1941 a number of German generals conspired to overthrow the *Fuehrer* but were baffled by how to carry out the coup.[460]

The British and American War Organization
During the Arcadia conference of United States and British military leaders in Washington, D.C. in December 1941 and January 1942, the two countries agreed to a unified approach to waging war against the Axis countries, and that Germany must be the first of the Axis nations to be defeated. This "Europe First" policy was based largely on (a) Britain's inability to spare troops from Europe to fight the Japanese in the Pacific, (b) uncertainty about how long the Soviet Union would be able to hold out against the Germans, (c) recognition that Japan did not have the capacity to seriously threaten the United States homel-

---

[455] *Curse*, 66-67, *Masters*, 63, *Fateful Choices*, 382, *Inferno*, 100, *Reich*, 893-97.
[456] *Fateful Choices*, 385, 420-21, *Reich*, 893-94.
[457] *Fateful Choices*, 384-86.
[458] *Reich*, 900.
[459] *Inferno*, 488.
[460] *Reich*, 903-08.

and, and (d) an appreciation that of all the Axis enemies, only Germany could simultaneously be attacked by Britain, the Soviet Union and the United States. Despite the Europe First doctrine, the Americans and British agreed that it was essential to maintain supply lines to the Pacific outpost of Australia and try to keep India out of Japanese hands.[461]

They also agreed that the British and American war effort was to be directed by a Combined Chiefs of Staff composed of the service chiefs of both England and the United States. The chiefs of staff of each nation continued to report to their commander-in-chief, but the Combined Chiefs of Staff reported as a body to the dual authority of President Roosevelt and Prime Minister Churchill.[462]

Roosevelt and Churchill rejected de Gaulle's demand that the Free French have comparable representation on the Combined Chiefs of Staff, noting that Canada, Australia, New Zealand, Holland, Belgium, Denmark and Norway, too, lacked such a seat.[463]

The American Joint Chiefs of Staff, created in early 1942, acted as Roosevelt's principal military advisors during World War II. Admiral William D. Leahy served as chairman. Other members were Army General George Marshall, Navy Admiral Ernest J. King and Army Air Force General "Hap" Arnold.[464]

The British Chiefs of Staff were headed by General Sir Alan Brooke, and included Admiral of the Fleet Sir Dudley Pound, Chief of Air Staff Sir Charles Portal and Lord Louis Mountbatten, who was Director of Combined Operations. They met almost daily throughout the war.[465]

The first full meeting of the Combined Chiefs of Staff of Britain and the United States took place in Washington on January 23, 1942.[466]

From January 1942 until his death in November 1944, Sir John Dill served successfully as Churchill's and the British Chiefs of Staff's personal representative to the Americans in Washington. By an act of Congress recognizing his substantial contributions to the United States, Dill was buried in Arlington Cemetery, the only non-American

---

[461] *Soldier's Story*, 184, 186, *Masters*, 69-86, *Eagle*, 123, *Inferno*, 196, *Ike*, 250-59, *Crusade*, 27-28, *Supreme Commander*," 22-25, 30-35, *Crucible*, 180-181, 195-197.

[462] *Soldier's Story*, 184, *Eagle*, 125, *Supreme Commander*, 27.

[463] *Masters*, 76.

[464] *Masters*, 97, *Eagle*, 125, *Supreme Commander*, 28.

[465] *Masters*, 102-14.

[466] *Masters*, 91.

ever to receive that honor.[467]

When several nations join forces to defeat an enemy, it is essential that each member has trust and confidence in the decisions of the group. This requires the setting aside of purely nationalistic interests and a willingness to allow individuals from one country to command troops of another.[468]

Churchill observed: "There is only one thing worse than fighting with allies, and that is fighting without them!" On the other hand, General Mark Clark, who commanded Allied troops in Italy, said, "I think Napoleon was right when he came to the conclusion that it was better to fight allies than to be one of them." General Eisenhower appreciated that "[h]istory testifies to the ineptitude of coalitions in waging wars," but applauded the "near perfection in allied conduct of [World War II] operations" in Europe.[469]

To carry out the Allied mission, the United States would now have to produce planes, ships, weapons, vehicles, food, clothing, landing craft, construction materials and myriad other things for all of the countries opposing the Axis forces.[470]

As 1941 closed, the Axis forces in Europe found themselves arrayed against new, powerful and resolute foes who were determined to prevail, whatever the cost.

THE EUROPEAN BATTLES INTENSIFY (1942)

Considerations as the Year Began

To defeat Germany, the Western Allies recognized that they needed to advance in three successive steps: (a) control the Atlantic seas and defeat the U-boats, (b) dominate the skies, and (c) invade the enemy's shores.[471]

Churchill recognized that the nighttime bombing accuracy of British planes over German targets was quite poor. In 1942, Britain's bombing strategy changed to what some called terror bombing. A target list of fifty-eight German cities with populations over 100,000 was compiled. The new objective was to bomb residential centers where workers lived, hoping that civilian losses would destroy morale and

---

[467] *Masters*, 55-56, 76, 529-30, *Ike*, 256.
[468] *Crusade*, 29-30.
[469] *Masters*, 573, *Battle*, 434, *Crusade*, 4, 451.
[470] *Crusade*, 29, 42.
[471] *Engineers*, 216.

cause citizens to rise up against the Nazis. Churchill appointed Air Marshal Arthur Harris to head the British Bomber Command.[472]

Determined to show Americans, the British and Stalin that the United States was an active participant in opposing Hitler, Roosevelt instructed his military advisors that American soldiers must be fighting Germans somewhere by the end of 1942.[473]

German Aggression

On January 21, Rommel's forces counterpunched the British Eighth Army in Libya, driving the British back almost 300 miles toward Egypt in just three weeks. The combatants then paused for a while.[474]

Also on January 21, German General Model's forces in the Soviet Union counterattacked the Red Army from positions west of Moscow. The enemies battered each other for weeks in snow and freezing weather, but neither side achieved a decisive victory. Moscow still lay outside Germany's grasp.[475]

The War Against Jews Continues

By the time Operation Barbarossa had been under way for six months, the Germans had killed hundreds of thousands of Soviet Jews — most of whom were shot to death. An estimated 5,000,000 Jews in Soviet territory remained.[476]

Once Germany had declared war against the United States, Hitler recognized that the predicted world war had arrived. In keeping with his January 30, 1939 threat, he then vowed to bring about "the annihilation of the Jewish race in Europe," which the Nazis called "the final solution."[477]

In March 1942, after abandoning Hitler's plan to deport an estimated 3,500,000 European Jews to the Soviet Union, the Germans began killing them at gas chambers in the Polish towns of Belsec, Sobibor, Treblinka, Chelmno and Auschwitz-Birkenau.[478]

During the summer and early fall of 1942, the Germans removed 310,322 Jews from the Polish city of Warsaw and sent them to be

---

[472] *Air Masters*, 54, 479-80.
[473] *Supreme Commander*, 36.
[474] *Inferno*, 133, *Montgomery*, 130, 148.
[475] *Inferno*, 172-74, *Reich*, 909.
[476] *Fateful Choices*, 459, 463, *1944*, 256.
[477] *Fateful Choices*, 466, *1944*, 266-271.
[478] *Fateful Choices*, 464-67, *Bloodlands*, 273, *Reich*, 967-74.

gassed at concentration camps.[479]

The Ongoing Battle for the Atlantic

The Battle of the Atlantic pitted German U-boats against Allied efforts to ship troops, equipment and supplies from the United States to Britain, the Soviet Union and North Africa. To hunt Allied freighters and oilers, Admiral Dönitz stationed long-distance U-boats off the North American coast from Canada to the Caribbean.[480]

During 1942, U-boats sank 1,160 merchant ships in the Atlantic — one every eight hours. Merchant seamen in the Atlantic in the spring of 1942 had a higher mortality rate than soldiers fighting the Japanese at Bataan in the Philippines. For the full war, the death rate for American merchant seamen matched the death rate for United States Marines.[481]

In February 1942, the Germans modified their secret Enigma code, thereby impeding until December 1942 Britain's ability to decipher German messages to U-boats.[482]

In late February, two German battle cruisers, *Scharnhorst* and *Gneisenau*, and the heavy cruiser, *Prinz Eugen*, sailed from Brest in France through the English Channel past British mines and ships to refuge in the German port of Wilhelmshaven. Hitler wanted the ships close to Norway where he expected the Allies to attempt an invasion of the European mainland. The return of the ships to Germany led to severe criticism of the porous British naval defenses.[483]

March 1942 was the worst month of the war in terms of Allied shipping sunk by German submarines, with at least 273 merchant ships destroyed. In May and June, Germans sank 1,000,000 tons of shipping in the waters off the east coast of the United States.[484]

Where to Strike First Against the Axis Forces

In April 1942, British and American military leaders met in London to again discuss an Allied cross-Channel invasion. The Americans favored an attack in 1943 ("Bolero"), whereas Churchill preferred to wait until Germany was weaker. The British expressed support for the

---

[479]   *Reich*, 975, *1944*, 389.
[480]   *WW II Story*, 167-78, *Air Masters*, 73.
[481]   *Battle*, 5, *WW II Story*, 170-75.
[482]   *Masters*, 92-3, *Inferno*, 274, 277, *WW II Story*, 176.
[483]   *Inferno*, 265, *Reich*, 914.
[484]   *Masters*, 92, *Inferno*, 274, 277, *Crusade*, 28.

American plan but then dragged their feet, in part because Britain had lost almost 1,000,000 dead in World War I and because her World War II forces had already been driven from the Continent three times — from Dunkirk, from Norway, and from Greece.[485]

On April 26, 1942, Hitler caused the Reichstag to grant him absolute power over all Germans regardless of what any other law provided. He also acted as both Commander in Chief of the Army and Supreme Commander of the Armed Forces.[486]

In May 1942, Soviet Foreign Minister Molotov met with Roosevelt to urge the Allies to quickly establish a "second front" by invading Western Europe, thereby drawing off some of the German pressure on the Soviet Union. Although he knew it would not happen, Roosevelt said he would consider forming a second front that year.[487]

On May 27, 1942, Rommel's Afrika Korps resumed Germany's North Africa offensive against the poorly led British. By June 21, he had captured Tobruk and two days later was inside Egypt. By the end of June, Rommel was at El Alamein, sixty-five miles from Alexandria and the Nile delta, and had captured tens of thousands of Allied troops.[488]

As of June 1942, Germany had defeated Britain wherever the two had battled on land: in Norway in April 1940, in France and Belgium in June 1940, in Greece in April 1941, and in Africa in May and June 1942. British military morale was very low.[489]

The very first in-person meeting among Roosevelt, Churchill, Marshall and Brooke occurred at the White House on June 21, 1942.[490]

Churchill again argued against a prompt Allied invasion of France. He advocated invading North Africa in Morocco, Algeria and Tunisia for several reasons: (a) it would trap Germany's Afrika Korps between the invading forces and the British forces already fighting in Egypt, (b) Allied control of North Africa would reopen the Mediterranean shipping routes to the Suez Canal, (c) untested American troops would gain combat experience in conditions less harsh than a frontal assault against Germany, (d) Vichy France might be persuaded to help the Allies, and (e) the attack could be launched in 1942, thereby helping

---

[485] *Masters*, 137, 166, *Dawn*, 12-13, *Ike*, 178, *Crusade*, 48, *Supreme Commander*, 40.
[486] *Reich*, 867, 909.
[487] *Masters*, 175, *Curse*, 69-70.
[488] *Reich*, 911, *Ike*, 276, *Montgomery*, 148-49.
[489] *Masters*, 4, *Inferno*, 135-36, 354-56, *WW II Story*, 53, *Montgomery*, 132-34.
[490] *Masters*, 1.

the Soviets by establishing an early second front against the Germans.[491]

American military leaders were strongly opposed to Britain's North Africa proposal and in July 1942, General Marshall and Admiral King hinted to Churchill that the United States might switch to a "Pacific First" policy. This was done in an effort to push the British into agreeing to an earlier cross-Channel invasion. But in late July, Roosevelt sided with Churchill, announcing that the Germans should first be attacked in North Africa ("Operation Torch"), even though Marshall had warned Roosevelt that doing so meant a 1943 invasion of France was improbable.[492]

The immediate objective of Operation Torch was to occupy Vichy French Morocco and Algeria, then Tunisia. The broader objective was to take from the enemy "complete control of North Africa from the Atlantic to the Red Sea."[493]

In 1942, many French citizens were hostile to Britain. They blamed the French defeat on Britain's refusal to send aircraft to France when Germany attacked, resented Britain's withdrawal at Dunkirk and refusal to surrender, and were angered by Britain's support of de Gaulle, who continued to oppose the Axis countries. In an effort to persuade the French that the North African campaign was not a British venture, and thereby perhaps persuade the Vichy French not to resist, an American would command Operation Torch.[494]

In the summer of 1942, General Dwight Eisenhower was appointed Commander-in-Chief of Allied Forces in the Mediterranean Theater, including the Allied invasion of North Africa. Two and on-half years earlier, Eisenhower had been a lieutenant colonel with no combat experience. He had, however, graduated from West Point in 1915, served many years on General MacArthur's staff, and was known as a charming hard worker. A chain smoker, Eisenhower consumed three packs of Camel cigarettes a day.[495]

Eisenhower promptly appointed American General Mark Clark to be the chief planner for Operation Torch. His job was to figure out how to ship more than 100,000 soldiers to North Africa over thou-

---

[491] *Dawn*, 13, *Inferno*, 364-65.
[492] *Masters*, 242, 253-5, 284, *Dawn*, 14-16, *Inferno*, 364, *Montgomery*, 134, *Supreme Commander*, 66-75.
[493] *Dawn*, 22, *Supreme Commander*, 85.
[494] *Clark*, 66.
[495] *Soldier's Story*, 17, *Masters*, 287, *Dawn*, 18, 59-60, *Battle*, 51, *Generals' War*, 10, *Ike*, 273, 278, 302.

sands of miles of restless ocean infested by U-boats.[496]

For his chief of staff, Ike selected Brigadier General Walter Bedell Smith, a tough, trustworthy and abrupt officer who ably filled that role for the rest of the war.[497]

The proposed Allied invasion of North Africa was based upon several risky assumptions: Spain would remain neutral, the French in North Africa would offer no more than token resistance, and the Germans would not invade Spain to take control of its airfields.[498]

Determining what stance Vichy France would take when faced with the Allied invasion of North Africa involved much planning and debate. French military figures who could be influential included (a) Admiral Darlan, who had resigned as Pétain's successor but remained the head of Vichy France's armed forces, (b) General Juin, who commanded France's ground and air forces in North Africa, and (c) General Giraud, who had no connection with the Vichy regime but might be able to persuade the French military to side with the Allies. Most members of the French military disliked and distrusted the aloof and arrogant de Gaulle.[499]

British Naval Operations

In May 1942, the British invaded the 1,000 mile long Vichy-controlled island of Madagascar off the east coast of Africa. Confronted by hostile French troops and naval forces, the British sank one French ship and three French submarines. The French did not surrender the island until November 5, 1942, and in that process suffered over 500 casualties to almost 400 for the British.[500]

The British, using mostly Canadian troops, launched an exploratory attack on the French Channel port of Dieppe on August 19, 1942. A small German convoy spotted the Allied ships and the element of surprise was lost. The Canadians suffered 907 killed and 1,874 wounded; the British suffered 550 casualties and lost 99 planes. The Germans had 591 casualties. The disaster at Dieppe made clear the risks involved in Operation Torch.[501]

That same month, the British launched Operation Pedestal, in

---

[496] *Clark*, 67-68, *Supreme Commander*, 79.
[497] *Supreme Commander*, 81-82.
[498] *Clark*, 74-75, *Supreme Commander*, 86.
[499] *Clark*, 72-73.
[500] *Inferno*, 391-92.
[501] *Masters*, 272-73, *Inferno*, 318, *Clark*, 70, *Montgomery of Alamein* ("*Montgomery*"), Alun Chalfont, Atheneum (1976), 125-28.

which fourteen merchant ships, accompanied by British warships, sought to deliver vital supplies to the besieged Mediterranean island of Malta. The island had an airbase from which the British were bombing Axis supply shipments to North Africa. During three days of attacks from German and Italian forces in the Mediterranean, nine British merchant ships and numerous warships went down, but some needed supplies got to Malta.[502]

War Continues in the Soviet Union

Hitler's 1942 plan for the German offensive against the Soviet Union focused on the southern front. He hoped to gain control of the Caucasus oil fields, the wheat fields of east Ukraine, the Donets industrial area above the Crimea, and Stalingrad. The two nations would battle over the crucial food and oil each needed to prevail. Hitler predicted that the Soviet Union would fall in 1942 and that Britain would cease its resistance in 1943.[503]

Because German casualties in the Soviet Union during 1941 exceeded 1,100,000, Hitler needed fresh troops. Some fifty-two divisions of moderately skilled soldiers were gathered from Germany's allies and satellites such as Hungary, Romania and Italy.[504]

In May 1942, the Germans, under Field Marshal Manstein, continued their attack on Red Army forces in the Crimea. After a 245 day siege which began in 1941 and cost the Germans 25,000 dead, the city of Sevastopol fell in early July. The Germans then controlled all of the Crimean peninsula. The Red Army lost 170,000 as prisoners.[505]

Also in May, the Germans repelled a Red Army thrust further north at Kharkov, causing the Soviets to lose more than 250,000 soldiers.[506]

During the summer Hitler elected, despite the objections of his generals who worried about stiffening Soviet defenses, to simultaneously pursue major offensives against both the Soviet's Caspian oil fields and Stalingrad.[507]

On August 23, 1942, the Germans began an all-out offensive to capture the city of Stalingrad, home to 600,000 Russians, 40,000 of

---

[502] *Inferno*, 288-91, *Reich*, 912-13.
[503] *Reich*, 909-10.
[504] *Reich*, 909-11.
[505] *Inferno*, 294-95, *WW II Story*, 70, *Reich*, 914, *Air Masters*, 62.
[506] *Inferno*, 295.
[507] *Reich*, 916-18, *Montgomery*, 135-37.

whom were killed the first day. Stalin, concerned that if Stalingrad fell the Germans would turn north to capture Moscow, ordered a battle to the death. By September 27, two-thirds of the city was in German hands. In November, the Red Army counterattacked with over 1,000,000 men and trapped 250,000 German soldiers within the city after Hitler refused to permit a retreat. The battle raged on for the rest of 1942. (During that time, the Soviets killed 13,500 of their own Red Army troops for deserting or failing to shoot other deserting soldiers). Germany's efforts to supply by air its surrounded and starving soldiers were not successful. In the Stalingrad fight the Red Army lost 155,000 dead.[508]

On December 29, Hitler reluctantly ordered the German forces that had attempted to capture the Caucasus oil fields to retreat so as to avoid a second Stalingrad.[509]

In the north, the Germans continued their siege of Leningrad until late August 1942, when they tried to occupy the city. The Soviets threw the Germans back and the siege continued, but the city's inhabitants were able to receive some food. By the time the siege ended in early 1944, between 632,000 and 1,000,000 Leningrad residents had died.[510]

The Red Army's soldier losses fighting the Axis forces in 1942 exceeded even those of the disastrous 1941.[511]

By the end of 1942, eighteen months after Germany first attacked the Soviet Union, the Germans had taken about 3,000,000 war prisoners — roughly sixty-five percent of the existing Red Army forces.[512]

Summer and Fall Battles in North Africa

On July 1, the Germans attacked British forces, commanded by General Auchinleck, in the first battle of El Alamein in Egypt. But Rommel failed to achieve a breakthrough toward Cairo, in part due to Britain's advance knowledge of Axis movements through Ultra intercepts of secret German communications.[513]

In late August, worn but aggressive Rommel forces attacked the British once more, this time at Alam Halfa, south of El Alamein.

---

[508] *Masters*, 275-76, 305, 349, *Inferno*, 296-97, 299-305, 309-13, *WW II Story*, 70-76, *Reich*, 918-19, 925-28.

[509] *Reich*, 928.

[510] *Inferno*, 306-07.

[511] *Inferno*, 298.

[512] *Curse*, 59.

[513] *Inferno*, 356, *Montgomery*, 133, 135, 150.

Again forewarned by Ultra intercepts, the recently resupplied British Eighth Army troops commanded by newly-appointed Lt. General Bernard Montgomery held the Germans off. Montgomery, however, did not counterattack.[514]

On October 23, 1942, Montgomery's larger and better-armed forces launched an attack on Italian and German troops at El Alamein, Egypt. By November 10, the weakly-supplied Axis forces had been expelled from Egypt and had retreated 700 miles past El Agheila in Libya. They suffered more than 50,000 killed, wounded or captured. This second battle of El Alamein was the first and last solely British land victory in the Second World War, all subsequent victories being achieved by joint Allied forces.[515]

The American Air War Against Germany Begins

The American Eighth Air Force, flying four-engine B-17 bombers, began to arrive in England in July 1942. The group, then commanded by General Carl Spaatz, flew its first dangerous daylight mission against Germany that summer. The Eighth Air Force was at that time the only American fighting force that was actually battling the Germans.[516]

The B-17 Flying Fortress was a high speed, heavily armed long range plane designed in the 1930s when many Americans were still firmly isolationist.[517]

The U.S. Army Air Corps had failed to develop simultaneously a long range fighter plane that could accompany the B-17 on distant bombing runs. Several reasons contributed to this omission: (a) military funding was scarce before World War II, (b) military planners did not appreciate that newly-developing radar would alert an enemy to the approach of bombers in time to launch defensive fighters, and (c) it was thought that any fighter equipped to fly long distances would be slower and less maneuverable, rendering it unable to keep up with the very fast B-17 and also vulnerable to nimble enemy fighters.[518]

In October 1942, a portion of the Eighth Air Force was assigned the duty of bombing submarine pens the Germans had built in Britta-

---

[514] *Inferno*, 356, *Reich*, 919, *Montgomery*, 151-52, 166-67.

[515] *Masters*, 289-91, 294, *Dawn*, 66, 418, *Inferno*, 359-64, *WW II Story*, 53-56, *Reich*, 921, *Montgomery*, 170, 184-90, 340.

[516] *Air Masters*, 62, 64, 70.

[517] *Air Masters*, 40-41.

[518] *Air Masters*, 41-42.

ny on the Atlantic coast of France. The Nazi bases were heavily defended, American losses were substantial, and only minimal damage was done to the concrete pens.[519]

During its first year of bombing, over 1,600 Eighth Air Force crewmen were taken from duty due to frostbite, and some 1,200 others were removed due to battle wounds.[520]

The Germans sought to ward off the American daylight bombing attacks with antiaircraft guns and fighters. Between the fall of 1942 and the next spring, the Germans doubled the number of fighters facing the Allied bombers.[521]

During the initial ten months that the Eighth Air Force flew missions against the Germans, 188 bombers were lost and fifty-seven percent of the crew members were either killed or missing in action.[522]

American Dissatisfaction

In the early November 1942 elections, the Democrats lost fifty-three congressional seats in voting by Americans troubled by the lack of a major United States response to Germany's war declaration and economic hardships at home. Still, Democrats retained control of all three branches of government.[523]

Operation Torch

In an effort to persuade the Vichy French military forces in North Africa not to resist the Allied invasion, U.S. General Mark Clark travelled by submarine to a secret October 22 meeting in North Africa with French General Mast, who claimed to have influence over the French North African military. In return for Clark's agreement that General Giraud would command North African French forces at an appropriate time after the landing, Mast provided information on the strength and location of French units and supplies.[524]

But in a November 7 meeting with Eisenhower in Gibralter, Giraud insisted on immediate command of the entire invasion force in return for his cooperation. Eisenhower refused and, after many hours of discussion, offered to recognize Giraud as commander of all French

---

[519] *Air Masters*, 75-76, 120.

[520] *Air Masters*, 90-92.

[521] *Air Masters*, 107, 139.

[522] *Air Masters*, 143.

[523] *Dawn*, 32, *Masters*, 290, *1944*, 333.

[524] *Clark*, 78-89, *Supreme Commander*, 99-100, 108-09.

forces in North Africa and governor of that area. Giraud finally accepted these terms.[525]

On November 8, 1942, the Allies commenced simultaneous amphibious assaults at eight places in North Africa ("Operation Torch"). More than 100,000 troops, transported from Britain and the United States and supported by almost 400 ships, landed in Vichy French Morocco and Algeria.[526]

General George Patton commanded the 34,000 American troops who on October 24, 1942 had set out for French Morocco from Hampton Roads, Virginia. From Britain, 72,000 United States and British troops embarked for Algeria, 33,000 to land at Algiers and 39,000 at Oran.[527]

On November 8, on the Atlantic coast of French Morocco, (a) 6,000 American assault troops landed at Safi, a town 140 miles south of Casablanca, (b) 9,000 were put ashore at the town of Mehdia, 80 miles north of Casablanca, and (c) almost 20,000, commanded by Patton, landed at Fedala, a fishing village just north of Casablanca.[528]

The Vichy French in Fedala fired on the Allied ships and landing craft from shore batteries, ships in the harbor and submarines. Allied fighter planes and ships responded, sinking or crippling sixteen Vichy French ships, costing the French 490 dead and 969 wounded.[529]

On November 8, Vichy France broke off diplomatic relations with the United States and Premier Pétain announced that his forces would oppose the Allied invasion.[530]

American efforts to persuade the French at Fedala and Mehdia to surrender were rejected, and the battle continued. After three days of combat, however, the French asked for a ceasefire in Mehdia.[531]

The victory in French Morocco, which afforded the Allies an Atlantic base in Africa, including a harbor and airport, cost the United States 337 killed, 637 wounded, 122 missing and 71 captured.[532]

Oran, a town in Algeria, was one of the three Allied landing zones controlled by the Vichy French. On November 8, Allied naval vessels attacked Vichy French ships in and near the Oran harbor, sinking or

---

[525] *Supreme Commander*, 114-17.
[526] *Masters*, 291, *Dawn*, 30-31, *Inferno*, 364.
[527] *Dawn*, 38, 40, 50-51, 57.
[528] *Dawn*, 105, 135, 141.
[529] *Dawn*, 131-35.
[530] *Reich*, 923-24.
[531] *Dawn*, 138, 143, 147, *Inferno*, 364.
[532] *Dawn*, 150, *Inferno*, 364.

damaging five. The French scuttled twenty-seven other ships and killed more than 300 Allied troops in the battle.[533]

Also on November 8, almost 40,000 Allied soldiers, some led by President Teddy Roosevelt's son, landed east and west of Oran with a plan to envelop the Algerian city. They faced resistance from Vichy French troops but by the end of the first day had Oran nearly surrounded.[534]

On the same day at Algiers, 33,000 Allied soldiers landed on beaches east and west of the city, meeting sparse French resistance.[535]

By November 10, some 37,000 Allied troops controlled a beachhead in Algeria seventy miles wide and fifteen miles deep.[536]

Vichy French forces in North Africa were commanded by Admiral Jean Francois Darlan, a Nazi collaborator, who happened to be in Algiers when the Allied troops landed. The French forces would follow orders from Darlan, but would give no weight to any orders from Giraud. After two days of resistance, under pressure from the Allies Darlan ordered all Vichy French forces in Africa to surrender. Several hours later, Pétain, concerned that the Germans might occupy the portion of France then under Vichy control, fired Darlan and repudiated the ceasefire agreement. The Allies then threatened to place Darlan under arrest if he retracted the ceasefire order.[537]

Beginning at midnight on November 10, troubled by the ceasefire in North Africa, German and Italian troops crossed the armistice line and invaded Vichy France. This action gave the French military leaders in North Africa an excuse to renounce their allegiance to Pétain since he was now a virtual prisoner of the Axis.[538]

On November 11 and 12, German U-boats sank or disabled six United States ships off the coast of Casablanca, killing 140 Americans.[539]

The French military in North Africa agreed to a ceasefire across North Africa on November 11. Two days later, Eisenhower recognized Darlan as head of all civil affairs in French North Africa and Gi-

---

[533] *Dawn*, 72-77.
[534] *Dawn*, 78-91.
[535] *Dawn*, 99-100.
[536] *Dawn*, 129.
[537] *Dawn*, 120-23, *WW II Story*, 162, *Clark*, 90-101, *Reich*, 924-25, *Supreme Commander*, 120-21.
[538] *Clark*, 100, *Reich*, 924, *1944*, 341.
[539] *Dawn*, 154-56.

raud as head of French military forces[540]

On November 16, French forces in North Africa for the first time fought German forces, evidencing their new commitment to the Allies.[541]

On November 22, the French forces in North Africa, represented by Darlan, signed a formal agreement in which they committed to assist the Allies in driving Axis forces out of Africa in return for the Allies' pledge to liberate France and restore the French empire.[542]

German troops tried to seize Vichy warships in the French port of Toulon on November 27. Admiral de Laborde, commanding the French fleet, decided to scuttle his ships rather than turn them over to either the Allies or the Germans. Three battleships, seven cruisers and thirty-two destroyers went down.[543]

Allied losses in the somewhat disorganized November 1942 invasions of North Africa were approximately 1,000 dead and 1,200 wounded. French killed and wounded totaled about 3,000.[544]

By the end of November, the public was criticizing the Allies for making a Roosevelt-approved armistice deal with Vichy France's Admiral Darlan, who was viewed in many quarters as a scoundrel. Eisenhower, too, was criticized for spending too much time on political issues and too little on military plans designed to drive Axis troops out of Tunisia.[545]

Darlan, who had failed to have the French fleet delivered to the Allies and had been an embarrassment to the Allies, was shot and killed on December 24, 1942 by a Frenchman seeking to restore the French monarchy. On December 26, a French firing squad killed the quickly-convicted assassin. General Giraud then succeeded Darlan as high commissioner in French North Africa and head of the French North African Army.[546]

The Germans Mean to Hold Tunisia

Hitler immediately recognized that if the Allies took North Africa they would have a platform for invading southern Europe. In Novem-

---

[540] *Dawn*, 149, 156-58, *Masters*, 297-98, *WW II Story*, 162, *Clark*, 100-08, *Supreme Commander*, 122-27.

[541] *Clark*, 108.

[542] *Clark*, 109.

[543] *Dawn*, 217, *Reich*, 925, *Supreme Commander*, 135.

[544] *Dawn*, 159.

[545] *Dawn*, 197-200, *Supreme Commander*, 129-34, *1944*, 343.

[546] *Dawn*, 251-53, 256, *Masters*, 311, 344, *Clark*, 115, *Supreme Commander*, 147.

ber he issued a brief order: "North Africa, being the approach to Europe, must be held at all costs." The Germans promptly strengthened the Axis forces in Vichy French-controlled Tunisia.[547]

The Vichy French debated whether to side with the Nazis or the Allies. Eventually, most French forces in Tunisia surrendered to the Germans without much of a fight.[548]

As the Allies headed east from Algeria on a broad front to try to take Tunisia, the Germans and Italians, commanded by Field Marshal Kesselring, prepared to move west to drive the Allies out of North Africa.[549]

The Allied mid-November advance on the Axis-held Tunisian cities of Bizerte and Tunis was slowed by poor planning and rookie troops and leadership, including Eisenhower's inexperienced command.[550]

By November 25, there were 16,000 German and 9,000 Italian soldiers in Tunisia, and new troops were arriving at the rate of 1,000 per day.[551]

From November until mid-December, Allied and Axis forces parried back and forth seeking control of Tunisia. Some 9,000 French North African Army troops, commanded by Generals Juin and Barré, fought with the Allies. The French North African Army was separate and distinct from the Free French forces that de Gaulle claimed to lead.[552]

By December, although there were 180,000 American troops in North Africa, only about 12,000 were at the front in Tunisia. They were joined by about 20,000 British soldiers and poorly-equipped French troops. The number of Axis troops facing them in Tunisia had climbed to 56,000. For eleven days in the middle of December, both sides consolidated their positions and waited for the battles to start anew.[553]

Meanwhile, the Germans forced thousands of Tunisian Jews to perform slave labor in the city of Tunis building trenches and other defensive fortifications.[554]

---

[547] *Dawn*, 164-65, *Inferno*, 365.
[548] *Dawn*, 164-66, 176, *Inferno*, 365.
[549] *Dawn*, 166-68.
[550] *Dawn*, 171, *Supreme Commander*, 137-43.
[551] *Dawn*, 183-84, 219.
[552] *Dawn*, 179, 201-235, *Masters*, 344.
[553] *Dawn*, 237-39.
[554] *Dawn*, 239-40.

Throughout November and December, French General Giraud demanded that he supplant Eisenhower as supreme commander in North Africa, a demand that was repeatedly rejected.[555]

In late December, Eisenhower concluded that weather conditions would delay for several weeks additional Allied efforts to take Tunis. His goal of quickly overrunning Tunisia and expelling the Germans and Italians from North Africa gave way to the recognition that the Allies were in for a lengthy fight.[556]

After the British success at El Alamein and the Allied invasion of North Africa, an elated Churchill said, "Now this is not the end. It is not even the beginning of the end. But it is, perhaps, the end of the beginning."[557]

In December 1942, while the western Allies were fighting six German divisions in Africa, the Red Army faced 183 German divisions on the Eastern Front. A division in World War II included about 14,000 men, a minority of whom were in the infantry. An infantry division consisted of eighty-one rifle platoons, each with a strength of about forty men. An army contained about 350,000 men.[558]

As 1942 ended, the Allied and Axis forces continued to fight in many European and African theaters, but which side would prevail could not yet be clearly foreseen.

THE TIDE BEGINS TO TURN IN EUROPE (1943)

The Casablanca Conference

Roosevelt, Churchill and the Combined Chiefs of Staff met in Casablanca, Morocco in mid-January 1943 to discuss their global war strategy. Stalin declined to attend because the battle for Stalingrad was still raging. Roosevelt and Churchill quickly confirmed "Germany First," and agreed to continue sending supplies to the Red Army, bomb German cities day and night, and suppress German U-boats. After much debate, they also agreed to the Allied invasion of Sicily in the summer of 1943, continuing military attacks against Japan supported by thirty percent of America's war production, and a cross-Channel invasion of France in 1944. In anticipation of the cross-Channel invasion, they directed that 938,000 U.S. troops should be gathered in the

---

[555] *Dawn,* 64-66, 247.
[556] *Dawn,* 249-50, *Supreme Commander,* 147.
[557] *Dawn,* 159, *WW II Story,* 54.
[558] *Soldier's Story,* 445, *Masters,* 304.

United Kingdom before 1943 ended.[559]

As the Combined Chiefs of Staff met in Casablanca, Montgomery's army chased Rommel's forces west in Libya. On January 23, the British took the city of Tripoli.[560]

On January 24, 1943, President Roosevelt, in Churchill's presence and with his stated agreement, announced at Casablanca that the Allies would insist upon unconditional surrender by Germany, Japan and Italy.[561]

The Battle for Tunisia Continues

By January, the Tunisian combat lines extended roughly 200 miles down the middle of the nation from the Mediterranean south into the Sahara, with British troops in the north, Americans in the south, and French in the middle. Tunis and Bizerte, two Mediterranean cities under Axis control, lay to the east of the front. General Giraud refused to integrate his French units into the overall Allied command structure until January 24, after the French had suffered thousands of casualties in a bad beating by the Germans.[562]

As 1943 started, Eisenhower was troubled by his American troops' lack of toughness and training, and the failure of his officers to enforce discipline. He issued stern training orders designed to strengthen the troops and their leaders.[563]

In mid-January 1943, Kay Summersby, a 34 year old comely divorced Irish woman who served as Eisenhower's driver, arrived in Algiers, renewing rumors that she and Ike were having an affair, even though she was then engaged to an American colonel (later killed by a mine in Tunisia).[564]

In late January, Allied troops, commanded by American General Fredendall, sought without success to advance against the Germans in central Tunisia.[565]

By February, German Field Marshal Rommel's forces totaled about 190,000 men, some 50,000 of whom were Italian. Only about

---

[559] *Soldier's Story*, 190-91, *Masters*, 320-36, *Dawn*, 269, 283-289, *Inferno*, 419, 428, *Air Masters*, 111-13, *Supreme Commander*, 158-65.

[560] *Montgomery*, 195, 340.

[561] *Dawn*, 293-95, *Guns*, 380, *Masters*, 343, *Curse*, 166, *Eagle*, 222, *Generals' War*, 123.

[562] *Dawn*, 275, 302, 305.

[563] *Supreme Commander*, 152-54.

[564] *Dawn*, 329-30, *Battle*, 57, *Generals' War*, 38, 45-48.

[565] *Dawn*, 301-17.

one-third of the total were true combat soldiers.[566]

In the week-long mid-February 1943 battle of Kasserine Pass in central Tunisia, Rommel's attacking Germans suffered 959 casualties, whereas the retreating American Army suffered 6,600 killed, wounded or missing. (Lt. Colonel John Waters, Patton's son-in-law, was one of the Americans captured by the Germans). After pushing the Allies back eighty-five miles toward Algeria, Rommel withdrew due to troop exhaustion and insufficient supplies. This was one of the worst defeats the United States Army suffered in World War II, reflecting disorganized leadership and inexperienced troops. But the Americans had now been tested in battle and realized that Rommel and the Germans were not invincible.[567]

After the Kasserine Pass debacle, Eisenhower removed from command Fredendall and several other officers, partly to divert focus from his own inexperienced leadership. General Patton took Fredendall's place for about a month, then General Omar Bradley was given command of the United States Army's II Corps.[568]

After the Allies landed in North Africa, de Gaulle moved his Free French headquarters from London to Algiers.[569]

In early March 1943, de Gaulle sought to visit French troops in North Africa. Because the visit might upset the delicate balance between Vichy and Free French forces, Churchill refused and threatened to have de Gaulle arrested. In April 1943, a plane transporting de Gaulle from London to Glasgow was apparently sabotaged, but he was not injured. In frustration in May, Churchill pondered whether it would be best to eliminate de Gaulle altogether as a political figure.[570]

By March, both Allied and Axis forces recognized that the contest for Tunisia and all of North Africa had come down to a shrinking battlefield in eastern Tunisia. Montgomery had in the last four months moved his British Eighth Army more than 1,000 miles west from Egypt into western Libya. Rommel's forces in central Tunisia now faced Montgomery from the east and American troops from the west. In northern Tunisia, Axis troops commanded by German General von Arnim faced General Anderson's British First Army.[571]

---

[566] *Dawn*, 320.
[567] *Masters*, 352, *Engineers*, 146, *Dawn*, 339-92, 412, *Inferno*, 366, *WW II Story*, 163, *Supreme Commander*, 166-74.
[568] *Dawn*, 399-403, 483-87, *Supreme Commander*, 175, 185.
[569] *Generals*, 136.
[570] *Masters*, 352-53, *Generals' War*, 133.
[571] *Dawn*, 398, 409.

On March 9, 1942, an exhausted and dispirited Rommel secretly left North Africa on sick leave. He never returned to that theater of war.[572]

Following his questionable winter performance as commander-in-chief in North Africa, Eisenhower became more focused as spring arrived, spent less time on political matters, and espoused several central themes: Allied unity, the certainty of victory, and the righteousness of the Allied cause.[573]

While American supplies poured into North Africa to support the Allied effort, Axis troops had to depend on Italian ships sailing supplies from Italy. Between November 1942 and May 1943, the Allies sank 243 Italian ships in the Mediterranean and damaged another 242. After bearing the burdens of war for the last three and one-half years, the Germans simply could not match the American supply train.[574]

In mid-March, some 170,000 British and Commonwealth troops, commanded by the egotistical and opinionated Montgomery, moved westward in southern Tunisia and attacked the Mareth Line, defended by 85,000 Axis troops. On April 6, after two weeks of back-and-forth fighting, in which the British suffered 600 dead and 2,000 wounded but took some 5,000 Italian POWs, the Axis troops began to withdraw north toward Tunis and Bizerte.[575]

Simultaneous with Montgomery's attack from the west, Patton's II Corps, moving east in a two-pronged formation, attacked the center of the Axis forces. Over a five day period, the right prong, led by Generals Allen and Roosevelt, fought and defeated experienced German troops in what General Bradley said was the "first solid, indisputable defeat we inflicted on the German army in the war." The left prong, led by General Ward, made some progress and was then stalemated by the Germans for days, resulting in Ward being removed from command.[576]

On April 7, Montgomery's British troops moving west in Tunisia met American troops moving east, creating a single Allied Tunisian battle line pursuing the Axis forces that were retreating north toward Tunis.[577]

---

[572] *Dawn*, 410-11, *Inferno*, 367, *Montgomery*, 197.
[573] *Dawn*, 412, 465-66, *Supreme Commander*, 180-82.
[574] *Dawn*, 415.
[575] *Dawn*, 421-430, 464, *WW II Story*, 164, *Montgomery*, 200-01.
[576] *Dawn*, 431-53, *Supreme Commander*, 185.
[577] *Dawn*, 465.

Unity among Allied leadership proved challenging as the Americans tended to dislike the British and the British tended to believe that the Americans lacked military skills. Montgomery said of Eisenhower: "he was good probably on the political line; but he obviously knows nothing whatever about fighting." Eisenhower said of the waspish Montgomery: "I can deal with anybody except that son of a bitch," and he "will never willingly make a single move until he is absolutely certain of success."[578]

A poorly designed and executed Allied attempt in early April to block the retreat of Axis troops being chased from the south by Montgomery and Patton failed. Those Axis troops successfully moved north and joined the German forces occupying Tunis and Bizerte.[579]

The Battle for North Africa Ends

The plan to finally drive Axis forces out of Tunisia and North Africa called for more than 300,000 Allied troops to attack in three main groups along a 140 mile front. The British were to come toward Tunis and Bizerte from both the south and southwest, and the American troops, now commanded by General Omar Bradley, were to proceed from the west. (Patton had been relieved so that he could concentrate on the forthcoming invasion of Sicily). French troops were among the Allied forces driving to Tunis.[580]

Beginning in mid-April, the Allies attacked some 250,000 poorly supplied Axis troops cornered in and near Tunis. Concerned, Hitler and Mussolini ordered their soldiers to hold their positions "at all costs."[581]

It was apparent to Mussolini that after North Africa the Allies would invade Italy. Thus, for months he implored Hitler to reach an accord with Stalin so that Axis troops on the Eastern Front could return to Europe to oppose the Allies. Hitler rejected Mussolini's prayer.[582]

By May 13, 1943, the American and British forces in North Africa had defeated the Axis forces, and in the process had taken 238,243 prisoners of war, half of them German.[583]

---

[578] *Dawn*, 466, 476-79, *Supreme Commander*, 177-.

[579] *Dawn*, 468-76.

[580] *Dawn*, 481-85.

[581] *Dawn*, 488-90, *Inferno*, 367.

[582] *Reich*, 995-96, *Dawn*, 490, *Battle*, 139.

[583] *Curse*, 72, *Dawn*, 478, 525-26, *Inferno*, 367, *Supreme Commander*, 189.

Allied casualties in the invasion of North Africa and the Tunisian campaign exceeded 70,000 — about 38,000 British, 19,000 French and 18,000 American.[584]

Pushing Axis forces out of North Africa (a) gave the Allies control of ports and airfields from Casablanca to Alexandria, (b) stalled Axis threats against Middle East oil fields, (c) reopened the Suez canal for the first time since 1941, (d) dissuaded Spain from entering the war, (e) exposed the southern flank of occupied Europe to further Allied attacks, and (f) weakened Mussolini's position at home.[585]

The Warsaw Ghetto is No More

When the Germans realized in early 1943 that almost 60,000 Jews still lived in the Warsaw Ghetto, they ordered them removed to the concentration camp at Treblinka by February 15. The Jews fought back with guns and Molotov cocktails. It was not until mid-May that the Warsaw Ghetto was crushed. All of the Jews died either in the battle or, after capture, in extermination camps.[586]

By resolution dated March 9, 1943, the United States Senate expressed its indignation at the "atrocities" and "mass murder of Jewish men, women and children." Still, while expressing concern for European Jews, Roosevelt was hesitant to take strong military action aimed at destroying concentration camps in Germany and Poland.[587]

Allied Advances in the North Atlantic Sea War

By early 1943, Admiral Dönitz had 300 U-boats operating in the Atlantic, often in wolf packs. During the first three weeks of March, the Germans sank ninety-seven merchant ships in the North Atlantic, most of them near Greenland in the 600 mile gap between British and American air coverage.[588]

In late March 1943, however, the Allies significantly improved their defenses against German U-boat attacks in the Atlantic through planes that could stay airborne longer, better radar, improved anti-submarine weapons, intercepted secret German naval radio messages, and strengthened naval escorts of merchant convoys.[589]

---

[584] *Dawn*, 536.
[585] *Battle*, 5, *WW II Story*, 164, *Dawn*, 490.
[586] *Reich*, 974-79, *1944*, 388-91.
[587] *1944*, 375-388, 451.
[588] *WW II Story*, 176.
[589] *Engineers*, 72, *Battle*, 5, *Inferno*, 278, *WW II Story*, 175-78, *Reich*, 1007.

In addition, the American Eighth Air Force bombed submarine construction yards in Germany in an effort to slow the building of new U-boats.[590]

Germany lost forty-seven U-boats in the Atlantic in May 1943, three times the number sunk just two months earlier.[591]

By June, Admiral Dönitz had withdrawn his U-boats from the North Atlantic to safer waters near Europe, and privately admitted that "We had lost the Battle of the Atlantic." He also lost two of his sons in U-boat defeats.[592]

During the summer of 1943, 3,500 Allied merchant vessels packed with needed personnel, arms and supplies crossed the Atlantic without one being sunk. Only sixty-seven were lost during the final four months of the year, while sixty-four U-boats were sent to the bottom during that period.[593]

Fighting on the Eastern Front

On January 31, 1943, the Red Army won the Battle of Stalingrad after some eight months of hand-to-hand fighting. Of the 91,000 German soldiers who surrendered, fewer than 10,000 ever returned home. Two months earlier, the Axis forces in Stalingrad had numbered 285,000.[594]

In February, Soviet troops captured the Ukrainian city of Kharkov, about 250 miles west of Stalingrad, only to have it retaken by German forces a month later.[595]

In March, Hitler reluctantly authorized German troops to withdraw from an area near Moscow, shortening the German battle line by 250 miles and concentrating his strength.[596]

In April 1943, the Germans publicized world-wide their discovery of a mass grave in the Katyń forest near Minsk containing the bodies of 4,000 of the 25,000 Polish officers the Soviet Union had executed following its 1939 invasion of Poland.[597]

In May 1943, Germans fighting in western Ukraine found and publicized more mass graves, this time almost 10,000 corpses of people

---

[590] *Air Masters*, 114.

[591] *Battle*, 5, *Inferno*, 278.

[592] *WW II Story*, 177, *Reich*, 1007, *Air Masters*, 147.

[593] *Battle*, 5, *WW II Story*, 177, *Reich*, 1007.

[594] *Curse*, 72, *Masters*, 275-76, 305, 349, *Inferno*, 372, *Reich*, 929-32.

[595] *Inferno*, 371.

[596] *Inferno*, 373.

[597] *Curse*, 50-51, 73, *Inferno*, 23, *Bloodlands*, 286-87.

thought to have been killed by the Soviet secret police during Stalin's purges.[598]

By June, Hitler had built up his Axis forces in the Soviet Union to more than 3,000,000. In early July, he directed 900,000 of his southern troops to push the Red Army bulge above Kharkov back east past Kursk. The Russians opposed this effort with 1,300,000 troops. After thrusts and counterattacks, in July the Germans were forced to retreat. In August the Red Army retook Kharkov and held it. In fifty days of fighting, the Germans had sustained a major defeat and suffered 500,000 casualties.[599]

The Trident Conference

For two weeks in May of 1943, Churchill, Roosevelt and the Combined Chiefs of Staff met in Washington, D.C. ("Trident"). They agreed on (a) a cross-Channel invasion, (b) increased aerial bombing of Germany, (c) the invasion of Sicily, (d) bombing the Ploesti oil fields in Romania, (e) an air campaign against Burma, (f) seizure of New Guinea and the Marshall, Caroline, Solomon and Aleutian islands, and (g) flying 10,000 tons of supplies from India to China each month.[600]

A significant Trident debate involved whether to invade mainland Italy after taking Sicily. The Americans felt doing so would delay the critical cross-Channel invasion of France and consume precious resources feeding Italian civilians once Italy surrendered. The British argued that because the Allies would not be ready to invade France until May 1944, once Sicily was taken it was important to keep the Allied troops occupied so that Stalin would feel that the Western Allies were sharing some of the war's burdens. Also, taking the Italians out of the war would force Hitler to send more German troops to defend Italy, thereby weakening German defenses elsewhere.[601]

As Trident drew to a close, the parties agreed to a compromise on Italy. The Americans received British commitments that a cross-Channel invasion would be launched by May 1944 and that seven Allied divisions would be transferred from the Mediterranean to England once Sicily fell so that they could prepare for the invasion of France. The British received an American commitment that General Eisenhower would plan whatever operations after taking Sicily that seemed

---

[598] *Curse*, 176, 206.
[599] *Inferno*, 375-80, *WW II Story*, 486, *Reich*, 1006.
[600] *Masters*, 358, 371.
[601] *Battle*, 13-16, *Inferno*, 428-29.

"best calculated to eliminate Italy from the war and to contain the maximum number of German forces."[602]

At Trident and thereafter, Churchill sought unsuccessfully to persuade the Americans to invade the Greek islands once mainland Italy had been taken.[603]

Churchill and Roosevelt agreed that de Gaulle was not trustworthy and was damaging the Allied war efforts. Despite the fact that Britain had given the Free French considerable amounts of money, de Gaulle admired the Soviet Union over Britain and the United States. De Gaulle's London headquarters were discovered to have betrayed to the Gestapo French officials who were not deemed sufficiently loyal to him.[604]

The Sicily Campaign

Sicily, the largest island in the Mediterranean, is located ninety miles from Tunisia and just two miles from mainland Italy.[605]

Operation Husky, in planning since January 23, called for the July 10, 1943 amphibious invasion of Sicily. The island, thought to be held by some 300,000 Axis troops (mostly Italian), would be invaded by two Allied armies — 80,000 troops in Patton's U.S. Seventh Army and a like number of troops in Britain's Eighth Army, with reinforcements from both nations to follow. More than 3,000 vessels, large and small, would ferry Allied troops and supplies to a 100 mile long stretch of the southeastern coast of Sicily. The British would land to the east; the Americans thirty-five miles to the west.[606]

In June, the Allies captured from Italian forces the small fortified island of Pantelleria, located sixty miles southwest of Sicily, in the process obtaining a useful airfield and over 11,000 POWs.[607]

By July 1943, Allied Forces Headquarters in Algiers, responsible for planning the invasion of Sicily, was staffed by almost 4,000 officers and 8,000 supporting staff. They understood that an amphibious landing on a hostile shore was the most demanding operation in war — wading ashore under fire, moving off the beach to a secure area, then moving inland.[608]

---

[602] *Battle*, 20-24, *Masters*, 422, *Supreme Commander*, 211.
[603] *Masters*, 371-72, 425, 433, *Battle*, 21, 309.
[604] *Generals' War*, 132-34, *Dawn*, 292.
[605] *Battle*, 7, 52.
[606] *Battle*, 32-33, 53-54, 75, 87, *Inferno*, 430, *WW II Story*, 215-16.
[607] *Battle*, 33, *Supreme Commander*, 214-15.
[608] *Battle*, 31, 52.

Operation Husky was the largest amphibious invasion in World War II.[609]

General Patton commanded the American soldiers landing in Sicily and Admiral Hewitt commanded the American naval forces. Both leaders had worked well together in the earlier American amphibious invasion of French Morocco in North Africa.[610]

During the evening of July 9-10, 1943, the Allies flew more than 3,000 paratroopers to drop zones in southern Sicily. Their mission was to block Axis counterattacks against Allied troops landing on the beaches.[611]

On July 10, seven Allied divisions made an amphibious landing in southeastern Sicily.[612]

The Germans were surprised by the Sicily invasion. This was due in part to a British scheme in which a uniformed man's body with a briefcase locked to his wrist was dumped into the ocean off the southern coast of Spain in April 1943. In the briefcase were forged documents suggesting that the Allies would invade Sardinia and Greece rather than Sicily. As hoped, the Spanish discovered the body and documents and turned them over to the Germans, who believed the documents were legitimate.[613]

On July 11, additional American paratroopers being flown to Sicily were thought by Allied troops to be enemy forces and were subjected to friendly fire, causing 410 casualties.[614]

On July 13, 1943, facing strong Axis resistance on his right flank, Montgomery unilaterally ordered his British troops on the left flank to occupy a highway in the section of Sicily that had been assigned to Patton and the Americans. This delayed Patton's advance and may have prevented the Americans from cutting off a vital escape route for 60,000 Axis forces moving from west to east across the top of Sicily. General Bradley characterized Montgomery's decision as "the most arrogant, egotistical, selfish and dangerous move in the whole of combined operations in World War II." To preserve Allied unity, Eisenhower decided not to intervene.[615]

By July 18, Montgomery's forces moving up the east coast of Sicily

---

[609] *Battle*, 55, *Supreme Commander*, 216.
[610] *Battle*, 42.
[611] *Battle*, 76, *Supreme Commander*, 219.
[612] *Battle*, 55, 86-87, *Masters*, 384-85.
[613] *Battle*, 91.
[614] *Battle*, 109, *Inferno*, 430, *Soldier's Story*, 133.
[615] *Battle*, 123-24, 130, *Inferno*, 433, *Soldier's Story*, 135-38, *Montgomery*, 208.

were stalemated. Patton, however, drove 100 miles up the center of Sicily and by July 23 had captured the city of Palermo on the north coast.[616]

The city of Messina sits in the northeastern corner of Sicily and just a few miles from the Italian mainland. Messina would be the jumping off point for Axis troops seeking to escape from Sicily.[617]

After taking Palermo, Patton turned his forces east toward Messina in two parallel lines, one along the coast and the other inland. For his own glory and that of the U.S. Army, the egocentric and irascible Patton wanted desperately to take Messina before Montgomery got there, even if doing so cost more lives.[618]

On August 3, while visiting a military hospital in Sicily, Patton encountered an American soldier suffering from battle anxiety but no wounds. Patton exploded, slapping the man with his gloves, calling him a coward, pulling him out of bed and sending him back to his unit. On August 10, he struck another hospitalized unwounded soldier who complained of battle anxiety.[619]

On August 10, Patton, over the objections of Generals Bradley and Truscott, insisted on an American amphibious landing on the northeastern coast of Sicily some ten miles behind German lines. After one and one-half days of costly fighting, the Germans pulled back toward Messina.[620]

In five days, beginning on August 11, German General Kesselring evacuated 40,000 German and 70,000 Italian troops across the two mile wide Straits of Messina to the Italian mainland, with little Allied opposition in what some have called a mini-Dunkirk.[621]

On the morning of August 17, 1943, as the last Germans departed, Patton and his conquering American troops entered the city of Messina to the welcoming applause of its citizens, and, importantly to Patton, ahead of Montgomery's British troops.[622]

After thirty-eight days of combat in Sicily, the Allies had sent the Germans into retreat. During the campaign, the Americans suffered 8,800 casualties, including 2,237 dead. The British had 12,800 casualties, including 2,721 killed. Axis casualties totaled almost 29,000, with about

---

[616] *Battle*, 129, 131-35, *Inferno*, 433, *Montgomery*, 214-15, *Supreme Commander*, 222-23.
[617] *Battle*, 166.
[618] *Battle*, 142-44.
[619] *Battle*, 147-49, *Generals' War*, 59-60, *Supreme Commander*, 228.
[620] *Battle*, 162-64.
[621] *Battle*, 164-68, *Engineers*, 243, *Inferno*, 434.
[622] *Battle*, 169-170, *Inferno*, 434.

9,000 killed. Some 140,000 Axis soldiers were taken as prisoners.[623]

While the Germans fought hard in Sicily, the Italians clearly did not. Although the Allied forces lacked coordination and were critical of each other, they acquired valuable knowledge of how to conduct an amphibious operation.[624]

About a week after Sicily fell, Eisenhower, noting a lack of "good judgment and self-discipline," privately censored Patton for striking the two subordinates, directed him to apologize to the individual soldiers, and questioned whether Patton would have any further role in the war. In the following days, Patton apologized to the two soldiers and, in meetings with thousands of his troops, expressed regret for his cussing, criticizing and loud talking. Some soldiers accepted his regrets, others did not.[625]

Despite Eisenhower's efforts to keep Patton's misdeeds and the reprimand out of the press, by December they had become public knowledge. Much public criticism of Patton (and Eisenhower) followed. Still, when Roosevelt met Patton in Sicily on December 8, the President told him "you will have an army command in the great Normandy operation." Several weeks later, Eisenhower ordered Patton to the United Kingdom to take command of the new Third Army.[626]

Because Eisenhower doubted Patton's ability to keep the secret, Patton was not told of Ultra — that the Allies had broken the German military code.[627]

During the invasion of Sicily, several soldiers in Patton's army shot and killed dozens of German and Italian prisoners. The soldiers claimed as a defense that Patton, in a speech to his troops, had told his men to take no prisoners. When questioned about this in March 1944, Patton denied having made the statement.[628]

In mid-July 1943, Supreme Allied Commander Eisenhower decided that once Sicily fell, the Allies would invade the 800 mile long mainland of Italy at the Gulf of Salerno, which lies 178 miles northeast of Sicily. Churchill and Roosevelt promptly concurred.[629]

---

[623] *Battle*, 172-73.
[624] *Inferno*, 431, 435, *Supreme Commander*, 227.
[625] *Battle*, 170-72, *Generals' War*, 60, *Supreme Commander*, 229-31.
[626] *Battle*, 293-97, *Generals' War*, 61-62, *Supreme Commander*, 311-12.
[627] *Generals' War*, 91.
[628] *Generals' War*, 96-97, *Battle*, 116-21.
[629] *Battle*, 137, 181, *Supreme Commander*, 237-38.

Mussolini Defanged

Italian combat casualties had grown to almost 300,000 when, on July 18, 1943, a dispirited Mussolini cabled Hitler to object to sacrificing Italy and its people principally for the purpose of delaying a direct Allied attack on Germany. Mussolini's meeting with Hitler the next day provided no benefit to Italy.[630]

On July 19, 400 Allied heavy bombers dropped thousands of tons of bombs on Rome's rail yards, upsetting Italy's king and shaking Italian morale.[631]

Fascist leaders in Italy were unhappy with Mussolini. Less than a week after Allied bombers struck Rome, the Fascist Grand Council of Italy convened for the first time in over three years. It voted in favor of restoring the constitutional monarchy paired with a democratic parliament, and returning command of the military to the king.[632]

On Sunday, July 25, 1943, King Victor Emmanuel III informed fifty-nine year old Mussolini that he was the most hated person in Italy and must resign. Upon leaving the meeting with the seventy-three year old monarch, Mussolini was arrested by Italian government forces. Fascism in Italy lost power as quickly as *il Duce*.[633]

In a July 28 radio broadcast, Roosevelt made clear that despite the removal of Mussolini, the Allies would insist upon an unconditional surrender from Italy.[634]

On September 12, 1943, Nazi airborne commandos, using gliders and led by Captain Otto Skorzeny, rescued Mussolini from captivity in northern Italy. After meeting with Hitler, Mussolini was designated as the head of a puppet nation in the Alps called the Italian Social Republic.[635]

Conspiring to Unseat Hitler

A number of Germans, including General Beck and several political and social leaders, continued in 1943 to seek a way to rid their nation of Hitler. At least six unsuccessful assassination attempts were made that year, including one on March 13 that failed when a time bomb on his plane failed to detonate.[636]

---

[630] *Battle*, 139, *Reich*, 996.
[631] *Supreme Commander*, 238.
[632] *Reich*, 996-97, *Supreme Commander*, 239, *1944*, 396.
[633] *Masters*, 390, *Battle*, 137-41, *Inferno*, 433, *Reich*, 997-98.
[634] *Supreme Commander*, 239.
[635] *Battle*, 244-45, *Inferno*, 434, *Reich*, 1003-05.
[636] *Reich*, 1014-22, *1944*, 480.

The conspirators' efforts in 1943 to persuade the Allies to offer Germany moderate peace terms if Hitler were removed met with no success. Some questioned the validity of the German inquiries. Moreover, the Allies had already announced that they would settle for nothing less than unconditional surrender.[637]

Troubled that Mussolini's overthrow in Italy might spawn similar action in Germany, Hitler, who was by then suffering from exhaustion and poor health, increased his security. The Gestapo arrested dozens of suspected conspirators. Several plots in 1943 to kill Hitler by means of bombs carried by assassins failed because, as a protective device, he made a practice of unexpectedly changing his schedule.[638]

The Quadrant Conference

Churchill, Roosevelt and the Combined Chiefs of Staff met again in Quebec, Canada in August 1943 ("Quadrant"). By this time, the Allied African campaign had succeeded, Mussolini had been deposed, Allied forces had taken Sicily, and the Red Army was on a promising summer offensive against the Germans. The debate continued over the timing of the invasion of France, with the British hesitating to give it "overriding priority," as General Marshall sought. Nonetheless, they agreed that (a) Operation OVERLORD was to be the primary European U.S./British ground and air effort against Germany with a May 1944 launch date, (b) the Allies would attack southern mainland Italy, and (c) southern France would be invaded at about the same time as the cross-Channel invasion.[639]

The Americans' eagerness to confront Germany in France was driven in part out of concern that Stalin might enter into a peace treaty with Germany which would allow the Nazis to concentrate all of their forces on the western front.[640]

At the Quadrant conference, Churchill recognized that the United States would supply the majority of troops engaged in the cross-Channel invasion and agreed with Roosevelt's proposal that an American should have overall command of Operation OVERLORD.[641]

---

[637] *Reich*, 1017-18, 1033.
[638] *Reich*, 998, 1018-28, *1944*, 357-58.
[639] *Soldier's Story*, 194-96, *Masters*, 406, *Battle*, 180-81.
[640] *Soldier's Story*, 254.
[641] *Masters*, 395-98.

Italy Surrenders

Prompted by Italian diplomatic overtures, the Allies met secretly with representatives of Italy in Lisbon, Portugal on August 19 to discuss terms for a possible Italian surrender. Italy was given until the end of August to decide whether to accept the Allied terms — surrender or face total ruination.[642]

Italy's king and government had to assess whether, as the war continued, Italy would suffer more by siding with the Germans or yielding to the Allies.[643]

On September 1, 1943, Italy hinted that it would surrender but its representative was not given authority to sign an armistice.[644]

After further Allied threats, the Italian government signed an armistice with the Allies on September 3, 1943, but agreed that no public announcement of the agreement was to occur until the day of the forthcoming Allied landing at Salerno.[645]

For the next several days Italy waivered on whether to honor the armistice and surrender. Frustrated, at 6:30 p.m. on September 8, Eisenhower publicly announced that Italy had surrendered and that all Italians who act to help eject Germans from Italian soil will be supported by the Allies. He also broadcast a proclamation that Italy's representative had previously made announcing that Italian forces should end hostile actions against the Allies.[646]

Faced with the public disclosure of their earlier capitulation, King Emmanuel and leaders of the Italian government decided at 7:45 p.m. that evening to publicly confirm the surrender.[647]

After siding with the Germans for 1,184 days, Italy had placed its fate in the Allies' hands.[648]

As six divisions of German troops entered Rome from the south, King Emmanuel, his family and other Italian governmental leaders fled the city (now controlled by Field Marshal Kesselring) and relocated to southern Italy.[649]

Italy's surrender meant that (a) its remaining navy, including five battleships, eight cruisers, many destroyers and twenty-one subma-

---

[642] *Battle*, 187, *Supreme Commander*, 255.

[643] *Battle*, 188.

[644] *Battle*, 188-89, *Supreme Commander*, 260.

[645] *Masters*, 390, *Battle*, 189, *Reich*, 1000-01, *Supreme Commander*, 260.

[646] *Battle*, 195, *Inferno*, 436, *Supreme Commander*, 262-65.

[647] *Battle*, 195, *Supreme Commander*, 267.

[648] *Battle*, 195.

[649] *Battle*, 195-96, *Reich*, 1002, *Supreme Commander*, 268.

rines, sailed to Allied ports and fell under Allied control and (b) its list-less and poorly equipped army of 1,700,000 stopped fighting.[650]

At the insistence of Roosevelt and Churchill, Italy declared war on Germany on October 13, six weeks after surrendering to the Allies.[651]

Following Italy's surrender, Italians carried out revenge killings on between 5,000 and 8,000 Fascists.[652]

Germany Punishes Italian Troops

Following Italy's surrender, Germany interned 600,000 Italian soldiers who had been fighting with the Axis forces and sent them to Germany to serve as slave labor in mines and factories.[653]

After Italy surrendered, a 12,000 man Italian army force in Greece battled the Germans for five days at the cost of 1,250 Italians dead. After the Italians surrendered on September 22, 1943, the Germans shot dead more than 6,000.[654]

The Allied Invasion of Mainland Italy

British General Sir Harold Alexander, who had been the senior commander of the Allied ground forces in Sicily, was appointed commander-in-chief of all Allied forces in Italy.[655]

In Operation Baytown, British troops, led by General Montgomery, crossed the Straits of Messina and landed in Calabria in mainland Italy on September 3, 1943. The British landing was unopposed because by that time all but 8,000 German troops had been withdrawn from that part of southern Italy.[656]

On September 9, 1943, additional British troops landed at Taranto in southeastern Italy.[657]

Operation Avalanche

The objectives of Operation Avalanche were to land additional troops in Salerno, Italy, seize the nearby city of Naples, and eventually establish airbases in the area of Rome and farther north.[658]

---

[650] *Masters*, 415, *Battle*, 243-44, *Reich*, 1002, *Supreme Commander*, 268-69, 278.
[651] *Masters*, 390, *Inferno*, 444, *Supreme Commander*, 281.
[652] *Curse*, 285.
[653] *Battle*, 243, *WW II Story*, 217, *Reich*, 1006.
[654] *Battle*, 243.
[655] *Masters*, 413, *Battle*, 124.
[656] *Engineers*, 244, *Battle*, 179-82, *Inferno*, 436.
[657] *Engineers*, 244.
[658] *Battle*, 184.

Instead of the normal allotment of three to five months, planning for Avalanche was compressed into forty-five days. Due to limited shipping capacity, American General Mark Clark's landing force was restricted to three divisions, less than half of the force that invaded Sicily. In addition, air support for the Salerno invasion was limited. While the twenty-two miles of beaches in Salerno Bay were well-suited to receive an invasion force, the landing area was surrounded by mountains, exposing invading troops to fire from higher ground.[659]

Following Mussolini's overthrow, the Germans had moved additional troops into Italy, now totaling about fifteen divisions. There were some 135,000 German soldiers near Naples. The Allies assumed Hitler would have the Germans draw a defensive line across northern Italy from Pisa to Rimini, above Rome. But the Germans did not have time after the Italian surrender and before the Salerno landing to withdraw their troops to the north. Thus, they stayed and fought.[660]

On Thursday, September 9, 1943, General Clark's Fifth Army, composed of one American and one British corps (a total of about 55,000 soldiers) made an amphibious landing at Salerno, Italy. Two British infantry divisions landed on the left. The Americans landed one division twelve miles to the right and held another division in reserve.[661]

Just before the invasion, Allied troops learned of Italy's surrender and many assumed there would be little or no resistance to their landing. But the Germans had 17,000 men, as well as planes and mines, waiting to defend the Gulf of Salerno.[662]

Within two days the Allies had established a beachhead, but at the cost of 1,000 casualties and only after having landed the U.S. Army's last reserves.[663]

On September 10, General Alexander urged British General Montgomery to quickly push north from Calabria to threaten the southern flank of the German forces facing the stalled Allied troops in Salerno. Montgomery agreed, then declared a two day rest period for his troops.[664]

By September 12, 28,000 American soldiers were ashore, and about

[659] *Battle*, 184-86.
[660] *Battle*, 185, 203, *Clark*, 131-33, *Supreme Commander*, 276.
[661] *Masters*, 410-11, *Battle*, 197-99, 202, *Inferno*, 436, *Supreme Commander*, 269.
[662] *Battle*, 200, 203-05, *Clark*, 132-33.
[663] *Battle*, 211, 214.
[664] *Battle*, 214, *Clark*, 135-36.

twice that number of British troops had landed. The Salerno beachhead was now forty miles wide but only averaged six miles in depth. Moreover, it was divided in the middle by the Sele River, offering the Germans a way to split the invasion forces.[665]

On September 13, the Germans launched a major counterattack, concentrating on the Sele River valley which divided the British and American troops. The Allies had no ready reinforcements and Montgomery's slow moving Eighth Army was still sixty miles to the south. A concerned Clark considered withdrawing from the Salerno beaches, something the Allies were neither trained nor equipped to do.[666]

But on September 13, 1,300 Allied paratroopers were airlifted to the beaches of Salerno. Within a few days they, supported by heavy naval shelling and Army Air Force bombs, helped stall the German counterattack. General Clark travelled to the Sele River front on September 14 to encourage his soldiers. By September 17, the Germans were withdrawing from Salerno and heading north to fight again elsewhere. In ten days of fighting, the Allies had suffered about 9,000 casualties, including more than 1,200 deaths. The Germans suffered 3,500 casualties, of whom about 630 had been killed.[667]

Montgomery's forces did not arrive until September 19, after most of the Salerno fighting was over.[668]

By the end of September, the Allies had landed thirteen invasion divisions in Italy and had captured airfields from which to further attack the Germans. While some of the Allied commanders revealed their inexperience at Salerno, valuable lessons were learned that would lead to better planning for the invasion of Normandy in 1944. And, two of the Allied goals for attacking mainland Italy — to take the nation of Italy out of the war and to require Hitler to station many German troops there — had been achieved.[669]

The Germans, too, had learned lessons. Kesselring concluded that his troops could sustain a lengthy delaying action in Italy in terrain well-suited to defense.[670]

---

[665] *Battle*, 220-23, *WW II Story*, 218.

[666] *Battle*, 222-28, *Inferno*, 436-37, *Clark*, 137-39, *Supreme Commander*, 270.

[667] *Battle*, 235-36, *Inferno*, 438-39, *Clark*, 136-38, *Supreme Commander*, 270-72, 274.

[668] *Battle*, 232, *Clark*, 139-40.

[669] *Battle*, 234-37, *Supreme Commander*, 283, 289.

[670] *Inferno*, 439-40, *Supreme Commander*, 276.

Hitler Ponders Peace

In August and September 1943, as Germany endured increasing losses in Italy and on the Eastern Front and as its citizens became more demoralized by Allied bombings of their homeland, Hitler pondered whether he could successfully negotiate a reasonable peace accord with either Stalin or Churchill. Hitler felt that it would be difficult to wring favorable terms from Stalin because the Germans were in retreat on the Eastern Front. And even though he sensed that the Allies would not want a Communist Europe, which could result if the Red Army swept west, he thought Churchill too hostile and the British not yet weak enough to negotiate acceptable terms.[671]

Naples is Taken

The Allies entered Naples on October 1, 1943. Before they arrived the Germans, seething at the Italian surrender, had destroyed much of the city, including piers, train tunnels, sewers, water systems and hotels. In addition, the Germans planted time bombs throughout the city, and sank dozens of vessels in the port, impeding the Allies' ability to ship in needed supplies for the nearly half million Allied troops in Italy.[672]

In the following weeks and months, the Allies helped restore Naples, where theft, prostitution and begging were rampant, and provided some food for its starving citizens.[673]

On October 4, after Naples fell, Hitler ordered Kesselring to continue to fight the Allies south of Rome rather than retreating to a position north of the Eternal City. Hitler sent two infantry divisions to bolster Kesselring's forces.[674]

The Fate of Italian Jews

While in power, Mussolini had not pursued Jews in Italy with the fervor Hitler desired. In September 1943, after Mussolini was deposed, Heinrich Himmler ordered the Gestapo chief in Rome to arrest all Jews in the city.[675]

On September 26, the Jewish leaders of Rome were told that to avoid deportation of 200 Jewish men they would have to deliver over

---

[671] *Reich*, 1011-12.
[672] *Battle*, 239-42, 245, *Clark*, 146.
[673] *Battle*, 246-47.
[674] *Clark*, 148.
[675] *Battle*, 475, *Bloodlands*, 274-75.

100 pounds of gold within thirty-six hours. The Jews complied.[676]

Nonetheless, on October 16, German storm troopers rounded up 1,200 Roman Jews, only sixteen of whom survived World War II. Even though the arrested Jews were held just a block from the Vatican, Pope Pius XII offered no opposition to the roundup.[677]

During World War II, Italian citizens hid almost 5,000 Jews in convents, monasteries and the Vatican. Although almost 8,000 Italian Jews were killed during the war, nearly 40,000 survived.[678]

The Allies Move Toward Rome

By early October, the Germans had withdrawn their forces from the Mediterranean islands of Sardinia and Corsica. In Italy, Hitler had twenty-five divisions facing eleven Allied divisions.[679]

On October 13, the Allies started their advance from Naples toward Rome. About twenty miles north of Naples, they fought the Germans at the Volturno River, successfully crossing it by October 20. Rome lay 130 road miles ahead.[680]

In the fighting between September 3 and October 20, American Fifth Army casualties were 15,000; the British Eighth Army suffered 3,000.[681]

It soon became evident that the Germans would not do what the Allies had anticipated — retreat to the northern Italian Apennines and force the battle there. Instead, commanded by Kesselring, they would resist in three successive defensive lines drawn across the eighty-five mile width of Italy below Rome, anchored by the mountain ridge at Monte Cassino.[682]

The conditions the Allies faced going into the Italian winter were brutal — mines, booby traps, mountains, twenty inches of rain in the final three months of 1943, thick mud, intense cold (Rome is at the same latitude as Chicago) and a determined and skilled enemy.[683]

As agreed at the May 1943 Trident conference, by year end seven Allied divisions in Italy were to be sent to Britain to prepare for the invasion of Normandy in 1944. The Allied strength in Italy was

---

[676] *Battle*, 475-76.
[677] *Battle*, 476, *WW II Story*, 217.
[678] *Battle*, 476, *WW II Story*, 217.
[679] *Supreme Commander*, 283, 289.
[680] *Battle*, 249-51, *Supreme Commander*, 289.
[681] *Battle*, 251.
[682] *Battle*, 254-55, *Clark*, 150.
[683] *Battle*, 252-56.

shrinking while the opposing German forces grew stronger.[684]

As winter approached, the Allies suffered serious supply shortages. The damaged port of Naples limited the flow of goods and the Allies had misgauged the severity of the weather and the need for warm clothing.[685]

On November 13, General Clark decided that his forces should pause their Rome campaign for at least two weeks.[686]

The Eureka Conference

From November 28 to December 1, 1943, Churchill, Roosevelt and Stalin and their war staffs met in Teheran, Iran ("Eureka").[687]

Prior to that meeting, the British and American leaders and their advisors gathered in Cairo, a conference that was also attended by Chinese Generalissimo Chiang Kai-shek and his wife. Churchill continued to press at Cairo for a military campaign in the eastern Mediterranean and for the Normandy invasion to be put off for five or six weeks.[688]

Roosevelt traveled to Africa to attend Eureka on the battleship *Iowa*. In the Atlantic near Bermuda on November 14, a torpedo traveling at forty-six knots came at the *Iowa* but detonated in the wake of the heeling battleship. When Admiral King learned that an American destroyer had accidently fired the torpedo during a drill, he ordered the ship back to the United States with her entire crew under arrest.[689]

At the Teheran conference, Stalin insisted that (a) Operation OVERLORD be the primary effort of 1944 for the Western Allies, (b) Italy was secondary, (c) Turkey would not enter the war, and (d) southern France needed to be invaded before OVERLORD. He also pressed for dismembering Germany after the war and having the Soviet Union retain Lithuania, Latvia, Estonia and parts of Poland. (Turkey remained neutral throughout most of the war despite Allied efforts to convince that nation to declare war against Germany).[690]

At Teheran, Stalin also made clear his view that until an Allied supreme commander was appointed for Operation OVERLORD, he would not take seriously the Western Allies' commitment to a cross-

---

[684] *Battle*, 255, *Clark*, 148.
[685] *Battle*, 265.
[686] *Battle*, 266.
[687] *Masters*, 443—54, *Curse*, 76.
[688] *Masters*, 420, 423, 429, *Generals' War*, 19-22, *Supreme Commander*, 303-05.
[689] *Battle*, 268, *Admirals*, 329-30, *Supreme Commander*, 303.
[690] *Masters*, 417-18, 444, *Curse*, 76-81, *Battle*, 310, *Generals' War*, 23.

Channel invasion. He added that if the Allies did not open a second front in Europe in 1944, the Soviets might make a separate peace with Germany[691]

Stalin's appearance at the Teheran conference was his first time out of the Soviet Union since 1918, and the last time he ever flew in a plane.[692]

Stalin had all of the guest rooms at the Teheran conference bugged by Soviet secret police.[693]

After the Teheran conference, American and British leaders met again in Cairo. The Americans resisted Churchill's renewed attempts to have the Allies invade the Balkans. But the participants did agree that in Italy the Allies would capture Rome and then advance to a line about 200 miles north of the Italian capital.[694]

Many assumed during the summer and fall of 1943 that General George Marshall, who was serving as U. S. Army Chief of Staff, would become the Supreme Commander of the Normandy invasion and Eisenhower would take his place as Army Chief of Staff.[695]

As to who would have supreme command of Allied forces in the Normandy invasion, Roosevelt believed that if General Marshall were to be given the assignment he should, considering his stature as a brilliant and iron-willed general and presidential advisor, also command the Italian campaign. For political reasons, Churchill opposed taking control of the Italian campaign from British General Alexander. He also opposed having Marshall command the Normandy invasion while remaining on the Combined Chiefs of Staff, believing that in that situation the role of the CCS would become insignificant since Marshall would control all important decisions himself.[696]

When the time came to decide who should be Supreme Commander of American and British forces in Operation OVERLORD, Churchill suggested General Marshall. Because of his invaluable advice and service to the President, Roosevelt concluded that it was essential to keep Marshall near him and favored Eisenhower as head of OVERLORD. On December 6, back in Cairo, Churchill approved. Roosevelt then told a stoic and quietly disappointed Marshall, "I felt I could

---

[691] *Masters*, 448, *Generals' War*, 23, *Supreme Commander*, 306, *1944*, 69.

[692] *Masters*, 444, *Curse*, 76, *Generals' War*, 23.

[693] *Curse*, 76, *Generals' War*, 22, *1944*, 19.

[694] *Battle*, 308-10.

[695] *Masters*, 395, 414, 448, *Battle*, 269, *Supreme Commander*, 296, 298-301.

[696] *Masters*, 423-24, 428, *Generals' War*, 19-22, *Supreme Commander*, 302, 306.

not sleep at night with you out of the country." On December 7, 1943, Roosevelt informed Eisenhower that he had been chosen to command OVERLORD.[697]

On several earlier occasions, without first clearing it with Roosevelt, Churchill had promised British General Sir Alan Brooke that he would be appointed Supreme Commander of Operation OVERLORD. Brooke was quite upset when Churchill reneged.[698]

As Supreme Commander, Eisenhower selected brilliant and blunt American General Walter Bedell Smith as his chief of staff, and the skilled and modest British Air Chief Marshal Tedder to be deputy commander of OVERLORD.[699]

Eisenhower wanted the patient and self-restrained British General Alexander to head all Allied ground forces in OVERLORD. Because the British rejected this request on the basis that they wanted Alexander to continue in his role commanding the Italian campaign, Eisenhower reluctantly selected haughty Field Marshal Montgomery.[700]

Eisenhower appointed Lt. General Omar Bradley to command the U.S. First Army and General Patton to command the U.S. Third Army in the Normandy invasion.[701]

Poison Gas

Troubled by reports that the Germans might use poison gas if their situation became desperate, an American transport ship, S.S. John Harvey, containing 1,350 tons of mustard gas bombs (to be used only in retaliation for such an attack) arrived in the eastern Italian port of Bari in late November 1943.[702]

On December 2, German planes bombed the port, sinking seventeen ships and damaging eight others. During the attack, the John Harvey blew up, spreading mustard gas throughout the town of Bari.[703]

Over 100 deaths and 600 illnesses from poison gas followed. The United States censored details of the attack and kept the presence of

---

[697] Soldier's Story, 205-06, Masters, 448-53, Battle, 310, Generals' War, 27-28, Supreme Commander, 302-09.

[698] Masters, 381-82, 395-97, Generals' War, 45, Admirals, 327.

[699] Soldier's Story, 206, Generals' War, 38, 42, 71, Supreme Commander, 310.

[700] Soldier's Story, 207-08, Inferno, 515, Generals' War, 40, 163, Supreme Commander, 314.

[701] Soldier's Story, 5, 8, 210, Supreme Commander, 310-14.

[702] Battle, 270-71.

[703] Battle, 274-76.

mustard gas secret for many years after the war ended.[704]

Churchill's Health and Musings

On November 30, 1943, Churchill celebrated his sixty-ninth birthday. For almost two weeks in December, he was in bed suffering from pneumonia and heart fibrillations.[705]

While recuperating, Churchill pondered the current status of the war against the Axis forces and Britain's place in the conflict. He recognized that America's role had grown and would be predominant in both the Normandy and southern France invasions. He was determined that the Italian campaign, in which the British played a major part, not become secondary to the other two campaigns. Thus, he pushed hard for another amphibious invasion of Italy, this time at Anzio.[706]

Dealing with De Gaulle

In mid-December, de Gaulle decided to arrest and possibly execute three Vichy administrators who had opposed him. Because the three had been very helpful to the Allies during the invasion of North Africa, Eisenhower, Churchill and Roosevelt were quite troubled by de Gaulle's actions and urged the general not to proceed with trials against the trio.[707]

On December 30, de Gaulle promised Eisenhower that he would not bring the three to trial until after a properly constituted government had been established in France, provided Eisenhower promised to allow French troops to be the first to enter Paris after the Germans were driven out. Eisenhower reluctantly agreed.[708]

The Continuing Allied Air War Against Germany

"Strategic bombing" involves broad strikes intended to damage an enemy's industry, civilian morale and its communications. "Tactical bombing" is more limited and focuses on directly supporting the combat actions of a nation's military forces.[709]

Lt. General Carl Spaatz commanded the U.S. Eighth Air Force,

---

[704] *Battle*, 277-78.
[705] *Masters*, 446, *Battle*, 307-11.
[706] *Clark*, 158-60.
[707] *Supreme Commander*, 315-16.
[708] *Supreme Commander*, 316-17.
[709] *Air Masters*, 31.

which concentrated on day bombing raids over Germany. Eisenhower characterized Spaatz as one of his best officers, loyal, cooperative, modest and selfless.[710]

The U.S. Army Air Forces had about 350,000 members in December 1941. Eighteen months later, that number had grown to over 2,100,000.[711]

Night and day in 1943, Allied strategic bombers hit German cities like Kiel, Dortmund and Hamburg, causing major damage to factories, homes and morale.[712]

As Roosevelt observed, "Hitler built walls around his 'Fortress Europe' but he forgot to put a roof on it."[713]

Allied planes were fitted with the Norden bombsight, a revolutionary device that permitted very accurate high-altitude bombing. During the war the U.S. Army Air Forces purchased 90,000 units at a cost of $10,000 each.[714]

Churchill considered Allied bombing of Germany important, among other reasons, because it helped mollify Stalin's unhappiness about Allied delays in invading Europe. In effect, it was a "second front" in Europe.[715]

An important consequence of Allied air attacks on Germany was that the enemy was forced, for defensive purposes, to keep fighter planes and anti-aircraft guns at home instead of in Soviet Union airspace.[716]

In late July 1943, more than 700 British night bombers, using both high-explosive and incendiary bombs, struck the German city of Hamburg. Out of a population of close to 2,000,000, at least 41,000 were killed in the fire storm. Many of the dead were charred beyond recognition and a quarter million homes were destroyed. Almost sixty percent of the city was obliterated.[717]

To confuse the strong radar-guided antiaircraft defenses around Hamburg, the British dropped packets of aluminum strips that created false radar images. Still, the British lost eighty-seven planes in the

---

[710] *Generals' War*, 67-69, *Air Masters*, 25.
[711] *Air Masters*, 160, 164.
[712] *Reich*, 1008-10.
[713] *Air Masters*, 202.
[714] *Air Masters*, 39, 68.
[715] *Inferno*, 461, *Air Masters*, 481.
[716] *Inferno*, 464-65.
[717] *Guns*, 355, *Inferno*, 467, *WW II Story*, 259, *Air Masters*, 180-84.

raid.[718]

During ten days of Hamburg bombing in the summer of 1943, more German civilians died than all the British who were killed by the German *Blitzkrieg* during the war.[719]

A shaken but stubborn Hitler refused to visit Hamburg after the bombing or even meet with the city's valiant rescue workers.[720]

Supplementing the British raids, U.S. Army Air Force B-17s flew six dangerous bombing missions against Germany during the final week of July 1943, losing 1,000 men and about 100 planes.[721]

Germany obtained oil, an essential ingredient in any war, in two ways: from factories in Germany that produced synthetic oil, and from oil fields captured abroad, especially the Ploesti oil fields in Romania. But Hitler's failure to take the Soviet oil fields in the Caucasus deprived him of much-needed additional supplies.[722]

On August 1, 178 American B-24 bombers set off from Libya to fly across the Mediterranean, Albania, Yugoslavia and Romania to the Ploesti oil fields which were vigorously defended by German flak guns and 250 fighters. In a low altitude bombing run, sixty percent of Ploesti's production capacity was destroyed, but 310 Americans were killed and 130 others wounded. Only thirty-three of the planes making the thirteen and one-half hour trip were airworthy the next day.[723]

On August 17, 146 American B-17 bombers took off from England bound for Regensburg, Germany, where Messerschmitt fighter planes and engines were assembled. Due to range limitations, their fighter escorts turned back as the bombers reached the German border. Inside Germany, the unescorted B-17s faced more than 100 angry German fighters. Once they successfully bombed the Regensburg plants, the 122 surviving American planes headed south and, after a total of eleven hours in the air, landed in Algeria. Killed in that mission were 240 B-17 crewmembers.[724]

On that same August 17, more than 200 American B-17 bombers, unprotected by fighter escorts while over Germany, attacked vital German ball-bearing plants in Schweinfurt, causing a significant but

[718] *Air Masters*, 180-83.

[719] *Air Masters*, 182, *WW II Story*, 259.

[720] *Air Masters*, 183.

[721] *WW II Story*, 266, *Air Masters*, 185.

[722] *Air Masters*, 187, 311-14.

[723] *Air Masters*, 188-92, *Supreme Commander*, 247.

[724] *Air Masters*, 193-98, *WW II Story*, 273.

temporary loss of production.[725]

Also on that August 17, the British bombed at night the secret German flying bomb facility at Peenemünde on the coast of the Baltic Sea.[726]

On October 14, "Black Thursday," more than 300 unescorted American Eighth Air Force B-17s again bombed Schweinfurt, wiping out two thirds of the city's ball bearing production. More than 100 Germans planes were destroyed or damaged in the fighting that day. Eighteen percent, 642, of the participating American crew members were killed, wounded or missing. Between the two raids on that city, the Americans had lost 207 planes and suffered damage to another 142.[727]

Beginning in November 1943, B-17s fitted with improved radar were able to fly despite overcast skies. While bombing accuracy was somewhat limited, the B-17s flew more missions and faced fewer German fighters and less flak.[728]

In late 1943, British Chief Air Marshal Arthur Harris sent Churchill a memo stating that of forty-seven German cities, nineteen had been "virtually destroyed" and another nineteen "seriously damaged. He confidently claimed that with another 15,000 bomber flights over German cities, Hitler would be finished.[729]

By year end 1943, 334 of Germany's single-engine fighters had been destroyed in fights over Western Europe. Hitler found replacement planes and pilots hard to come by.[730]

In late 1943, Hitler moved many fighters back to Germany from northern France and Holland in order to use them to defend against Allied bombing runs over German cities. This was of considerable benefit to the Allies for it meant fewer planes available to oppose the forthcoming invasion of Normandy.[731]

Overall, 131 German cities and towns were bombed during the war, killing about 400,000 and leaving more than 7,000,000 homeless.[732]

---

[725] *Inferno*, 468, *WW II Story*, 272-74, *Air Masters*, 185-86, 198-201.

[726] *Air Masters*, 201, *WW II Story*, 314.

[727] *Inferno*, 468, *Air Masters*, 208-11.

[728] *Air Masters*, 234-36.

[729] *Guns*, 355, *Inferno*, 469, *Generals' War*, 67.

[730] *Air Masters*, 204, 237.

[731] *Air Masters*, 237.

[732] *Guns*, 358, 536, *Inferno*, 465.

Further German Naval Losses

On December 26, the British Navy attacked and sank the German battleship *Scharnhorst* off the northwest coast of Norway, costing the Germans nearly 2,000 lives.[733]

In June 1944, the American escort carrier *Guadalcanal* captured a surfaced German U-boat in the Atlantic and secretly towed it to Bermuda after taking possession of its codebooks and crew.[734]

The War at Year End in Italy

As 1943 came to a close, General Clark's Fifth Army renewed its effort to push the Germans out of their positions in Italy southwest of Rome. Beginning on December 7, Allied troops fought to seize the mountain village of San Pietro Infine. After ten days and nights of bloody fighting, they took the town.[735]

On the east side of Italy, Montgomery's Eighth Army moved north toward the Adriatic town of Ortona in December. By the end of December, his predominantly Canadian forces had captured Ortona, but at a cost of 2,300 casualties, including 500 dead.[736]

At the end of 1943, the Germans, with 300,000 troops in Italy, noted with satisfaction that the Allied advance toward Rome had moved at the lethargic rate of about six miles per month.[737]

On December 31, Montgomery departed Italy for London, having been ordered to command an army group in the forthcoming Normandy invasion, and a weary Eisenhower, under orders from Marshall, flew home to the United States for rest before taking overall command of the Normandy effort.[738]

The War at Year End in the Soviet Union

On November 3, 1943, because he needed troops in Italy and for the expected Allied invasion of France, and feeling that he had enough troops in Russia to protect Germany, Hitler declined to send more reinforcements to the Eastern Front.[739]

By November 6, 1943, the Red Army had pushed the Germans

---

[733] *Battle*, 314.
[734] *WW II Story*, 178-84.
[735] *Battle*, 283-292, *Clark*, 151.
[736] *Battle*, 301-06.
[737] *Battle*, 314-15.
[738] *Battle*, 316-17, *Supreme Commander*, 318.
[739] *Inferno*, 508.

west and retaken Kiev in Ukraine.[740]

By the close of 1943, the Soviets had regained one-half of the territory lost to the Germans since June 1941 and were approaching the Polish and Romanian borders.[741]

GERMANY IN RETREAT (1944)

Manpower and Effectiveness

In January 1944, Britain had in uniform a total of about 4,900,000 English and Dominion troops and America had over 10,500,000.[742]

By December 1944, a total of 12,000,000 were in the American armed forces and 5,000,000 were in Britain's.[743]

Approximately two-thirds of America's troops were assigned to Europe, reflecting America's adherence to the "Germany First" agreement.[744]

In 1943-44, the combat effectiveness of German troops was deemed twenty to thirty percent better than that of British and American troops; on a man-to-man basis the Germans inflicted 50% more casualties than they suffered when fighting the British and Americans. On a man-to-man basis, the Germans' effectiveness against the Soviets was stunning: the Germans inflicted casualties at a three-to-one ratio. Contributing to the German strength were the outstanding professionalism of most German officers, a decade of Nazi indoctrination, and the knowledge that fleeing battle or deserting was answered by execution.[745]

Blacks in the American Military

By January 1944, there were 755,000 blacks in the United States Army, up from fewer than 4,000 in September 1939. Of 633,000 Army officers, only 4,500 were black.[746]

The United States Navy had 82,000 black enlisted sailors, but no black officers. The Marine Corps had no black officers during World War II, and had rejected all black enlistments until President Roosevelt

---

[740] *Inferno*, 383-84, *Reich*, 1007.

[741] *Inferno*, 384, *Reich*, 1007.

[742] *Masters*, 432.

[743] *Guns*, 408.

[744] *Masters*, 468.

[745] *Masters*, 354, 467, *Inferno*, 328.

[746] *Battle*, 381, 383.

objected.[747]

While the 1940 Draft Act banned racial discrimination, only 250 blacks sat on the country's 6,400 draft boards.[748]

During the war, the Army established three black divisions. The 2nd Cavalry served in Africa, but saw no combat. The 93rd Infantry was assigned to the Pacific. The 92nd Infantry was sent to Italy in the late summer of 1944 and fought the enemy there, although some reports said they ran from fire. General Mark Clark ascribed their perceived weaknesses to discrimination and a lack of education.[749]

Blacks were barred by Army Air Force policy from flying with the American Eighth Air Force, which was formed a month after Pearl Harbor for the purpose of bombing Germany.[750]

In 1942, the Army Air Force was ordered to accept blacks at the rate of about ten percent. Those placed in uniform were assigned solely to ground support units — quartermaster, ordinance, engineering and transportation.[751]

The 99th Fighter Squadron, trained at a segregated base in Tuskegee, Alabama, was composed entirely of black pilots, commanded by Lt. Colonel Benjamin O. Davis, a thirty year old African-American graduate of West Point and the son of the Army's only black general. Prior to World War II, only nine black Americans had commercial pilot licenses and fewer than 300 had private pilot licenses.[752]

During World War II, 450 Tuskegee Airmen shot down 108 enemy planes. Sixty-six Tuskegee Airmen were killed in combat and thirty-three were taken as POWs.[753]

The Eastern Front

In January 1944, the Soviets finally liberated Leningrad from the German siege. By that time about 1,000,000 of its residents had died.[754]

From January to March, the Red Army attacked German positions elsewhere in the Soviet Union but, faced with harsh weather and ruthless opposition, made little progress.[755]

---

[747] *Battle*, 381, *WW II Story*, 368.
[748] *Battle*, 382.
[749] *Battle*, 383, *Generals' War*, 382-83, *WW II Story*, 246-50, *Clark*, 224, 228, 236-37.
[750] *Air Masters*, 3, 5, 230.
[751] *Air Masters*, 230-31.
[752] *Battle*, 383-84.
[753] *WW II Story*, 477.
[754] *Inferno*, 508, *Bloodlands*, 173.
[755] *Inferno*, 508-09.

After a sustained Soviet attack, the Germans withdrew from the Crimea on May 12.[756]

By May, 2,200,000 Axis troops in the Soviet Union were defending a line that was at its shortest only 560 miles from Berlin.[757]

The Italian Campaign Continues

Caserta Palace, a 1,200 room ancient structure about twenty miles north of Naples, housed some 15,000 soldiers and served as headquarters for General Clark's Fifth Army and General Alexander's 15th Army Group. Clark told his diary: "Never before in the history of warfare have so few been commanded by so many."[758]

By 1944, the Germans had stationed about twenty divisions, one seventh of the entire German army, in Italy, with the result that German defenses in France and elsewhere were weaker. Even Stalin conceded that the campaign in Italy was relieving some pressure on the Eastern Front.[759]

The Anzio Battle

At Churchill's persistent urging, the Allied military leaders agreed in early January 1944 to land two divisions on the beaches of Anzio on the western Italian coast, about thirty-five miles south of Rome and about 100 miles above the southernmost German lines. The theory of Operation Shingle was that an Anzio landing would force the Germans to remove troops from defensive positions in the south, enabling the American Fifth Army there to break through and move north to meet up with the amphibious forces at Anzio. Perhaps the Germans might even withdraw to a defensive position north of Rome.[760]

Many of the ships needed to land and supply the Anzio invasion force were scheduled to be withdrawn from the Italian campaign in February and sent to support the forthcoming Normandy invasion. This meant that the forces landing at Anzio would have to move off the beaches quickly and join up with the Allied forces moving up from the south.[761]

As a prelude to the Anzio landings, on January 20, Allied troops in

[756] *Inferno*, 509, *WW II Story*, 488-89.

[757] *Inferno*, 510.

[758] *Battle*, 372-74, 376.

[759] *Masters*, 459, *Battle*, 317.

[760] *Battle*, 323-28, 363.

[761] *Clark*, 160-63.

southern Italy attacked the German defensive lines about fifty miles below Rome and attempted to cross the Rapido River (25-50 feet wide and 9-12 feet deep) near Monte Cassino. The Germans responded by moving troops south from Rome, meaning that those soldiers were not readily available to oppose the Anzio landings. However, after several days of battle and some 2,000 casualties, the Allies had made little progress moving north.[762]

On January 22, 1944, two Allied divisions, commanded by American Major-General John Lucas, landed on the beaches of Anzio, expecting to face no more than 31,000 German soldiers. By the end of the first day, the Allies had landed 36,000 soldiers with only thirteen killed.[763]

The landing came as a surprise to the Germans, but Field Marshal Kesselring promptly ordered troops from Rome, northern Italy, France, Germany and the Balkans to move toward Anzio. Within three days, portions of eight German divisions were in the area of Anzio, with another five on the way.[764]

By January 25, 40,000 American and 16,000 British troops occupied the Anzio beaches. As January ended, the Germans had 71,000 troops encircling the beachhead.[765]

On January 27-28, 1944, the 99th Fighter Squadron, about two dozen black Tuskegee Airmen, shot down twelve German planes and damaged several others over the beaches of Anzio, with the loss of just one American pilot.[766]

By February, the number of Allied troops at Anzio had grown to 92,000. The Germans hemmed them in on a dug-in beachhead only eight miles deep and about fifteen miles wide. Using persistent artillery and aircraft strikes, the Germans stalled them there for the next four months. The Allies suffered some 800 casualties a day. General Lucas was criticized for moving too slowly off the beach, but many believe that his caution saved numerous lives and avoided a disaster at Anzio.[767]

In fighting from February 16-20, eight German divisions reduced the size of the Allied beachhead by three to four miles. But Allied artil-

---

[762] *Battle*, 339-50, *Clark*, 164-65, 167-69.
[763] *Battle*, 351-63.
[764] *Battle*, 364-65, *Clark*, 172-73.
[765] *Battle*, 368, 387.
[766] *Battle*, 381-85.
[767] *Masters*, 459, 464, *Battle*, 370-72, 412-14, 418, *Clark*, 178-79.

lery, bombs and naval fire, and a counterattack on February 19, reduced some of the German gains. Nonetheless, General Clark, reacting to pressure from London and Washington, removed General Lucas from command on February 22.[768]

During the first month of the Anzio campaign, Allied and German forces combined suffered 40,000 casualties out of a total of 200,000 troops. In February alone, 1,900 Americans were killed at Anzio.[769]

While the opposing forces at Anzio were stalemated at the end of February, the Germans were being weakened. The German Fourteenth Army had 133,000 men on March 9. Six weeks later, battle casualties and transfers to Cassino reduced that force by 43,000, while Allied numbers at Anzio grew.[770]

The Battle for Monte Cassino

Italy's sixth-century spacious and majestic Benedictine abbey of Monte Cassino sits on a rocky pinnacle some 1,500 feet above the floor of the nearby valley and about fifty miles south of Rome. In late 1943, the Germans removed to Rome (and later Berlin) most of the art treasures of the abbey, but a number of monks remained in residence there.[771]

In December 1943, Hitler declared that Monte Cassino would form an essential part of Germany's southern Italy defense — the Gustav line. Thus, Kesselring heavily fortified the abbey and the surrounding area with bunkers, pillboxes and dugouts manned by troops ordered to fight to the death.[772]

American and French forces sought in late January and early February to take control of the town of Cassino and the nearby abbey, and then move west to the Liri Valley to open up a route toward Rome. After weeks of bitter winter fighting, their objective was unachieved, despite 8,000 French and 10,000 American casualties.[773]

On February 11, the worn and depleted Americans pulled back and were replaced by New Zealand, Indian and British troops commanded by Lt. General Freyberg, a New Zealander. Frustrated by the German advantage provided by possession of the abbey of Monte Cas-

---

[768] *Battle,* 427-29, *Inferno,* 511, *WW II Story,* 230, *Clark,* 188, 191.
[769] *Battle,* 428, 431.
[770] *Battle,* 486, 490.
[771] *Battle,* 398-99, *Inferno,* 441-42, 511, *WW II Story,* 231-32.
[772] *Battle,* 399-400.
[773] *Battle,* 399-405.

sino, Freyberg proposed bombing the ancient structure, which all understood would cause considerable public dismay.[774]

On February 14, the Germans and Allies near Monte Cassino agreed to a one-day truce so that each side could gather its dead from the battlefield.[775]

Under continuing pressure from General Freyberg to spoil the abbey and spare Allied lives, General Alexander authorized the bombing of Monte Cassino. But first, on February 14, Allied gunners fired twenty-four shells over the abbey spreading leaflets warning residents to move out to escape the forthcoming bombing.[776]

On February 15, Allied planes and artillery bombed German-surrounded Monte Cassino, killing from 100-400 civilians in the process.[777]

The leader of the Monte Cassino abbey, Abbot Diamare, revealed a few days after the bombing that no German soldiers or weapons had been within the walls of the abbey. The U.S. Army's history of World War II lamented that the bombing of Monte Cassino achieved "nothing beyond destruction, indignation, sorrow, and regret."[778]

During the morning of March 15, Allied aircraft bombed the nearby town of Cassino (population formerly 22,000) for over three hours. Then Allied artillery sent almost 200,000 rounds into the area. The objective was to obliterate Cassino and its German occupants, so that Freyberg's forces could then take the town.[779]

That afternoon, Freyberg's troops attacked on foot and in tanks. By March 19, the battle for Cassino was stalemated. Eight days after the bombardment, Freyberg pulled back having suffered thousands of casualties. The third Allied attempt in two months to puncture the Gustav line by taking Cassino had failed.[780]

The Allies reluctantly decided to wait until May and better weather to again try to break through the German southern Italy defense and join up with Allied forces on the beaches of Anzio. This decision meant that Operation Anvil, the invasion of southern France, would have to be delayed because the troops and ships needed to carry out

---

[774] *Battle*, 411-12, *Clark*, 181-86.

[775] *Battle*, 405.

[776] *Battle*, 432-35, *Clark*, 186.

[777] *Masters*, 435, 467, *Clark*, 186-87.

[778] *Battle*, 440, *Inferno*, 511.

[779] *Battle*, 453-61, *Clark*, 196.

[780] *Battle*, 464-73, *Clark*, 196-97.

Anvil were tied down in Italy.[781]

The Pleasures and Perils of Naples

Allied troops on liberty in Italy in 1944 usually repaired to Naples, mostly for "I & I" — intercourse and intoxication.[782]

In the destitute city, thousands of hungry women turned to prostitution, each earning a few dollars a night. The venereal disease rate among American soldiers exceeded ten percent, and the strain of gonorrhea in Naples proved especially difficult to cure. Twenty "personal ablution centers" in Naples were open twenty-four hours a day, offering post-sex soldiers soap, water and iodine. Fifteen percent of all of the American hospital beds in Italy were filled with VD patients. Five hundred Naples hospital beds were filled by infected prostitutes in buildings called "whorespitals."[783]

The impoverished denizens of Naples were adept at theft. Estimates were that twenty percent of all cargo brought in by Allied supply ships was stolen, and that two-thirds of the Neapolitan economy was derived from those pilfered goods. According to one report, an entire train and its load of sugar simply disappeared.[784]

For a week in late March, nearby Mt. Vesuvius erupted spewing lava and volcanic ash, killing twenty-six people, destroying parked airplanes and fouling equipment for miles.[785]

German Executions

In late March 1944, fifteen uniformed American soldiers landed near La Spezia, Italy with orders to blow up the nearby train tunnel on the Genoa line. They were captured by the Germans and promptly executed.[786]

On March 23, Italian partisans killed thirty-three Germans and wounded sixty-eight. In reprisal, Hitler ordered ten Italians killed for each dead German. The next day the Germans killed 335 innocent Italians and left their bodies in a cave.[787]

In September, the Germans executed 1,830 Italian civilians, including priests, women and children, in the towns of Marzabotto and Ca-

---

[781] *Clark*, 197-98.
[782] *Battle*, 446.
[783] *Battle*, 447-49.
[784] *Battle*, 451.
[785] *Battle*, 483-84.
[786] *Battle*, 499, *Reich*, 956.
[787] *Inferno*, 445.

solari in punishment for the hostile actions of local partisans.[788]

Roosevelt's Failing Health

By March, 1944, Roosevelt was suffering from a range of maladies — congestive heart failure, hypertension, acute bronchitis, an enlarged heart and a heart murmur. In February of 1940 he had suffered a mild heart attack. He may even have had stomach cancer. He was taking digitalis each day. These grave facts were kept from the public.[789]

Beginning on April 9, at his doctors' insistence, an exhausted Roosevelt retreated to a friend's estate in South Carolina for a month's rest and recuperation.[790]

Roosevelt was too ill to attend the funeral of Navy Secretary Frank Knox, who died of a heart attack on April 28, 1944.[791]

The Liberation of Rome

Under Operation Diadem, scheduled to commence May 11, (a) the Eighth Army, commanded by British Lt. General Leese and having more than 250,000 troops (including 56,000 Poles), would attack the German Gustav Line at Cassino, (b) American General Clark's more than 250,000 man Fifth Army (including Juin's 100,000 French corps) would simultaneously attack the Germans west of Cassino, and (c) once the Gustav Line was broken, General Truscott's Allied forces would advance off the beachhead at Anzio.[792]

Kesselring's Axis forces in Italy then totaled 412,000 men in twenty-three divisions. Nine of those German divisions were on the Cassino front and five were at Anzio. The German strategy in Italy was a simple one — exhaust the Allies.[793]

Beginning at 11:30 p.m. on May 11, troops from the British Eighth Army attacked the Germans in and around Cassino, the same places the Americans and then the New Zealanders had attacked months earlier. The fighting was brutal — in four days the Allies advanced only four miles at the cost of over 4,000 casualties.[794]

Fifteen miles to the west, the Americans also began their attack on May 11. During the first twenty-four hours they fired 174,000 artillery

---

[788] *Inferno*, 446.
[789] *1944*, 48, 86-89, 157.
[790] *1944*, 90-91.
[791] *1944*, 156.
[792] *Battle*, 509-10, *Inferno*, 512, *Clark*, 200-02.
[793] *Battle*, 516, 518.
[794] *Battle*, 521-25.

shells at the Germans who were in the hills. After two days of slow progress, hardy French (and Moroccan) troops under General Juin had advanced seven miles across a sixteen mile wide front. To their left, the Americans were also making good progress. By May 18, the French forces were six miles ahead of the British Eighth Army on their right, but on that day the British finally captured Cassino and the abbey. The Gustav line had been ruptured.[795]

As the Germans fell back, the fighting continued. Kesselring belatedly brought in reinforcements from Anzio and other areas, but they could not halt the Allied advance toward Rome.[796]

North at Anzio, the American Fifth Army's attack, which began in the morning of May 23, faced strong German resistance. By the close of the first day, Truscott's forces had suffered almost 2,000 casualties, including 334 killed — the largest one-day loss in the entire Italian campaign. But the Germans, too, had suffered heavy losses, including 1,500 captured.[797]

On May 25, after advancing north sixty miles, some of the Allied forces that had punctured the Gustav Line joined up with Fifth Army forces from Anzio. The Anzio beachhead was, after 125 days of brutal warfare, finally secure.[798]

On that same day, the prideful and publicity-seeking Clark, bent on beating the British to Rome, cut an order directing his Anzio troops to move northwest toward that ancient city. In doing so, he contravened a direct order from his superior, General Alexander, aimed at cutting off German escape routes toward northern Italy. Clark did not alert Alexander to his new order until his attack had begun.[799]

Clark spent the rest of his life defending his impertinent decision, which did not become publicly known until the Italian campaign had receded from the headlines. The official British military history observed that Clark's "thirst for glory spoiled the fulfillment of Alexander's plan in order to obtain for himself and his army the triumph of being first to enter Rome." Churchill wrote: "Glory in this battle, already great, will be measured not by the capture of Rome or the juncture with the beachhead, but by the number of German divisions cut

---

[795] *Battle*, 521, 526-33, *Clark*, 203-04.
[796] *Battle*, 533-36.
[797] *Battle*, 542-43, *Clark*, 208.
[798] *Battle*, 544-45, *Clark*, 208.
[799] *Battle*, 546-51, *Inferno*, 512, *WW II Story*, 235, *Clark*, 205-18.

off ...".[800]

In late May 1944, General Marshall's twenty-six year old step-son was killed by a German sniper during the Fifth Army's drive from Anzio toward Rome. Marshall sorrowfully visited his grave in Italy on June 17.[801]

Adhering to Clark's controversial order, Fifth Army forces pushing northwest toward Rome from Anzio during the final week of May encountered stiff German resistance. By June 1, however, the Fifth Army was making good progress.[802]

By May 31, the British forces in the Eighth Army were still twenty-five miles south of the Anzio forces and moving quite slowly. During the last half of May, advancing Moroccan soldiers under General Juin's command went on a binge raping hundreds and hundreds of Italian women ranging from ages twelve to seventy-five. Eventually, fifteen of the soldiers were executed and another fifty-four were jailed, but Allied relations with the Italians had been severely damaged.[803]

On June 2, Kesselring reported to Hitler that in the last three weeks his forces had suffered 38,000 casualties. Despite Kesselring's proposal to destroy all bridges, and rail, power and industrial sites around the Eternal City, on June 3, Hitler decided that there should not be a battle of Rome — it would be an open city. The remaining German troops streamed north to where the supply lines were shorter and the mountains taller.[804]

Soldiers from Clark's Fifth Army entered Rome during the morning of June 4, 1944 and were greeted by thousands of cheering Italians.[805]

The next day General Clark made his own appearance in Rome. During a press conference in the center of town, he praised the Fifth Army but made no mention of the British Eighth Army, causing even his American subordinates considerable discomfort.[806]

Between May 11, when Operation Diadem began, and June 4, Allied casualties were 18,000 Americans (including more than 3,000 dead), 12,000 British, 9,600 French and 4,000 Poles. German casualties

[800] *Battle*, 548-51.
[801] *Masters*, 483, 493, *Battle*, 554, *Admirals*, 338-39.
[802] *Battle*, 551-55, 558-64, *Clark*, 212.
[803] *Battle*, 555-58.
[804] *Battle*, 568, 579, *Inferno*, 512-13, *Clark*, 213-14.
[805] *Masters*, 481, *Battle*, 570-71, *Clark*, 214-15.
[806] *Battle*, 573-74, *Clark*, 215-16.

during that time were estimated at 52,000, including 5,800 killed.[807]

After two days of merriment, on June 6, the same day the Allies invaded Normandy, General Alexander ordered the Fifth and Eighth Armies to follow the retreating Germans north toward Pisa and Florence where they were establishing the next defensive battlement — the Gothic Line.[808]

After Rome fell, the Allies weakened General Clark's Fifth Army by transferring out several divisions to meet the requirements of Anvil, the invasion of southern France.[809]

Brazil declared war against Germany in 1944 and sent 25,000 soldiers to Italy to serve in the Fifth Army under Clark's command.[810]

On August 12, the Germans withdrew from Florence after destroying all bridges except the 14th century Ponte Vecchio.[811]

As winter approached, the war in Italy turned largely into a holding operation. In December, Churchill informed Clark that he had been elevated to command all Allied ground troops in Italy, an honor reflecting Clark's overall service in Italy.[812]

Not far from Rome one can find the seventy-seven acre Sicily-Rome American Cemetery in which almost 8,000 United States veterans of the Italian campaign are buried.[813]

In the full twenty-month war in Italy, the Germans suffered between 435,000 and 536,000 casualties compared to 312,000 for the Allies. American casualties in Italy totaled 120,000, of whom 23,501 were killed.[814]

Opinions are mixed as to the wisdom of Churchill's insistence that the Allies confront Germany in Italy. He wrote that the main task was "to draw off and contain the greatest possible number of Germans" and this goal had been achieved. Others asserted that the Italian campaign was a strategic diversion that became a "grinding war of attrition whose costs were justified by no defensible military or political purpose." Italy did provide critical training to Allied forces soon to invade Normandy and helped meet Stalin's demand for a second front in

---

[807] *Battle*, 572-73.
[808] *Battle*, 576, 580, *Guns*, 36, *WW II Story*, 236.
[809] *Clark*, 220-21.
[810] *Clark*, 226, 228.
[811] *Clark*, 225.
[812] *Battle*, 580-81, *WW II Story*, 246-54, *Clark*, 227-36.
[813] *Battle*, 578.
[814] *Masters*, 460, *Battle*, 581.

1943.[815]

The Air War Against Germany Continues

In early 1944, P-51 Mustangs, newly-developed long range American fighters, arrived in Europe to escort Allied bombers in runs against distant enemy cities. The P-51s, with a top speed of almost 440 miles per hour, protected Allied aircraft from less capable German fighters, and enhanced the safety and success of Anglo-American bombing runs.[816]

During 1944, Germany's primary weapon against Allied bombing was antiaircraft flak (a 17 pound shrapnel grenade), which that year destroyed over 6,000 Anglo-American planes and damaged 27,000 others. On average, more than 8,000 flak shells were required to destroy a single Allied heavy bomber.[817]

On February 3, 1944, more than 900 American bombers attacked the German capital, Berlin, killing up to 25,000 civilians. On February 13-14, Allied planes dropping explosive and incendiary bombs struck Dresden, sparking a fire storm that killed at least 25,000 residents. These raids were intended to convince the average German civilian that the war was lost and to bring about a quicker peace.[818]

In late February 1944, a bombing offensive by almost 4,000 Allied planes flying from Britain and Italy was launched against industrial and military sites in Germany, including Regensburg and Schweinfurt again. Significant damage was done to Germany's war production, but at the cost of 226 Allied bombers, twenty-eight fighters and 2,600 crewmen.[819]

During the February 1944 air battles, the Luftwaffe lost over one-third of its single engine fighters and almost twenty percent of its fighter pilots. Still, Germany continued to manufacture many new fighters.[820]

In the first half of 1944, casualty rates for every 1,000 Allied bomber crewmen serving six months in combat were 712 killed and 175 wounded — an 89 percent casualty rate.[821]

Three times in March the Americans bombed Berlin, each time

[815] Battle, 582-84, Inferno, 513.
[816] Engineers, 126-33, Inferno, 471, Battle, 495, Air Masters, 249-54.
[817] Guns, 350, Air Masters, 316.
[818] WW II Story, 479-80, Guns, 534-35, Air Masters, 265-67.
[819] Battle, 495-96, Air Masters, 260-64.
[820] Battle, 496, Generals' War, 125, WW II Story, 276-77, Air Masters, 264.
[821] Guns, 351, Generals' War, 123.

encountering heavy German fighter and flak defenses. A total of 153 United States bombers were lost during the trio of raids.[822]

In April 1944, Allied bombers again struck oil fields under German control in Ploesti, Romania and elsewhere, significantly reducing the amount of aviation fuel available to the Germans from mid-1944 on. Accompanying many of those bombers were Tuskegee Airmen, black American P-51 fighter pilots known as the Red Tails.[823]

In April 1944, 613 American bombers were lost in raids over Germany.[824]

In early 1944, only one in four Eighth Air Force bomber crews flying from Britain over Germany was expected to complete the minimum of twenty-five missions. Then the mission minimum was raised to thirty. Morale was so bad that some U.S. crews flew to neutral countries (usually Sweden or Switzerland) where they were held for the rest of the war.[825]

Generals Spaatz and Harris resisted turning over control of their American and British bomber forces, which were engaged in strategic attacks on Germany, to be used to tactically bomb French and Belgian transportation facilities in advance of the Normandy invasion. Eisenhower ended the dispute and ordered the bombers to operate under OVERLORD command. Churchill expressed concern that when the tactical bombing in France began in April, many unintended civilian deaths would occur. President Roosevelt and the commander of the Free French Forces, however, concurred that military considerations should prevail. River bridges and the rail system in northern France were obliterated, impeding Hitler's ability to speed reinforcements to Normandy.[826]

Even after command of bombers was transferred to the OVERLORD team, in May several damaging Allied raids were carried out on German cities and the Ploesti oil fields.[827]

Martin Bormann, Hitler's secretary and trusted aid, notified local authorities in May 1944 that no German citizen would be punished for killing downed Allied airmen. Forty-seven captured Allied flight offic-

---

[822] *Air Masters*, 276.

[823] *Engineers*, 137, *Inferno*, 471, *WW II Story*, 469-70, 473-77, *Air Masters*, 192.

[824] *Air Masters*, 276.

[825] *Battle*, 496, *Generals' War*, 316, *Air Masters*, 246, 266, 331-47.

[826] *Generals' War*, 77-84, 126, *WW II Story*, 279, *Air Masters*, 288-91, *Supreme Commander*, 363-76.

[827] *Air Masters*, 290.

ers were killed by Germans in September 1944.[828]

Preparing for the Normandy Invasion

Stalin continued in 1944 to insist that the Allies commence a cross-Channel attack on the Germans to relieve pressure on the Red Army. Conversely, because Germany's forces in France would be at least as large as the invasion force, it was important to the Western Allies that the Red Army maintain pressure on Axis soldiers in the Soviet Union to prevent any major troop transfers to France.[829]

The Western Allies faced several grave risks if the 1944 invasion of Normandy failed. It would take many months before they would be equipped and ready to attempt a subsequent landing. In the meantime, Stalin might either negotiate a truce with Hitler or continue his drive west through Europe, ultimately resulting in Soviet control of Germany, Denmark, the Netherlands and France.[830]

Eisenhower recognized that the Allies needed the support of French resistance fighters in the invasion and that to gain that support he had to deal with de Gaulle and his French Committee of National Liberation. Roosevelt disliked de Gaulle (who he thought was anti-American) and said he did not want to influence the decision who would govern France after the war by supporting de Gaulle. To help Britain resist the advance of Soviet interests in Western Europe, Churchill wanted a strong post-war France and felt that de Gaulle offered the best choice in this regard. Eisenhower had to cope with these differences in planning for OVERLORD and determining who would control French civil affairs once the Germans were driven out.[831]

Because they were contributing the majority of troops and supplies to the European war effort after the Normandy invasion, the Americans enjoyed dominance over the British in strategy decisions. However, because the majority of the invading soldiers were British, General Montgomery had overall command of the Allied invasion ground forces.[832]

The most logical place for the Allies to invade the European mainland was at Pas de Calais in eastern France. It was close to Germany, near the excellent port of Antwerp, within range of planes flying from

---

[828] *Inferno*, 472, *Reich*, 954-55, *Air Masters*, 383-85.
[829] *Soldier's Story*, 201, *Generals' War*, 114.
[830] *Supreme Commander*, 329-30.
[831] *Supreme Commander*, 377-87.
[832] *Masters*, 577-78, *Generals' War*, 163, *Supreme Commander*, 451-52.

Britain, very near England and would avoid the inevitable destruction that would result from fighting the Germans across a wide swath of northern France. Because all of these advantages were known to the Germans, too, much Allied thought went into alternative landing sites.[833]

Ultimately, Normandy was selected as the place for the invasion. It was less obvious, had firm beaches that would accommodate tanks, was near England, was protected from the Atlantic Ocean's high waves by the Cotentin peninsula, and faced weaker German defenses.[834]

In an effort to mislead Germany as to where the invasion would take place, the Allies created a phantom army based in England commanded by General Patton, and sought to persuade the Germans that Allied forces would enter either through Scandinavia or Pas de Calais.[835]

As Eisenhower prepared for OVERLORD, he and other Allied leaders fretted about rumored secret German weapons — pilotless aircraft or long-range rockets — being installed at Peenemünde on the Baltic coast and on the French coast. They could be used to attack Allied troops gathering in southern England for the invasion.[836]

In April, during dinner at a public restaurant in London (and after several drinks), General Miller, an American air force officer, mentioned the planned Normandy invasion date. Eisenhower had Miller arrested, busted to lieutenant colonel and sent home.[837]

Toward the end of April, Patton, having been warned not to make controversial statements, made a speech to a small group of British women during which the press claimed he said that after the war the British and Americans would rule the world. This report generated concern in Congress and elsewhere that Stalin might be offended. In fact, Patton had included the Soviets, although apparently *sotto voce*. Publicity over his latest misconduct almost cost him his new Normandy command.[838]

For Operation OVERLORD, the Allies mustered 8,000 doctors, 600,000 doses of penicillin and 800,000 pints of blood (segregated by white and black donors).[839]

---

[833] *Supreme Commander*, 331-32.
[834] *Supreme Commander*, 332-33.
[835] *Soldier's Story*, 344, *Engineers*, 256-57, *Inferno*, 519, *Supreme Commander*, 394, 401.
[836] *Generals' War*, 115, *Supreme Commander*, 412-14.
[837] *Generals' War*, 89, *Supreme Commander*, 403.
[838] *Generals' War*, 104-05, 107-09, *Supreme Commander*, 342-45.
[839] *Guns*, 24, *Inferno*, 390, *Supreme Commander*, 413.

Of the American GIs arriving in Europe in 1944, nearly half were teenagers, one in three had only a grade school education, and only one in ten had attended college for at least a semester.[840]

On May 15, Eisenhower convened a high-level meeting to discuss the invasion plans and risks. In attendance were King George VI, Churchill, South Africa's Prime Minister, Generals Bradley, Patton, Montgomery and Crerar, and many other leaders.[841]

Because the Allies found General de Gaulle to be an extremely difficult person to work with, and for security reasons, they excluded him from planning for the Allied invasion of Europe.[842]

On the eve of the Normandy invasion, Churchill was outraged when de Gaulle refused to record a radio broadcast asking the French to obey the liberators. De Gaulle declared that "I cannot follow Eisenhower." Eisenhower said "To hell with him." Churchill called de Gaulle "a false and puffed up personality." It was said of de Gaulle that an essential element of his diet had long been the hand that fed him.[843]

After several days of bad weather that delayed the Normandy invasion, Eisenhower was told there would be about twenty-four hours of fair weather beginning late on June 5. He alone made the agonizing decision to proceed with the invasion on June 6. Had OVERLORD not been launched on June 6, it would have to have been delayed until at least June 19.[844]

The tides at the beaches in Normandy rose and fell nineteen feet twice each day. Landing at high tide was not suitable because Rommel had planted underwater obstacles in the beach. Low tide exposed all of the German wood and metal beach defenses, causing landing craft to be grounded more than 400 yards offshore. Thus, a landing shortly after low tide was selected, as this would give the first men ashore an opportunity to destroy the obstacles and clear the beach for subsequent landings at higher tides.[845]

In anticipation of the possible failure of the Normandy invasion, a weary and anxious Eisenhower prepared a note saying that "Our landings in the Cherbourg-Havre area have failed to gain a satisfactory foothold and I have withdrawn the troops. My decision to attack at this

---

[840] *Guns*, 19.
[841] *Generals' War*, 117, *Supreme Commander*, 398-99.
[842] *Guns*, 34, *Generals' War*, 136-37, *Supreme Commander*, 382-83.
[843] *Guns*, 35, *Masters*, 487, *Generals' War*, 137-38, *Supreme Commander*, 384-87.
[844] *Generals' War*, 143-44, *Supreme Commander*, 415-17.
[845] *Soldier's Story*, 260-61, *Supreme Commander*, 392-94.

time and place was based upon the best information available. The troops, the air and the Navy did all that bravery and devotion to duty could do. If any blame or fault attaches to the attempt it is mine alone."[846]

Normandy is Invaded

The D-Day invasion was supported by seven battleships, twenty-three cruisers, more than 100 destroyers and 1,000 other fighting ships. In all, the Allies used almost 7,000 seagoing craft to deposit 150,000 soldiers on the sands of Normandy.[847]

Shortly before the invasion, British Air Marshal Leigh-Mallory, who opposed flying paratroopers to the Cherbourg peninsula in Normandy, predicted to Eisenhower that the airborne operations would be a complete failure and would cause the loss of three-quarters of the men. Eisenhower elected to proceed and was relieved that on D-Day fewer than three percent of the paratrooper planes were downed.[848]

The Allied troops were scheduled to land on the beaches at about 6:30 a.m., after bombers had attacked German positions and paratroopers had parachuted into Normandy.[849]

The average rifleman's pack in the Normandy invasion weighed 68.4 pounds.[850]

The British and Canadians landed on their three assigned beaches to the east with minimal opposition. Similarly, Americans landing on western-most Utah beach, at the base of the Cotentin Peninsula, suffered relatively small losses of men and material.[851]

In the roughly five mile wide Omaha Beach landing area, however, American V Corps troops, commanded by General Gerow, faced eighty-five German machine gun nests, mines in the beach, and some 3,700 wood pilings and metal barriers. An underwater demolition team was supposed to have destroyed the obstacles and created sixteen lanes for landing craft to approach the beach, but they destroyed just five.[852]

In the early morning of June 6, German officers in Normandy wanted to immediately move needed panzer forces into the area to oppose the Allied landing. They were blocked by a standing order from

---

[846] *Guns*, 39, *Generals' War*, 144, *Supreme Commander*, 392, 418.
[847] *Guns*, 29, *Engineers*, 253, *Inferno*, 516, *Generals' War*, 146.
[848] *Generals' War*, 142, 157, *Montgomery*, 232, *Supreme Commander*, 407, 418-19.
[849] *Generals' War*, 148.
[850] *Guns*, 27.
[851] *Generals' War*, 150.
[852] *Generals' War*, 151, *Soldier's Story*, 227, *Guns*, 65.

Hitler that required his personal approval before panzer forces could be transferred. Hitler slept until 3:00 p.m. that day. By the time he woke and approved the request, the panzer force's opportunity for success had passed.[853]

By the end of D-Day, the Allies had moved between one-half and three miles inland and had established a beachhead in Normandy.[854]

Field Marshal Rommel was in charge of German defenses on the Channel coast from Holland to the Loire River and commanded 500,000 men. Having concluded that the bad weather in early June precluded any invasion, he had gone home to Germany to celebrate his wife's fiftieth birthday.[855]

In the fighting on D-Day, 2,500 Americans, 1,641 Britons, 359 Canadians, 37 Norwegians, 19 Free French, 12 Australians and 2 New Zealanders were killed.[856]

From the small Blue Ridge Mountain town of Bedford, Virginia, came nineteen soldiers who were all killed during the first fifteen minutes of fighting at Omaha Beach, representing the largest per capita war loss of any American town or city.[857]

By June 7, most of the dead soldiers on the beaches had been removed to temporary cemeteries.[858]

During the invasion efforts on June 6-7, some 3,000 French citizens of Normandy were killed by bombs, naval fire and other weapons. Thereafter, some angry French citizens took up weapons against the Allies.[859]

Air superiority during the Normandy invasion was critical. The Allies flew 13,688 sorties on D-Day; the Germans just 319.[860]

Within six days after D-Day, the Allies had landed some 326,000 men and 54,000 vehicles on the Normandy beaches.[861]

De Gaulle was angered by America's unwillingness to recognize him as head of the new French government without a vote of the French people. Thus, de Gaulle undercut Allied efforts in Normandy,

---

[853] *Reich*, 1038.

[854] *Inferno*, 518, *Montgomery*, 234.

[855] *Guns*, 79, 81, *Reich*, 1037, *Supreme Commander*, 420.

[856] *Masters*, 487, *Inferno*, 518, *Generals' War*, 159-60.

[857] *WW II Story*, 301-02.

[858] *Generals' War*, 160.

[859] *Guns*, 85, *Inferno*, 518, *Generals' War*, 204-06, *The Duel for France: 1944* ("*Duel*"), Martin Blumenson, Da Capo Press (1963), 53.

[860] *Masters*, 489, *Guns*, 80, *Engineers*, 135, 227, 252-53, *Generals' War*, 72.

[861] *Engineers*, 276, *WW II Story*, 305.

including refusing to allow hundreds of French liaison officers to accompany invasion forces and refusing to back new Allied French currency that his representatives had previously approved. On June 14, de Gaulle made a speech in Bayeux in which he said that it was the French who were reconquering their lost territory, "with the aid of the Allies." When he learned of the distorted comment, Eisenhower was livid.[862]

Moving Inland Against the Germans

On June 17, Rommel and von Rundstedt met with Hitler in a bunker in Soissons, France to discuss the military situation in Normandy. Rommel pointed out that the Allies had air, land and sea superiority, and that the struggle was hopeless unless Hitler agreed to remove German forces from the range of Allied naval guns and organize panzer units for a counterattack. Hitler insisted that German forces stand and fight. Rommel also predicted that the German fronts in Normandy and the Soviet Union would soon collapse, and urged Hitler to seek peace. Hitler told Rommel not to worry about the overall course of the war.[863]

By June 18, American troops had established a line across the Cotentin Peninsula and were moving north to take from the Germans the isolated city of Cherbourg, thirteen miles away.[864]

Between June 19 and 24, 1944, violent storms struck Normandy and destroyed important Allied man-made Mulberry harbors there used for landing men and critical supplies.[865]

The Germans surrendered Cherbourg on June 23, but only after destroying the facilities in the port, thereby delaying the Allies' ability to offload critical supplies in the harbor.[866]

After the Allies captured Cherbourg, two bordellos quickly opened, one of which was designated for "whites only." (Similarly, in India the British set up segregated brothels for their black African soldiers).[867]

After taking the port of Cherbourg, the Allies' plan in OVERLORD was to move south off the beaches of Normandy and out of the

---

[862] *Generals' War*, 168, 202-04, *Supreme Commander*, 479.
[863] *Reich*, 1039-40, *Duel*, 8-9, *Supreme Commander*, 431.
[864] *Guns*, 111, *Generals' War*, 177-78, *Supreme Commander*, 430.
[865] *Masters*, 494, *Generals' War*, 51, 182, *Supreme Commander*, 431.
[866] *WW II Story*, 306.
[867] *Guns*, 122, *Inferno*, 399.

Cotentin Peninsula, then pivot to the east, and move toward Paris and Germany. The British forces were to take the French city of Caen and protect the American flank west of Caen from attack by any German forces arriving from the east.[868]

U.S. Military Intelligence (G-2) failed to warn Generals Marshall and Eisenhower about the Normandy *bocages* — deep, thick, ancient farm field hedgerows that gave German defenders excellent cover and led to considerable Allied bloodshed.[869]

While the Allies had excellent artillery, their efforts in Normandy were complicated by the fact that their Sherman, Churchill and Cromwell tanks were poor opponents for the well-armored and better-weaponed German Panther and Tiger tanks. The inability of Allied tanks to compete with those of the Germans created morale problems within Allied ground troops.[870]

On June 29, Rommel and von Rundstedt again met with Hitler, this time in Germany, to try to persuade him to end the war. Hitler rejected the proposal and two days later replaced von Rundstedt with Field Marshall Kluge.[871]

On July 10, 1944, after many delays and intense Allied heavy bombing, British General Montgomery's troops finally took a portion of Caen from the Germans, but not the airfields south of the city. In May, Montgomery's plans had called for his forces to capture Caen on D-Day. On July 7, after a full month of fighting, an impatient Eisenhower wrote to Montgomery urging him "to prevent a stalemate."[872]

British Air Chief Marshal Arthur Tedder noted in his diary, concerning Montgomery's slow progress in taking Caen, "[t]he problem is Monty, who can be neither removed nor moved to action." By late July, Tedder favored replacing Montgomery.[873]

The Americans, moving south from the heavily hedge-rowed, swampy and vigorously-defended Cotentin Peninsula, finally took the French Norman city of Saint-Lô on July 18, 1944. They suffered about 40,000 casualties in seventeen days. Falling back, the Germans left bo-

---

[868] *Soldier's Story*, 317-18, *Inferno*, 536, *Generals' War*, 176-78, 180-81, 190.

[869] *Masters*, 490, *Inferno*, 520, *Generals' War*, 156, *WW II Story*, 307-10, *Supreme Commander*, 430.

[870] *Inferno*, 521-22, *Generals' War*, 184, 199-201.

[871] *Reich*, 1041.

[872] *Masters*, 502, *Inferno*, 536, *Generals' War*, 165, 172-77, 187-90, 218, *Guns*, 124, *Duel*, 46-47, *Supreme Commander*, 399, 427, 434.

[873] *Guns*, 125, *Generals' War*, 189, 215-21, *Montgomery*, 238, 243, *Supreme Commander*, 438.

dies and souvenir weapons that had been booby-trapped.[874]

General Omar Bradley headed the American ground forces in the Normandy invasion. Eisenhower said Bradley had "brains, a capacity of leadership, and a thorough understanding of the requirements of modern battle." During the first two months of the Normandy invasion, Bradley removed from command nine American generals for performance reasons.[875]

President Theodore Roosevelt's son, Theodore, Jr., who was part of the U.S. invasion force at Normandy, died of a coronary thrombosis on July 12, 1944. He subsequently was awarded the Congressional Medal of Honor.[876]

On July 17, Rommel sustained a skull fracture in France in a car accident caused by Allied strafing. Although he survived, his role as a German commander in World War II was over. His duties were assigned to Field Marshal Kluge.[877]

Germany's Army Group B, responsible for defending against the Normandy invasion, suffered some 100,000 casualties during the first six weeks of battle.[878]

On July 18, following Allied saturation bombing of German positions south of Caen, Montgomery's forces attacked Axis troops there. After two days of strong German resistance, the risk-averse Montgomery called off the assault. Eisenhower, hinting that the British were not carrying their weight, pressed Montgomery to renew his attack.[879]

On July 25, some of the more than 1,800 Allied bombers assigned to tactically bomb German positions near Saint-Lô (on the southern base of the Cotentin Peninsula) mistakenly struck Allied positions, killing 111 Americans (including U.S. General McNair) and wounding about 500 others.[880]

By the end of July, the American troops, aided by tanks and fighter-bombers, had broken out of Saint-Lô and were driving southwest into crumbling German defenses below the Cotentin Peninsula. Still, the Germans fought with stunning vigor and their V-1s rained down

---

[874] *Guns*, 127-30, *Masters*, 503, *Inferno*, 536, *Generals' War*, 184, 193, 210, *Duel*, 17-28, 49-63, *Supreme Commander*, 459.

[875] *Guns*, 126, *Duel*, 16, 21, 44, 48, 75, *Supreme Commander*, 423.

[876] *Guns*, 126-27.

[877] *Guns*, 132-33, *Generals' War*, 235, *Reich*, 1041-42, *Duel*, 60.

[878] *Guns*, 130, *Duel*, 65, *Supreme Commander*, 460.

[879] *Generals' War*, 197-98, 212-13, 215-18, *Duel*, 69-72, *Supreme Commander*, 439.

[880] *Generals' War*, 225-26, *WW II Story*, 318-21, *Air Masters*, 305-07, *Duel*, 80-91.

on England.[881]

Renewed Efforts to Remove Hitler

During the second half of 1943, conspirators on the *Fuehrer*'s general staff continued their plans to rid Germany of Hitler. Early in 1944 they persuaded Rommel to join in the plot. Their plan was to arrest Hitler and try him for war crimes, seek a reasonable armistice with the Western Allies, eliminate Nazi rule, and continue the war against the Bolshevik Soviet Union. But they soon realized that the Allies would hold firm to their demand for an unconditional surrender.[882]

As the summer of 1944 drew near, the conspirators recognized that Germany faced an impending Allied invasion in Europe, Rome was falling, and the Red Army approaching from the east carried with it the threat of Bolshevism. They also knew that the Gestapo was investigating the conspirators. Faced with these urgent conditions, they revised their plan, called Valkyrie. Now Hitler would be assassinated, an anti-Nazi government would be formed, the Home Army would take responsibility for control of civilian matters throughout Germany, and the military would be persuaded not to oppose the coup. Hope for something better than an unconditional surrender was abandoned.[883]

On July 20, the German conspirators, operating through severely wounded war veteran Colonel Claus von Stauffenberg, tried to kill Hitler by exploding a time bomb near him during a meeting. Protected by the heavy base of an oak conference room table, Hitler was moderately wounded but survived. Many others in the room were killed or gravely wounded.[884]

Less than three hours after the explosion, Hitler proceeded with a planned meeting with Mussolini — the last they ever had.[885]

Following the explosion, the conspirators were slow to activate the steps needed to gain control of the army, the national radio network, the telephone lines and government in Berlin. As a result, the coup failed. Stauffenberg and three other senior military conspirators were shot and killed by a firing squad the evening of the explosion.[886]

At 1:00 a.m. the next morning, Hitler informed a German radio

---

[881] *Generals' War*, 229, *Air Masters*, 307-08, *Duel*, 92-128, *Supreme Commander*, 459-68.
[882] *Reich*, 1028-33.
[883] *Reich*, 1028-36, 1042, 1047.
[884] *Masters*, 509, *Dawn*, 464-65, *Inferno*, 533, *General's War*, 210, 235, *Reich*, 1048-55.
[885] *Reich*, 1055, 1057.
[886] *Reich*, 1057-68.

audience that he had survived the plot and was eliminating the criminal conspirators.[887]

On August 8, 1944, eight conspirators, including Field Marshal von Witzleben, were convicted and hanged by piano wire.[888]

Field Marshall Kluge, relieved of his duties in France on August 17 and ordered home to Germany, knew that he was suspected of participating in the conspiracy. He committed suicide by taking poison the next day.[889]

On October 14, 1944, when given the choice between facing charges for high treason for his involvement in the Hitler assassination attempt on July 20, or killing himself, a state funeral and no harassment of his family, Rommel elected to commit suicide by ingesting the poison Hitler's messengers had supplied. The public was told that Rommel had suffered a cerebral embolism tied to battle wounds.[890]

Overall, some 7,000 alleged conspirators were arrested and charged with crimes. Those sent to death numbered 4,980. Some of those arrested were freed by Allied troops in 1945.[891]

Command of American Ground Forces in Normandy

On August 1, 1944, the U.S. Third Army came into being in Normandy. It was led by Lieutenant General Patton, who had for some time doubted whether he would ever again be given command of an army. The daring and impetuous Patton favored "a good plan violently executed now" over "a perfect plan next week."[892]

To preserve for a little longer the hoax that Patton was in Britain preparing to lead an invasion of France at Pas de Calais, Eisenhower prohibited any public disclosure that Patton was leading the Third Army.[893]

Patton's niece, Jean Gordon, joined him in London in July and remained with him for most of the duration of the war. They attended social events together and were rumored to be lovers. Two weeks after Patton died in December 1945 following an auto accident in Germany,

---

[887] *Reich*, 1069.
[888] *Reich*, 1070-71.
[889] *Reich*, 1075-76, *Duel*, 287-89.
[890] *Reich*, 1077-79, *Guns*, 182, *Duel*, 79.
[891] *Reich*, 1072-74.
[892] *Guns*, 149, *Soldier's Story*, 355, *Inferno*, 536, *Generals' War*, 233, *Duel*, 158.
[893] *Duel*, 158-59.

she committed suicide.[894]

The 12th Army Group, which included Patton's U. S. Third Army and Hodges' U. S. First Army, was also created on August 1, 1944. It was commanded by General Omar Bradley. Before August 1, Bradley had commanded the U. S. First Army.[895]

During the invasion of Sicily, General Patton had been General Bradley's commander. After the Normandy invasion, Bradley was Patton's commanding officer.[896]

Driving the Germans Out of Normandy

Within days after its creation, Patton's Third Army, supported by Allied fighter bombers, had moved south past the Norman town of Avranches. It then split, with one division moving west toward the city of Brest in Brittany and the other south toward the cities of Rennes and Le Mans.[897]

Patton's forces moving into Brittany were assisted by some 20,000 male and female members of the French Forces of the Interior, who engaged in guerrilla actions against the Germans there.[898]

Hitler ordered the 200,000 or so German soldiers defending Brittany to retreat into fortresses guarding the Atlantic ports there and fight "to the last man, to the last cartridge." His goals were to deny the Allies access to the harbors there and to soak up Allied forces that otherwise would participate in the drive toward Germany.[899]

By August 6, Third Army troops had moved across Brittany and had sealed the Germans within the Brittany fortresses guarding the port cities of Brest, Lorient and Vannes. The American forces had not, however, liberated the valuable harbors there.[900]

Because Patton's troops had stalemated the Germans pocketed in Brittany, other Allied troops in Normandy could pivot east and seek to push the Germans out of France.[901]

---

[894] *Generals' War*, 185, 191, 240, 353, 392, 412, *Patton: The Man Behind the Legend, 1885-1945* ("*Patton*"), Martin Blumenson, William Morrow and Company (1985), 244-45, 261, 265, 307.

[895] *Guns*, 149, 220, 222, *Soldier's Story*, 361, *Generals' War*, 232, *Supreme Commander*, 468.

[896] *Soldier's Story*, 355, *Generals' War*, 64.

[897] *Generals' War*, 234, *Air Masters*, 308, *Supreme Commander*, 468-70.

[898] *Duel*, 164-65.

[899] *Duel*, 156-57.

[900] *Duel*, 182-83, *Supreme Commander*, 470.

[901] *Duel*, 203-04.

As the Allies advanced, Hitler faced two choices: (a) end the fighting in Normandy and withdraw to a defensive line at the Seine River or (b) try to stabilize the German defensive lines in Normandy. He chose the second option.[902]

Thus, beginning August 6, Hitler personally ordered a German counterattack west toward Avranches (at the base of the Cotentin Peninsula) designed to separate the First and Third U.S. Armies. After several days of intense fighting the counterattack was thwarted, in part because the Allies had been forewarned by an Ultra intercept and had air superiority.[903]

As Hitler pondered what to do next with his forces, General Bradley realized that the counterattacking German troops had become vulnerable to encirclement some twenty-five miles to the east. More than 100,000 German soldiers west of Falaise, France were in a pocket shaped like a U on its side with the opening facing east. Allied troops — Montgomery's British, Canadian and Polish moving south and Patton's American and French moving north — were ordered to close the gap and encircle the enemy troops. The cautious Montgomery was, however, slow to compress the opening from the north. Patton offered to close the gap by moving his troops north into Montgomery's area. On August 13, a frustrated Bradley, claiming concern that Allied forces might attack each other, ordered Patton not to venture into the British area unless requested to do so by Montgomery. No such request ever came and the gap remained open for several more days. The failure to close the fifteen mile wide gap triggered many questions about Allied decision-making.[904]

Recognizing their dilemma, an estimated 30,000 to 100,000 frantic German troops escaped from the gap in the Falaise Pocket before it finally closed on August 19. Still, the Allies killed 10,000 Germans and captured another 50,000. Most of the retreating Germans' weapons were abandoned or destroyed.[905]

The tattered and exhausted Germans who escaped the Falaise Pocket scrambled eastward. Within a week most had retreated across the Seine and were edging toward the Rhine River, 250 miles to the

---

[902] *Duel*, 198-99.
[903] *Generals' War*, 236, 242, *Duel*, 211-12, 227-37, *Guns*, 158-59, *Supreme Commander*, 472-74.
[904] *Soldier's Story*, 376-77, *Guns*, 157-70, *Inferno*, 536-38, *Generals' War*, 241-46, *WW II Story*, 324-25, *Duel*, 238-80.
[905] *Guns*, 164-69, *Inferno*, 538, *Air Masters*, 310, *Duel*, 310-12, *Supreme Commander*, 477-78.

east. Meanwhile, the Allied forces chasing them approached Paris.[906]

Paris Liberated

General Dietrich von Choltitz commanded some 20,000 German troops in Paris in August 1944. Hitler had ordered that the city "must not fall into the hands of the enemy except as a field of ruins."[907]

Eisenhower considered bypassing the ancient French capital out of concern that attacking a defended Paris would (a) require lethal street fighting, (b) destroy the City of Light, (c) divert the Allies from pursuing the retreating Germans, and (d) impose upon the Allies the duty to feed the 2,000,000 inhabitants, thereby reducing supplies needed by his combat troops.[908]

As the Vichy French government collapsed, de Gaulle insisted that his French National Committee of Liberation was the only legitimate provisional French government. However, many members of the French underground were left-leaning and opposed de Gaulle's claim. Roosevelt, too, had opposed giving recognition to the FNCL without a public vote. However, on July 11, after meeting with de Gaulle, Roosevelt said he was willing to view the FNCL as the "dominant" political authority in France until there were elections.[909]

Eisenhower had reluctantly promised de Gaulle months earlier that when the Allies were ready to liberate Paris, French troops would be allowed to lead the way into town. However, Ike was concerned that by doing so the Allies might be influencing an internal French debate over who should lead the government.[910]

In mid-August, restive Parisian rail workers and policemen began labor strikes and Communists launched attacks against occupying German patrols. De Gaulle feared the Germans might brutally retaliate against Paris as they had in Warsaw, and he worried that the insurrection would advance the cause of French Communists.[911]

Pressured by de Gaulle and sensing that the Germans might not fight hard for Paris, on August 22 Eisenhower agreed that Allied troops, including French soldiers, should take the city. General Bradley favored allowing French troops to enter Paris first to help them

---

[906] *Duel*, 322-28, 368.
[907] *Guns*, 175-76.
[908] *Reich*, 1085-86, *Duel*, 329-30, *Supreme Commander*, 482.
[909] *Duel*, 330, *Guns*, 173, *Supreme Commander*, 377, 479-83.
[910] *Guns*, 173, *Generals' War*, 253-55, *Duel*, 330, *Supreme Commander*, 483.
[911] *Guns*, 173, *Duel*, 332-34, *Soldier's Story*, 387-90, *Supreme Commander*, 276, 483.

A CONCISE HISTORY OF THE SECOND WORLD WAR

restore some pride after four years of German occupation.[912]

Late on August 24, 1944, after slowly overcoming pockets of German resistance outside Paris, French General Leclerc entered the city with several tanks and halftracks. American troops entered Paris in force several hours later.[913]

General von Choltitz recognized that Paris could not long be defended. He had remarked cynically to his staff that "Ever since our enemies have refused to listen to and obey our *Fuehrer*, the whole war has gone badly." On August 25, rather than destroy Paris, von Choltitz surrendered the city and ordered a cease fire. For this, the Nazis tried him for treason *in absentia* in April 1945.[914]

On August 25, de Gaulle returned to Paris, established his headquarters there, and proclaimed that the city had been "liberated by itself, liberated by its people with the aid of the armies of France, with the help and support of all of France ...." He never mentioned the more than 50,000 American, British, Canadian and Polish lives that had been lost in France since D-Day. The prideful French seemed unwilling or unable to admit that they had not alone liberated Paris.[915]

In 1944, the French Communist Party was one of the largest Bolshevik organizations in Europe.[916]

Soon after de Gaulle returned to Paris, concerned that French Communists would take over the city, he asked Eisenhower to assign two divisions of American troops to Paris. Focused on defeating Germany, but eager to let Parisians know that it was the Allies who had driven the Germans back, Eisenhower ordered one division to parade through Paris on August 29. To encourage stability, he also permitted Leclerc's troops to remain in the city for about two weeks. [917]

On August 30, 1944, the seat of the Free French government was relocated from Algiers to Paris.[918]

Following the liberation of Paris, French citizens, in what was called "the purification," summarily executed up to 40,000 French men and women alleged to have collaborated with the Germans during the

---

[912] *Guns*, 173-74, *Duel*, 332-45, *Soldier's Story*, 390-92, *Supreme Commander*, 485.
[913] *Guns*, 175, *Inferno*, 539, *Duel*, 350-58, *Soldier's Story*, 392, *Supreme Commander*, 485-86.
[914] *Guns*, 175-78, *Soldier's Story*, 388-93, *Curse*, 91, *Reich*, 1085-86, *Duel*, 348.
[915] *Guns*, 179, *Generals' War*, 255, *Paris*, 367-68, *Duel*, 363-66.
[916] *Curse*, 282, *Paris*, 346-47.
[917] *Guns*, 184-85, *Generals' War*, 331, *Paris*, 314, *Duel*, 362, *Supreme Commander*, 487.
[918] *Masters*, 512.

occupation.[919]

After the Germans departed, Paris became a primary destination for GIs while on leave. Some 13,000 prostitutes plied their craft there. Soldier venereal disease rates increased sevenfold, leading Eisenhower to order all brothels off-limits.[920]

After taking Paris, the Allies estimated that Germany would be defeated by year end 1944.[921]

On October 23, the United States, Great Britain, the Soviet Union and several other nations gave diplomatic recognition to the French provisional government headed by de Gaulle.[922]

Operation Bagration

On June 22, 1944, about two weeks after D-Day, some 2,000,000 Red Army troops launched Operation Bagration, a massive summer offensive against two-thirds of the entire German army, which was spread across a 1,400 mile Soviet front.[923]

Seven hundred thousand Soviet troops attacked the center of the German line and by July 4, Minsk had been taken. To the north, the Soviet advance reached Riga on the Baltic Sea.[924]

By the end of July, the Red Army had moved well into Latvia and eastern Poland. This was the third time during World War II that these lands had been invaded by hostile forces.[925]

The Soviet Union also drove deep into Finland and, under an armistice signed September 2, 1944, took for itself land in eastern Finland.[926]

Beginning on September 14, 1944, the Red Army assigned some 900,000 troops to clear the Baltic states of German soldiers.[927]

Axis soldier deaths suffered fighting the Soviets in Operation Bagration were 142,079 in June, 169,881 in July, and 277,465 in August of 1944. During that time the Red Army suffered 243,508 deaths.[928]

Still, it was estimated that during the entire year of 1944, German

---

[919] *Guns*, 178, *Curse*, 179, 282, *Inferno*, 637, *Paris*, 349-54.

[920] *Guns*, 400-01.

[921] *Masters*, 511, *Inferno*, 539.

[922] *Supreme Commander*, 490.

[923] *Inferno*, 528, *Guns*, 131.

[924] *Inferno*, 528.

[925] *Inferno*, 530-32, *Masters*, 504-05, *WW II Story*, 489, *Bloodlands*, 277-280, *Reich*, 1085.

[926] *Inferno*, 531, *WW II Story*, 489, *Reich*, 1085.

[927] *Curse*, 203.

[928] *Curse*, 84, *Engineers*, 203, 208, *Inferno*, 510, 531.

troops killed three Red Army soldiers for every German lost.[929]

Allied Attacks on German Oil Production

Seeking to cut off Germany's supply of oil from both Ploesti and its domestic synthetic fuel manufacturing plants, the Allies began a major strategic bombing effort in May 1944. Planes flying from Italy bombed Ploesti, while others from England attacked the synthetic oil plants clustered near Berlin.[930]

The Americans and British launched over 500 separate attacks against German oil supply sources. By summer's end, German oil production was down about ninety percent.[931]

But during the June, July and August raids, the Allies lost over 1,500 bombers, more than 650 fighters and over 1,200 men.[932]

By choking off Germany's synthetic oil production, the Allies also impeded Hitler's ability to make synthetic rubber and chemicals used to produce ammunition.[933]

By the end of summer, German tanks and trucks in France had to be abandoned due to a lack of fuel, and pilot training was halted for the same reason.[934]

Another benefit achieved by Allied bombing of Germany was that in 1944 Hitler was forced to assign 800,000 troops and two-thirds of his air force to air defense of the homeland.[935]

Operation Dragoon

Stalin had suggested at the Teheran conference that the Western Allies invade France from the south at about the same time as the Normandy invasion. The theory was that this would divide Hitler's western forces. Stalin's goal apparently was also to keep the Allied forces in the Mediterranean from invading the Balkans, an area he sought to control after the war. In an effort to preserve portions of the British pre-war empire, Churchill tried to persuade the Americans to invade the Balkans rather than southern France. Roosevelt supported Stalin's position.[936]

---

[929] *Masters*, 467.
[930] *Air Masters*, 310-21.
[931] *Air Masters*, 315, 320-21.
[932] *Air Masters*, 318, 321.
[933] *Air Masters*, 313-14.
[934] *Air Masters*, 328.
[935] *Air Masters*, 481.
[936] *Generals' War*, 257-61, *Supreme Commander*, 445-58.

The Allied invasion of southern France, which Eisenhower wanted as support for the Normandy invasion, was called Operation Dragoon (previously "Anvil"). The fact that Marseille was the best port in France was a prime reason Ike insisted on Dragoon.[937]

The British opposed withdrawing seven divisions of troops from the Italian campaign, under the command of British General Alexander, to include them in the Dragoon invasion of southern France. The Americans insisted that the troops be transferred to support the Normandy invasion, causing Churchill considerable dismay.[938]

Churchill continued well into August to argue against Dragoon and the Americans just as firmly insisted that the operation take place.[939]

By the end of Operation Dragoon's D-Day (August 15, 1944), some 77,000 U.S. Seventh Army troops had landed along the Riviera in southern France, and 9,000 American and British airborne troops had parachuted a few miles inland. The Free French also took part. Allied casualties were about 500, with 95 dead.[940]

American troops involved in Operation Dragoon were commanded by Major General Lucian Truscott, Jr., who had previously commanded troops in the invasions of Sicily and Anzio.[941]

The French troops involved in Operation Dragoon were commanded by General De Lattre, who had been loyal to German-controlled Vichy France from 1940 until November 1942. He then opposed Germany's occupation of southern France, was court-martialed and sentenced to ten years in prison. He escaped in September 1943, and was appointed by de Gaulle to head the French army in exile.[942]

Of the Axis troops taken prisoner in Dragoon, about forty percent were Soviets who had agreed to fight with the Germans against Stalin.[943]

Within ten days after landing, the Operation Dragoon troops moving north had made contact with General Patton's Third Army at Dijon.[944]

---

[937] *Guns*, 192, *Masters*, 586, *Generals' War*, 260, *Supreme Commander*, 457.

[938] *Masters*, 495-500, *Battle*, 579.

[939] *Generals' War*, 263-66, *Supreme Commander*, 455-57.

[940] *Guns*, 199, *Masters*, 508.

[941] *Guns*, 196, *Battle*, 586.

[942] *Guns*, 202.

[943] *Generals' War*, 265.

[944] *Masters*, 508, *Reich*, 1086.

By September 14 — in one month — the forces involved in the Allied invasion of southern France had advanced 300 miles north to the northern Swiss border.[945]

German casualties in France between D-Day and the end of August, 1944, neared 500,000.[946]

The German Air War Against Britain

Starting in mid-June 1944, the Germans launched devastating nightly attacks on London using a new weapon, V-1 flying bombs that could travel at a speed of 400 miles per hour. Between June 12 and the end of August, some 8,000 "buzz bombs" were aimed at London. One defense against V-1s was for an airplane to fly close and change the bomb's direction by tipping its wings. Only about twenty percent were destroyed before striking targets.[947]

By late July 1944, British casualties from German V-1 flying bombs exceeded 18,000, including 6,184 killed. The British considered using gas warfare to eliminate the V-1 launching sites but Eisenhower refused.[948]

Between September 8, 1944 and March 28, 1945, the Germans fired over one thousand V-2 rockets on England, causing almost 3,000 British deaths and 6,500 serious injuries. The British had no defense against the V-2s, which could travel at speeds faster than sound, other than to destroy the launch sites.[949]

In an effort to destroy German bases from which V-2s were launched, the Allies experimented with having pilots fly explosive-laden bombers toward the sites, bail out over friendly territory, and then by remote control direct the unmanned bombers toward the target. In an early attempt, a modified B-24 blew up before the pilots could bail out, killing Lt. Joseph Kennedy, Jr., brother of the future American president (who had, a year earlier, been wounded in a PT boat battle with the Japanese).[950]

Events in Hungary, Poland, Finland and the Balkans

In the spring of 1944, in pro-Nazi Hungary, Hitler's forces sent

---

[945] *Guns*, 215, *Masters*, 508, *Inferno*, 558-59, *Supreme Commander*, 499.

[946] *Guns*, 181, *Reich*, 1086, *Supreme Commander*, 514.

[947] *Masters*, 489-90, *Generals' War*, 168-71, *WW II Story*, 313-17, *Air Masters*, 297-99.

[948] *Air Masters*, 299, *Masters*, 504, *Supreme Commander*, 442, 445.

[949] *Guns*, 405, *Masters*, 513, 563, *Generals' War*, 292, *WW II Story*, 317, *Air Masters*, 417.

[950] *Generals' War*, 293, *Air Masters*, 299-303.

434,000 Hungarian Jews to the Auschwitz concentration camp where almost ninety percent met death. This led to requests to the British and Americans to bomb and destroy the killing facilities at Auschwitz. No such attack took place, arguably out of concern that many prisoners would have been killed in the process and because the risky invasion of Normandy was underway.[951]

Following a Polish uprising in Warsaw in August and September 1944, the Germans killed another 200,000 Poles. The Red Army halted its advance through Poland as the massacre was underway, apparently because the Soviets wanted to insure that the Polish government had different (i.e., not anti-Communist) leaders once the war ended.[952]

Intending to take control of Balkan nations before the Western Allies could exercise influence there, Stalin ordered the Red Army to attack Romania on August 20, 1944. Romania surrendered three days later. Upon that defeat, Germany lost the Ploesti oil fields, its only significant source of natural oil.[953]

On August 26, Bulgaria formally quit the war, causing the Germans to withdraw from there. On September 5, the Soviet Union declared war on Bulgaria, which gave up four days later.[954]

Finland severed its ties with Germany on September 2, 1944.[955]

After taking Bulgaria, Stalin attacked Yugoslavia, which yielded on October 19.[956]

Concerned that the Soviets would next invade Turkey and Greece, Churchill again expressed frustration that Allied troops had been sent to southern France instead of the Balkans.[957]

By October, the Germans had begun their evacuation of Greece and its islands.[958]

Germany's 1944 loss of control over Romania (oil), Finland (nickel and copper) and Yugoslavia (copper) meant that its supply of important natural resources was being choked off.[959]

---

[951] *Air Masters*, 322-27, *1944*, 168-173, 201, 471.
[952] *Soldier's Story*, 493, *Curse*, 90, *Inferno*, 569, *WW II Story*, 491, *Bloodlands*, 298-307, 310, *Air Masters*, 325-26, *1944*, 464-65.
[953] *Inferno*, 531-32, *Reich*, 1085, *Supreme Commander*, 510.
[954] *Reich*, 1085, *Inferno*, 532, *Supreme Commander*, 510.
[955] *Guns*, 248-49, 390, *Bulge*, 2, *Supreme Commander*, 510.
[956] *Inferno*, 532, *Supreme Commander*, 510.
[957] *Masters*, 504-05.
[958] *Inferno*, 533, *Bulge*, 2, *Supreme Commander*, 510.
[959] *Bulge*, 3.

The Battle for Brest

In August, 30,000 Germans troops still controlled the hemmed-in French port city of Brest on the Atlantic coast. Hitler had ordered them to fight to the last man. Needing additional port facilities from which to supply their troops, the Allies opened their attack on August 25.[960]

Street-to-street fighting in Brest continued until September 18, when the stubborn Germans finally surrendered to the U.S. Ninth Army. Before yielding, however, Hitler's troops destroyed the port facilities — bridges, wharfs, dry docks, cranes and all other elements that might have been of value to the Allies. As a consequence, Brest provided no relief to the Allied effort to deliver supplies to their combat troops.[961]

The Western Allies Drive Toward Germany

Upon crossing the Seine, the Allies ordered four armies to attack the Germans on a broad front. The First Canadian Army (under General Crerar) was to move north and clear the enemy out of the Channel coast area. Below the Canadians, the Second British Army (under Dempsey) was responsible for driving northeast into Belgium and toward the Netherlands. The American First Army (under Hodges) was to move northeast below the British troops toward Luxembourg and south of Brussels. Patton's American Third Army, south of the other three, was to advance toward the 100-mile distant Rhine River below Luxembourg.[962]

Over British opposition (including Montgomery's), Roosevelt and Marshall insisted that Eisenhower replace Montgomery as commander of all Allied ground forces in Western Europe effective September 1, 1944. Montgomery retained command of the British-Canadian 21st Army Group under Eisenhower's overall command. To salve Montgomery's pride and minimize the view that he had been demoted, Churchill promoted Montgomery to the rank of field marshal — the military equivalent of Eisenhower's five star rank. This action irritated the Americans and embarrassed many British military leaders.[963]

For many months, Eisenhower had favored attacking Germany in

---

[960] *Duel*, 368-69.

[961] *Duel*, 369-72, *Guns*, 220.

[962] *Duel*, 373-74, 378, 383, *Guns*, 224, *Supreme Commander*, 493.

[963] *Masters*, 510-12, *WWII History*, 34, *Inferno*, 539, *Generals' War*, 250, 267, *Guns*, 225, *Supreme Commander*, 505-06.

two thrusts along a broad front above and below the Ardennes Forest in Belgium. The northern jab would be aimed at the industrial Ruhr valley some sixty miles east of the Rhine and east of the Netherlands. The southern thrust would target Frankfurt and the Saar, another German industrial center. Ike's theory was that by attacking in this manner, the Germans would be spread across a wide front and the Allies could keep them off balance by shifting emphasis as combat needs dictated.[964]

But in August, as the Allies approached German territory, Montgomery argued in favor of a primary attack (headed by him) against the Germans concentrated on the northern front and aimed at Berlin. Montgomery also asked to have Hodges' entire First Army moved north to his right flank. Further, he sought to have priority in all supplies, which meant taking them from the American forces to the south. Bradley, who commanded the American armies, favored continuation of the original dual thrust plan with his troops pushing from positions south of Montgomery's.[965]

On August 23, Eisenhower agreed to give Montgomery's mission priority and assigned Hodges' First Army to him. Patton's southern advance was to be slowed and given limited supplies. As his supplies dwindled, Patton nonetheless pushed his troops toward the German border.[966]

On September 2, Patton and Bradley sought to persuade Eisenhower to allow their armies to continue to press the Germans south of Montgomery's position — at the Siegfried Line, the western wall of Germany's defense. Eisenhower again pondered whether (a) precious supplies should be diverted to Patton's and Bradley's forces and (b) the main push against the Germans should still come from Montgomery in the north.[967]

Following the September 2 meeting with Bradley and Patton at Chartres, the plane flying Eisenhower back to headquarters had to make an emergency landing. He transferred to a two-seat plane and continued his flight to the Cotentin Peninsula. Eisenhower's pilot was unable to find the Cotentin airstrip and made a forced landing on the

---

[964] *Guns*, 222-24, *Soldier's Story*, 396-400, *Guns*, 244.

[965] *Soldier's Story*, 396-400, 434-35, *Masters*, 510, 532, *Generals' War*, 250-53, *Supreme Commander*, 505-06.

[966] *Soldier's Story*, 400-01, *Generals' War*, 268-69, *Montgomery*, 248-49, *Supreme Commander*, 506-08.

[967] *Generals' War*, 270-71, *Guns*, 225-26, *Supreme Commander*, 508-09.

beach in Normandy. In the process of helping the pilot push his plane away from the rising tide, Eisenhower injured his knee, requiring a cast and two weeks of limited activity.[968]

By September 4, the advancing British, supported by Hodges' troops, had captured Brussels and Antwerp, taking more than 25,000 prisoners in the process.[969]

Among Montgomery's assignments was elimination of the V-1 launching sites on the northern coast of France. After the Canadians neutralized those launch pads in early September, the Germans began dispatching the lethal flying weapons from the Netherlands.[970]

On September 4, noting the relative ease with which Montgomery was proceeding, Eisenhower again concluded that the attack on Germany should contain two thrusts — crossing the Rhine in the north and busting through the Siegfried Line farther south. He believed that a broad front would spread thin the German defenses and lead to enemy confusion. While the northern thrust would continue to have priority, Ike authorized additional supplies for Patton's Third Army. Ike quickly rebuffed Montgomery's complaints about the change in emphasis.[971]

On September 10, Montgomery and Eisenhower met again — Montgomery insisting that they meet at his headquarters. After the seething and impertinent Montgomery characterized Ike's double-thrust policy as "rubbish" and claimed to have been betrayed, Eisenhower scowled, "Monty, you can't speak to me like that. I'm your boss." Montgomery apologized, but then incorrectly concluded that Eisenhower had once again agreed to put the brakes on the American advance toward Germany below Luxembourg.[972]

Eisenhower characterized Montgomery as "a psychopath," "egocentric" and "not an honest man."[973]

In mid-September, American forces under General Hodges probed the strength of Germans along the Siegfried Line, but made little progress. Again, Montgomery peevishly but unsuccessfully asked Eisenhower to order Bradley to halt all Allied action south of his north-

---

[968] *Guns*, 226.

[969] *Generals' War*, 269, *Duel*, 392, *Soldier's Story*, 408, 415, *Guns*, 230-31, *Supreme Commander*, 508.

[970] *Generals' War*, 248, 252, *Duel*, 374, 394-95.

[971] *Soldier's Story*, 410-12, *Generals' War*, 272, *Guns*, 227-28, *Duel*, 395, *Supreme Commander*, 509, 511-13.

[972] *Generals' War*, 276-77, *Guns*, 243-47, *Montgomery*, 258, *Supreme Commander*, 515.

[973] *Guns*, 247.

ern area.[974]

By mid-September, the Germans had reorganized their retreating forces and placed them in defensive positions along the Siegfried Line.[975]

As the Allies advanced and Germany faced more troop desertions, Axis soldiers were warned that if they deserted, their families would be shot.[976]

Market Garden

At the September 10 meeting with Eisenhower, Montgomery proposed to send his troops from Belgium into Holland to seize a bridgehead over the Rhine River. Seeing the plan as daring, Eisenhower agreed to Montgomery's "Market Garden" proposal.[977]

Montgomery's ambitious "Market Garden" plan called for dropping almost 35,000 airborne Allied soldiers into the Netherlands behind German lines, near the Rhine River, and above the German Siegfried Line. Montgomery argued that if the Rhine were crossed in this northern portion of the front, Allied forces could then rush into Germany. The invasion of Holland, which began on September 17, became the largest airborne operation in World War II.[978]

A major objective of Market Garden was to capture bridges over the Waal and Rhine Rivers at the towns of Arnhem and Nijmegen and to have other troops march northeast up a narrow corridor to join them. Montgomery's plan failed. After about ten days of hard fighting against skilled German troops, the surviving Allied soldiers withdrew west back across the Rhine downstream from Arnhem. Several days later, the Germans blew up the bridge at Nijmegen.[979]

Allied casualties in Market Garden totaled some 12,000 airborne soldiers, plus 261 planes and 658 air crewmen.[980]

During Market Garden, Montgomery monitored the battle through radio reports and liaison officers. He never visited either the battle site or his field commanders; he was having his portrait painted.

---

[974] *Generals' War*, 279-85, *Montgomery*, 258.

[975] *Duel*, 409-12.

[976] *Reich*, 1088.

[977] *Generals' War*, 276-77, *Guns*, 243-47, *Montgomery*, 258, *Supreme Commander*, 515-16.

[978] *Guns*, 260, 288, *Soldier's Story*, 416-19, *Inferno*, 558-59, *Reich*, 1089.

[979] *Inferno*, 559-61, *Guns*, 275, 283-89, *Soldier's Story*, 416-19, *Generals' War*, 281, *Supreme Commander*, 524.

[980] *Guns*, 286, *Inferno*, 561, *Generals' War*, 282.

Market Garden was the last strategic proposal from Montgomery that Eisenhower unequivocally accepted.[981]

While some Market Garden objectives were achieved and one-fifth of the Netherlands was liberated, overall the operation was considered to have been poorly planned and executed. The Allies had fought hard to win strategically worthless ground. After the battle, the Germans ordered some 145,000 Dutch civilians to move out of their homes in Arnhem and nearby areas.[982]

The Shortage of Supplies

Germany had not been forced to defend its home soil since Napoleon's time. With the fast-moving Allies now across the Seine and drawing nearer the German border, Hitler's military leaders were puzzled by why, in September 1944, the Allies halted their advance.[983]

The daily supplies per U. S. soldier in Europe in 1944 averaged 66.8 pounds, composed of 33.3 pounds of fuel, 8 pounds of ammunition, 7.3 pounds of construction material, 7.2 pounds of food, and additional weight for medical and other supplies. Combined, the Allied invasion troops needed 20,000 tons of supplies daily.[984]

By September, the Allies had advanced from Normandy several hundred miles east toward Germany. However, their supplies were still entering France from Normandy in the west and even more distant Marseille in the south. This caused serious delays in delivering fuel, ammunition and other needed supplies, and virtually halted the Allied advance by September 10. The French rail system, having been bombed in preparation for D-Day, was of little help. Thus, supplies had to move by some 6,000 two-and-a-half-ton trucks driven round the clock, mostly by African-American soldiers, in a system called the Red Ball Express. Of the approximately 800,000 gallons of gas the Allies used in France each day, some 300,000 were required to fuel the Red Ball Express.[985]

Between Antwerp, Belgium and the North Sea was the eighty mile estuary of the Scheldt River, which in September and October 1944 was held by German troops. Until it was cleared, no Allied shipping

[981] *Guns*, 281, 288, *Montgomery*, 253.

[982] *Inferno*, 561, *Guns*, 275, 287-88.

[983] *Reich*, 1087-88.

[984] *Guns*, 240, *Duel*, 399, *Supreme Commander*, 493.

[985] *Inferno*, 559, *Guns*, 241-42, *Soldier's Story*, 405, *Masters*, 492, *Generals' War*, 270, *WW II Story*, 328, *Reich*, 1089, *Air Masters*, 358, *Duel*, 399- 403.

could reach Antwerp.[986]

Field Marshal Montgomery had been assigned responsibility for taking the port near Antwerp which, upon capture, would significantly shorten Allied supply lines. But Montgomery gave this job a low priority, focusing instead on Market Garden.[987]

On October 5, Brooke criticized Montgomery for placing the Market Garden attack ahead of the capture of Antwerp's critical port.[988]

Four days later, a frustrated Eisenhower, who was about to turn fifty-four, cabled Montgomery: "Unless we have Antwerp producing by the middle of November our entire operations will come to a standstill. I must emphasize that ... I consider Antwerp of the first importance, and I believe that the operations ... require your personal attention."[989]

By late October, the supply problem was growing worse. The Red Ball system of trucking supplies from the open ports had been so hard on equipment that 9,000 trucks had been used up before November arrived.[990]

Montgomery eventually assigned the task of taking the Scheldt estuary to the Canadian First Army. In the process of removing the Germans, the Canadians sustained almost 13,000 casualties.[991]

The port of Antwerp was not finally opened for Allied shipping until November 28. The delay in taking the Scheldt has been called the "worst single mistake of the campaign."[992]

Hitler promptly ordered 7,000 V-1 and V-2 rockets fired at the port of Antwerp to disrupt Allied supply efforts, causing 10,000 casualties.[993]

General Bradley believed that if Montgomery had cleared the Scheldt and opened the port of Antwerp instead of pursuing Market Garden, the Allied advance on Germany would have proceeded months faster and with less resistance. Between early September and

---

[986] *Guns*, 233-34, 302-04, *Inferno*, 563.
[987] *Guns*, 221, 232-34, 241-42, 245, 302-04, 329, *Soldier's Story*, 412, *Inferno*, 559, 562, *Generals' War*, 269, *Montgomery*, 250.
[988] *Supreme Commander*, 526.
[989] *Guns*, 304, *Generals' War*, 305, *Supreme Commander*, 524-25.
[990] *Generals' War*, 302, *Supreme Commander*, 495.
[991] *Guns*, 329, *Inferno*, 563-64, *Supreme Commander*, 526.
[992] *Guns*, 329, *Inferno*, 564, *Generals' War*, 308.
[993] *Generals' War*, 308.

A CONCISE HISTORY OF THE SECOND WORLD WAR

mid-December, Germany tripled its forces on the western front.[994]

Adding to the Allied supply problems in the fall of 1944, organized thieves stole tons of food and clothing and thousands of gallons of gas and delivered them to the French black market.[995]

The Allied supply effort was commanded by the pompous and fastidious American General J. C. H. Lee, who was disliked by Eisenhower, Patton, Bradley and others, but not replaced.[996]

Octagon and Tolstoy

Churchill, Roosevelt and their military staffs met again in Quebec in September 1944 ("Octagon"). The British once more urged an invasion of the Balkans, with the goal of reaching Vienna before the Russians, but General Marshall made it clear that no American troops would be involved in such a landing. He favored a strong advance against Germany from the west.[997]

In Quebec, Roosevelt and Churchill approved a post-war plan, advanced by Secretary of the Treasury Morgenthau, calling for (a) the destruction of Germany's industrial power and (b) only a subsistence level of food for German citizens. Others opposed converting Germany into nothing more than an agrarian nation, fearing it would generate another war and be inhumane. When word of the plan leaked to the press, Nazi propaganda highlighted it, increasing German military resolve.[998]

In October 1944, Churchill and Stalin met in Moscow ("Tolstoy"). Roosevelt did not attend because of the forthcoming November presidential election. At the conference Churchill gave Stalin a free hand in dealing with Romania in exchange for British freedom to put down a Communist insurgency in Greece. Shortly thereafter, British troops moved into Athens. Churchill also ceded to Stalin substantial influence over Poland and other eastern European countries.[999]

On November 7, 1944, President Roosevelt was reelected to his fourth term, receiving 25,600,000 votes against Thomas Dewey's 22,000,000.[1000]

---

[994] *Soldier's Story*, 423-25.
[995] *Soldier's Story*, 428.
[996] *Guns*, 237, *Generals' War*, 329-34.
[997] *Masters*, 514-17.
[998] *Generals' War*, 295-99.
[999] *Masters*, 526-28, *Curse*, 90-94.
[1000] *Masters*, 528, *1944*, 491-92.

Allied Attacks Against the Siegfried Line

On October 28, Eisenhower ordered a general offensive against Germany along a 200 mile front. One aspect of this plan called for American General Hodges' First Army, assisted by General Simpson's Ninth Army, to make a thrust toward the Roer River and then aim for the German city of Cologne. Another was that Patton's forces would attack further south.[1001]

Hodges decided that his forces should attack Germany's fortified Siegfried Line in the dense Hürtgen Forest (about eleven miles long and five miles wide).[1002]

In months of fighting there, 120,000 Allied troops suffered 33,000 casualties in what one historian characterized as "the most ineptly fought series of battles of the war of the West."[1003]

The Battle of the Hürtgen Forest lasted until February 1945, and was at that time the longest running combat site in United States military history.[1004]

The tired and unimaginative General Hodges has been described as the American army's least impressive commander in World War II. Eisenhower, however, described Hodges in March 1945 as having done more than any other army commander in bringing about victory.[1005]

On November 8, Patton's troops, south of Hodges's, attacked the German line near Metz. After twelve days of fighting, Metz was surrounded but nearby German forts continued to resist and the Siegfried Line there remained unbroken.[1006]

In mid-November, Montgomery and Brooke recognized that a war-weary Britain needed the fighting to end soon and were frustrated with the deliberate pace of Eisenhower's battle plan and the lack of immediate success. At a meeting on November 28, and by letter on November 30, Montgomery informed Ike that his two-pronged battle plan had "failed; and we have suffered a strategic reverse." Eager to get to Berlin before winter, Montgomery asserted that (a) there should be a primary thrust into Germany north of the Ardennes Forest, (b) he should have full command of all Allied forces north of the Ardennes, and (c) Bradley should be ordered to report to him, adding that

---

[1001] *Generals' War*, 317-18, *Guns*, 312.

[1002] *Guns*, 310-12, 316, *WW II Story*, 333-36.

[1003] Guns, 325.

[1004] *Monuments Men*, 164.

[1005] *Inferno*, 563, *Guns*, 312-14, *Supreme Commander*, 621-22.

[1006] *Generals' War*, 313-14, *Air Masters*, 359, *Guns*, 345-49, *Bulge*, 36-37.

"[t]hings have not been so good since you separated us."[1007]

On December 1, the normally composed Ike angrily wrote to Montgomery rejecting the claim that his broad attack plan had failed. He noted the great Allied victory in Normandy, the successful effort to drive the Germans out of France, and suggested that had Montgomery broken out of Caen more quickly the Allies' September supply problems would have been avoided.[1008]

At a tense meeting on December 7, Eisenhower again rejected many of Montgomery's proposals. He stated that Bradley's First and Third Armies would continue to press the Germans in a broad front in and below the Ardennes Forest. Ike also refused to give Montgomery command of all Allied forces north of the Ardennes Forest, but agreed that Bradley should lend his U.S. Ninth Army to Montgomery for the primary drive in the north.[1009]

In London on December 12, Churchill and Brooke tried to persuade Eisenhower to alter his plan. Eisenhower lacked confidence in Montgomery and was concerned that the Allied forces in a single thrust could be surrounded and destroyed by German soldiers fighting to protect their homeland. Also, the sustained failure to free the port in Antwerp meant that supplies were slow to arrive to the forces near the German border. Furthermore, Ike knew that General Marshall would insist that American troops play a significant role in driving the Germans back. Thus, Ike held to his deliberate broad thrust plan.[1010]

Eisenhower and Montgomery both recognized that under Ike's plan there was a thinly defended 75-100 mile section between Bradley's two armies facing the Ardennes Forest. When Eisenhower questioned Bradley about this vulnerability on December 7, Bradley acknowledged the risk but said he could not strengthen that section without weakening Patton's and Hodges' offensives. He added that if the Germans attacked there the Allies could attack the enemy flanks and stop them before reaching the Meuse River. He also said that as a precaution, he had avoided placing any significant supply depots in that area.[1011]

[1007] *Generals' War*, 320-26, *Guns*, 383-85, *Montgomery*, 261-62, *Supreme Commander*, 530, 546, 584-85.

[1008] *Supreme Commander*, 547-48.

[1009] *Generals' War*, 327, *Guns*, 387-89.

[1010] *Generals' War*, 326-29, *Supreme Commander*, 529-33, 551.

[1011] *Supreme Commander*, 552, *Generals' War*, 327.

The Battle of the Bulge Begins

In late 1944, Hitler reasoned that his best method of curtailing the Allied advance from the west was to recapture the not-to-distant city of Antwerp and cut off Allied supply lines. This was the impetus for the Battle of the Bulge, a German counterattack through an eighty mile front running from southern Belgium to Luxembourg, that Hitler had been secretly planning since August. The German forces were commanded by Field Marshal von Rundstedt.[1012]

To prevail, Hitler was counting on surprise, bad weather that would thwart Allied flights, and his troops' ability to capture needed fuel supplies from the Allies.[1013]

At dawn on December 16, 1944, Hitler launched the Battle of the Bulge sending almost 250,000 soldiers and 900 tanks against the thinly defended Allied line in the Ardennes Forest in southeastern Belgium. His aim was to split the United States and British forces and isolate four Allied armies north of the Ardennes Forest.[1014]

Hitler's tactics included sending into Allied territory some 2,000 English-speaking German commandos dressed as American soldiers. They caused considerable confusion by changing road signs and cutting telephone lines. Many of those who were captured were shot immediately; others were court-martialed and then executed.[1015]

The Battle of the Bulge, undertaken in deep snow during the coldest Belgian winter in memory, was a surprise to the Allies and was characterized as the worst U. S. intelligence failure since Pearl Harbor. Due to extraordinary German precautions, there had been no warning from Ultra and the Allies had disregarded other signs of a buildup.[1016]

Four reasons contributing to the Allied failure of intelligence were: (a) not knowing whether or where the Germans would counterattack, (b) the Allies' focus on offense rather than defense, (c) the belief that the cautious von Rundstedt, not Hitler, was controlling the strategy and would not accept the severe losses Allied air supremacy would inflict, and (d) the belief that the fuel shortage in Germany precluded any counterattack.[1017]

On December 17, an American truck convoy with 150 GIs surren-

---

[1012] *Guns*, 394-96, *Soldier's Story*, 455, *Generals' War*, 338, *Air Masters*, 370, *Bulge*, 17.

[1013] *Masters*, 534, *Soldier's Story*, 455, *Air Masters*, 371, *Bulge*, 22.

[1014] *Guns*, 419-20, *Masters*, 532-33, *Curse*, 105, *Soldier's Story*, 464, *Generals' War*, 339, *WW II Story*, 338, *Air Masters*, 371.

[1015] *WW II Story*, 340, *Reich*, 1091-92, *Bulge*, 558, *Supreme Commander*, 561.

[1016] *Guns*, 412, *Masters*, 534, *Ultra Secret*, 177-78, *Generals' War*, 336, 340.

[1017] *Supreme Commander*, 554-55.

dered to a German SS panzer unit near Malmédy, Belgium. The Germans lined up the Americans in a field and, using machine gun fire and pistol shots to the heart or head, killed most of them.[1018]

On December 19, 1944, nearly 8,000 American soldiers surrendered to the Germans in the Ardennes Forest.[1019]

Eisenhower accepted full blame for the Allied intelligence failure and General Bradley admitted that he had greatly underestimated the enemy's intentions and offensive capabilities.[1020]

In reaction, Eisenhower, sensing an opportunity to profit from the Germans' aggressiveness, dispatched 250,000 troops and 50,000 vehicles to counter the German thrust. He ordered General Bradley to move his whole Third Army, which Patton commanded, north to close the gap from the south, and temporarily assigned command of Bradley's two northern armies, the First and the Ninth, to British Field Marshal Montgomery in the north. A furious Bradley, concerned that transferring two of his armies to Montgomery suggested a weakness in American war efforts, threatened to resign but then concurred.[1021]

In just a few days, Patton brilliantly moved his entire Third Army almost 100 miles north over icy roads and on December 22 attacked the Germans on the south side of the bulge.[1022]

On December 21, 18,000 U.S. Army soldiers commanded by Brigadier General McAuliffe were surrounded by 45,000 German troops in the critical crossroads town of Bastogne. When offered surrender terms by the Germans, McAuliffe replied "Nuts!" The surrounded soldiers resisted capture until Allied assistance came from Patton's Third Army on December 26. Of McAuliffe's troops, 482 died and 2,449 were wounded.[1023]

Prior to December 22, overcast weather prevented Allied planes from confronting the German forces. The weather then cleared for the next five days, during which the fuel-thirsty Germans suffered from repeated Allied air attacks and needed supplies were delivered to friendly Allied troops.[1024]

[1018] *WW II Story*, 345-47, 358, *Guns*, 423-24, *Generals' War*, 367, *Reich*, 1095-96.

[1019] *Masters*, 534, *Bulge*, 170.

[1020] *Supreme Commander*, 555, *Soldier's Story*, 459.

[1021] *Masters*, 534, *Soldier's Story*, 476-78, *Guns*, 448, *Generals' War*, 349-351, *Bulge*, 334, 423-24, *Supreme Commander*, 556, 563-64.

[1022] *Soldier's Story*, 472-73, *Generals' War*, 356-57, *Bulge*, 486-88.

[1023] *Guns*, 455-56, 467, *Soldier's Story*, 482, *Generals' War*, 357, *WW II Story*, 349, *Reich*, 1093, *Bulge*, 468, 481.

[1024] *Inferno*, 574, *Guns*, 470, *Reich*, 1093, *Air Masters*, 372, *Bulge*, 468-70, 649.

By the last week in December, the German thrust, or bulge, had moved sixty miles deep into Allied territory but was running out of steam.[1025]

U.S. battle casualties in Europe went from 1,000 per day in October 1944, to 2,000 in November, and 3,000 in December. Of these losses, eighty-three percent were in the infantry.[1026]

Although the Germans had some 105 divisions battling the Western Allies in late 1944, they still had 149 divisions facing the Red Army. Eisenhower was troubled by the Red Army's failure in December to attack the enemy, which would have relieved German pressure in the Bulge. For almost a month, Stalin simply watched instead of providing help.[1027]

On December 28, Eisenhower met with Montgomery to discuss ways to counter the German thrust. Eisenhower believed he had received Montgomery's commitment to attack the German bulge forces from the north starting on January 1, 1945. Montgomery spent time during the meeting arguing again that he should have operational command. In essence, Montgomery sought to replace Eisenhower as supreme commander of all Allied ground forces.[1028]

On December 29, Montgomery cavalierly wrote to Eisenhower saying that, "One commander must have powers to direct and control the operation; you cannot possibly do it yourself, and so you would have to nominate someone." Montgomery added that without "one man directing and controlling ... we will fail again," and enclosed a proposed order for Eisenhower to sign designating Montgomery as the commander.[1029]

On December 30, Montgomery's chief of staff informed a furious Eisenhower that Montgomery would not attack the Germans from the north until at least January 3. After Montgomery breached his perceived promise to counterattack on January 1, 1945, leaving Patton's Third Army exposed, Eisenhower threatened to fire Montgomery and replace him with General Alexander. Upon being informed by his aide that he was about to be fired, Montgomery quickly apologized and kept his job, but his relationship with Eisenhower was further wea-

---

[1025] *Guns*, 468, *Inferno*, 574, *Bulge*, 672-73, *Supreme Commander*, 571.

[1026] *Guns*, 408-09.

[1027] *Masters*, 535, *Generals' War*, 339, 363, 372, *Supreme Commander*, 572, 600.

[1028] *Guns*, 470-71, *Generals' War*, 364, *Bulge*, 612, *Montgomery*, 265, *Supreme Commander*, 572.

[1029] *Guns*, 471, *Generals' War*, 364, *Montgomery*, 266.

kened. Eisenhower later said of Montgomery, "He's just a little man. He's just as little on the inside as he is outside."[1030]

THE FINAL YEAR OF COMBAT IN EUROPE (1945)

The Battle of the Bulge Continues

On New Year's Day, the German air force attacked Allied air bases in Holland, Belgium and northern France, destroying or damaging more than 450 planes, the majority of which were still on the ground. The Germans, however, paid a severe price for their aggression — they sacrificed over 400 planes and 237 pilots.[1031]

Also on January 1, German troops attacked in an effort to retake the Alsatian capital city of Strasbourg which, because of its French history, de Gaulle considered to be "sacred ground." American General Devers commanded the Allied forces there, including French soldiers under General De Lattre.[1032]

Eisenhower proposed to have the Allies withdraw from Strasbourg to a more defensible line. When de Gaulle learned of this, he ordered General De Lattre on January 2 to remain in Strasbourg regardless of Allied orders. The next day, de Gaulle told Eisenhower that withdrawing from Strasbourg could bring down the French government, and threatened to deny the Allies access to French railroads and communications if there were a withdrawal. With Churchill's approval, Eisenhower reluctantly cancelled his order to withdraw from Strasbourg.[1033]

On January 3, 1945, Montgomery finally ordered the U.S. First Army to counterattack the German bulge from the north.[1034]

In a January 7 press conference, Montgomery took substantial personal credit for blunting the German advance, giving little recognition to the American troops who had been temporarily assigned to him. Bradley and other Americans were incensed by Montgomery's conduct and countered his misleading tale.[1035]

Faced with fierce Allied resistance, on January 8, 1945, Hitler authorized a withdrawal from the westernmost portion of the Bulge. On

---

[1030] *Guns*, 471-73, *Ultra Secret*, 177, *Generals' War*, 365-67, *Montgomery*, 267, *Supreme Commander*, 573-75.

[1031] *Air Masters*, 373-74.

[1032] *Guns*, 475-78, *Generals' War*, 368, *Supreme Commander*, 576-78.

[1033] *Guns*, 474-81, *Generals' War*, 368, *Supreme Commander*, 578-79.

[1034] *Masters*, 535, *Generals' War*, 370-71, *Supreme Commander*, 576.

[1035] *Guns*, 482-84, *Generals' War*, 373-75, *Montgomery*, 264, *Supreme Commander*, 579-80.

January 16, Patton's troops from the south met up with First Army forces from the north and the Bulge was closed. By January 28, the last German troops were cleared from the Bulge.[1036]

On January 17, the U.S. First Army reverted from Montgomery's command to General Bradley.[1037]

Because there was a shortage of white infantrymen during the Battle of the Bulge, African-Americans were allowed to serve in formerly all-white units. By February, approximately 4,500 black Americans had signed up for combat duty.[1038]

Some 600,000 American GIs fought in the Battle of the Bulge. Of those, more than 60,000 were wounded, 19,246 died, and more than 23,000 were taken prisoner.[1039]

The British, who played a smaller role, suffered 1,400 casualties in the battle.[1040]

German casualties in the Battle of the Bulge were estimated at 100,000 or more, including 36,000 who became POWs. In addition, the Germans lost almost all of the tanks and aircraft they had dedicated to the counterattack.[1041]

In January 1945, as the Battle of the Bulge drew to a close, President Roosevelt celebrated his 63rd birthday. He suffered from severe high blood pressure, congestive heart failure and anemia, and had experienced a mild heart attack in August 1944.[1042]

The Soviets Advance Toward Germany

As 1945 began, the Soviets had some 6,000,000 soldiers and 10,000 tanks deployed against Germany on a front running from the Baltic Sea to the Adriatic.[1043]

On January 12, the Soviets began their long anticipated winter offensive against Axis forces on the Eastern Front.[1044]

By January 17, 1945, the center portion of the Red Army's offensive had reached Warsaw, Poland.[1045]

[1036] *Guns*, 486, *Masters*, 535, *Generals' War*, 378, *Reich*, 1095.

[1037] *Soldier's Story*, 492, *Guns*, 586.

[1038] *WW II Story*, 504, *Supreme Commander*, 560.

[1039] *Guns*. 488, *Masters*, 535, *Generals' War*, 379, *WW II Story*, 358, *Air Masters*, 375.

[1040] *Masters*, 535.

[1041] *Inferno*, 574, *Masters*, 535, *Soldier's Story*, 492, *Reich*, 1095.

[1042] *Guns*, 497-98.

[1043] *Inferno*, 586, *WW II Story*, 490, *Air Masters*, 409.

[1044] *Generals' War*, 377, *Reich*, 1097, *Air Masters*, 378.

[1045] *Soldier's Story*, 493, *Bloodlands*, 313, *Reich*, 1097.

Hungary, a nation of 9,000,000 citizens, had sided with the Germans. In December 1944, when the Red Army advanced on Budapest, Hitler refused to permit his troops there to withdraw. Between December 30 and the end of February, the Soviets fought Germans and Hungarians until the Red Army prevailed. Throughout, Germans continued to kill Jews — 105,453 Jews died or disappeared from Budapest between October and February. After Budapest fell, Russian troops raped and pillaged, conduct Stalin said was their reward for their sacrifices. As a result of these abuses, in February 1945, the Hungarian ban on abortions was lifted.[1046]

The battle for Budapest cost the Soviets 38,000 dead and 250,000 wounded. Thirty-eight thousand civilians were killed. The German/Hungarian forces lost 40,000 dead and 63,000 captured.[1047]

The Red Army reached the German border on February 8, 1945, having advanced 275 miles in less than thirty days.[1048]

The Yalta Conference

In January 1945, just before conferring with the other Allies at Yalta, Soviet Premier Stalin offered his perspective on the west. The great depression had divided capitalist nations into two factions — one Fascist and the other democratic. The Soviet Union had entered into an alliance with the democratic side in order to stop Hitler's Fascist aggression, but in the future Stalin would oppose the democratic capitalists, too.[1049]

In early February 1945, prior to meeting with Stalin in Yalta, Roosevelt and Churchill gathered on the Mediterranean island of Malta to discuss strategies for ending the global conflict. This was the most heated British/American conference of the war. The British still favored a single Allied thrust, commanded by Montgomery, against German troops north of the Ruhr valley. Eisenhower and the Americans argued for a duel thrust aimed at enveloping the industrial Ruhr, with General Bradley commanding the southern forces. Ike believed that under his plan most of the remaining German forces would be destroyed west of the Rhine, leading to less resistance in Germany and an earlier Allied victory.[1050]

[1046] *Inferno*, 577-84, *Soldier's Story*, 493, *Iron Curtain*, 31.
[1047] *Inferno*, 584.
[1048] *Monuments Men*, 239, *WW II Story*, 491, *Reich*, 1097.
[1049] *Curse*, 96.
[1050] *Guns*, 223, 495-501, *Soldier's Story*, 513, *Supreme Commander*, 580-85, 605, 609.

At Malta, with the Battle of the Bulge fresh in their minds, the British, through Field Marshal Brooke (Churchill's prime military advisor), criticized Eisenhower and his approach to defeating the Germans. Brooke had misgivings about Ike's plan for a dual-pronged attack on Germany, and questioned whether Ike was too busy, not strong enough for the job, and too influenced by the last person who had spoken to him. Brooke also sought to enhance Montgomery's day-to-day battle command role. Making it clear that he resented the criticism of Ike, on February 1, 1945, General Marshall (Roosevelt's chief military advisor) bluntly told Brooke that Montgomery was an "over-cautious commander who wants everything" and was an "impudent and disloyal subordinate" who treated American officers with "open contempt." After the debate, both the American two-pronged battle plan and Eisenhower's role as supreme commander continued in effect.[1051]

Argonaut, the Yalta meeting among Churchill, Stalin and Roosevelt (and their staffs), which began on February 4 and ended six days later, addressed both military plans to end the war and post-victory political arrangements. Roosevelt and Churchill had agreed to exclude de Gaulle from the Yalta meeting. Churchill said, "I cannot think of anything more unpleasant and impossible than having this menacing and hostile man in our midst." Nonetheless, Roosevelt, who neither trusted nor liked de Gaulle, favored giving France a postwar occupation zone in Germany despite its modest contribution to victory.[1052]

Roosevelt's health and appearance were quite poor at the Yalta conference.[1053]

Before the Yalta conference began, the Soviet intelligence services set up secret listening devices in all of the facilities. One of their objectives was to develop psychological profiles of the main participants.[1054]

The Soviets reported at Yalta that their army had advanced 300 miles west against the Germans in three weeks at a cost of 400,000 Soviet casualties — roughly four times the Allied losses in the Battle of the Bulge.[1055]

Stalin's negotiating strength at Yalta derived largely from (a) the Soviet Union having killed far more German soldiers than all other

---

[1051] *Guns*, 502-03, *Masters*, 540-545, *Generals' War*, 383, *Supreme Commander*, 586.

[1052] *Guns*, 510-11, 518, *Masters*, 548, *Generals' War*, 131, 387, *Paris*, 206, 313.

[1053] *Masters*, 549, *Guns*, 507, *Generals War*, 383, *Curse*, 95.

[1054] *Curse*, 97.

[1055] *Guns*, 512-13.

Allied nations combined, (b) the loss of some 26,000,000 Soviet lives, (c) Roosevelt's poor health, and (d) the fact that the Red Army was already occupying land in Poland and Eastern Europe.[1056]

Churchill told the House of Commons that Soviet forces did "the main work of tearing the guts out of the German army."[1057]

At Yalta, Stalin, citing the staggering Soviet war losses, insisted on controlling Eastern European countries, including Poland, purportedly as protection against future German invasions of the Soviet Union. In addition, he wanted Poland's borders to be reconfigured. While displeased with the stance, Britain and the United States did not feel that they had the power to resist Stalin's argument. In response to Churchill's interest in democracy, the Soviets disingenuously promised that there would be "free elections" in Poland within a month.[1058]

During Yalta, the participants also confirmed the Allies' unconditional surrender policy toward Germany and Japan, and mapped out zones of control in a defeated Germany for the United States, Britain, France and the Soviet Union. Stalin agreed to declare war on Japan three months after Germany's surrender in exchange for regaining control over territory lost to the Japanese during the 1904-05 Russo-Japanese war.[1059]

Churchill and Roosevelt believed that Stalin was acting in good faith at Yalta, but within a few months came to recognize that the Soviet leader would not honor his promises.[1060]

Charles Bohlen, a World War II advisor to Roosevelt on the Soviet Union, observed that the President did not understand that Stalin's mistrust of and enmity toward the United States were "based on profound ideological convictions."[1061]

The Yalta parties also laid the groundwork for establishing the United Nations, a Roosevelt pet project.[1062]

Upon learning shortly after Yalta that the parties had agreed to Communist control of his native land, Polish General Anders, whose troops were then fighting the Germans in Italy, asked what incentive there was for him and his men to continue. In the hope that the Yalta terms might be altered, he agreed to continue to fight. The irony was

---

[1056] *Guns*, 523, *Masters*, 559, *Curse*, 95-97.

[1057] *Guns*, 195.

[1058] *Guns*, 516-17, *Inferno*, 576, 590, *Bloodlands*, 313-15.

[1059] *Masters*, 550, 558, *Curse*, 98-102, *Guns*, 517, *WW II Story*, 492.

[1060] *Guns*, 521-22, *Masters*, 557, *Curse*, 110-112.

[1061] *Curse*, 71.

[1062] *Curse*, 100, *Guns*, 518.

that Britain and France had gone to war to protect Poland from Germany, only to see it taken over by the Soviet Union.[1063]

The Closing Days of War in Europe

Early in 1945, some high-level members of the German military tried unsuccessfully to negotiate a separate peace with the Western Allies. Stalin learned of these efforts and accused the United States and Britain of negotiating behind his back. Roosevelt assured Stalin that there would be no separate peace or end to the war short of unconditional surrender.[1064]

In January 1945, German officials concluded that Allied bombing in 1944 had resulted in Germany making thirty-six percent fewer tanks, thirty-one percent fewer military planes, and forty-two percent fewer trucks.[1065]

Throughout early 1945, Allied bombers continued to attack the German rail and water transportation systems. Coupled with the damage being done to Hitler's oil supplies, Germany's industry was buckling at the knees, its troops were being denied essential supplies, and many of its planes and tanks were stilled for lack of fuel.[1066]

On February 3, over 900 American B-17s and about 450 fighters bombed the center of Berlin in a strategic attack intended to demoralize German civilians and hopefully speed the war's end. German flak destroyed twenty-five B-17s, while bombs killed thousands of Berliners and rendered another 120,000 homeless. This was just one of 363 times the Allies bombed Berlin during World War II.[1067]

On January 20, Eisenhower outlined his three-pronged Rhineland campaign plan: (a) advance from the German border to the Rhine and destroy all enemy forces fighting west of the Rhine, (b) cross the Rhine in a broad front and (c) destroy German forces remaining east of the Rhine and drive toward Berlin.[1068]

On February 8, General Montgomery's forces in the north began their advance toward the Rhine River. Facing stubborn German resistance, they reached the Rhine on March 2 after killing 6,000 Germans and taking another 30,000 as prisoners.[1069]

[1063] *Guns*, 517, *Inferno*, 576, *Clark*, 240.

[1064] *Curse*, 110-111, *Clark*, 241, *Supreme Commander*, 627.

[1065] *Air Masters*, 467.

[1066] *Air Masters*, 375-76, 460-61,469, *Supreme Commander*, 615-16.

[1067] *Air Masters*, 420-26, *Guns*, 534.

[1068] *Supreme Commander*, 609-12.

[1069] *Guns*, 542, *Generals' War*, 385-86, *Supreme Commander*, 613-14.

A CONCISE HISTORY OF THE SECOND WORLD WAR

Farther south, on February 9, the Germans opened the floodgates on a 170 foot high Roer River dam, swamping the valley below and blocking the advance of American Ninth Army troops there for two weeks.[1070]

In mid-February, de Gaulle informed Eisenhower he wanted to withdraw three French divisions from the Allied line, apparently to quell Communist opposition in the heart of France. After reluctantly allowing two divisions to withdraw, Eisenhower said of the French, "I must say that next to the weather I think they have caused me more trouble in this war than any other single factor."[1071]

On February 13, more than 800 British bombers struck the largely undefended, but militarily important, city of Dresden with explosive and incendiary bombs, killing at least 35,000 people and immolating the city. The next day, 311 American B-17s again bombed Dresden, Germany's seventh largest city. The day after that, over 200 American B-17s struck the Dresden suburbs.[1072]

During February 22-23, more than 3,500 Allied bombers and almost 5,000 companion fighters bombed and gunned rail yards, train stations, bridges, cars, barges and other targets in towns across Germany.[1073]

Some within the military and others at home in the United States characterized the Berlin and Dresden raids as terror bombing aimed at killing civilians rather than destroying military targets. In response, General Spaatz on March 1 issued a new directive asserting strongly that only military objectives were to be targeted.[1074]

General Hodges' American First Army forces crossed the Rhine River in strength on March 7, 1945 at the surprisingly still intact bridge at Remagen, just fifteen miles south of Bonn. Upon learning of this crossing, a furious Hitler directed General Kesselring to replace von Rundstedt as theater commander.[1075]

On March 19, Hitler issued an order that all military, industrial, transportation and communications facilities in Germany were to be demolished so as not to fall into enemy hands. Implementation of this astonishing directive, which would have destroyed the German econ-

---

[1070] *Guns*, 536-38, 542, *Generals' War*, 387, *Supreme Commander*, 613.

[1071] *Supreme Commander*, 614-15.

[1072] *Air Masters*, 427-41.

[1073] *Air Masters*, 442.

[1074] *Air Masters*, 445.

[1075] *Curse*, 108, *Inferno*, 589, *Soldier's Story*, 510-11, *WW II Story*, 495-98, *Reich*, 1101, *Guns*, 542, 546-51, *Supreme Commander*, 618-19.

omy, was thwarted by several high ranking German army officers.[1076]

At the southern side of the Allied front, Patton's troops crossed the Rhine at Oppenheim (near Frankfurt) on March 22, about a day before Montgomery's British, Canadian and American troops crossed further north at Wesel, above the Ruhr valley.[1077]

As the Western Allies moved deeper into Germany they burned 4,000,000 gallons of gas each day.[1078]

General Patton's son-in-law, Colonel Waters, who had been captured by the Germans in Africa in 1943, was being held in a German POW camp. In March 1945, Patton sent a rescue mission into German-controlled territory in an attempt to rescue Waters. After liberating Waters, the American task force was overtaken by German troops. Fifty-seven Americans were killed, wounded or missing, and all others were captured. Waters, too, was wounded. Patton evaded accepting responsibility for the unsuccessful mission and, with the war's victory so close, his commanders elected not to reprimand him.[1079]

On March 28, 1945, Eisenhower took General Simpson's U. S. Ninth Army back from Montgomery and placed it again under General Bradley's command. Concerned that Montgomery's remaining British forces would not have enough strength to carry out offensive action, an angry Churchill protested unsuccessfully to Eisenhower, the Joint Chiefs of Staff and Roosevelt.[1080]

By early April, the Western Allies had encircled the Rhine-Ruhr region and captured some 320,000 German troops whose commander, Field Marshal Model, then committed suicide.[1081]

The main Allied thrust, commanded by Bradley, then moved across the middle of Germany toward a meeting with the Soviets at the Elbe River.[1082]

Early in April, a German factory test pilot flew one of the new Messerschmitt jets to Frankfort and turned it over to the Americans. The fast-flying jets had, through the end of March, downed sixty-three

---

[1076] *Reich*, 1102-04.

[1077] *Inferno*, 589, *Generals' War*, 394, *Guns*, 542, 557-58, 570, *Reich*, 1101.

[1078] *Guns*, 568.

[1079] *Guns*, 568-576, *Soldier's Story*, 541-43, *Generals' War*, 395.

[1080] *WWII History*, 37, *Soldier's Story*, 492, *Generals' War*, 400-02, *Supreme Commander*, 629, 636-40.

[1081] *Curse*, 108, *Inferno*, 589, *Generals' War*, 396, *Reich*, 1105, *WW II Story*, 500, *Supreme Commander*, 650.

[1082] *Supreme Commander*, 640-41, 644.

B-17s.[1083]

On April 17, some 600 B-17s struck Dresden once more, obliterating its rail yards and cutting the last north-south rail line in Germany.[1084]

In early April, 1945, 1,500,000 Western Allied troops in Italy, commanded by General Mark Clark, renewed their attacks against the German Gothic line. On April 23, the Fifth Army broke through the Gothic Line near Bologna. Genoa fell on April 27. The next day the German commander sought to negotiate a local surrender of almost 1,000,000 Axis troops.[1085]

During the month of April 1945, 10,677 U.S. soldiers were killed in action in Europe.[1086]

In April, United States troops found in a German mine 250 tons of gold valued at $500,000,000. The mine was in a part of eastern Germany that the Soviet Union would control after the war, and thus the gold and other loot were quickly removed to territory the United States would govern.[1087]

To Montgomery's considerable anger, he was assigned by Eisenhower to move his forces into northern Germany to protect Denmark from a possible Soviet occupation. On May 2, his troops reached Lübeck on the Baltic and achieved their objective just two hours ahead of the Red Army.[1088]

Sex With German Women

After crossing into Germany, Western Allied soldiers had sex with German women, some consensual, some not. Venereal disease rates soared as desperate German females traded their bodies for goods.[1089]

U.S. soldiers were warned against fraternizing (copulating) with German women. Eager GIs argued that copulation without conversation was not fraternization. The practical General Patton advised his Third Army soldiers that "so long as they keep their helmets on [,] they are not fraternizing."[1090]

[1083] *Generals' War*, 382, *Air Masters*, 448-49.

[1084] *Air Masters*, 437.

[1085] *Battle*, 580-81, *WW II Story*, 509-13, *Clark*, 227-36, 243-45, *Guns*, 616.

[1086] *Guns*, 596.

[1087] *Guns*, 587-88, *Generals' War*, 404.

[1088] *Inferno*, 589, 592, *Guns*, 617, *Supreme Commander*, 652-53.

[1089] *Inferno*, 584-85.

[1090] *Guns*, 545.

The Taking of Berlin

After Eisenhower wrote directly to Stalin in late March to say that his Western Allied troops would halt their advance at the Elbe River, an angry Churchill objected and pressed Eisenhower to send his forces further east to Berlin before the Red Army got there.[1091]

Because the Allies had already agreed at Yalta that the Soviet Union would control eastern Germany once the war ended, Eisenhower believed it made little sense for the Americans and British to cross the Elbe River and race to Berlin knowing they would suffer casualties in the process and still have to turn over captured territory to the Soviets. Moreover, advancing to Berlin could generate friction with Stalin.[1092]

General Omar Bradley estimated that once Allied forces had reached the Elbe River, moving the last 60 miles across Germany to capture what was left of the repeatedly-bombed Berlin before the Soviets did so would have cost as many as 100,000 U.S. casualties. The Red Army was then thirty miles from Berlin with 1,250,000 men. Thus, Eisenhower elected not to try to beat the Soviets to Berlin and the Joint Chiefs of Staff supported his decision.[1093]

To Stalin, having the Red Army conquer Berlin was an important means of redressing the devastation Germany had wreaked on the Soviet Union. He also wanted to deny Berlin to Britain and the United States, and acquire the Nazi's nuclear weapons scientists and research materials at the Kaiser Wilhelm Institute for Physics in Dahlem, near Berlin.[1094]

Between April 16 and May 8, 1945, the Red Army lost 78,291 dead and 274,184 other casualties in the final efforts to defeat Germany. They had previously lost 32,846 dead and suffered 106,969 other casualties in taking Vienna, a battle that ended on April 15.[1095]

In April, Eisenhower diverted two of his armies in Germany south toward Austria in order to block the Nazis from trying to establish a final war redoubt there.[1096]

[1091] *Curse*, 108-11, *Generals' War*, 399-400, *Montgomery*, 270, *Supreme Commander*, 627-29, 632-.

[1092] *Masters*, 561, 568-69, *Inferno*, 589-90.

[1093] *Guns*, 578-79, *Monuments Men*, 308, *Soldier's Story*, 535, *Curse*, 108, *Generals' War*, 399, *Supreme Commander*, 629-36.

[1094] *Curse*, 115, *Inferno*, 590.

[1095] *Curse*, 116, *Guns*, 609, *Inferno*, 600.

[1096] *Inferno*, 590, *Reich*, 1105-06, *Montgomery*, 270, *Supreme Commander*, 651.

The Concentration Camps

On April 12, 1945, the U.S. Third Army, commanded by Patton, discovered and liberated the Ohrdruf-Nord slave labor camp, which was a sub-camp of Buchenwald. Before abandoning the camp a day earlier, SS guards murdered over 4,000 prisoners there.[1097]

When Patton, known as "Old Blood and Guts," first saw the conditions and prisoners at the Ohrdruf Nazi work camp — dead bodies, skeletal survivors, gallows and whipping blocks — he ducked behind a building and threw up.[1098]

On April 13, Eisenhower ordered each Allied unit near Ohrdruf to visit the concentration camp so that the soldiers would know what they were fighting against. He also arranged for members of Congress and members of the British Parliament to visit the camps to witness the horrid conditions.[1099]

When the British army arrived at the Bergen-Belsen concentration camp near Hamburg, Germany on April 15, 1945, they discovered 10,000 corpses and over 40,000 starving prisoners reduced to eating the dead. Of those liberated from the camp, 13,000 soon died of their injuries — at a rate of 1,000 per day.[1100]

At the Buchenwald concentration camp and its sub-camps, which held over 100,000 captives in March, the Germans had murdered at least 56,000 of the prisoners.[1101]

The Americans came to the concentration camp at Dachau, near Munich, in late April 1945. They found 2,310 corpses and thousands of starving inmates. At least twenty-eight German SS troopers who had surrendered were gunned down by Allied soldiers at Dachau. No prosecution followed, a decision America justified on the grounds of battle stress and the horrors found at Dachau.[1102]

Records from the Auschwitz-Birkenau concentration camp reveal the following about people sent to the camp: of 1,100,000 Jews, 100,000 survived; of 140,000 non-Jewish Poles, half survived; of 23,000 gypsies, 2,000 survived; and all 15,000 Soviet POWs died.[1103]

Of the 714,211 prisoners in concentration camps in January 1945,

---

[1097] *Ike*, 574, *Monuments Men*, 309, *Guns*, 602.

[1098] *Ike*, 574, *Monument Men*, 295-96, *Soldier's Story*, 539, *WW II Story*, 521.

[1099] *WW II Story*, 521, *Supreme Commander*, 659.

[1100] *Guns*, 601-02.

[1101] *Guns*, 603.

[1102] *Guns*, 612-13, *WW II Story*, 516-17.

[1103] *Inferno*, 486.

almost half were dead by May.[1104]

Prisoners of War

By 1945, the Germans held 95,000 American prisoners of war, more than one-third of whom were fighter pilots and bomber crew-members.[1105]

In January of that year, as the Red Army approached Germany from the east, Hitler ordered that Allied POWs in camps east of Berlin be moved west, often in forced long winter marches. He intended to use those POWs as hostages in an effort to negotiate a suitable truce with the Western Allies.[1106]

As Eisenhower's troops advanced through Germany in 1945 they liberated tens of thousands of sick, hungry and exhausted POWs.[1107]

Roosevelt and Truman

On April 12, 1945, a withered President Roosevelt suffered a massive cerebral hemorrhage and died in Warm Springs, Georgia.[1108]

During his presidency, Roosevelt had chosen not to inform Vice President Truman about the substance of his meetings with Churchill and Stalin, and did not inform him about U.S. efforts to develop an atomic bomb.[1109]

After being sworn in as president, Truman wisely elected to retain Roosevelt's entire cabinet.[1110]

On April 25, 1945, President Truman received from War Secretary Stimson a report explaining that within a few months the United States would complete work on an atomic bomb.[1111]

Because more than 200 Americans spied for the Soviets during World War II, by 1945 Soviet intelligence had been aware for several years of U.S. efforts to develop an atomic bomb.[1112]

On April 26, Heinrich Himmler, who headed the SS, tried through an agent to arrange a German surrender to the Western Allies. President Truman responded saying that the only acceptable terms

---

[1104] *Inferno*, 600.
[1105] *Air Masters*, 493.
[1106] *Air Masters*, 493, 500-02.
[1107] *Air Masters*, 504-06.
[1108] *Masters*, 566, *Curse*, 112, *1944*, 526-27.
[1109] *Curse*, 137-38.
[1110] *Curse*, 138.
[1111] *Curse*, 141.
[1112] *Curse*, 142-43.

were the unconditional surrender of all German forces to the United States, Britain and the Soviet Union.[1113]

Berlin Falls

On April 25, 1945, units of the Red Army met units of the U.S. Army along the Elbe River in Germany. This was the same day that the Red Army completely encircled Berlin. Thereafter, Soviet/German fighting continued in Berlin, city block by city block.[1114]

On April 30, 1945, the Red Army surrounded the Reichstag in Berlin, the last symbol of German power. German soldiers within surrendered the next day.[1115]

Mussolini's Death

On April 28, 1945, while trying to escape to Switzerland, Mussolini was captured by Italian partisans near Lake Como, Italy and shot dead. His mangled body was then hanged upside down at a gas station.[1116]

Hitler's Death

Hitler, at the age of 56, committed suicide on April 30 by shooting himself in his Berlin bunker. German supporters then burned the body along with that of his newly-wed wife, Eva Braun, who had just committed suicide by taking poison.[1117]

On May 1, Joseph Goebbels, Hitler's loyal propaganda minister, poisoned his six young children and then, at his request, he and his wife were shot by an SS official.[1118]

Hitler's will directed that Grand Admiral Karl Dönitz succeed him as head of the German state.[1119]

A week before his death on April 30, Hitler ordered the SS to arrest for high treason Hermann Göring, who was then Reich Marshal and second in command of Germany. Hitler was upset because on April 23, Göring had notified Hitler that he was prepared to take command of the German government if Hitler lost his freedom to act.

[1113] *Supreme Commander*, 660.

[1114] *Curse*, 116, *Inferno*, 602, *Reich*, 1106, *Supreme Commander*, 653.

[1115] *Curse*, 116, *Inferno*, 604.

[1116] *Fateful Choices*, 131, *Inferno*, 604, *Battle*, 585, *WW II Story*, 513, *Reich*, 1131.

[1117] *Guns*, 614, *Masters*, 569, *Curse*, 116, *Inferno*, 604, *WW II Story*, 525-26, *Reich*, 1111, 1123, 1133-34.

[1118] *WW II Story*, 526, *Reich*, 1133.

[1119] *Guns*, 621, *Inferno*, 609, *Reich*, 1129, 1134.

Göring nonetheless survived the war.[1120]

Several days before his suicide, Hitler concluded that Himmler had also betrayed him by secretly seeking to negotiate an armistice with the British. Himmler was promptly expelled from his government position and the Nazi party.[1121]

Germany Surrenders

The end of the war for Germany came in a variety of steps. On April 29, German General Wolff unilaterally negotiated the unconditional surrender of his massive army in Italy, effective May 2.[1122]

During the next several days, a number of German generals sought to surrender their forces to just the Western Allies. This was done out of fear of retribution from the Red Army and in an effort to force a wedge between the Western Allies and the Soviets. Intent on avoiding such a conflict, Eisenhower refused to accept the surrender of any German forces facing the Red Army.[1123]

On May 4, 1945, German forces in the Netherlands, north Germany, and Denmark surrendered to the British.[1124]

On May 5, Kesselring's army group north of the Alps put down their arms.[1125]

Early on May 7, with Admiral Dönitz's approval, Germany unconditionally surrendered in Reims, France, 335 days after D-Day. Eisenhower announced: "The mission of this Allied force was fulfilled at 0241 local time, May 7, 1945."[1126]

For years Hitler had insisted that the German army in World War I was never actually defeated because Germany had signed the armistice on French soil, not after being driven back to its homeland. To avoid a repetition of this argument, the Soviets insisted that Germany surrender on German soil. On May 8, 1945, Germany again surrendered in Karlshorst, near Berlin.[1127]

Had Germany not surrendered when it did, the United States was

---

[1120] *Monuments Men*, 324, 345, *Ultra Secret*, 186, *Reich*, 1116.

[1121] *Reich*, 1126.

[1122] *Inferno*, 609, *Reich*, 1138, *Crusade*, 424, *Guns*, 616.

[1123] *Supreme Commander*, 660-63.

[1124] *Master*, 570, *Inferno*, 609, *Reich*, 1138, *Crusade*, 425, *Montgomery*, 272-73, *Supreme Commander*, 661.

[1125] *Reich*, 1138, *Supreme Commander*, 662.

[1126] *Guns*, 625, *Soldier's Story*, 553-54, *Curse*, 117, *Inferno*, 609, *Reich*, 1138-39, *Supreme Commander*, 663, 668.

[1127] *Guns*, 629, *Curse*, 117, *Inferno*, 609, *Air Masters*, 506-07, *Reich*, 1139.

planning to drop an atomic bomb in order to end the war in Europe.[1128]

Events Following the German Surrender

On May 23, after being captured by the British, Heinrich Himmler poisoned himself.[1129]

Defeated Germany was promptly divided into separate zones of occupation under military control. On June 5, 1945, the United States, Great Britain, the Soviet Union and France issued a declaration assuming supreme governmental authority over four sections of Germany, each to be controlled by one of the victors. The Soviet Union controlled lands in eastern Germany. France monitored sections in southwest Germany near the Rhine River. Britain controlled parts near Holland and south of Vienna. The remainder fell to the United States, including the cities of Munich, Stuttgart, Frankfurt and Bremen. The City of Berlin was placed under joint control of all four.[1130]

As soon as the fighting in Europe ended, plans had to be made for the prompt transfer of millions of American troops and their equipment to the Pacific in the effort to defeat the still-fighting Japanese. Meanwhile, sufficient Allied forces had to be stationed in Germany to assure that peace there was maintained.[1131]

On July 14, 1945, the Supreme Headquarters Allied Expeditionary Forces ("SHAEF"), which General Eisenhower headed, was phased out of existence.[1132]

The Potsdam Conference

Stalin, Churchill and recently sworn-in President Truman gathered to discuss World War II issues at a conference in Potsdam, Germany from July 17 to August 2, 1945. This was the first time Stalin and Truman had met.[1133]

On July 26, 1945, following surprising election results in Britain, Clement Atlee replaced Winston Churchill as Prime Minister. Shortly thereafter, Atlee took Churchill's place in the Potsdam discussions.[1134]

President Truman announced at Potsdam that the United States

[1128] *Air Masters*, 454.

[1129] *Reich*, 1141.

[1130] *Crusade*, 431, 433, Curse, 289.

[1131] *Crusade*, 428-29.

[1132] *Crusade*, 435.

[1133] *Curse*, 157.

[1134] *Curse*, 157, *Iron Curtain*, 105.

sought no reparations from Germany. This was consistent with the position Roosevelt and Churchill had taken at Yalta. But at Yalta, Stalin claimed that his country was due $10 billion in reparations from Germany over a ten year period.[1135]

In addition to matters pertaining to the war with Japan (addressed in Part 3 below), the leaders at Potsdam discussed where the border between Germany and Poland should be drawn. Thousands of Poles had recently moved into what was previously eastern Germany and had forced out many ethnic Germans. Stalin wanted Poland to include a considerable portion of eastern Germany's land and, after some heated discussion, his position prevailed.[1136]

Post D-Day Casualties

Between D-Day and the war's end, the Western Allied forces in Europe suffered more than 750,000 casualties, including some 165,000 dead. Western Allied naval casualties totaled 10,000, with half of those killed. Air casualties were 62,000, again with half killed.[1137]

American dead and wounded in the European theater of war after D-Day amounted to almost 400,000, including 8,230 on the first day, June 6, 1944.[1138]

[1135] *Curse*, 290, *Iron Curtain*, 34-35, *Guns*, 515-16.
[1136] *Curse*, 159-61, *Iron Curtain*, 117.
[1137] *Guns*, 636-37.
[1138] *Guns*, 85.

Part 3

War in the Pacific

BECAUSE this writing divides the war into two theaters of combat and discusses them separately, the reader must now turn the Pacific calendar back some eight years to 1937.

Japan's ambition for additional territory and resources became evident in 1931 when, following a localized military confrontation with China, the island nation asserted control over portions of mainland Manchuria. During the following several years, Japan's aggressive relationship with the Chinese persisted without turning into a declared war. However, in 1937 circumstances changed. Power-thirsty Japan widened its assault on China by attacking major cities and killing hundreds of thousands of Chinese. Western nations sided with the reeling Chinese and imposed severe trade restrictions that pained Japan but did not alter its behavior. All-out war in the Pacific was brewing.

JAPAN STARTS A WAR AGAINST CHINA (1937)

"The China Incident"

Prince Konoye Fumimaro became Japan's Prime Minister in June 1937. In his view there were two basic causes of war: the unfair distribution among nations of (a) land and (b) resources. According to his philosophy, lasting peace would occur only after such imbalances were eliminated, by territorial expansion if necessary. The path to national prosperity that Japan intended to follow in Asia would soon become clear.[1139]

By 1937, Japan had grown frustrated by China's unwillingness to submit to Japanese control. In July, following a minor incident in Peking and fueled by the voices of aggressive citizens at home, Japan invaded mainland China. Army leaders assured the Emperor that "The China Incident," as the Japanese called the conflict, would last no more than three months. Although Chiang Kai-shek's Nationalist Chinese troops resisted Japan's attacks, Peking quickly became the first Chinese

---

[1139] *Fateful Choices*, 97, 106-07, *Conspiracy*, 12, 887.

off
A CONCISE HISTORY OF THE SECOND WORLD WAR   223

city to fall.[1140]

In August, the Japanese attacked Shanghai, one of the world's largest cities, killing almost 250,000 Chinese civilians in the process. After opposing the Japanese army for several months in Shanghai, Chiang Kai-shek and his Kuomintang army retreated up the Yangtze River to Nanking, capital of the Chinese Nationalist government.[1141]

In October, Japan sought without success to persuade the Chinese people to abandon their "continued nationalism," their "anti-Japanese sentiments," and their allegiance to Chiang Kai-shek, and instead accept Japanese control.[1142]

Japanese soldiers continued to chase the Chinese army up the Yangtze and in December 1937 took Nanking. Chiang Kai-shek again refused to surrender and withdrew with his troops to Hankow, 350 miles further up the Yangtze River. Over a six week period, the Japanese brutally murdered 200,000 Nanking civilians and Chinese POWs. Local women and girls were raped at the rate of 1,000 per day. These Japanese atrocities, known as the "Rape of Nanking," generated in western nations considerable hostility against Japan and moral support for China.[1143]

On December 12, 1937, Japanese bombers repeatedly attacked the United States gunboat *Panay* which sank in the Yangtze River near Nanking. The bombers also damaged three American tankers, killed two sailors and wounded more than a dozen others. Seeking to avoid an immediate confrontation with America, Japan quickly apologized and paid reparations.[1144]

Japan Strengthens its Navy

The Japanese plan in any potential conflict with the United States was first to seize the Philippines and Guam. This would force America to send its fleet across the vast Pacific to try to recapture those islands. Japan, fighting closer to home, would then intercept the United States ships where and when it chose, expecting to defeat the Americans in a decisive battle. To prevail in such a fight, Japan recognized that it needed a robust navy with powerful warships, excellent weapons and

---

[1140] *Engineers*, 224, 287, *Fateful Choices*, 4, 91, 97-98, 376, *Eagle*, 43, *Inferno*, 188, *Conspiracy*, 6, *Crucible*, 91.

[1141] *Fateful Choices*, 98, *Conspiracy*, 4, 6, 10.

[1142] *Conspiracy*, 10, 17, 35, 51, 56.

[1143] *Fateful Choices*, 98, 377, *Inferno*, 188, *Conspiracy*, 4, 28, 45, 48, 56-57, *Crucible*, 91.

[1144] *Eagle*, 63, *Conspiracy*, 34-35, *Crucible*, 114.

superior training.[1145]

In 1937, Japan secretly began construction of two immense battleships, the *Yamato* and the *Musashi*, both targeted for completion in 1941.[1146]

Japan was also building what, by the end of the 1930s, would become the world's biggest fleet of large, fast aircraft carriers.[1147]

THE SINO-JAPANESE WAR EXPANDS (1938)

In January 1938, after Nanking fell and Chiang Kai-shek rejected harsh peace terms, Japan severed all diplomatic relations with the Nationalist Chinese government. Prime Minister Konoye announced that Japan intended to "eradicate" Chiang's regime.[1148]

During the following months, Japan's army brutally extended its control over large portions of China.[1149]

In May 1938, reasoning that Japan would continue to dominate China, Hitler gave diplomatic recognition to the puppet government Japan had established in Manchukuo. This was a significant reversal because previously Germany had backed China.[1150]

On October 21, 1938, Japanese troops invaded the main southern Chinese city, Canton. Four days later, Japanese troops took Hankow.[1151]

In late 1938, after Japan explicitly rejected the "Washington Conference" principles that limited warship construction, America signaled its support for Chiang Kai-shek by making the first of many loans to the Nationalist Chinese.[1152]

The Japanese Army had great respect for Germany's military, but considered the United States and Britain to be relatively unthreatening due to their lack of robust armed forces and their unsettled domestic policies. Significantly, the Japanese Army considered any war with Britain or the United States to fall within the responsibility of the Japanese Navy.[1153]

[1145] *Eagle*, 44-47.
[1146] *Eagle*, 47, *Crucible*, 102-104.
[1147] *Sword*, 75, *Engineers*, 314.
[1148] *Fateful Choices*, 99, *Conspiracy*, 17.
[1149] *Fateful Choices*, 99.
[1150] *Fateful Choices*, 100.
[1151] *Conspiracy*, 904.
[1152] *Fateful Choices*, 100, *Pacific*, 4.
[1153] *Eagle*, 38.

At the close of 1938, (a) Japan, with 600,000 troops in China, controlled the five largest cities there; (b) 62,000 Japanese soldiers had been killed since the conflict began; and (c) Chiang Kai-shek had moved his capital again, this time even further up the Yangtze to Chungking in western China. The "China Incident" had turned into a long-running stalemate.[1154]

THE CONFLICTS IN ASIA CONTINUE (1939)

On January 4, 1939, a tired Prime Minister Konoye resigned and was replaced by Baron Hiranuma, an avowed anti-Communist.[1155]

In early 1939, Japan's seizure of several islands off the southern coast of China revealed that Japan intended to extend its influence even farther south. This caused considerable concern among the governments of Britain, France and the Netherlands, as they had colonial possessions in the area. The Dutch responded by cutting back on imports from Japan.[1156]

In April, Hitler urged Japan to align itself militarily with Germany and added that if Hirohito was unable to commit, he would move to strengthen Germany's ties with the Soviet Union. Hirohito was concerned that striking a full military deal with Hitler would further alienate America and western European nations. He eventually offered to enter into a military alliance with Germany, but imposed conditions that Hitler found unacceptable. Thus, no pact was signed and Hitler pursued a nonaggression deal with Stalin.[1157]

Under the existing 1936 Anti-Comintern Pact between Japan and Germany, Hitler was obligated to assist Japan if hostilities arose between Japan and the Communist Soviet Union. To test whether Hitler would honor his obligations, Hirohito decided in May to start a small conflict with the Soviet Union. He sent some troops into Outer Mongolia, a Soviet protectorate. These hostilities on the eastern flanks of the Soviet Union were threatening to Stalin. To gain some security against Japan's threat, on August 23, 1939, the Soviet Union and Germany entered into the notorious nonaggression pact that included plans to dismember Poland. In doing so, Hitler simply ignored the Anti-Comintern pact with Japan. Hirohito fumed at the treachery and

---

[1154] *Fateful Choices*, 99, *Conspiracy*, 896, 904.
[1155] *Conspiracy*, 907.
[1156] *Fateful Choices*, 100, *Conspiracy*, 908.
[1157] *Conspiracy*, 910-11, *Fateful Choices*, 100-01.

concluded that Hitler could not be trusted.[1158]

Tientsin was an open trading port in China in which the British and French had a commercial interest. In June 1939, the Japanese set up a naval blockade around Tientsin, further aggravating relations with those two European nations.[1159]

In July 1939, because of Hirohito's continuing military aggression against China, the United States cancelled its thirty year old trade agreement with Japan. This rupture in relations was significant because the United States provided about one-third of Japan's imports, especially scrap iron and oil.[1160]

In September, as Hitler and Stalin moved against Poland, Japanese and Soviet troops continued to clash in Mongolia. In October, after Japan's army was thrown back with some 17,000 of its soldiers killed, Japan signed a peace treaty on Moscow's terms. This defeat ended arguments in Japan that, in its quest for additional resources, its military should strike north against the Soviet Union rather than south.[1161]

JAPANESE TERRITORIAL EXPANSION (1940)

Like Britain, Japan was an island nation with limited natural resources. But Britain had established an empire of colonies across the globe from which it obtained needed oil, ore and other materials. In the Far East alone, Britain controlled British Malaya, British Borneo, Burma, Australia, New Zealand and India. In contrast, Japan had to depend on world trade for its well-being.[1162]

The war spreading through Europe in 1940 stimulated Japan's appetite for expansion in Asia. Japanese leaders saw an opportunity to strengthen their nation's self-sufficiency through conquests of nearby countries, and in the process weaken the western powers — Britain, America, France and the Netherlands — that had colonies there.[1163]

Influenced by Germany's easy victories against the French, Dutch and others in Europe, Japan prepared plans in mid-1940 for a military occupation of the Dutch East Indies should diplomatic efforts to assure access to that area's resources fail. Japan, led by Emperor Hirohito,

---

[1158] *Conspiracy*, 875, 911-18, *Fateful Choices*, 100-01.
[1159] *Fateful Choices*, 100.
[1160] *Fateful Choices*, 100, *Eagle*, 64.
[1161] *Fateful Choices*, 100, 332, *Inferno*, 189, *Conspiracy*, 913-19, *Bloodlands*, 116-17.
[1162] *Fateful Choices*, 126, *Eagle*, 66.
[1163] *Fateful Choices*, 110, 377, *Eagle*, 62, *WW II Story*, 79, *Conspiracy*, 921-22.

hoped to gain control of the Dutch East Indies without triggering a war with the United States, but recognized that "sooner or later military action against the United States may become inevitable."[1164]

Earlier that year, a Japanese navy study had concluded that attacking the East Indies would lead to a lengthy war with the United States in which the Japanese "chances of winning would be nil." But the navy never shared this conclusion with Japan's political leaders. Ironically, Admiral Yamamoto, who commanded the Japanese fleet and had considerable responsibility for planning the anticipated war, was one of the firmest opponents of attacking the United States.[1165]

Japan's leaders did recognize that in a protracted war with the United States their nation "will be in great trouble," but believed Japan could negotiate a successful resolution following a blitz attack against America.[1166]

The *Zero* Japanese fighter plane entered service in 1940. It was superior to any American plane at the time, but its speed, climbing ability and firepower came at the expense of thin armor and the absence of self-sealing fuel tanks, rendering the *Zero* vulnerable to attack.[1167]

In May 1940, hoping to deter the Japanese from aggression in the East Indies, President Roosevelt ordered the U. S. Navy to base most of its Pacific fleet in Hawaii rather than California.[1168]

In mid-July 1940, Japan made two ominous decisions: to establish stronger links with Germany and Italy, and to expand into southern Asia. The first was expected to strengthen Japan's defensive position *vis-a-vis* Russia and deter the United States from hostilities against Japan. The second would assure supplies from the Dutch East Indies and, by blockading Burma, weaken the Nationalist Chinese by making it harder for American aid to reach Chiang Kai-shek.[1169]

Japan's leaders debated and then rejected the notion of entering into an alliance with the United States. In that case Japan would have to end its war with China and give up its hopes for expansion in Asia.[1170]

In September 1940, following a brief skirmish with French troops, Japan established several military bases in French Indochina (now Viet

---

[1164] *Fateful Choices*, 112-17, *Inferno*, 189-90, *Conspiracy*, 924, 932, 953.

[1165] *Eagle*, 76, *Conspiracy*, 953-60, 1010, *Slept*, 10-11.

[1166] *Fateful Choices*, 121, *Conspiracy*, 958, 1004.

[1167] *Eagle*, 46-47, *Inferno*, 239, 459, *Sword*, 85, *Crucible*, 51-52, 94.

[1168] *Slept*, 37-39, 70.

[1169] *Fateful Choices*, 116, 123, *Conspiracy*, 929-32.

[1170] *Fateful Choices*, 122-25, *Inferno*, 191, *Conspiracy*, 942.

Nam) with permission coerced from the weak Vichy French regime. Japan planned to use these bases for further territorial expansion and to cut off a supply route to Chiang Kai-shek in China.[1171]

On September 27, 1940, Japan, Italy and Germany entered into the Tripartite Pact which committed each signatory to assist the others if attacked by the United States. The Japanese hoped this would deter the United States from interfering with Japan's plan to seize the Dutch East Indies.[1172]

Painfully aware of how European appeasement of Hitler had failed, the United States had no interest in accommodating Japanese expansion or abandoning American support for Nationalist China.[1173]

In response to the Tripartite Pact, the United States imposed a complete embargo, effective October 16, 1940, on the export of iron and scrap metal to Japan. The United States also continued aid to Chiang Kai-shek.[1174]

As 1940 drew to a close, Japan's list of perceived American insults included: (a) the United States' recognition and support of Chiang Kai-shek in China, (b) American aid to Great Britain — a nation at war with Japan's allies, Germany and Italy, and a nation maintaining colonies across Asia, (c) Roosevelt's decision to bar exports of many war materials to Japan, (d) a United States immigration policy that blocked Japanese from immigrating and barred citizenship to all Japanese except those born in America, and (e) the presence in the Pacific of a large and expanding United States naval fleet.[1175]

Although the United States broke the Japanese secret "Purple" diplomatic code (sometimes called "Magic") in September of 1940, its ability to read Japanese diplomatic messages was limited — only about half of Purple-coded transmissions could be decrypted. In October, Japan adopted a new Admiral's Code for top-secret naval fleet messages which was so complex that even its personnel had difficulty using it. The United States did not break that code until the war was almost over. Japan, however, continued to use the Purple code for its diplomatic communications.[1176]

[1171] *Fateful Choices*, 124, *Engineers*, 287, *Eagle*, 62, *Inferno*, 190-91, 395, *Conspiracy*, 926, 937, 944, *Judgment*, 113-14.

[1172] *Fateful Choices*, 123, 125, *Eagle*, 64, *Inferno*, 189, *Conspiracy*, 943, 945.

[1173] *Fateful Choices*, 127-28.

[1174] *Fateful Choices*, 124-25, *Inferno*, 189, *Conspiracy*, 945.

[1175] *Slept*, 5.

[1176] *Ultra Secret*, 168, *Eagle*, 157, 448-49, *Conspiracy*, 954, 979-83, *Judgment*, 42, 44, *Dawn*, 80-81.

Japan's Goals and Alliances

In order to confirm their self-image as a major power, the Japanese still believed in 1941 that they must seize the oil fields of the Dutch East Indies, and eliminate British and American military bases in the western Pacific. In other words, Japan intended to dominate the Far East.[1177]

Admiral Yamamoto developed a preliminary plan for a surprise attack on the military facilities at Pearl Harbor in the Hawaiian Islands. He recognized that as the weaker nation, Japan's only chance for success was to strike first. After he submitted his blueprint to the Emperor in late November 1940, Hirohito ordered a detailed review of the concept. The conclusion of that review was "that the attack would be extremely hazardous but would have a reasonable chance of success."[1178]

Simultaneous with development of the Pearl Harbor strategy, Japan's army was creating plans for attacking sites in Southeast Asia.[1179]

Hitler urged Japan in the spring of 1941 to attack British-controlled Singapore, believing that doing so would cause the United States to focus on the Pacific region rather than Europe.[1180]

In April 1941, a Japanese-Soviet Neutrality Pact was signed in Moscow. The treaty removed the threat of Soviet action against Japan's northern border, thereby encouraging Japan's expansionist goals elsewhere in the Pacific. The treaty also paved the way for what Japan hoped would be a coalition among Japan, Germany, Italy and the Soviet Union which would deter western powers from interfering with Japan's planned expansion in Asia.[1181]

Emperor Hirohito concluded that Japan should engage in negotiations with the United States in 1941 in an effort to resolve their differences. He had two main goals. At best, America would agree to persuade Chiang Kai-shek to cede to Japan Manchuria and nearby provinces in exchange for Japan's withdrawal from other parts of China, and the United States would agree that Japan had special rights to acquire oil, rubber, tin, nickel and trade from Southeast Asia. If so, Japan

---

[1177] *Engineers*, 290, *Fateful Choices*, 380.

[1178] *Conspiracy*, 954-55, *Slept*, 98.

[1179] *Conspiracy*, 956-57.

[1180] *Fateful Choices*, 401-02, *Conspiracy*, 964, 966, *Slept*, 116.

[1181] *Fateful Choices*, 270, 331, *Eagle*, 68, *Pacific*, 4, *Conspiracy*, 960, 971, *Bloodlands*, 165.

would achieve its expansionist objectives without war. At worst, by negotiating with the United States, Japan would gain time to prepare for Yamamoto's attack and America would not sense that war was coming.[1182]

In May 1941, the Germans warned Japan's Foreign Service bureau that the United States was apparently reading messages sent using Japan's Purple diplomatic code. The Japanese opened an investigation into the potential security breach. Ironically, the investigation instructions (using the Purple code) alerted the United States to Japan's concerns. In late May, the Japanese Foreign Ministry curiously concluded that there had been no breach of the Purple code.[1183]

Hitler's June 22, 1941 massive surprise attack on the Soviet Union destroyed hopes for a coalition among Japan, Germany, Italy and the Soviets and, to Japan's great disappointment, drove Stalin into alliances with Britain and the United States. This turn of events made a Japanese move south more dangerous because the Soviet Union was no longer aligned with all of the Axis nations.[1184]

Despite the Japanese-Soviet Neutrality Pact, for several weeks Japan considered whether to drop its southern expansion plans and instead attack its northern traditional foe, the Soviet Union, while Stalin was frantically resisting Germany's massive invasion.[1185]

By August 1941, Japan had concluded that it would not then attack the Soviet Union, and had sent 40,000 troops to occupy the rest of Indochina. Control of Indochina furthered Japan's plan to cut off supplies moving to Chiang Kai-shek over the Burma Road, a 700 mile dirt corridor running through jungles and mountains from Burma to Chiang Kai-shek's wartime capital in Chungking. The taking of Indochina, which was quite unsettling to the United States, also opened Japan's path to seizing the Dutch East Indies' oil resources.[1186]

American Aid to China

In 1941, the United States provided aid to China and Chiang Kaishek under the Lend-Lease law, and began to send squadrons of American pilots, under the command of Colonel Chennault, known as the

---

[1182] *Conspiracy*, 960-61, 969, 973.

[1183] *Conspiracy*, 979-83, *Judgment*, 45-46, *Slept*, 118-19.

[1184] *Fateful Choices*, 331-32.

[1185] *Fateful Choices*, 331-32, 377, *Conspiracy*, 990-95.

[1186] *Inferno*, 191, *Fateful Choices*, 332-33, *Conspiracy*, 1007, *Eagle*, 327, *Slept*, 142-147, 173-74.

"Flying Tigers," to fly missions against the Japanese in occupied China.[1187]

Lend-Lease materiel delivered to China had to travel 12,000 miles by ship to ports on the west coast of India, then 1,500 miles by rail to Calcutta, then by narrow gauge rail to airfields in Assam for the long and dangerous flight to China over the "Hump" — the Himalayas.[1188]

The Chinese Kuomintang government under Chiang Kai-shek was corrupt, inefficient and unaggressive. It had fought little with the Japanese since 1938, preferring instead to survive the war with Japan and be ready to oppose the forces of the Chinese Communists led by Mao Tse-tung.[1189]

Out of fear that they would compromise the secret, the United States refused to share with Chiang Kai-shek and his Kuomintang government information gathered from breaking the Japanese codes, including the fact that the Japanese had broken the Chinese code.[1190]

American Concerns and Negotiations

On January 27, 1941, the United States ambassador to Japan, Joseph Grew, reported to the State Department in Washington a rumor that "the Japanese military forces planned, in the event of trouble with the United States, to attempt a surprise attack on Pearl Harbor using all of their military facilities." Although the United States military had long recognized the possibility of a Japanese surprise attack on Pearl Harbor, it viewed Grew's reported rumor as hearsay having "no credence" and concluded that "no move against Pearl Harbor appears imminent or planned for the forseeable [sic] future."[1191]

But, in late January, Navy Secretary Knox had remarked:

> If war eventuates with Japan, it is believed easily possible that hostilities would be initiated by a surprise attack upon the Fleet or the Naval Base at Pearl Harbor.
>
> In my opinion, the inherent possibilities of a major disaster to the fleet or naval base warrant taking every step, as rapidly as can be done, that will increase the joint readiness of the Army and Navy to withstand a raid of the character mentioned

---

[1187] *Eagle*, 325.
[1188] *The Burma Campaign* ("*Burma*"), Frank McLynn, Yale University press (2011), 115.
[1189] *Eagle*, 326, 338, *Inferno*, 414.
[1190] *Burma*, 200.
[1191] *Slept*, 30-36, 45-47.

above.[1192]

Due to the shortage of supplies in 1941 and the military's pressing war-related needs elsewhere, a number of the proposed measures for increasing protection of Pearl Harbor, including more reconnaissance planes and radar screening equipment, were not readily available.[1193]

In May, Roosevelt ordered the Navy to transfer from the Pacific fleet about one-quarter of the vessels based there so that they would be available in the Atlantic to support the passage of vital transport ships to Britain. Although this weakened the perceived deterrent effect on Japan of the Pacific fleet, it was consistent with the Europe First doctrine and deemed essential to the survival of Britain.[1194]

Troubled by Japan's growing aggression, President Roosevelt recalled General Douglas MacArthur from retirement in July 1941, and named him commander of the U.S. Army Forces in the Far East.[1195]

In July 1941, Roosevelt also ordered the Army of the Philippine Republic into the service of the United States.[1196]

Because the United States had broken the Japanese Purple diplomatic code used to send messages from Tokyo to the Japanese embassy in Washington, D.C., Roosevelt understood in mid-1941 that Japan still intended to advance toward Southeast Asia, and was not inclined to attack the Soviet Union from the east at least until it was sure Hitler could defeat Stalin.[1197]

By the first of August 1941, Roosevelt had frozen all Japanese assets in the United States and blocked all oil, scrap iron and machine tool shipments to Japan. Several days later, Britain, Canada, the Philippines, New Zealand and the Netherlands adopted identical rules. In effect, Japan was under a total oil embargo, heightening its need for oil from the Dutch East Indies. At that point, Japan had barely enough resources to carry out two full years of warfare.[1198]

In early August 1941, Japan proposed that Prime Minister Konoye, who had retaken office in 1940, meet with Roosevelt to discuss ways of

---

[1192] *Slept*, 45.

[1193] *Slept*, 55-69, 188.

[1194] *Slept*, 127-133.

[1195] *Tears in the Darkness* ("*Tears*"), Michael Norman, Farrar, Strouse and Giroux (2009), 17, *Eagle*, 69, 72.

[1196] *Engineers*, 287, *Eagle*, 68-69, *Slept*, 170.

[1197] *Fateful Choices*, 299-300, *Eagle*, 446, *Inferno*, 358, *Conspiracy*, 980-81, *Slept*, 174-77.

[1198] *Fateful Choices*, 300, 333, *Eagle*, 75, *Pacific*, 4, *Conspiracy*, 1003-06, *Sword*, 76, *Slept*, 167-69, *Crucible*, 116.

bridging differences between Japan and the United States. Aware of Japan's aspirations from breaking the Japanese code, the United States took the position that diplomacy could begin only after Japan ceased her expansionist actions and her hostilities in China.[1199]

On September 6, 1941, based on recommendations from the Prime Minister and the heads of the army and navy, Emperor Hirohito concluded that Japan would have to go to war against the United States (and Britain and the Netherlands) if the two countries were unable to reach agreement within the next six weeks (*i.e.,* by October 15). Japan's position was that the United States would have to stop supporting Chiang Kai-shek, not expand its military presence in the Far East, and provide Japan with resources.[1200]

The autumn negotiations between Japan and the United States broke down primarily because Japan refused to withdraw from China. Japan felt that accepting the United States' proposal would mean giving up gains in China and Manchuria, abandoning plans for expansion to the south, and a humiliating return of Japan to its relatively powerless status in the 1920s.[1201]

The Japanese appreciated in the fall of 1941 that they would have difficulty winning a war against the United States lasting more than two years because they would lack required oil, steel and other natural resources. But Japan's hope was that its expansion into Southeast Asia, coupled with a surprise attack on the United States, the end of Allied aid to Chiang Kai-shek, Axis advances in Europe, and a German declaration of war against the United States would force America to negotiate for peace.[1202]

The Japanese added two new identical aircraft carriers, *Shokaku* and *Zuikaku*, to their Pacific fleet in August and September, respectively, giving Japan a total of six large carriers.[1203]

In 1941, after unsuccessfully arguing against a Japanese war with the United States, Admiral Yamamoto completed plans for an unconventional surprise air attack on Pearl Harbor aimed at destroying the U.S. Navy's Pacific fleet in one blow. His objectives were to keep the Navy out of the western Pacific for at least six months while Japan seized territory, and to cripple American morale. Having been edu-

---

[1199] *Fateful Choices,* 335-37, 348, *Eagle,* 77, *Crucible,* 121.
[1200] *Fateful Choices,* 339-46, *Eagle,* 77, *Conspiracy,* 1015-18, *Slept,* 205, 209, *Crucible,* 122.
[1201] *Fateful Choices,* 350-54, 380, *Conspiracy,* 1020.
[1202] *Fateful Choices,* 340-41, 358, 366, *Inferno,* 191-92, *Slept,* 14.
[1203] *Slept,* 199-200.

cated in the United States, Yamamoto appreciated the untapped power of the United States and understood that a more conventional approach to war with the Americans would surely lead to a Japanese defeat.[1204]

The Japanese plan for a carrier-based air attack on Pearl Harbor was influenced by Britain's successful carrier-based air attack on the Italian fleet in Taranto, Italy in November, 1940.[1205]

Recognizing that Japan's negotiations with the United States were making no progress and that war was approaching, Prime Minister Konoye resigned again on October 16, 1941. He was replaced by General Tojo Hideki, an ardent advocate for Japan's continuing occupation of China. As a precaution, Emperor Hirohito told Tojo to ignore the six week deadline set on September 6 and directed him to carefully reexamine Japan's policy regarding the United States.[1206]

Early in November, after further studying the issue, Hirohito and his hawkish government concluded that, to assure Japan's self-preservation and self-defense, and establish a new order in Asia, it would go to war against the United States, Britain and the Netherlands except in the unlikely event that a negotiated resolution with the United States occurred by December 1, 1941.[1207]

On November 3, the American ambassador to Japan, Joseph Grew, warned Washington that in his opinion Japan would probably risk "national *hara kiri*" rather than yield to foreign pressure, and that "Japan's resort to measures which might make war with the United States inevitable may come with dramatic and dangerous suddenness."[1208]

On November 20, the Japanese ambassador met with Secretary of State Hull to present Japan's final negotiating position which called for the United States to lift its embargo and supply Japan with all of the oil it needed. In return, Japan offered only to move its troops from southern Indochina to the north and not to advance further into southern Asia or the south Pacific. Japan expressed no willingness to depart China, renounce the Tripartite Pact, or promise not to supply Hitler. Although Hull considered the Japanese proposal outrageous, to

---

[1204] *Eagle*, 78-82, *Conspiracy*, 1057-58, *Slept*, 18, 21, 340, *Crucible*, 69-70.

[1205] *Pacific*, 5, *Sword*, 86, *Slept*, 40, 320.

[1206] *Fateful Choices*, 109, 354, *Conspiracy*, 1028-29, *Slept*, 278.

[1207] *Fateful Choices*, 364-66, *Conspiracy*, 1049-54, *Slept*, 326.

[1208] *Slept*, 334-35.

gain time to strengthen the military he did not immediately reject it.[1209]

On November 24, based on intercepted Japanese messages, the U.S. Chief of Naval Operations warned all of his commanders in the Pacific that "a surprise aggressive movement [by Japan] in any direction including attack on Philippines or Guam is a possibility."[1210]

At a meeting on November 25, Roosevelt (according to Stimson) observed that:

> [W]e were likely to be attacked perhaps next Monday, for Japs are notorious for making an attack without warning, and the question was what we should do. The question was how we should maneuver them into the position of firing the first shot without allowing too much danger to ourselves.

Secretary of State Hull responded that heavily armed and expansionist Japan, not the United States, was in complete control of the situation.[1211]

On November 26, 1941, a large Japanese fleet, including six aircraft carriers, secretly departed Japan for its anticipated attack on Pearl Harbor, and many Japanese submarines left the Marshall Islands for the same destination. (Twenty-seven other submarines had sailed from Japan on November 18 with orders to reassemble near Pearl Harbor). Their two main objectives were to destroy all American carriers in Oahu and at least four battleships, and to wipe out American air power there.[1212]

Several days earlier, a large Japanese task force had departed Japan *en route* to anticipated attacks against the Philippines, Malaya and other military objectives in Southeast Asia. When the United States learned of this armed movement south shortly before December 7, its officials reasoned that any Japanese attack would likely occur there.[1213]

Ironically, the limits the London and Washington Naval treaties imposed on the size of the Japanese fleet encouraged the Japanese to carry out a surprise attack on the ships at Pearl Harbor in an effort to eliminate the American advantage in naval strength.[1214]

[1209] *Slept*, 363-64, 369.

[1210] *Eagle*, 96, *Slept*, 370.

[1211] *Slept*, 371-72.

[1212] *Eagle*, 85, *WW II Story*, 79, *Pacific*, 5-6, *Conspiracy*, 1057-58, *Slept*, 295-99, 339, 374.

[1213] *Slept*, 433-35, 464, 470.

[1214] *Sword*, 84.

On November 27, 1941 (Thanksgiving), aware from reading secret Japanese diplomatic messages that war was likely, the Chief of Naval Operations again cabled American naval commanders in the Pacific.

> This dispatch is to be considered a war warning. ...[A]n aggressive move by Japan is expected within the next few days. The number and equipment of Jap troops and the organization of naval task forces indicates an amphibious expedition against either the Phillipines [sic] or KRA peninsula or possibly Borneo. Execute an appropriate defensive deployment....

In addition, Washington ordered all aircraft carriers and half of the Army planes at Pearl Harbor to leave.[1215]

On the same Thanksgiving day, Army General Marshall's cable advised General Short in Hawaii that negotiations with Japan were faltering, that "hostile action possible at any moment," and that he was to "undertake such reconnaissance and other measures as you deem necessary" without alarming the civilian population.[1216]

On November 28, Admiral Halsey departed Pearl Harbor for Wake Island with the carrier *Enterprise*, three heavy cruisers, five destroyers and many planes. On December 5, the carrier *Lexington*, three cruisers, nine destroyers and eighteen more planes left Pearl Harbor for Midway Island. The third American carrier in the Pacific fleet, *Saratoga*, was in San Diego. Remaining in Pearl Harbor were eight old, slow battleships and eight aged cruisers that were basically obsolete weapons.[1217]

Although the United States had recognized for years that Pearl Harbor might be the target of a surprise attack from Japan, government officials in Washington thought the Japanese would first attack the Philippines or Malaya, not Hawaii.[1218]

By the end of November 1941, the U.S. Army garrison in the Philippines had almost tripled its strength to 31,000 troops.[1219]

Even though he had received the "hostile action" warning contained in the Army's November 27 message, General MacArthur believed that the Japanese would not attack American bases until at least

---

[1215] *Judgment*, 85-86, 262-63, 287, *Inferno*, 192, *Conspiracy*, 1064-66, *Eagle*, 96, *Slept*, 406.

[1216] *Judgment*, 84-85, 262-63, 287, *Eagle*, 96, *Slept*, 402.

[1217] *Conspiracy*, 1064-66, *Admirals*, 204, *Slept*, 410, 420, *Rising Sun*, 42.

[1218] *Conspiracy*, 1066-67, 1083, *Slept*, 362-63.

[1219] *Tears*, 17.

April 1942.[1220]

On December 1, Japan concluded that negotiations with the United States had failed. Neither side had been willing to weaken its position on China. The huge Japanese task force, commanded by Vice Admiral Nagumo, continued on course for Pearl Harbor with an anticipated attack date of December 7, 1941.[1221]

One week before the attack on Pearl Harbor, the Japanese changed their standard naval code and their warships altered their call signals. Although viewing this enhanced radio security as ominous, American code-breakers were not able to break the new code until shortly after December 7.[1222]

By December 3, the United States had gathered additional information strongly suggesting that war was imminent: Japan had ordered its diplomats in Washington, London, Manila, Hong Kong and embassies elsewhere to destroy all secret documents and most of their secret code machines.[1223]

On December 3, in meetings with Tokyo's Tripartite Pact companions — Berlin and Rome — Japanese diplomatic representatives asked theoretically whether Germany and Italy would declare war on the United States if Japan did so. Within a few days, Hitler and Mussolini both promised to do so.[1224]

On December 6, U.S. Navy Department intelligence officers prepared a report on the location of Japan's major warships that erroneously placed all of the vessels about to attack Pearl Harbor in port in Japan.[1225]

Late on December 6, after reading the segment of an intercepted Japanese diplomatic message that the United States had been able to decode, Roosevelt said "This means war." The full message was not received and decoded in Washington until after midnight and was not shown to Roosevelt, Hull or General Marshall until the next morning. On December 7 at about noon (6:30 a.m. in Hawaii), General Marshall ordered that a message be promptly sent to all Pacific military theaters warning them to be on alert because in about an hour Japan planned to give the United States an ultimatum and had ordered the destruction of

---

[1220] *Tears*, 18, *Eagle*, 75, *Pacific*, 10, *Conspiracy*, 1065, *Judgment*, 141, 143.

[1221] *Fateful Choices*, 369-72, 378, *Pacific*, 6, *Conspiracy*, 1075.

[1222] *Eagle*, 449, *Conspiracy*, 1075, 1077, *Slept*, 353, 439-441.

[1223] *Judgment*, 69, 234-39, *Slept*, 437, 447-48.

[1224] *Conspiracy*, 1076, *Reich*, 889-90, *Slept*, 558.

[1225] *Reich*, 892, *Slept*, 440.

A CONCISE HISTORY OF THE SECOND WORLD WAR

its code machines. Because the atmosphere was disrupting the War Department's radio connection to Hawaii that morning, Marshall's message was sent by commercial cable. Although the cable did not arrive in Hawaii for several hours, other Pacific military leaders, including those in the Philippines, received the warning on time.[1226]

Japan Attacks Pearl Harbor

On December 7, 1941, at about 7:55 a.m. in Hawaii, 181 Japanese fighters, dive-bombers and torpedo planes diving out of the sun attacked the anchored American fleet and the airbase at Pearl Harbor. Less than an hour later, another wave of 170 Japanese warplanes blasted the same targets.[1227]

While the second wave of Japanese planes was attacking Pearl Harbor, Japanese diplomats in Washington, D.C. delivered to Secretary of State Cordell Hull a written message citing alleged United States wrongs and announcing that negotiations were over between the two nations. After deliberately studying the message (which he had already seen in decoded Magic form), Hull curtly declared that the Japanese document was "crowded with infamous falsehoods and distortions" and ordered the diplomats out of his office.[1228]

It was not until some eight hours after the first attack on Pearl Harbor that Emperor Hirohito signed documents formally declaring war against the United States.[1229]

When the war began, the average Japanese carrier pilot had about 700 hours of training — more than twice that of U.S. Navy carrier pilots.[1230]

Although America's three aircraft carriers in the Pacific fleet (*Lexington, Saratoga* and *Enterprise*) were not in Pearl Harbor on December 7, the Japanese surprise attack sank five battleships, damaged many other ships, destroyed 188 planes, killed 2,403 servicemen and wounded 1,178 others. Fortunately for the United States, no U.S. Navy submarines were damaged in the attack, and Pearl Harbor's crit-

---

[1226] *Fateful Choices*, 372-73, *Eagles*, 94-95, *Conspiracy*, 1080, 1084, *Judgment*, 80-82, 136-38, 143, 164, 217, 281, *Slept*, 474-75, 485, 494-95, 502, 567.

[1227] *Curse*, 66, *Fateful Choices*, 373, *Eagle*, 1, 6, *WW II Story*, 79-85, *Conspiracy*, 1085-93, *Slept*, 530.

[1228] *Conspiracy*, 1082, 1094-95, *Slept*, 554.

[1229] *Fateful Choices*, 374, *Slept*, 558.

[1230] *Eagle*, 148, *Slept*, 190-91, *Crucible*, 51.

ical fuel oil storage tanks remained largely unhurt.[1231]

The Japanese lost just nine war planes during the first raid and twenty during the second. Another seventy-four Japanese planes were damaged during the American counterattack that day. These losses, the success already achieved, and uncertainty as to where the threatening American carriers were persuaded the Japanese to head home without launching a third attack.[1232]

At the time of the Pearl Harbor attack, Admiral Kimmel commanded the Navy's Pacific fleet. Lieutenant General Short headed the Army's Hawaiian Department and was responsible for the defense of Pearl Harbor and all ships berthed there. Both officers had received warnings of a possible Japanese attack, but took few precautions, apparently believing that hostilities would be initiated in the Far East, not Hawaii. Within ten days after the Japanese bombings, both commanding officers had been relieved of their positions for "dereliction of duty" and "errors of judgment." Several months later they were permitted to retire, but with the understanding that courts-martial would follow "at such time 'as the public interest and safety' permits."[1233]

Some historians contend that by December 4, Roosevelt and his inner circle knew of Japanese plans to attack Pearl Harbor, but withheld the information from Short and Kimmel to assure that the isolationist United States would enter the war. Others reply that Kimmel and Short had received multiple warnings that a Japanese sneak attack on Pearl Harbor was possible and that they, as "sentries," failed to carry out their responsibilities to protect the base and its vessels.[1234]

While Japan's bombing of Pearl Harbor shocked and infuriated Americans, it was a strategic error for Japan because it did not destroy the United States' ability to wage war. Indeed, at the time of the attack the U.S. Navy was building fifteen battleships, eleven carriers, fifty-four cruisers, 193 destroyers and seventy-three submarines. Moreover, the Navy had access to a fourth carrier, *Yorktown*, which was then deployed in the Atlantic but was quickly moved to the Pacific.[1235]

On December 8, President Roosevelt told Congress in a five minute speech heard by a radio audience of sixty million Americans:

[1231] *Engineers*, 315, *Fateful Choices*, 374, *Eagle*, 2, 6, 88, 104, *WW II Story*, 99, *Conspiracy*, 1090-93, *Admirals*, 222-23, *Slept*, 539, *Crucible*, 159.

[1232] *Slept*, 544-45.

[1233] *Eagle*, 1, 3, 96-100, *Inferno*, 193, *Conspiracy*, 1064-1082, *Judgment*, 201-05, 224-45, *Admirals*, 224, *Slept*, 65, 589-613, 636, 653.

[1234] *Judgment*, 224-45, *Slept*, 739-53, 855-66.

[1235] *Inferno*, 193-94, 196, *Pacific*, 6, *Crucible*, 203.

Yesterday, December 7, 1941 — a date which will live in infamy — the United States of America was suddenly and deliberately attacked by naval and air forces of the Empire of Japan.

The American declaration of war came from Congress less than an hour later, with just one dissenting vote. Britain declared war on Japan the same day.[1236]

The day before, Roosevelt had authorized the U.S. Navy to commence unrestricted submarine warfare against Japan, including sinking merchant vessels. This repudiated a 1930 international agreement barring submarines from sinking merchant ships unless arrangements had been made to assure the safety of their passengers and crew.[1237]

Japan's decision to carry out a surprise attack on Pearl Harbor was taken without first consulting Hitler, who was delighted but would have preferred a Japanese invasion of the Soviet Union from the east. Nonetheless, Germany declared war on the United States four days after Pearl Harbor, even though it had no duty to do so under the Tripartite Pact (which required action only if the United States attacked Japan). Italy followed Hitler's lead several hours later.[1238]

Following the attack on Pearl Harbor, Roosevelt asked the Soviet Union to declare war on Japan. Because the Red Army was then in a death struggle to prevent German troops from entering Moscow, an anxious Stalin said he would not be in a position to take on Japan until after the Germans had been driven back.[1239]

Japan Attacks Guam and Wake Island

A few hours after bombing Pearl Harbor, Japan attacked the American-owned island of Guam in the Mariana Islands. Guam was quickly defeated.[1240]

The Japanese simultaneously attacked Wake Island, a tiny and flat American-controlled atoll 600 miles from Japan's Marshall Islands. The island, a way station on the route to the Philippines, was defended by

---

[1236] *Fateful Choices*, 374-75, *Eagle*, 7, *Conspiracy*, 1096, *Crucible*, 35-36.

[1237] *Eagle*, 479-80.

[1238] *Curse*, 66, *Reich*, 885, 892-94, *Fateful Choices*, 416-18, *WW II Story*, 100, *Crucible*, 59-60.

[1239] *Curse*, 66, *Eagle*, 552.

[1240] *Eagle*, 54, 101, *Inferno*, 227, *WW II Story*, 112, *Conspiracy*, 1095, 1105.

about 450 U.S. Marines, a dozen fighter planes, and several hundred American construction workers. On December 11, the Americans on Wake repulsed a Japanese landing force of 450 soldiers, sinking several ships and killing over 500 Japanese in the process. On December 23, approximately 1,000 angry Japanese soldiers landed on Wake. When it became clear that the United States would not be able to deliver timely reinforcements, the remaining Americans on Wake surrendered. The Japanese lost more than 800 dead and 300 wounded fighting for the island, while the Americans suffered about 200 casualties.[1241]

Japan's seizing of Wake and Guam meant that the Philippine Islands had become isolated from the United States and were now vulnerable to a Japanese invasion.[1242]

Japan's Air Attack on the Philippines

The thousands of islands that make up the Philippines stretch along the South China Sea for more than a thousand miles. Following the Spanish-American War of 1898, the United States took possession of the islands. In 1934, Congress granted full independence to the Philippines, effective in 1946. Although America maintained naval and army bases in the Philippines, it recognized that if Japan attacked, the islands would fall because the forces stationed there were insufficient to defeat a major incursion and many weeks would pass before the American fleet could transport reinforcements 7,000 miles across the Pacific.[1243]

The Far East U.S. Army Air Force commander, Major General Brereton, knew from intelligence reports that, in the event of war, Japanese bombers would likely attack the Philippines from bases on Formosa (now Taiwan), some 500 miles away. After receiving Washington's November 27 war warning, Brereton was prepared to send Army Air Force planes to bomb Formosa in the event of an attack.[1244]

The Japanese had planned a surprise aircraft bombing of Clark Field (near Manila) to take place at first light, shortly after their Pearl Harbor attack some 5,000 miles to the east. However, a dense fog shrouded Formosa, delaying the bombers' takeoff for more than six hours. The Japanese pilots now knew that a vigorous defense of the

[1241] *Eagle*, 101-06, *Inferno*, 227, *WW II Story*, 112-13, *Pacific*, 13-14, *Conspiracy*, 1125, *Rising Sun*, 56-57, 60-63, *Crucible*, 139-147.

[1242] *Eagle*, 106, *WW II Story*, 112.

[1243] *Tears*, 39-41, *Eagle*, 56, 73-74, *Pacific*, 10, *Crusade*, 21, *Slept*, 576-77.

[1244] *Tears*, 20.

targets was most likely.[1245]

American military leaders in the Philippines received word of the Japanese attack on Pearl Harbor at about 2:30 a.m. on December 8 (the same day as the attack; the Philippines are across the International Dateline). General MacArthur and Admiral Hart, commander of the Navy's Asiatic Fleet, alerted their commands a short time later, but no immediate defensive actions were taken.[1246]

Shortly after learning of the Pearl Harbor attack, General Brereton rushed to MacArthur's headquarters and asked for permission to arm and send the B-17 bombers based at Clark Field toward Formosa. MacArthur's chief of staff told Brereton to wait for MacArthur's approval. None came. At 7:15 a.m. an impatient Brereton returned to MacArthur's headquarters and renewed his request. Again he was told to wait.[1247]

General "Hap" Arnold, head of the Army Air Force, upon hearing that the Army's destroyed planes at Pearl Harbor had been parked wingtip to wingtip, called General Brereton and warned him not to make the same error at Clark Field.[1248]

Between 8:00 and 9:00 a.m., Clark Field received notice that Japanese planes were headed its way. Because MacArthur still had not acted, the local officers ordered the American bombers at Clark to take off, without bombs, and cruise above the field.[1249]

At approximately 11:00 a.m., MacArthur finally authorized a reconnaissance flight over Formosa to be followed by bombing missions. The bombers and their companion fighters aloft were promptly called back to Clark Field for arming and refueling. By 11:30, most were on the ground. The crews then went to lunch.[1250]

When the Japanese planes, fifty-three bombers and forty-five fighters, arrived at Clark Field shortly after noon, almost ten hours after the Pearl Harbor attack, they found the American warplanes neatly parked on the runway. By the end of the attack, seventeen of nineteen B-17s and most of the fighters had been destroyed or damaged, some 100 men killed and over 250 wounded. Japanese planes also destroyed American fighters at nearby Iba airfield. Half of MacArthur's best Phi-

---

[1245] *Tears*, 25-27, *Conspiracy*, 1101.

[1246] *Tears*, 18-19.

[1247] *Tears*, 21, *Eagle*, 107, *Pacific*, 10, *Conspiracy*, 1101-02.

[1248] *Tears*, 21.

[1249] *Tears*, 21, *Conspiracy*, 1102.

[1250] *Tears*, 21-22, *Eagle*, 107, *Pacific*, 11-12, *Conspiracy*, 1102.

lippine planes had been wiped out with ease on the first day of battle.[1251]

Japan's Invasion of the Philippines

Two weeks later, some 43,000 Japanese troops, many hardened
from fighting in China, landed on Luzon, the main Philippine island,
in what was at that time the largest amphibious landing in history.
They and their tanks promptly confronted American (12,000) and Philippine (68,000) troops. MacArthur announced, "My gallant divisions
are holding ground and denying the foe the sacred soil of the Philippines. We have inflicted heavy casualties on his troops, and nowhere is
his bridgehead secure. Tomorrow we will drive him into the sea."[1252]

In fact, within a day the Japanese were driving MacArthur's ill-
prepared forces back. Within a few days the defending troops had begun a 150 mile retreat south to the Bataan peninsula. Lacking adequate
supplies, the Allied troops were soon on half-rations.[1253]

On December 23, 1941, when MacArthur informed President
Quezon that the American troops would retreat to Bataan and not defend Manila, Quezon felt betrayed. MacArthur was reneging on his
earlier promise to Filipinos that America would defend the entire isl-
and of Luzon. In turn, a disturbed MacArthur had recently discovered
Quezon's secret attempt to deliver a message to the invading Japanese
forces.[1254]

To avoid its destruction by the Japanese, Manila was declared an
open city on December 24. Under pressure from MacArthur, Quezon
and his government then withdrew from Manila to the Philippine fortress of Corregidor just south of the Bataan peninsula.[1255]

On Christmas Eve 1941, General MacArthur and his family arrived at Corregidor, an island about the size of New York City's Central Park.[1256]

Unlike Admiral Kimmel and General Short following the attack
on Pearl Harbor, MacArthur was not relieved of duty despite botching
the Philippines' defense. Although his failure to prepare for and resist
the Japanese attack was a twin to the derelictions of Kimmel and

---

[1251] *Tears*, 26-27, 31, *Inferno*, 227, *Eagle*, 107, *WW II Story*, 102, *Conspiracy*, 1102-03, *Crucible*, 48-49.

[1252] *Inferno*, 227-28, *Conspiracy*, 1129-32, *Eagle*, 111, *Tears*, 46, 49, 60, *Crucible*, 238-239.

[1253] *Tears*, 46, 49, 60, *Eagle*, 108-111, *Inferno*, 227-28, *Conspiracy*, 1129-35.

[1254] *Tears*, 121-25, *Inferno*, 230, *Conspiracy*, 1129-35, 1141, *Eagle*, 115-16.

[1255] *Conspiracy*, 1133-34, *Tears*, 49.

[1256] *Tears*, 121-25, *Inferno*, 230, *Conspiracy*, 1129-35, 1141.

Short, President Roosevelt, recognizing that the American public viewed MacArthur as a hero, did not censor him. Rather, Roosevelt arranged for MacArthur to receive the Congressional Medal of Honor in March.[1257]

Japan Attacks Elsewhere in Southeast Asia

On December 8, 1941 (the same day as the Pearl Harbor attack), the Japanese landed in northern Malaya, and the first of their bombs struck the British-controlled city of Singapore, which is on the southern tip of Malaya.[1258]

Also the victim of a December 8 attack, Hong Kong fell to the Japanese on Christmas day. The invaders chopped off hands, tongues and ears of victims, bayoneted nurses and doctors, and raped women.[1259]

On December 10, 1941, the new British battleship HMS *Prince of Wales* and older cruiser HMS *Repulse*, which had left port in Singapore to search for an enemy convoy, were sunk by Japanese planes off the coast of Malaya with the loss of 840 sailors. As a result, the Japanese navy had achieved complete supremacy in the Pacific and the South China Sea.[1260]

The Japanese took control of British Borneo late in December 1941.[1261]

The United States Girds for Battle

Stunned and infuriated by the sneak attack on Pearl Harbor while Japanese diplomats were simultaneously talking "peace" in Washington, the people of United States reacted with a determination that washed away all isolationist sentiment. Now the vast economic and industrial might of the United States would join the war against the Axis.[1262]

On December 14, Army Chief of Staff Marshall asked General Eisenhower to outline what military steps the United States should now take in the western Pacific. Eisenhower responded that America, with its wounded Pacific fleet, could not adequately supply the Philippines,

---

[1257] *Admirals*, 226-27, *Eagle*, 116-19, *Crucible*, 49.

[1258] *Inferno*, 199-200, *WW II Story*, 101, *Pacific*, 7-10, *Conspiracy*, 1086.

[1259] *Eagle*, 128, *Inferno*, 207, 212, *WW II Story*, 113, *Conspiracy*, 1095, 1100, 1126-29.

[1260] *Masters*, 64-5, *Inferno*. 201, *Eagle*, 128, *Pacific*, 9, *Conspiracy*, 1106-17, *Reich*, 901, *Crucible*, 53-57.

[1261] *Eagle*, 128.

[1262] *Slept*, 582-83, *Crucible*, 61-62.

which would therefore eventually fall to Japan. Consequently, he said it was essential to assure that Australia remained under Allied control and to secure the islands between the United States and Australia which served as way-stations.[1263]

On December 30, Roosevelt appointed the brilliant, stubborn and pugnacious Admiral Ernest King to command all three U.S. Navy fleets — Atlantic, Pacific and Asiatic. Three months later the President added the top Navy job, Chief of Naval Operations, to King's responsibilities.[1264]

On December 31, Admiral Chester Nimitz assumed command of the U.S. Navy's Pacific fleet. His orders were to (a) secure the communication and supply lines between the west coast and Hawaii and Midway, and (b) maintain a lifeline between the United States and Australia.[1265]

THE FIRST FULL YEAR OF TOTAL WAR IN ASIA (1942)

Japan Continues its Asian Advance

As 1942 arrived, the Japanese were operating six heavy aircraft carriers and five light carriers. They recognized that their numerical advantage over the Americans in carriers would not last because the United States was able to build ships more quickly. Thus, it was essential for Japan to preserve its temporary advantage by avoiding unwise carrier losses.[1266]

On January 11, a Japanese submarine torpedoed the USS *Saratoga* while the carrier was about 420 miles southwest of Hawaii. The wounded warship limped to Puget Sound, Washington for six months of needed repairs, leaving the United States with just three carriers afloat in the Pacific.[1267]

In January 1942, the Japanese invaded the South Pacific island of New Britain and seized from Australia the port of Rabaul. The Japanese then turned Rabaul into a major naval and air force base from which they could threaten the American naval supply route to Australia.[1268]

[1263] *Ike*, 244-45, *Crusade*, 21-22.
[1264] *Admirals*, 212-20, 235, 238, *Slept*, 615.
[1265] *Admirals*, 221, *Rising Sun*, 65, *Crucible*, 169.
[1266] *Sword*, 58-59, 418-19.
[1267] *Rising Sun*, 67-68, *Crucible*, 200.
[1268] *Inferno*, 232, *Conspiracy*, 1142, *Admirals*, 231-33.

After almost a month of bombing, on January 20, two divisions of Japanese troops entered Burma from Siam (now Thailand). Their objectives were to secure Burma's oil and natural resources, and to close the Burma Road to China that the Allies were using to supply Chiang Kai-shek. Within a few weeks, the British, Indian and Burmese troops stationed there were in retreat. Burma had been a British colony for fewer than seventy years and harbored many citizens who resented the British and welcomed the Japanese.[1269]

On January 24, four U.S. Navy destroyers snuck up on a Japanese convoy near Balikpapan on the east coast of the oil-rich Indonesian island of Borneo. After several passes, the Americans torpedoed and sank three or four troop transports and a patrol boat in what was the first Japan/United States naval battle of World War II.[1270]

At the end of January, American pilots flying from the carriers *Enterprise* and *Yorktown* attacked Japanese bases in the Marshall Islands. The raids did little damage but boosted Navy morale and provided valuable combat training.[1271]

In early February 1942, President Roosevelt assigned Lieutenant General Joseph W. Stilwell to (a) serve as chief of staff to Chiang Kai-shek, (b) command all American forces in China, Burma and India, and (c) supervise distribution of Lend-Lease aid to China.[1272]

The United States bolstered China so that the Chinese would continue to resist the invading Japanese forces, preventing those enemy troops from being sent elsewhere to battle the Allies.[1273]

Singapore was the British Empire's strongest fortress in the Far East. Nonetheless, at least 70,000 British troops there surrendered to 35,000 Japanese troops on February 15, 1942. In seventy days the Japanese had crossed Malaya and taken Singapore, at a cost of only 3,506 dead, whereas about 7,500 British and Indian troops had been killed. Another 138,000 soldiers and civilians were taken prisoner.[1274]

In February, the Japanese, with a force of just 10,000 men, took the large Indonesian island of Sumatra after a brief battle with Dutch

---

[1269] *Eagle*, 328, 330-31, *Inferno*, 214-18, *WW II Story*, 126-28.

[1270] *Eagle*, 131-32, *Neptune's Inferno* ("*Neptune*"), James D. Hornfischer, Bantam Books (2011), 145, *Crucible*, 237.

[1271] *Eagle*, 149-50, *WW II Story*, 116, *Crucible*, 200-232.

[1272] *Eagle*, 329.

[1273] *Eagle*, 330.

[1274] *Masters*, 116-17, 169, *Inferno*, 207-10, *WW II Story*, 113, *Pacific*, 9-10, *Conspiracy*, 1118, 1143-53, *Crucible*, 244-252.

and British forces.[1275]

On February 19, the Japanese occupied Bali, near the east end of Java. On the same day, they sent 189 bombers to attack the northern Australia city of Darwin, killing almost 300 people, sinking ten ships and destroying twenty-three Allied planes.[1276]

The Australians, who feared an immediate Japanese invasion of their homeland, had only about 7,000 trained soldiers available to oppose such an incursion. Most Australian troops had previously been sent to fight with the British in England, Africa, India and the Far East. However, after considering the vastness of Australia and the challenges of supplying his troops there, Emperor Hirohito decided on February 23 that Japan should not attempt an invasion of Australia — at least until Burma had been secured.[1277]

On February 27-28, in battles near the Dutch East Indies, the Japanese sank almost all of the Pacific-based ships remaining under Dutch control. Not a single Japanese ship went down, but almost 3,000 Allied lives were lost.[1278]

The U.S. Navy attacked Japanese forces on Wake Island in February, and in New Guinea in March. In retaliation for the strike against Wake, the Japanese executed about 100 civilian construction workers who had been taken prisoner there in December.[1279]

By March 1942, American code breakers had made some progress in being able to read portions of the new standard Japanese naval code that had been installed the previous December.[1280]

After Singapore fell, Japanese amphibious forces sailed east toward the Dutch East Indies and the oil, rubber, timber, rice and metals there. On March 1, Japanese troops landed in strength on Java. One week later, the last Dutch forces there surrendered.[1281]

On March 11, Hirohito established a policy to deal with the many Jews who became part of the Japanese empire upon the capture of Singapore and Java. They would be treated as nationals where they resided, but subjected to special surveillance. No Jews would be allowed to move to Japan.[1282]

[1275] *Conspiracy*, 1155.

[1276] *Eagle*, 132, *Inferno*, 389, *Pacific*, 21, *Conspiracy*, 1155, *Crucible*, 254.

[1277] *Conspiracy*, 1156-57, *Sword*, 27.

[1278] *Conspiracy*, 1158, *Ike*, 262-63, *Inferno*, 213-14, *Crucible*, 254-263.

[1279] *Eagle*, 150, *WW II Story*, 113, 115, *Sword*, 31.

[1280] *Eagle*, 449, *Judgment*, 213, *Rising Sun*, 85-88.

[1281] *Eagle*, 134, 142, *Inferno*, 213-14, *WW II Story*, 114, *Conspiracy*, 1159.

[1282] *Conspiracy*, 1160.

In early 1942, the British worried that if the Japanese gained control of the Indian Ocean they would threaten Allied oil supplies in the Middle East and shut off the southern route to Russia through the Black Sea.[1283]

In early March 1942, Japanese forces in Burma captured Rangoon. Despite intervention by Nationalist Chinese troops, by May the Japanese had driven the Allies out of Burma. After four months in Burma, the Japanese had incurred 4,000 casualties compared to 13,000 for the British.[1284]

The British view in mid-1942 was that they would not have the strength to defeat the full Japanese occupying force in Burma until after the Germans had been defeated.[1285]

The fall of Burma and loss of access to the Burma Road meant that Allied supplies to China had to be flown from India over the 15,000 foot high Himalaya Mountains, called the "Hump," using overworked transport planes.[1286]

During the war more than 1,000 Allied planes were lost crossing the "Hump" — roughly one plane for each day of flying.[1287]

In late March 1942, two Japanese task forces sailed into the Indian Ocean, bombed British bases on Ceylon (now Sri Lanka), destroyed supply ships in the Bay of Bengal, and sank two British cruisers and a small carrier. The remainder of the British fleet there promptly withdrew west to Africa.[1288]

With Japan now in control of Southeast Asia and its navy sailing in the Indian Ocean, the Allies fretted about the potential loss of vital supply routes to Persian Gulf oil and their ability to continue to supply China from the Indian Ocean.[1289]

As the Japanese army advanced west toward India, a British colony, in the spring of 1942, many of India's 400,000,000 citizens opposed British control and saw little advantage in defeating the Axis forces if India remained a British colony. Mohandas Gandhi called for an immediate British withdrawal from India. During the summer of 1942, demonstrations and riots rocked India, with the result that over 1,000 rebels died and 100,000 were imprisoned. Britain was forced to keep

---

[1283] *Masters*, 155, *Pacific*, 16-17.
[1284] *Masters*, 124, *Eagle*, 331-32, *Inferno*, 220, *Conspiracy*, 1159.
[1285] *Masters*, 318.
[1286] *Eagle*, 333, *WW II Story*, 128.
[1287] *Burma*, 122, 434.
[1288] *Eagle*, 152, *Pacific*, 16-17, *Crucible*, 264-65.
[1289] *Crucible*, 264-66.

many soldiers there to enforce the peace.[1290]

The Philippines Battle Continues

Despite messages from Washington signaling that no meaningful military reinforcements were available to send to the Philippines, MacArthur told his troops on January 15:

> Help is on the way from the United States. Thousands of troops and hundreds of planes are being dispatched.... No further retreat is possible. We have more troops in Bataan than the Japanese have thrown against us; our supplies are ample; a determined defense will defeat the enemy's attack.[1291]

Reeling from the Japanese invasion, on February 8 Filipino President Quezon, with MacArthur's puzzling support, asked President Roosevelt to grant the Philippines immediate independence so that the nation could be a "neutral" in the war. Roosevelt promptly rejected the proposal and insisted that the United States continue to defend the islands.[1292]

In February 1942, General MacArthur accepted and kept a confidential $500,000 reward from President Quezon, who a month earlier had issued a peculiar executive order thanking MacArthur and his staff for "their magnificent defense" efforts in the Philippines. Some speculate that Quezon's motive was to strengthen MacArthur's support of the beleaguered country.[1293]

Despite being underfed and ill with malaria and other diseases, courageous American and Filipino troops, commanded in the field by Lieutenant General Wainwright, slowed for several months the Japanese advance south through the mountain jungles of the Bataan peninsula.[1294]

Only once did MacArthur leave Corregidor to visit his hungry and sick troops on Bataan, and then for just a day.[1295]

During his stay on Corregidor, MacArthur wrote or edited multiple Army press releases taking personal credit for American defensive

---

[1290] *Masters,* 118, 404, *Inferno,* xix, 404-13, *Eagle,* 336-37.

[1291] *Crucible,* 240-241.

[1292] *Ike,* 247, *Crusade,* 26, *Supreme Commander,* 18, *Crucible,* 242-243.

[1293] *Eagle,* 115-16, *Conspiracy,* 1133, *Crucible,* 243-244.

[1294] *Tears,* 114-120, *Inferno,* 229-30, *Conspiracy,* 1163.

[1295] *WW II Story,* 103, *Tears,* 122.

actions in the battle of Bataan. The American press treated him like a hero. Of 142 communiqués issued from his headquarters between December and March, 109 made no mention of anyone but him. They often went like this: "General MacArthur and his troops in the Bataan peninsula ..." or "General MacArthur's small air force ..." or "General MacArthur launched a heavy counterattack ...."[1296]

Some of the frustrated American troops on Bataan crafted the following ditty critical of MacArthur:

Dugout Doug MacArthur lies a shaking on the Rock,
Safe from all the bombers and from any sudden shock.
Dugout Doug is eating of the best food on Bataan
And his troops go starving on.[1297]

MacArthur and his family remained in the Corregidor fortress until March 11, 1942, when, under orders from President Roosevelt, they were secretly taken by PT boat 600 miles to the southern Philippine island of Mindanao and then flown 1,400 miles to Australia, where MacArthur brazenly announced, "I shall return." American General Jonathan Wainwright was left to command all Allied forces remaining in the Philippines.[1298]

On April 9, 1942, despite orders from General Wainright to fight to the death, General King, who commanded 76,000 sick, listless and starving American and Filipino troops on Bataan, remorsefully surrendered unconditionally to the Japanese. Before doing so, King sought assurances from the Japanese that his troops would be treated well. The Japanese proclaimed, "We are not barbarians." This was the largest surrender in United States Army history.[1299]

The Bataan Death March

After General King's surrender, the Japanese ordered his 76,000 troops and 26,000 civilians to march sixty-six miles out of Bataan to a railhead from which they were to be taken another forty miles by train to a POW camp. Hungry, thirsty and subject to robbery, abuse

---

[1296] *Eagle*, 118, *Tears*, 124, *WW II Story*, 103.

[1297] *Tears*, 121, *Eagle*, 117, *WW II Story*, 103.

[1298] *Tears*, 121-25, *Eagle*, 116-19, *Inferno*, 229, *WW II Story*, 102-04, *Conspiracy*, 1160-62, *Crucible*, 243-244.

[1299] *Tears*, 151, 155, *Eagle*, 135, *Inferno*, 229-30, *WW II Story*, 104-05, *Conspiracy*, 1164-65.

and slaughter, an average soldier's walk took five to seven days. An estimated 1,100 Americans and 5,000 Filipinos died on the Bataan Death March. Those who survived faced spending the rest of the war as POWs performing slave labor.[1300]

Japanese mistreatment of POWs was due in part to the view in Japan that anyone who surrendered was a disgraceful coward, and because Japan often assigned misfits and troublemakers to guard POW camps. The ancient Japanese *Bushido* code warned warriors: "Do not survive the dishonor of capture."[1301]

United States military leaders did not learn the fate of the Bataan Death March captives until the summer of 1943, after three officers escaped and made their way to Australia. The press was not informed of the Death March until early 1944. The belated newspaper reports sparked outrage among American readers.[1302]

America Bombs Tokyo

On April 18, 1942, sixteen twin-engine American B-25 medium bombers, led by Lt. Colonel James Doolittle, took off from the carrier *Hornet*, flew 650 miles west and bombed Tokyo in a surprise attack that had little military but substantial psychological impact on the Japanese. Fifteen of the planes then flew on to crash land out of fuel in China, while one landed in Russia. Seventy-seven of the eighty American crewmembers who participated survived the day's raid. The five-man crew that landed in Russia was allowed, after a year of captivity, to escape to Iran. Of eight who were subsequently captured by the Japanese, three were shot with Hirohito's approval, one died of torture in prison in 1944, and the remaining four were liberated in August 1945. During a four-month period following the Tokyo raid, the Japanese slaughtered about 250,000 Chinese in punishment for the few who had collaborated with the Americans in the Doolittle attack.[1303]

Roosevelt, in reply to a press conference question about where the planes that bombed Tokyo came from, drolly said "from our new secret base at Shangri-La."[1304]

The Tokyo attack emphasized the military importance of aircraft

---

[1300] *Tears*, 163, 168, 202, 293, 361, *Inferno*, 230, *WW II Story*, 106-112, *Conspiracy*, 1165-70, 1237-38.

[1301] *Eagle*, 398, *WW II Story*, 105, *Pacific*, 35.

[1302] *Eagle*, 398.

[1303] *Eagle*, 154-55, *Inferno*, 232, *WW II Story*, 116-18, *Pacific*, 17-18, *Conspiracy*, 1170-75, 1220, *Sword*, 42-43, *Crucible*, 281-301.

[1304] *Admirals*, 245, *Crucible*, 298.

carriers and convinced the Japanese that they must prevent any similar homeland attacks in the future. To achieve this goal and force the United States to negotiate a prompt end to the Pacific war, the Japanese developed a multi-pronged plan. First, they would send forces south to seize Port Moresby in New Guinea, thereby threatening Australia. Then they would seize the Aleutians and the mid-Pacific island of Midway, which America had held since 1867, hopefully triggering a battle in which America's Pacific carriers would be destroyed. Following a victory at Midway, the Japanese planned to regroup in the South Pacific to take New Caledonia, Fiji and Samoa, in the process isolating Australia. By the fall of 1942, the Japanese aimed to invade the outer islands of the Hawaiian chain.[1305]

Corregidor Falls

On May 6, 1942, General Wainwright sought to surrender the remaining 9,000 Americans and 2,000 Filipinos who were still under attack in the Philippine fortress of Corregidor. Because he was by then in command of all U.S. troops in the Philippines, the Japanese conditioned the Corregidor surrender on Wainwright's issuance of orders directing all American troops in the islands to surrender. Concerned for the well-being of America's POWs already in Japanese hands, on May 7 Wainwright announced by radio the total Philippine surrender.[1306]

The press in America found glory in the defense of Bataan and Corregidor, but in reality it was a defeat in which the Japanese had extended their reach in the Pacific. Eisenhower wrote in his diary, "Poor Wainwright! He did the fighting ... [MacArthur] got such glory as the public could find ...."[1307]

Despite Wainwright's Corregidor surrender orders, for the remainder of the war some 200,000 Filipinos and a few Americans engaged in guerilla warfare in the Philippines against the occupying Japanese and delivered valuable information about the enemy to the Allies.[1308]

The Battle of the Coral Sea

In early May 1942, American and Japanese naval forces clashed off

---

[1305] *Sword*, xvii, 26-28, 42-43, *Inferno*, 232, *Conspiracy*, 1174-75.

[1306] *Tears*, 234, *Inferno*, 230, *Conspiracy*, 1175-77.

[1307] *Inferno*, 230-31.

[1308] *Eagle*, 466-67, *Conspiracy*, 1177.

the southeast coast of New Guinea in the inconclusive Battle of the Coral Sea. Allied information gained from the broken Japanese naval code, JN 25, allowed the U.S. Navy to surreptitiously move two of its carriers and several other ships to confront a Japanese invasion fleet. The world's first carrier-versus-carrier battle was fought entirely by aircraft. The American carrier *Lexington* was sunk and *Yorktown* was damaged. The Japanese lost a new light carrier, *Shoho*, suffered serious damage to the heavy carrier *Shokaku*, and lost other smaller vessels and seventy-seven planes. American pilots mauled the air group from the Japanese heavy carrier *Zuikaku*. The Americans lost 543 dead and the Japanese lost over 1,000 killed. Following the battle, Japan abandoned its planned amphibious invasion of Port Moresby in Papua, New Guinea, which it viewed as the final step before attacking Australia.[1309]

During the Coral Sea battle, U.S. Navy aerial torpedoes were found to be slow, unreliable and often failed to explode even in a direct hit. This problem lingered until 1943.[1310]

The Japanese carriers *Shokaku* and *Zuikaku* lost so many planes and crew during the Coral Sea battle that they were unable to participate in the planned June battle of Midway Island. Unlike American carrier air groups, which were independent of the ships and therefore transferable from one to another, Japanese carrier air groups were permanently assigned to a particular carrier.[1311]

The Japanese incorrectly believed that in the Battle of the Coral Sea they had sunk or crippled the American carrier *Yorktown*, which they thought left the United States with just two carriers in the Pacific, *Hornet* and *Enterprise*, or at most three (if *Wasp* had been transferred from the Atlantic).[1312]

Japan Achieves its Expansion Goals

By June 1942, Japanese forces had reached the limits of their World War II advance — the border between Burma and India, control of the Indian Ocean, the oilfields of Java, Sumatra and North Borneo, New Guinea near northern Australia, and across the Pacific all the way to Hawaii. This was one of the largest empires ever assembled by one na-

---

[1309] *Engineers*, 292, *Ultra Secret*, 175, *Eagle*, 160-63, 449, *Inferno*, 233-36, *WW II Story*, 118-19, *Pacific*, 18-21, *Conspiracy*, 1178-83, *Sword*, 10, 60, 63, 418, *Admirals*, 246-49, *Rising Sun*, 103-190, *Crucible*, 314-22, 329-74.
[1310] *Inferno*, 236, *Conspiracy*, 1182.
[1311] *Sword*, 65, *Eagle*, 162-63.
[1312] *Eagle*, 162, 166, *Inferno*, 239, *Pacific*, 22, *Sword*, 32, 41-42, 66.

tion, and it was acquired at the relatively small cost of about 10,000 men and a few small ships.[1313]

These extraordinary victories delighted the Japanese public and reinforced the widely-held view that Japan was a nation destined by heaven to dominate Asia. The military's influence on Japanese politics was by now virtually unlimited. Political parties were dissolved, the state-controlled media touted the military's achievements, and the nation's governance was dominated by a single entity — the Imperial Rule Assistance Association that vetted and determined all candidates for elective office.[1314]

Having gained control over important sources of oil, rubber, tin and other natural resources, Japan essentially had achieved its war goals and could sit tight. The onus was on the Allies to dislodge and defeat the Japanese.[1315]

It is significant that the new territory Japan acquired included very little additional industrial capacity, such as shipbuilding, and that the raw materials it gained still had to be transported back to Japan by merchant ships vulnerable to attack by the U.S. Navy.[1316]

By the summer of 1942, Japan had stretched itself so far that its overburdened merchant vessels could not adequately supply all of its armed forces. Submarines that could have been used to attack American shipping were therefore diverted to supplying remote Japanese bases.[1317]

America Interns Japanese-Americans

About two months after the Pearl Harbor attack, President Roosevelt issued an Executive Order excluding persons of Japanese ancestry from the Pacific coast of the United States. Over 100,000 Japanese-American citizens and resident aliens living near the Pacific were rounded up, purportedly because they represented a threat to the United States. They were, without criminal charges or legal due process, involuntarily forced to leave their homes and businesses and placed in ten remote government-run shabby internment camps in Utah, Nevada and California.[1318]

[1313] *Engineers*, 292, *Pacific*, 21, *Sword*, 19-22, *Crucible*, 269.
[1314] *Crucible*, 270-71.
[1315] *Engineers*, 294, *Inferno*, 197.
[1316] *Sword*, 427.
[1317] *Engineers*, 293-94, *Eagle*, 486, *Sword*, 427.
[1318] *Eagle*, 408-09, *WW II Story*, 507, *1944*, 447.

In December 1944, the United States Supreme Court ruled that the President's exclusion of certain persons from the west coast was legal.[1319]

In a companion decision, the Supreme Court ruled that the incarceration of loyal and law-abiding American citizens, regardless of ancestry, was illegal.[1320]

Nisei in the Military

Americans of Japanese ancestry ("*Nisei*") were deemed by the Selective Service Department to be enemy aliens and not eligible to serve in the United States military — until January 1943, when Roosevelt erased the restriction.[1321]

Once *Nisei* were permitted to join the United States military, thousands enlisted. In September of 1943, the 100th Infantry Battalion, staffed by *Nisei*, fought valiantly in Italy, suffering 900 casualties out of 1,300 men.[1322]

The Army then established the 442nd Infantry Battalion composed of *Nisei*. They battled the enemy in France in 1944 and Italy the next year, and became the most decorated infantry unit in the United States Army.[1323]

Allied Defensive Options

In March 1942, the United States and Britain agreed to partition the world into three areas of accountability. The United States would have sole responsibility for the Pacific; Britain would have sole responsibility for the "middle area" from Singapore across the Indian Ocean to the Persian Gulf, the Red Sea and the Mediterranean; and the two nations would share responsibility for the Atlantic.[1324]

The drubbing that the United States suffered at Pearl Harbor, in the Philippines and elsewhere in the Pacific in 1941-42 forced the American military to acknowledge several painful lessons. First, the battleship had ceased to be the decisive naval vessel; carriers and submarines were the new weapons of importance. Second, the Pacific defense against Japan would have to be borne solely by the Americans;

[1319] *Korematsu v. United States*, 323 U.S. 214 (1944).

[1320] *Ex Parte Endo*, 323 U.S. 283 (1944), *1944*, 448.

[1321] *WW II Story*, 507, *Dawn*, 72.

[1322] *WW II Story*, 507-08, *Clark*, 228.

[1323] *WW II Story*, 507-08.

[1324] *Eagle*, 142, *Crucible*, 266-67.

the British and Dutch navies there had been neutered. Third, it was essential to safeguard the nation of Australia and the Pacific supply routes from the United States to Australia. Fourth, the "Germany First" strategy had to be flexible enough to allow the U.S. Navy to address these Pacific challenges.[1325]

In July 1942, President Roosevelt appointed Admiral William Leahy to serve as his senior military advisor, a role in which he acted both as the president's personal representative on the Joint Chiefs of Staff and as neutral JCS chairman arbitrating service rivalries. Leahy's appointment thwarted efforts by some to have MacArthur named supreme commander of all United States armed forces.[1326]

Because of service rivalries, in the spring of 1942 the United States divided command responsibility in the Pacific between the Army and the Navy. General MacArthur was appointed commander in chief of the Southwest Pacific Area, which included Australia, the Philippines, the Solomon Islands, New Guinea, the Bismarck Archipelago, Borneo and all of the Dutch East Indies except Sumatra. Admiral Nimitz was given command of the Central and North Pacific Ocean Areas. Admiral Ghormley commanded the South Pacific area. (In July, responsibility for an attack on the island of Tulagi in the Solomons was transferred from MacArthur to Nimitz). Overall, the Joint Chiefs of Staff, however, retained final authority over the entire Pacific theater and approved each significant operation.[1327]

In 1942, the Allies had four potential attack routes to Japan: (a) launch a counteroffensive in mainland China, (b) recover Burma, Thailand, Singapore, French Indochina and the Dutch East Indies and advance toward Japan from there, (c) push northward from Australia through New Guinea, the Solomon and Bismarck Islands, and the Philippines, and/or (d) cross the expanses of the Central Pacific.[1328]

A counterattack in China as the main approach to Japan was not feasible because necessary supplies would have to be transported from India over the Himalayas to China at too high a cost. Nonetheless, the Allies continued to support the Chinese Nationalist government of Chiang Kai-shek, thereby tying down in China millions of Japanese troops.[1329]

[1325] *Sword*, 39-40, *Eagle*, 143, 147.

[1326] *Admirals*, 269-72.

[1327] *Eagle*, 144, 186, *Ghosts*, 13, *Admirals*, 261, *Crucible*, 267-68.

[1328] *Engineers*, 295.

[1329] *Engineers*, 298.

Pursuing the Japanese mainly through Southeast Asia (Burma, etc.) was not feasible because much of that area was jungle with seasonal monsoons that would thwart troop and equipment movements.[1330]

Thus, the Americans decided to counterattack from the two remaining directions: Army forces under General MacArthur from the Southwest Pacific, and naval forces under Admiral Nimitz from the Central Pacific.[1331]

The United States had seven battleships assigned to the Pacific fleet in mid-1942. However, because of their thirst for fuel and the Navy's limited supply of both oil and tankers in the Pacific, the Navy had to choose between operating carriers or battleships. Due to their offensive capabilities, carriers were the clear choice.[1332]

The Battle of Midway

In March 1942, Admiral Yamamoto recognized that Japan was not then in a position to launch an amphibious attack on the Hawaiian Islands due to their considerable distance from Japan, the strength of American defenses there, and Japan's overextended shipping capacity. Thus, the aggressive admiral settled on the idea of attacking the American base on tiny Midway Island, a coral atoll located about 1150 miles northwest of Oahu, in hopes of provoking a confrontation with the remaining U.S. Navy warships in the Pacific fleet and destroying them in battle.[1333]

In May, the United States Navy, using the broken Japanese naval code, intercepted secret messages suggesting that Japan had dispatched a task force of 145 warships and over 600 planes to capture Midway. (The Japanese had planned to use a new naval code as of April 1, but delayed its implementation until June). The advance warning afforded equally-aggressive Admiral Nimitz an opportunity to avoid the trap.[1334]

Although the United States had not yet engaged in combat against the Germans in Europe, Nimitz was willing to confront the Japanese in a decisive battle at Midway because he believed his fighting personnel were at least as good as Japan's and he was confident that he had an advantage in intelligence gathering. To match up against planes

---

[1330] *Engineers*, 299-300.
[1331] *Engineers*, 301-02, 312.
[1332] *Neptune*, 22.
[1333] *Crucible*, 277-81.
[1334] *Ultra Secret*, 175-76, *Eagle*, 168, 450, *Inferno*, 239, *WW II Story*, 119-126, *Conspiracy*, 1184-85, *Sword*, 67, 92-93, *Crucible*, 302-07, 383-90.

A CONCISE HISTORY OF THE SECOND WORLD WAR

launched from four expected Japanese carriers, Nimitz counted on using planes from three U.S. carriers plus land-based planes flying from Midway.[1335]

The Japanese battle plan had four components: (a) an attack on the distant Aleutian Islands of Attu and Kiska on the first day in an effort to extend Japan's defensive perimeter, (b) the next day four Japanese carriers would launch a surprise air attack on Midway, (c) the following day Japanese troops would invade Midway, and (d) nearby Japanese battleships, submarines and carriers would await the expected American naval counterattack.[1336]

Japan's scheme suffered from several weaknesses. First, the attack on the insignificant Aleutians stripped valuable naval power away from the Midway battle scene. Second, the Japanese attack on remote Midway would have to be carried out without support from any land-based planes. Third, even if the Midway invasion succeeded, the Japanese fleet would have to retreat to Japan to replenish, leaving the island with little defense against a United States counterattack. Fourth, if Midway were taken, the Japanese would have difficulty supplying it from Japan because their merchant shipping was already overburdened. Finally, if taken, Midway was too small to provide a meaningful Japanese presence in that part of the Pacific.[1337]

Assuming they prevailed at Midway and destroyed most of the U.S. Navy's Pacific fleet, the Japanese intended to take Hawaii in late summer and then seize the Panama Canal and harass cities on the west coast of the United States. The thinking was that this would curtail America's support of Australia and, perhaps, persuade America to negotiate for peace.[1338]

On May 27, 1942, the damaged carrier *Yorktown* limped into Pearl Harbor from the Coral Sea battle. Told that needed repairs would take about ninety days, Admiral Nimitz insisted that the ship be ready to sail in three days. To carry out this order, 1,400 welders and other dockyard workers labored twenty-four hours a day to make temporary repairs.[1339]

Unbeknownst to the Japanese, the carriers *Hornet* and *Enterprise*,

---

[1335] *Sword*, 93-94.

[1336] *Sword*, 43-59, *Eagle*, 167, *Inferno*, 239, 358, *Conspiracy*, 1184, *Crucible*, 378-79.

[1337] *Sword*, 35-36, 52-59.

[1338] *Conspiracy*, 1183, *Sword*, 33, 38, *Admirals*, 253.

[1339] *Eagle*, 168-69, *Inferno*, 239, *Pacific*, 24, *Conspiracy*, 1186, *Sword*, 94, *Crucible*, 396-97.

together with twenty-two other warships, left Pearl Harbor on May 28 to sail to a point northeast of Midway, out of range of scout planes from the four Japanese carriers that were sailing toward Midway from the west. The patched-up *Yorktown* left Pearl Harbor two days later. Japanese submarines assigned to spot the movement of enemy ships from Pearl Harbor were late arriving and missed the passage of the U.S. Navy carriers.[1340]

During the morning of June 3, 1942, Japanese air craft attacked American installations in the Aleutian Islands. That same morning, American search planes from Midway (PBY Catalinas and B-17s) located Japanese troop transports and destroyers heading east to invade Midway Island. (The Japanese carriers, positioned many miles north of the invasion convoy, were not sighted by the United States planes and were unaware of the presence of enemy carriers). That afternoon, B-17 bombers attacked the Japanese troop ships but scored no hits.[1341]

At about 0430 on June 4, Admiral Nagumo, who commanded the Japanese carriers, (a) sent out seven reconnaissance planes in mostly eastern and southern directions, (b) dispatched 108 planes to attack Midway, and (c) assigned eleven fighters the duty of protecting his fleet from overhead. Nagumo held his remaining carrier planes in reserve to attack any United States ships that his search planes might locate.[1342]

Because none of the ships in Nagumo's fleet had radar, the Japanese relied on reconnaissance planes and destroyer escorts to detect enemy planes by sight.[1343]

Shortly after Nagumo sent his planes off to attack Midway, American scout planes located the Japanese carriers and warned Midway of the incoming enemy planes. Midway's aircraft immediately took off — bombers to strike the Japanese carriers and fighters to oppose the incoming Japanese planes. The yet undiscovered American carriers sailed southwest toward the Japanese warships.[1344]

Nagumo's planes attacked Midway at about 0600, but the damage was limited because the forewarned Americans had previously launched their planes and installed strong defensive weapons. The commander of the Japanese attack planes radioed Nagumo at 0700 that a second air attack on Midway was warranted. Significantly, Nagumo

[1340] *Eagle*, 169-70, *Conspiracy*, 1185-87, *Sword*, 92-98, *Crucible*, 401-02, 406.
[1341] *Eagle*, 170, *Inferno*, 240, *Conspiracy*, 1188, *Sword*, 106, *Crucible*, 406-08.
[1342] *Eagle*, 170, *Inferno*, 242, *Conspiracy*, 1188, *Sword*, 107-14, 128-32, 154.
[1343] *Sword*, 136, 186.
[1344] *Eagle*, 170, *Inferno*, 242, *Sword*, 133-35, *Conspiracy*, 1188-89.

lost sixty-eight of his carrier-based aircraft during the opening attack on Midway, leaving him with fewer planes than the Americans had. (He longed for the carriers and planes Yamamoto had sent to do battle in the Aleutians).[1345]

Shortly after 0700, Midway's torpedo planes and bombers attacked the Japanese carrier group but did little harm. Ironically, several of the Japanese carriers could travel faster than the speed of the poorly designed U.S. Navy torpedoes. Of thirty American attack planes, twenty-seven were either shot down or so damaged that they never flew again.[1346]

To attack Midway again, Nagumo would have to violate his standing orders and arm his standby planes with high-explosive bombs for land targets instead of torpedoes and armor-piercing bombs for any enemy ships that might be nearby. The rearming process could take from one to two hours. Because his reconnaissance planes had not yet discovered that American carriers were in the vicinity, at 0715 Nagumo ordered his planes rearmed for another land attack.[1347]

At 0745, a Japanese scout plane reported the presence of about ten American ships. Nagumo, eager to attack the American ships, immediately reversed course and ordered his planes rearmed with torpedoes and armor-piercing bombs. He wanted fighters to escort the bombers, but many of his fighters were then occupied providing air cover for the carrier fleet. Complicating matters, the Japanese planes returning from their attack on Midway were expected back at about 0815. They would need clear decks on which to land for refueling and rearming.[1348]

Between 0800 and 0830, while Nagumo was processing all of this information, additional dive-bombers and B-17s from Midway attacked the Japanese carrier group, but again with little success.[1349]

At about 0800, Admiral Spruance, commanding the U.S. Navy carriers *Hornet* and *Enterprise*, sent all 117 of his planes to attack the Japanese carriers that were about 150 miles away — close to the maximum range of the American planes.[1350]

Almost an hour later, Admiral Fletcher launched thirty-five of *Yorktown*'s planes and sent them to locate the Japanese carriers. He

[1345] *Eagle*, 171, *Inferno*, 242, *Conspiracy*, 1189-90, *Sword*, 149, 202-04, *Crucible*, 411.
[1346] *Eagle*, 171, *Inferno*, 242, *Conspiracy*, 1189-90, *Sword*, 149-152.
[1347] *Eagle*, 171, *Inferno*, 242, *Conspiracy*, 1191, *Sword*, 152-58, *Crucible*, 412.
[1348] *Eagle*, 172, *Inferno*, 243, *Conspiracy*, 1191-92, *Sword*, 159-73.
[1349] *Eagle*, 172, *Inferno*, 242, *Conspiracy*, 1191, *Sword*, 170, 176-80, 185.
[1350] *Eagle*, 173, *Conspiracy*, 1192-93, *Sword*, 173-74.

saved his remaining planes to deal with any contingency.[1351]

In the meantime, after taking aboard the surviving Japanese Midway attack planes, Nagumo's carriers sailed northeast seeking to place greater distance between themselves and the American carriers.[1352]

Fifteen torpedo bombers from *Hornet*, with no fighter protection, found three of Nagumo's carriers at about 0915, but their attack caused no meaningful damage. Within twenty minutes, Japanese fighters shot down all of the attacking *Hornet* planes and all but one of the American crew members had been killed. However, the attack impeded Nagumo's efforts to launch his planes to strike the American carriers.[1353]

At about 0940, fourteen torpedo bombers from *Enterprise*, also without fighter protection, attacked the Japanese carrier *Kaga*, but caused no damage. Japanese fighters destroyed most of those planes during the twenty minute battle.[1354]

Shortly after 1000, Admiral Nagumo's carriers were making preparations to send 108 torpedo planes off to attack the American carriers. It is unclear whether the Japanese planes were on the flight decks or below. What is clear is that the planes never got airborne.[1355]

At just that time, *Dauntless* dive-bombers and torpedo planes from *Yorktown* and *Enterprise*, supported by fighters, surprised the Japanese carriers and attacked the ships from opposite directions. Many of the American torpedo planes were destroyed by Japanese fighters, but the dive-bombers succeeded in striking the carriers *Kaga* (at least four hits), *Soryu* (at least three hits) and *Akagi* (at least one hit). After day-long efforts to save the wounded carriers failed, the Japanese reluctantly scuttled all three that evening.[1356]

A total of seventy American aircraft were lost during the morning's operations — about forty per cent of the planes launched. The Japanese lost about seventy-five per cent of their carrier planes.[1357]

At least three American airmen who had been shot down were captured that day by the Japanese, interrogated, and then killed.[1358]

The last Japanese carrier, *Hiryu*, had become separated from the

---

[1351] *Sword*, 189, *Eagle*, 173-74, *Conspiracy*, 1195.

[1352] *Eagle*, 173, *Sword*, 192, 199.

[1353] *Eagle*, 173-74, *Sword*, 205-10, *Conspiracy*, 1194, *Inferno*, 243-44.

[1354] *Eagle*, 174, *Inferno*, 243-44, *Conspiracy*, 1194, *Sword*, 205-16.

[1355] *Conspiracy*, 1195-96, *Sword*, 229-31.

[1356] *Eagle*, 174-75, *Inferno*, 245-46, *Conspiracy*, 1195-97, *Sword*, 216-63, 320-21, 331, 336-38, 353.

[1357] *Sword*, 269, 275.

[1358] *Sword*, 288, 320.

others during defensive maneuvers. By 1100, it had launched planes to attack *Yorktown*, some ninety miles away. At about 1210, after American fighters had shot down several Japanese dive-bombers, the remaining seven enemy planes bombed *Yorktown*, striking it three times. At about 1430, more Japanese planes from *Hiryu* attacked the crippled *Yorktown*, torpedoing it twice and forcing an "abandon ship" order.[1359]

Several hours later, twenty-six dive-bombers from *Enterprise* and *Yorktown* (flying from *Enterprise*) struck *Hiryu* (at least four hits) and left her sinking. The Americans had destroyed in one day four of the six Japanese carriers that had attacked Pearl Harbor six months earlier.[1360]

On June 5, 1942, Admiral Yamamoto ordered the remains of the Japanese task force to retreat west. In the process of turning, two Japanese cruisers collided and were slowed by damage. The next day, American bombers from *Enterprise* and *Hornet* sank one and seriously damaged the other.[1361]

On June 6, the United States naval task force called off efforts to find what was left of the enemy and headed home to Pearl Harbor.[1362]

On June 7, the empty *Yorktown*, which the U.S. Navy had under tow, was torpedoed and sunk by a Japanese submarine.[1363]

In a meager achievement, Japanese soldiers invaded the Aleutian islands of Kiska and Attu on June 7. The rest of the wounded Japanese Midway fleet set out for the week-long trip home. Of little strategic value, the Japanese occupied Kiska and Attu until August 1943.[1364]

The United States Navy prevailed in the Battle of Midway, sinking four Japanese carriers and a heavy cruiser, destroying some 280 Japanese planes and about half of their pilots, and damaging another cruiser. More than 3,000 Japanese sailors were killed, including over 700 almost irreplaceable aircraft mechanics. This was the first major defeat Japan's navy had suffered since 1592. The Americans lost the carrier *Yorktown*, a destroyer and 146 aircraft.[1365]

After Midway, the Japanese had only five carriers left. Before the

---

[1359] *Eagle*, 175, *Inferno*, 246-47, *Pacific*, 25, *Conspiracy*, 1197-98, *Sword*, 262-65, 292-99, 312-18.

[1360] *Eagle*, 175, *Inferno*, 247, *Conspiracy*, 1198, *Sword*, 318-19, 324-27, 345-48.

[1361] *Eagle*, 176, *Inferno*, 248, *Sword*, 346-49, 367-71.

[1362] *Eagle*, 176, *Sword*, 381-82.

[1363] *Inferno*, 248, *Conspiracy*, 1198, *Sword*, 372-75, 383, *Crucible*, 466-70.

[1364] *Eagle*, 181, *Sword*, 383-84.

[1365] *Masters*, 179, 241, *Engineers*, 292, 316, *Eagle*, 176, *WW II Story*, 125, *Conspiracy*, 1198, *Sword*, 18, 145, 417, *Crucible*, 476.

war ended in 1945, they were able to build only five new carriers, most of which were inferior in quality to the four lost at Midway.[1366]

Between April 1942 and April 1943, Japan lost 2,817 naval aircraft. Because of production difficulties, the Japanese aircraft industry was able to build only fifty-six carrier-based attack planes in 1942, causing a severe shortage in such aircraft available to the fleet and a reduction in the effectiveness of Japan's carriers.[1367]

To mask the devastating Midway defeat from the Japanese public, on June 10 Tokyo radio announced that Japan had won a great victory sinking two American carriers and destroying 120 planes while losing only one carrier, having another seriously damaged, and losing thirty-five Japanese planes. To preserve the false propaganda, wounded Japanese sailors from the Midway battle were impounded upon return to Japan and the healthy were quickly sent to remote battle stations without being afforded home leave.[1368]

Due to the intense inter-service rivalry between the Japanese army and navy, the army did not inform the navy before the Midway battle that the Americans had broken the naval operational code.[1369]

After its losses in the Battle of Midway, Japan apparently gave up any further thought of seizing the Hawaiian Islands.[1370]

Following the Battle of Midway, the Japanese navy did not fight another major sea battle with the United States until mid-1944.[1371]

Fighting on New Guinea

Beginning in 1942, coast watchers — usually local planters, missionaries or government officials on the Solomon Islands, New Guinea and the Bismarck Islands — sent valuable radio reports to the Allies about Japanese ship and aircraft movements.[1372]

By mid-July, 1942, General MacArthur's staff had received several reports that Japan was shipping a large force of soldiers to Papua, New Guinea, an island just above Australia. MacArthur and his staff gave the reports little weight and did not rush Allied troops there.[1373]

On July 21, 1942, 16,000 Japanese soldiers landed at Buna on the

---

[1366] *Conspiracy*, 1198, *Sword*, 391-92, 421.
[1367] *Sword*, 89-90, 420.
[1368] *Conspiracy*, 1201-02, *Sword*, 386-88, *Crucible*, 482-86.
[1369] *Neptune*, 45.
[1370] *Engineers*, 364, *Eagle*, 178.
[1371] *Eagle*, xiv.
[1372] *Eagle*, 458-59, *Inferno*, 256, *Neptune*, 4, 47.
[1373] *Eagle*, 188-89.

northern coast of New Guinea. They set out south on the Kokoda Trail to cross the rugged Owen Stanley Mountains toward Port Moresby, from which they planned to attack Australia, 200 miles further south. The rocky, steep and slippery Kokoda Trail climbed mountains that reached an elevation of 13,000 feet and was in places so narrow that only one man could pass. The men were carrying, in jungle conditions, weapons and supplies weighing sixty or more pounds.[1374]

Initially, Australian troops in New Guinea were assigned the job of resisting the Japanese salient. By September, Japan's forces had driven the Australians on the Kokoda Trail back almost to Port Moresby. U.S. Army Air Force bombers then attacked the Japanese supply lines, forcing the Japanese to withdraw to the north shore of Papua.[1375]

After six months of hard fighting, Australian and American troops drove the Japanese out of New Guinea, but at a high cost in lives — 8,500 American casualties (including 3,000 dead) and 21,000 Australian casualties. MacArthur has been criticized for his strategy of allowing the Japanese to land on New Guinea without opposition and later ordering his poorly supplied troops to attack the enemy head-on.[1376]

While MacArthur took personal credit for the Allied victory on New Guinea, he was never even close to the scene of battle. General Eichelberger, who led the troops at Buna, wrote:

> The great hero went home [to Australia] without seeing Buna before, during, or after the fight while permitting press articles from his GHQ to say he was leading his troops in battle.[1377]

The Guadalcanal Combat

The South Pacific Solomon island of Guadalcanal, sixty miles long by thirty miles wide, lies northeast of Australia about ten degrees below the Equator, and some 3,600 miles from Pearl Harbor. In mid-1942, the Japanese began construction of an airbase on that jungle island that threatened the American supply route to Australia.[1378]

The United States headquartered its South Pacific naval operations in Nouméa, the capital of the French-controlled island of New Cale-

---

[1374] *Eagle*, 189, *Inferno*, 249, 258-60, *Conspiracy*, 1207.
[1375] *Inferno*, 260, *Eagle*, 189-90.
[1376] *Eagle*, 189-90, 214-17, *Inferno*, 261, *WW II Story*, 157-59, *Conspiracy*, 1250.
[1377] *WW II Story*, 159.
[1378] *Eagle*, 185, 191-92, *Inferno*, 249, 255, *WW II Story*, 129, *Pacific*, 27, *Neptune*, 5, 20.

donia. The island's governing administration, which was not aligned with Vichy France, reluctantly permitted the Allied base there but severely limited its size. A presence on Nouméa was essential to the Allies' ability to protect the sea lanes to Australia.[1379]

On August 7, 1942, the Navy landed some 19,000 U.S. Marines on Guadalcanal and several nearby islands. Supplies for the Marines were being offloaded from transport and cargo ships under the command of Admiral Turner. Admiral Fletcher, a veteran of the hard-fought Coral Sea and Midway battles, commanded carriers and other ships that were responsible for protecting Turner's supply vessels. After providing two days of cover, Fletcher withdrew his task force about twelve hours ahead of schedule out of concern that Japanese planes from nearby bases and carriers would attack his vitally important carriers. Turner felt that he had been deserted.[1380]

On August 9, shortly after midnight, Japanese ships rounded nearby Savo Island and steamed undetected in the dark toward Admiral Turner's relatively unprotected ships. In less than an hour of fighting, the Japanese left four Allied cruisers sunk or sinking and two destroyers and a cruiser damaged. This was the worst American naval defeat since 1812. About 1,600 Allied sailors died. The next day an American submarine sank a Japanese heavy cruiser returning from the battle — the first major Japanese warship sunk by an American submarine. The surviving Allied ships then withdrew, leaving the Marines on Guadalcanal without needed supplies.[1381]

Admiral King called the Navy's Savo Island defeat the "blackest day of the whole war." To keep news of the loss from the public, approximately 500 survivors from the battle were held in quarantine in California for some time.[1382]

Like a tripod, to be successful the Guadalcanal campaign needed a coordinated approach from three separate elements of warfare. "For the infantry to seize and hold the island, ships had to control the sea. For a fleet to control the sea, the pilots had to fly from the island's airfield. For the pilots to fly from the airfield, the infantry had to hold the island."[1383]

[1379] *Neptune*, 37-38, 209.
[1380] *Eagle*, 191-95, *Inferno*, 249-50, *WW II Story*, 130, *Pacific*, 27-29, *Conspiracy*, 1207-08, *Neptune*, xxi, 50-53.
[1381] *Eagle*, 192-94, *Inferno*, 250-51, *WW II Story*, 130-31, *Conspiracy*, 1212, *Neptune*, 56-87.
[1382] *Neptune*, 91.
[1383] *Neptune*, xix.

Despite the Savo Island naval losses, the Marines quickly captured and completed construction of the Guadalcanal airstrip that the Japanese had begun, and by August 15 were receiving some supplies by air. Japanese troops remained on parts of the island and over the next two months each side sought with great difficulty to bolster its forces.[1384]

On August 24, in the Battle of the Eastern Solomons, American carrier-based planes sank the Japanese light carrier *Ryujo*, while enemy planes damaged the American carrier *Enterprise*.[1385]

In late August, the Japanese landed 6,000 men on Guadalcanal in an effort to retake the airstrip (which the Americans called Henderson Field). After two weeks of fighting, half of the Japanese soldiers and one-fifth of the Marines were dead.[1386]

American reinforcements landed on Guadalcanal on September 18, but in the process a Japanese submarine sank the carrier *Wasp*. This loss, which was also kept from the American public for months, left the United States with just two carriers in the Pacific, *Enterprise* and *Hornet*.[1387]

Naval skirmishes near Guadalcanal continued. On October 11, in the Battle of Cape Esperance, American ships sank a Japanese heavy cruiser and three destroyers and damaged another heavy cruiser. The Japanese damaged the American cruiser *Boise*.[1388]

A week later, aggressive Admiral Halsey was ordered to replace the nervous and weary Admiral Ghormley as commander of the South Pacific Area and South Pacific Forces. Upon arriving at Nouméa, Halsey learned that the Free French governor of New Caledonia was refusing to grant the Navy sufficient room on the island to carry out its operations unless the Navy first provided something more than just protection from the Japanese. An angry Halsey, accompanied by Marines, promptly seized the governor's office and started construction of needed military facilities on the island.[1389]

On October 23-24, 1942, the Japanese attempted an all-out attack on Guadalcanal. In hand-to-hand fighting, they were thrown back and lost over 3,000 dead.[1390]

On October 26, Japanese and American naval forces clashed again

---

[1384] *Eagle*, 195-97, *Inferno*, 249-53, *Conspiracy*, 1211, *Neptune*, 109-111, 132.
[1385] *Eagle*, 196, *Inferno*, 256, *Conspiracy*, 1218, *Neptune*, 114-18.
[1386] *Eagle*, 198-99, *Conspiracy*, 1218-19.
[1387] *Eagle*, 198-99, *Inferno*, 256, *Conspiracy*, 1218-19, *Neptune*, 132-37.
[1388] *Eagle*, 200-01, *Inferno*, 256, *Conspiracy*, 1220, *Neptune*, 157-88.
[1389] *Neptune*, 209, 212, *Admirals*, 293-97, *Eagle*, 209.
[1390] *Eagle*, 209-10, *Inferno*, 254-55, *WW II Story*, 151.

near Guadalcanal in the Battle of Santa Cruz Islands. The Japanese lost over 100 planes; the Americans seventy-four. The United States carrier *Hornet* was sunk and *Enterprise* damaged. The wounded *Enterprise* was the only American carrier left in the Pacific fleet. Two Japanese carriers and a cruiser were damaged.[1391]

As the early November Congressional elections approached, a concerned President Roosevelt told the military to be certain that "every possible weapon gets into that area to hold Guadalcanal."[1392]

On November 8, Admiral Halsey flew to Guadalcanal to personally examine the battle situation. When asked at a press conference how to win the war, his terse reply was, "Kill Japs. Kill Japs. Keep on killing Japs."[1393]

Another heated naval battle took place off the coast of Guadalcanal on November 12-13. This was the first time the Americans had used battleships there. A Japanese submarine sank the cruiser *Juneau*, killing 683 U.S. Navy sailors out of a crew of 700. Among the dead were the five Sullivan brothers from Waterloo, Iowa who had overcome military resistance to having family members serve together in combat.[1394]

During the next several months the Japanese and Americans continued to fight land and sea battles on and near Guadalcanal. On the final day of 1942, the Japanese reluctantly decided to withdraw. Five weeks later, all Japanese troops were gone from the island. In the fighting for Guadalcanal, 3,100 American soldiers perished. Almost 5,000 U.S. Navy sailors died in the many nearby sea battles as America lost two carriers, eight cruisers, fifteen destroyers and a troop transport ship. Twenty-five thousand Japanese soldiers, pilots and sailors died in the contest for Guadalcanal. Japan lost a carrier, two battleships, four cruisers, eleven destroyers, sixteen troop transport ships, and five submarines.[1395]

President Roosevelt's oldest son, James, served on Guadalcanal in 1942 as a Marine major.[1396]

The Allied victories in Guadalcanal and New Guinea were costly in casualties, but showed that Japanese soldiers were not unstoppable jungle fighters. From that time on, the Japanese were basically on the

---

[1391] *Eagle*, 211, *Inferno*, 256, *Conspiracy*, 1221, *Neptune*, 223-36.

[1392] *Conspiracy*, 1222, *Neptune*, 382.

[1393] *Conspiracy*, 1222.

[1394] *WW II Story*, 135, *Neptune*, 329-30, 345-52, 370-75.

[1395] *Eagle*, 211-14, *Masters*, 322, *Inferno*, 256-58, *WW II Story*, 142, *Conspiracy*, 1221-25, 1231, *Neptune*, 376, 403-08.

[1396] *Neptune*, 215.

defensive.[1397]

Pondering Peace Initiatives

Following Japan's defeat at Midway and its early difficulties on Guadalcanal, Japanese Foreign Minister Togo considered asking neutral nations to mediate peace negotiations. Togo recognized that the first step toward ending hostilities would require Japan to end the war with China. On August 25, 1942, he urged the Emperor to pursue negotiations with Chiang Kai-shek. Hirohito was not receptive. He believed that the war was not yet lost and that the distant territories Japan had captured would, at a minimum, provide battlegrounds that would keep the Allies from Japan's shores for many years.[1398]

On September 1, at Hirohito's urging, Prime Minister (and War Minister) Tojo agreed to remove Togo as Foreign Minister and add those responsibilities to his bulging portfolio. A few weeks later, the Foreign Minister duties were turned over to a low level diplomat.[1399]

America Continues to Press Japan

In 1942, the United States began fitting some of its ships with a new device, radar, which allowed a vessel to target distant enemy ships in the dark. The Japanese favored optical target spotting and were late in equipping their vessels with radar.[1400]

In August 1942, the Japanese again changed their standard secret naval code. Assisted by Japanese code books captured in the Solomon Islands, American code breakers were able to read much of the new code by early 1943.[1401]

By November 1942, American shipyards were capable of building 10,500 ton merchant vessels — "Liberty ships" — in about a week.[1402]

During 1942, U. S. submarines sank 180 Japanese vessels displacing approximately 725,000 tons. Japan was able to replace only 635,000 of those tons with new construction.[1403]

By the end of 1942, the United States had sent 460,000 troops to the Pacific to fight Japan. It had also dispatched tens of thousands of soldiers to oppose the Germans in North Africa and to bomb Germa-

---

[1397] *Eagle*, 218, 226.

[1398] *Conspiracy*, 1214-17.

[1399] *Conspiracy*, 1216-17.

[1400] *Neptune*, 102-04, *Sword*, xviii.

[1401] *Eagle*, 452-53, *Neptune*, 28-29, 240, 249-50.

[1402] *Masters*, 297.

[1403] *Eagle*, 483, *Conspiracy*, 1271.

ny.[1404]

During the final weeks of 1942, American P-38 fighters began to arrive in the Pacific theater. They were faster, heavier and bigger than the Japanese *Zero*, meaning that American pilots no longer had to run from a dogfight.[1405]

THE TIDE BEGINS TO TURN IN THE PACIFIC (1943)

Strengthening the U.S. Navy

As 1943 began, America had only one undamaged aircraft carrier, the *Saratoga*, operating in the Pacific.[1406]

By the fall of 1943, the U. S. Navy added to its Pacific fleet six new *Essex*-class carriers, each stocked with almost 100 planes, and six light carriers, each carrying about fifty planes. Both carrier types sported the new F6F *Hellcat* fighter which was faster, better armed, and better protected than the Japanese *Zero*.[1407]

The Casablanca Conference

Churchill, Roosevelt and the Combined Chiefs of Staff attended the January 1943 Casablanca strategy conference. Among other topics discussed, the Americans wanted a larger share of war materiel allocated to the Pacific campaign. Admiral King argued that thirty percent of Allied resources should be sent to the Pacific and seventy percent to the European conflict. The British opposed allocating such a significant proportion to the Pacific. Ultimately, the parties vaguely agreed that while Europe came first, the United States should continue its initiatives in the Pacific and be ready to launch a full-scale offensive against Japan once Germany had been defeated.[1408]

One of America's goals in the Pacific was to provide sufficient arms and supplies to the Chinese to assure that they continued to tie down a significant portion of the Japanese army there. At Casablanca, Britain reluctantly agreed that it would at some future time undertake a military advance from India into Burma (code-named Anakim) and try to secure a northern land route to China by which Chiang Kai-

---

[1404] *Eagle*, 221.
[1405] *Conspiracy*, 1249.
[1406] *Engineers*, 316.
[1407] *Eagle*, 257.
[1408] *Eagle*, 222, *Masters*, 320, *Inferno*, 419.

shek could be supplied.[1409]

MacArthur vs. Nimitz

In early 1943, United States Army and Navy leaders again wrestled with the issue of which military branch should have overall command of the Pacific forces, and what path they should follow to Tokyo in order to defeat the Japanese.[1410]

In late March 1943, the Joint Chiefs of Staff agreed that MacArthur would continue to have overall command of the forces advancing north from New Guinea, with Admiral Nimitz retaining control of those naval forces not specifically assigned to MacArthur. This decision eased collective planning for the Allied move to neutralize the powerful Japanese military base at Rabaul on New Britain Island, just north of New Guinea.[1411]

Burma

In early 1943, British forces moved down the coast of Burma intending to capture Akyab Island. The objectives included showing that the British were still fighting in that area and taking airfields on the island that could be used both to attack the Japanese in Rangoon and protect Calcutta, India. After several months of jungle fighting, the Japanese threw back the poorly trained and inexperienced British and Indian troops.[1412]

In February 1943, 3,000 British troops (called "Chindits"), commanded by General Wingate, snuck into the steamy Japanese-controlled jungles of northern Burma. The men knew going in that because there was no way to carry out badly wounded soldiers, those who suffered serious injuries would be put out of their misery. For three months the Chindits cut Japanese rail lines and attacked enemy outposts. Because only about two-thirds made it back to India, some historians question the military value of their actions. Churchill, however, maintained that the courageous Chindits demonstrated that British soldiers could hold their own in jungle fighting against the Japanese.[1413]

By April 1943, Churchill and Roosevelt had decided that a full-

---

[1409] *Masters,* 321, *Eagle,* 342-43, *Burma,* 160.
[1410] *Eagle,* 223.
[1411] *Eagle,* 223-26, *Inferno,* 420-21, *Ghosts,* 16-17.
[1412] *Masters,* 354, *Inferno,* 420.
[1413] *Eagle,* 348, *Inferno,* 420-21, *Burma,* 135.

scale military campaign in Burma ("Anakim") should at least be postponed. Roosevelt favored continuing air attacks on the Japanese in Burma and Churchill wanted to avoid more jungle warfare.[1414]

One challenge to American/British decision-making regarding Southeast Asia was Britain's interest in preserving its empire there, whereas the United States sought to cultivate friendly, disinterested relations with Asian nations.[1415]

Allied servicemen in the India/Burma campaign on leave often travelled to Calcutta, India, a city that had some 40,000 prostitutes and plentiful drugs and alcohol.[1416]

Yamamoto's Death

On April 13, 1943, American code breakers learned from a low-security message that five days hence Japanese Admiral Yamamoto would be flying from Rabaul to inspect a forward base in Bougainville in the Solomon Islands. The message was signed by Yamamoto's subordinate, who recently had been Hirohito's chief naval aide-de-camp.[1417]

Despite being credited with planning the stunning Pearl Harbor success, Yamamoto subsequently shouldered responsibility for the embarrassing Doolittle raid on Tokyo, the terrible naval defeat at Midway, Japan's failure to hold Guadalcanal, and its losses in New Guinea.[1418]

Concerned that the low-security message describing Yamamoto's flight plan might have been intercepted, several of Yamamoto's colleagues implored him to abandon the dangerous trip. Perhaps welcoming an honorable death, he refused.[1419]

On April 15, after pondering legal questions and whether an attack might reveal that the Japanese code had been broken, President Roosevelt approved the launching of a group of American P-38 fighters from Guadalcanal aimed at shooting down Yamamoto's plane.[1420]

The American fighters dispatched to intercept the flight arrived at Bougainville on April 18 just two minutes before Yamamoto's plane was scheduled to appear. They spotted his bomber and attacked. A

[1414] *Eagle*, 349.

[1415] *Eagle*, 352, *Burma*, 164.

[1416] *Eagle*, 404.

[1417] *Conspiracy*, 1248-49, 1253, *Eagle*, 453-54.

[1418] *Conspiracy*, 1249-52.

[1419] *Conspiracy*, 1254.

[1420] *Conspiracy*, 1255-56, *Admirals*, 315-16.

A CONCISE HISTORY OF THE SECOND WORLD WAR

machine gun bullet struck Yamamoto in the head, he was killed immediately and his plane crashed in the jungle.[1421]

Thirty-four days later, after recovering his body from the jungle wreck, the Japanese announced Yamamoto's "gallant death in a war plane." On June 5, Yamamoto was accorded just the second state funeral for a commoner in Japanese history.[1422]

The Trident Conference

As the battle for North Africa was coming to a successful conclusion, Roosevelt, Churchill and their staffs met at a conference ("Trident") in May 1943 in Washington, D.C. There the parties agreed on the invasion of Normandy in May 1944, continuing military operations in Italy, a delay in the British land campaign against the Japanese in Burma, and maintaining American pressure against Japan in the Pacific, including seizure of the Marshall and Caroline Islands nearer to Japan.[1423]

Island Warfare

On May 11, 1943, U.S. Army troops landed on Attu seeking to retake it from the Japanese, who had invaded the Alaskan island the previous June as part of the Battle of Midway. After seventeen days of hand-to-hand fighting, Attu came again under American control. Several months later, the Japanese abandoned the nearby island of Kiska.[1424]

In June, 1943, the Allies, employing newly developed amphibious landing craft, began their advance against Japanese forces in the Solomon Islands and New Guinea.[1425]

In July 1943, American soldiers were equipped with a new weapon to use against dug-in Japanese pillboxes in the Pacific — the flamethrower. Soldiers carrying the ninety-five pound weapon on their backs were vulnerable to instant incineration if a shell struck the fuel tank, and they suffered far higher casualty rates than riflemen.[1426]

Early in the Pacific war, Army Air Force bombers flying at their customary high altitudes had proved almost useless in damaging Japa-

---

[1421] *Conspiracy*, 1256-57, *Eagle*, 230, 453-54, *Ultra Secret*, 176.
[1422] *Conspiracy*, 1258, 1267.
[1423] *Eagle*, 254-55, *Inferno*, 428-29, *Masters*, 358-73.
[1424] *WW II Story*, 185-86, *Conspiracy*, 1265-66, *Admirals*, 324-25.
[1425] *Eagle*, 230-31, *Inferno*, 422, *Conspiracy*, 1269.
[1426] *Eagle*, 237, *WW II Story*, 587-88.

nese ships in the Pacific. This approach was altered in 1943 when Army Air Force planes, bombing from low altitudes, sank Japanese troop transports near New Guinea causing the loss of almost 3,000 Japanese lives.[1427]

In July, the American Joint Chiefs of Staff concluded that to tighten the noose on the Japanese, the Gilbert Islands should be taken before the Marshall and Caroline Islands.[1428]

In August 1943, British and American leaders met again at a conference in Quebec ("Quadrant"). Among other decisions, they determined that MacArthur was to continue to drive the Japanese out of New Guinea, but he should not seek to capture by land the Japanese fortress at Rabaul (later discovered to hold 100,000 troops). Rather, the base should be neutralized by air attacks and isolated. They also agreed that the atomic bomb under development at Los Alamos would not be used as a weapon unless both Britain and the United States consented.[1429]

On November 1, 1943, Admiral Halsey's ships landed 14,000 Marines on Bougainville, one of the Solomon Islands near the Japanese stronghold in Rabaul, and quickly established air bases there.[1430]

In late November 1943, 18,000 U.S. Marines made an amphibious landing on Tarawa, a three square mile atoll in the Pacific's Gilbert Islands peppered with almost 5,000 Japanese troops in pillboxes. A Navy task force, including nineteen carriers, twelve battleships and many support vessels, had bombarded the tiny island for hours but did little harm to the dug-in Japanese. In three days of extremely difficult fighting, in which almost all of the Japanese were killed, 1,027 Marines died and 2,292 were wounded. Many Marines were killed trying to wade one hundred or more yards to shore because their landing craft had, due to poor planning, become stuck on reefs. Tarawa taught America lessons on the intensity of Japanese resolve and the need to shed blood to seize islands. The extent of American casualties there also generated considerable anguish at home.[1431]

In December 1943, MacArthur's forces landed in two places on New Britain, but at the opposite end of the island from the powerful

---

[1427] *Eagle*, 226-28, *WW II Story*, 186, *Conspiracy*, 1251.

[1428] *Eagle*, 256, *Ghosts*, 17.

[1429] *Eagle*, 277-78., *Masters*, 406-07, *WW II Story*, 187-88.

[1430] *Eagle*, 244, *Conspiracy*, 1277.

[1431] *Engineers*, 344, *Eagle*, 259-66, *Inferno*, 422-24, *WW II Story*, 190-213, *Pacific*, 30-60, *Conspiracy*, 1285-86, *Ghosts*, 18.

Japanese base at Rabaul. Their objectives were to establish a PT boat base and seize an unfinished Japanese air base. They overcame modest Japanese opposition in about a month and then used the airbase to send bomber flights against Rabaul.[1432]

The Cairo and Teheran Conferences

Chinese Generalissimo Chiang Kai-shek and his wife attended the Allied conference in Cairo in November 1943 ("Sextant"), during which the parties discussed Operation Buccaneer, a proposed attack on the Andaman Islands in Burma in early 1944. The Combined Chiefs of Staff directed MacArthur to clear the Japanese out of New Guinea, and told Nimitz to advance to the Marshalls in January, the Carolines in July, and the Marianas in October. They made no decision regarding whether there should be an Allied landing in the Philippines.[1433]

At the November 1943 Teheran conference among Stalin, Churchill, Roosevelt and their military leaders, Stalin made significant promises: (a) to launch an offensive against Germany during the anticipated May 1944 Operation OVERLORD in order to discourage the Germans from moving troops westward from the Soviet front, and (b) to declare war on Japan once Germany was defeated. Stalin's agreement to attack the Japanese reduced the importance of having the Chinese continue to engage and occupy Japanese forces.[1434]

After meeting with Stalin in Teheran, Churchill and Roosevelt got together again in Cairo. They agreed to reduce Allied efforts to contest the Japanese in China, instead favoring advances against the enemy in the central and southwest Pacific.[1435]

Japan Isolated and Desperate

Following Mussolini's arrest, Italy's surrender in September 1943 and Germany's ongoing retreat in the Soviet Union, Emperor Hirohito realized that Japan would soon be fighting the Allies alone.[1436]

The Japanese strategy was to extract a brutally high human price from the Americans by fighting from island to island in hand-to-hand combat. Their objective was to force the United States to negotiate for

---

[1432] *Eagle*, 246-47, *WW II Story*, 186-88.
[1433] *Masters*, 436, 438, 442, *Eagle*, 279.
[1434] *Masters*, 443-51, *Eagle*, 369, 552.
[1435] *Eagle*, 354-55.
[1436] *Conspiracy*, 1271.

peace on terms less harsh than an unconditional surrender.[1437]

Hoping to free up Japanese troops from China and transfer them to Pacific bases where they could be used to resist powerful Allied forces, Hirohito sought in the fall of 1943 to negotiate a peace agreement with Chiang Kai-shek. The Emperor's overture was rejected. Chiang recognized that if he ended both his ties to the Allies and the war with Japan, he would then be forced to carry out his civil war against Communist Mao Tse-tung without international support.[1438]

JAPAN IN RETREAT (1944)

The Island War Continues

Some argue that by the end of 1943, it was unnecessary for MacArthur's forces to engage in further land battles because American naval and air superiority could bomb and blockade Japanese island troops into surrendering without hand-to-hand combat. But MacArthur's ego and his publicized promise to return to the Philippines prevailed.[1439]

Beginning in late December 1943 and continuing for some three months, Allied planes bombed the enemy base at Rabaul. As a consequence, Rabaul was no longer capable of serving effectively as a harbor for Japanese ships. All serviceable Japanese planes were withdrawn in February.[1440]

The Marshall Islands, located about 620 miles northwest of Tarawa, include dozens of islands spread out over an area of some 600 miles. In early February 1944, U.S. Marines and Army troops, supported by intense naval bombardment, made amphibious landings there against the Japanese on Roi-Namur and Kwajalein. After four days of combat the Japanese were toppled. The Americans lost almost 500 dead and 1,300 wounded, but far fewer casualties than at Tarawa. The Japanese suffered more than 2,700 casualties.[1441]

To thwart Japanese efforts to listen in on American battle communications, the Americans enlisted Navajo Indian "code talkers" to send combat messages in their native language that the enemy could not translate.[1442]

[1437] *Inferno*, 424-25.
[1438] *Conspiracy*, 1274-75.
[1439] *Inferno*, 425-26.
[1440] *Eagle*, 278, *Inferno*, 422.
[1441] *Eagle*, 268-71, *Inferno*, 425, *WW II Story*, 360-61, *Pacific*, 61-70.
[1442] *Pacific*, 69.

Truk Island, about 400 miles northwest of Kwajalein, was a Japanese naval and army stronghold. On February 17-18, 1944, U.S. Navy forces battered the island, destroying many ships and planes and removing Truk as a threat to Allied efforts to close in on Japan.[1443]

Beginning on February 17, American troops also made an amphibious landing on heavily-defended Eniwetok Atoll, some 330 miles northwest of Kwajalein. After five days of bloody fighting, the Japanese were routed with the loss of about 3,400 men. The Americans suffered 348 dead and 866 wounded.[1444]

In March, MacArthur's troops invaded and took Los Negros Island in the Admiralties north of New Guinea, further isolating the enemy base at Rabaul. The Japanese then attacked American airfields at Empress Augusta Bay on Bougainville, but were thrown back. Because the Allies controlled the Admiralties, the Japanese had to evacuate Madang, a vulnerable base on New Guinea.[1445]

In the spring and summer of 1944, MacArthur's troops gained control of most of New Guinea and the northern islands near it, which gave them land for airbases to be used in the effort to retake the Philippines.[1446]

Submarine Warfare

American submarines in 1941 had a range of about 10,000 miles, a top speed on the surface of twenty-one knots, and were quiet when submerged. Japanese submarines were larger, slower and louder when submerged.[1447]

From the moment World War II began, America used its submarines in the Pacific as offensive weapons. But they were operating with torpedoes that often had faulty firing pins and ran deeper than the depth set for them. It took the Navy until mid-1943 to eliminate the faults, after which torpedo damage inflicted on Japanese shipping grew tremendously.[1448]

By July 1944, some 100 U.S. Navy submarines were operating out of Pearl Harbor and another forty from Australia. Normally, no more than fifty were deployed at any one time.[1449]

[1443] *Pacific*, 71-72, *Conspiracy*, 1290.
[1444] *Pacific*, 73-76, *Conspiracy*, 1286.
[1445] *Eagle*, 281-84, *Inferno*, 425, *Conspiracy*, 1294.
[1446] *Eagle*, 286-94, *Inferno*, 425, *Conspiracy*, 1294.
[1447] *Eagle*, 481.
[1448] *Engineers*, 336-37, *Eagle*, 130, 485, *Neptune*, 427.
[1449] *Eagle*, 485, *Inferno*, 540.

During 1944, American submarines sank more than 600 Japanese ships displacing over 2.7 million tons. Half of Japan's merchant fleet and two-thirds of its tankers were sent to the bottom by year end 1944, almost completely cutting off oil imports from the East Indies. Breaking the secret Japanese shipping codes gave the Americans the location of each Japanese convoy in the Pacific.[1450]

During the entire war, some 16,000 men, just 1.6 percent of all Navy personnel, served in the United States submarine service. Those submariners caused about fifty-five percent of all of Japan's shipping losses — 1,300 vessels displacing over six million tons — fatally constricting Japan's ability to transport resources and personnel to and from the homeland.[1451]

Japan was slow to develop modern antisubmarine capabilities such as radar and airborne weapons. As a result, Japan sank only forty-one American submarines during the war. Although the mortality rate for American submariners was almost twenty-five percent, the naval blockade results they achieved against Japan were extraordinary.[1452]

Admiral Halsey, when asked what strategic instruments and machines were most important in felling the Japanese in the Pacific, said, "I would rank them in this order: submarines, first, radar second, planes third, bulldozers fourth."[1453]

The Burma and China Campaigns

U.S. General Stilwell, commanding American and Chinese troops, advanced in late 1943 from China into northern Burma intending to capture from the Japanese the town of Myitkyina, which had an airfield that could be used to shorten Hump flights to China. After many months of bitter jungle fighting, the Allies took Myitkyina on August 3, 1944.[1454]

During the campaign for Myitkyina, about 10,000 Kachin tribesmen, small wiry natives from northern Burma working with some 500 Americans, acted as guides, cleared trails, built bamboo bridges, located water holes, selected supply drops, helped downed Allied airmen, and harassed Japanese patrols.[1455]

[1450] *Eagle*, 486, *WW II Story*, 466, *Engineers*, 337-38.
[1451] *Inferno*, 540, *WW II Story*, 466, *Admirals*, 372.
[1452] *Inferno*, 540-41.
[1453] *Admirals*, 369.
[1454] *Eagle*, 355-61, *Inferno*, 542.
[1455] *Eagle*, 464.

Beginning in late 1943, American engineers and 15,000 American soldiers (mostly African-American) began constructing a new road connecting Ledo in eastern India with China. The Ledo Road was intended to ease the burden of flying supplies over the Hump.[1456]

In early 1944, the Japanese decided to attack the British in the towns of Imphal and Kohima on the border between southern Burma and India. By July, British troops led by General Slim had routed the Japanese, who suffered 53,000 casualties, including 30,000 dead.[1457]

In April 1944, the Japanese launched an offensive moving west in China aimed at defeating the Chinese Nationalists and eliminating airfields from which the Flying Tigers operated. Facing poorly trained and supplied Chinese troops with corrupt and unmotivated leaders, the Japanese made significant progress and, by late summer, were threatening the Kuomintang government.[1458]

Roosevelt tired of Chiang's reluctance to fight hard against the Japanese and sent him a message in July 1944, asking that General Stilwell command all Allied forces in China, including the Nationalist and Chinese Communist forces. An angry Chiang resisted and asked that Stilwell, whom he did not like, be replaced. With American forces having established airbases in the Marianas, MacArthur about to invade the Philippines, and Stalin having agreed to attack Japan after Germany fell, Roosevelt was somewhat less concerned about the situation in China. Thus, in October 1944, he agreed to replace Stilwell with General Wedemeyer.[1459]

Shortly after arriving, Wedemeyer agreed with Chiang's decision to bring two Chinese divisions back to China from Burma to resist the Japanese advance into western China. At about the same time the Japanese halted their advance, partly due to extended and exposed supply lines and partly out of fear that the Americans, now in the Philippines, would land troops on the Chinese coast.[1460]

By 1944, the Allies had significantly weakened the Japanese blockade of China. Hump flights to China had delivered just 3,700 tons of materiel in 1942 and 61,000 in 1943, but by October 1944 were capable of moving more than 30,000 tons per month.[1461]

[1456] *WW II Story*, 593, *Eagle*, 333.

[1457] *Inferno*, 542-45, *Eagle*, 361-62, *WW II Story*, 594, *Conspiracy*, 1293.

[1458] *Eagle*, 365-67, *Inferno*, 419.

[1459] *Burma*, 403-06, *Eagle*, 369, *Inferno*, 419, *WW II Story*, 594.

[1460] *Eagle*, 371.

[1461] *Eagle*, 370.

Beginning in July 1944, the new American B-29s, capable of flying 20,000 pound bomb loads 7,000 miles, began attacking Japan and Manchuria from bases in China. Due to inexperience in flying the new Superfortresses and inaccurate bombing, the planes did little serious damage. By year end, most B-29 flights from China were stopped because by then the Americans had B-29 bases in the Marianas which were easier to supply and defend.[1462]

At the end of 1944, the Ledo Road, a supply route over mountains and streams from Ledo to Kunming in western China, was completed. In January 1945, the initial truck convoy using the road entered China.[1463]

Political Intrigue

By 1944, President Roosevelt's health was quite poor — congestive heart failure, high blood pressure, anemia. In early July 1944, at the request of his regular physician, Roosevelt was examined by a specialist, Dr. Frank Lahey, who concluded that the President, if reelected, could not survive another four year term. Roosevelt's advisors then suggested that Vice President Wallace, who was deemed too liberal and supportive of labor, be replaced by either Senator Truman or Supreme Court Justice Douglas.[1464]

President Roosevelt dispatched Vice President Wallace to southeast Asia in 1944 to meet with Chiang Kai-shek for two reasons: to try to persuade Chiang to partner with the Chinese Communists to oppose Japan, and to keep Wallace out of the United States during the July Democratic convention.[1465]

Harry Truman was chosen as Roosevelt's Vice Presidential candidate at the 1944 Democratic convention.[1466]

In 1944, MacArthur considered running against Roosevelt as the Republican candidate, but gave up that aspiration when he realized he could not win the nomination.[1467]

On November 7, 1944, Roosevelt was elected to his fourth term as president.[1468]

[1462] *Eagle*, 488-92, *Ghosts*, 9.

[1463] *Eagle*, 370, *WW II Story*, 594.

[1464] *WWII History*, 6, *Guns*, 498, *Admirals*, 378, 424-25, *1944*, 476-77.

[1465] *Burma*, 388, *Eagle*, 377.

[1466] *Curse*, 137.

[1467] *Inferno*, 551.

[1468] *Admirals*, 426.

Saipan in the Marianas

Troubled by the relative ease with which the Americans had taken the Gilbert and Marshall islands, which were part of Japan's defensive ring, the Japanese gathered troops from China and Japan to bolster their forces in the Mariana Islands.[1469]

Beginning on June 15, 1944, just nine days after the Normandy invasion, an American amphibious force of 127,000 troops, commanded by Admiral Spruance, landed on the Japanese-controlled island of Saipan in the Marianas. Eight thousand U.S. Marines were put ashore in the first twenty minutes and 20,000 were landed by the first day's end. Once this fourteen-mile long mountainous island was taken, the Americans would have airbases from which their B-29 bombers could reach the Japanese homeland, 1200 miles away.[1470]

The 32,000 Japanese troops defending Saipan were subjected to two days of intense battleship bombardment before D-Day. Nonetheless, they put up a strong defense against the American invasion.[1471]

During the fighting on Saipan, Marine Lt. General Holland Smith, who commanded both Marine and Army divisions, relieved an Army general because his National Guard 27th Division was not making expected progress. This led to a serious inter-service controversy that lingered for years.[1472]

Among the Marines on Saipan were 800 African-Americans assigned to serve as laborers in military support units.[1473]

The Saipan battle ended on July 9, with more than 14,000 Americans killed or wounded and 30,000 Japanese soldiers dead.[1474]

On that same day, some 7,000 Japanese noncombatants, including women and children, committed suicide by jumping off the 220 foot Marpi Point cliff at the northern tip of Saipan. About a week earlier, an imperial order had been sent out promising those civilians who died on Saipan spiritual standing equal to that of Japanese soldiers who died in combat.[1475]

The Japanese fight to the death on Saipan altered the course of the

---

[1469] *Pacific*, 78.

[1470] *Engineers*, 140, 345, *Eagle*, 301-04, *Inferno*, 549, *Pacific*, 78-82, *Conspiracy*, 1295, 1299.

[1471] *Eagle*, 302-03, *WW II Story*, 364, *Pacific*, 79.

[1472] *Eagle*, 314-16, *WW II Story*, 376, *Pacific*, 84, 88.

[1473] *WW II Story*, 368.

[1474] *Eagle*, 317, *WW II Story*, 379, *Pacific*, 87-91, *Conspiracy*, 1301.

[1475] *Masters*, 519, *Eagle*, 317, *Inferno*, 550, *WW II Story*, 383-87, *Pacific*, 90-91, *Conspiracy*, 1300.

Pacific war in several ways. First, Japan's military leaders recognized that defeat was inevitable. Second, the Tojo government was replaced by that of General Kuniaki Koiso, who was convinced that Japan could prevail in the war if it made a sacrificial defense of the homeland. Third, Americans began preparations for a costly invasion of the Japanese home islands. Fourth, the Japanese government began efforts to convince its civilians that they should prepare for death in defense of their homeland.[1476]

After Saipan fell, members of the U.S. Navy Construction Battalion ("Seabees") began transforming the island into bases for both the Navy and the Army Air Force. The new port promptly became the second busiest anchorage in the world, and the air base was constructed to accommodate the new, long range B-29 bombers that would soon attack Japan. In November, those round trip bombing missions from Saipan to Japan began.[1477]

The Great Marianas Turkey Shoot

As American troops were landing on Saipan in June 1944, a large Japanese task force was sailing east through the Philippines headed for what it hoped would be a decisive air and sea battle with the U.S. Navy near the Mariana Islands. The Americans, under Admiral Spruance, had uncovered the plan through Ultra intercepts. Nine Japanese carriers were armed with 422 fighters and bombers, but their pilots had only about six months of individual training.[1478]

Fifteen American carriers were sent to confront the Japanese task force west of the Marianas. The American warships carried some 900 fighters and bombers, each piloted by a man with at least two years of training.[1479]

On June 19-20, 1944, Japanese and American carrier-based planes clashed in the Battle of the Philippine Sea. In what is known as the Great Marianas Turkey Shoot, the Japanese lost about 480 planes (including those destroyed on the ground), almost ten times as many as the Americans. From that time on, Japan's naval air threat was negligible.[1480]

Late in the afternoon of June 20, 216 American planes flying from

[1476] *WW II Story*, 387-390, *Conspiracy*, 1301-03.
[1477] *WW II Story*, 436-444, 529, *Pacific*, 149.
[1478] *Eagle*, 306, *Inferno*, 547, *WW II Story*, 369, *Pacific*, 84-85, *Sword*, 390.
[1479] *Eagle*, 306, *Inferno*, 547, *Pacific*, 85.
[1480] *Engineers*, 321-22, *Eagle*, 308-10, *Inferno*, 548, *Pacific*, 86, *Conspiracy*, 1295.

Admiral Mitscher's carriers, at the far reaches of their range found the Japanese task force, sank the carrier *Hiyo* and damaged three others. The Navy planes then headed back toward the carrier in darkness and with little fuel. Despite the risk of being located by the enemy, Mitscher bravely ordered all carrier lights to shine to help guide in his planes. About eighty American planes were lost due to lack of fuel or landing accidents, but most returned safely. All but forty-nine of the pilots and crew were recovered.[1481]

During the Great Marianas Turkey Shoot, U.S. Navy submarines sent two Japanese carriers, *Shokaku* and the brand new *Taiho*, to the bottom. The Americans also sank seventeen of the Japanese task force's submarines.[1482]

Guam in the Marianas

The Marianas island of Guam, some 120 miles south of Saipan, had been under American protection from 1898 until invaded by Japan in December 1941. On July 21, 1944, after a massive naval bombardment, Marine and Army troops made an amphibious landing on the thirty-four mile long island. It was defended by about 18,500 Japanese troops. After three weeks of brutal combat, almost all of the Japanese troops on Guam were killed. (A few surviving Japanese fought on, with the last emerging from a cave in 1972). America lost over 1,300 dead and almost 6,000 wounded.[1483]

Tinian in the Mariana Islands

Just three days after the invasion of Guam, more than 15,000 Marines and sailors made an amphibious landing on the island of Tinian, about three miles south of Saipan, in what the commanding officer, General Holland Smith, considered the most skilled landing of the campaign. The Americans seized control of Tinian from some 8,350 Japanese troops in less than two weeks.[1484]

In the battle for Tinian, American planes used a new weapon in the Pacific — napalm, a slow-burning, gelatinous type of gasoline.[1485]

Once the United States took control of the Marianas, the Japanese knew their homeland was vulnerable to bombing from airstrips on

---

[1481] *Eagle*, 310-12, *Inferno*, 548, *WW II Story*, 371-73, *Pacific*, 87.
[1482] *Eagle*, 310, *Inferno*, 547-48, *WW II Story*, 371, *Pacific*, 84-86.
[1483] *Eagle*, 319-20, *Inferno*, 550, *Pacific*, 78-79, 93-102, *Conspiracy*, 1301.
[1484] *Eagle*, 319, *Inferno*, 550, *Pacific*, 91-93, *Conspiracy*, 1301.
[1485] *Pacific*, 93, *Eagle*, 491.

those captured isles.[1486]

The Octagon Conference

During the American/British conference in Quebec in September 1944 ("Octagon"), Churchill offered to have British ships play an active part in the Pacific war once Germany surrendered. He apparently wanted to regain Britain's bases and colonies there. Admiral King was opposed (presumably because he did not want to share the hard-won success), but Roosevelt accepted the British proposal.[1487]

In Quebec, the Allies also agreed to abandon the 1943 plan to gain control of the South China coast and Formosa. Instead, they confirmed that (a) the U.S. Navy should attack the Palau Islands and (b) MacArthur should invade Leyte Island in the Philippines in October and Luzon Island in December, 1944.[1488]

Peleliu Island

MacArthur was determined to honor his "I shall return" pledge to the citizens of the Philippines and originally planned to invade the island of Mindanao. He insisted that the Navy protect his right flank from an enemy attack by securing the Palau Islands which lie east of Mindanao.[1489]

The initial American naval and air bombardment of the Palau island of Peleliu began in late March 1944. It drove out most enemy naval and air forces, but many land-based Japanese troops remained.[1490]

On September 15, 1944, after further naval bombardment, the Navy landed 9,000 members of the 1st Marine Division on Peleliu, a hot, jagged coral island occupied by 10,000 dug-in Japanese troops. The 1st Marines were veterans of deadly battles on Guadalcanal and New Britain. Clearing the Japanese out took until November (sixty-eight days longer than expected) and cost the United States 1,529 dead and 6,282 wounded. The Japanese had 9,615 casualties.[1491]

Some argue that there was no military value in taking Peleliu since the Japanese air fleet had already been largely destroyed. But MacArthur wanted his flank protected in the invasion of the Philippines and

---

[1486] *Inferno*, 551, *Masters*, 519-20.
[1487] *Masters*, 519-24, *Admirals*, 440-42.
[1488] *Eagle*, 418-20.
[1489] *Pacific*, 103-04.
[1490] *Pacific*, 106.
[1491] *Eagle*, 420-21, *Inferno*, 552, *WW II Story*, 393-412, *Pacific*, 103-145, *Conspiracy*, 1305, *Ghosts*, 32.

Admiral Nimitz declined to call off the invasion.[1492]

Ironically, after receiving reports that the Japanese had relatively few troops in Mindanao, MacArthur decided to bypass Mindanao and invade the more northern Philippine island of Leyte.[1493]

While the Marines were taking Peleliu, the Army invaded the atoll island of Ulithi without Japanese opposition. After the Seabees got to work, Ulithi provided a valuable anchorage for Navy vessels preparing for the invasion of Okinawa.[1494]

Returning to the Philippines

Despite arguments that the Navy's success in the Marianas had rendered an invasion of the Philippines unnecessary, MacArthur insisted on liberating all of the country's islands and its 17,000,000 people.[1495]

In September 1944, in preparation for an invasion, U.S. Navy planes from Third Fleet carriers attacked Japanese airfields in the Philippines for several days, destroying many enemy planes and damaging Japanese land installations.[1496]

When the Third Fleet returned on October 10 to bombard Luzon, Formosa and other nearby islands, the Japanese fought back, leading to days of intense fighting. But the enemy forces caused relatively little harm. Poorly trained Japanese pilots lost over 500 planes to fewer than 100 downed American planes.[1497]

On October 20, 1944, an Allied invasion force of 160,000 troops under MacArthur's command and supported by over 700 Navy ships, landed on the east coast of the Philippine island of Leyte. Within three days the troops were well entrenched, and MacArthur grandly announced, "People of the Philippines, I have returned!"[1498]

The Battle of Leyte Gulf

Although Japan's remaining aircraft carriers were largely impotent because most of their planes and skilled pilots had been shot down, its navy still had many battleships and cruisers. Short on oil and desperate, the Japanese decided to attack the American landing force on

---

[1492] WW II Story, 392, 396, 412, Pacific, 104, 145-46, Ghosts, 31-32.
[1493] Pacific, 103-04.
[1494] WW II Story, 557-60.
[1495] Inferno, 551, WW II Story, 390-92, Conspiracy, 1304.
[1496] Eagle, 424, Inferno, 551-52.
[1497] Eagle, 424, Conspiracy, 1307.
[1498] Eagle, 426-28, Inferno, 552, WW II Story, 413-15, Conspiracy, 1309-10.

Leyte and confront the U.S. Navy fleet in what Japan hoped would result in a decisive Japanese victory. Japan's military leaders recognized that if the Americans became rooted in the Philippines, they would be able to cut off Japan's remaining oil supplies from Southeast Asia.[1499]

From west of the central Philippines, the Japanese sent two battle-ship and cruiser task forces, one sailing through Surigao Strait and the other further north through San Bernardino Strait — both targeting American transports and warships operating in Leyte Gulf. Japan's almost empty carriers sailed as decoys north of the Philippines in an attempt to draw U.S. Navy ships away from Leyte Gulf.[1500]

The Japanese had recently changed their codes, preventing Ultra intercepts that might alert the Americans to the Japanese plan. How-ever, early on October 23, 1944, American submarines spotted the Jap-anese task force sailing through San Bernardino Strait, warned the Se-venth Fleet, and then attacked, sinking two cruisers and gravely da-maging another.[1501]

On October 24, land-based Japanese planes attacked and sank the American carrier *Princeton*, but suffered many lost planes in the process.[1502]

Meanwhile, American carrier planes located the remaining ships in the Japanese task force sailing through San Bernardino Strait, sinking the huge battleship *Musashi* (with over 1,000 sailors drowned) and da-maging three other battleships and two cruisers. Admiral Kurita, commanding that Japanese task force, decided to reverse course and move west out of range of the sting of American carrier planes.[1503]

Also on October 24, Admiral Halsey located the decoy Japanese carriers sailing to the north of the Philippines and took the bait. He moved his Task Force 34 away from protecting the eastern side of San Bernardo Strait and sailed north to pursue the Japanese carriers com-manded by Admiral Ozawa.[1504]

Meanwhile, American warships further south waited for the Japa-nese task force of battleships and cruisers, commanded by Admiral Ni-shimura, sailing through Surigao Strait. The American task force was comforted by the flawed belief that Halsey's Task Force 34 was pro-

---

[1499] *Eagle*, 422, 428-29, *WW II Story*, 416, *Conspiracy*, 1310, *Admirals*, 387-403.

[1500] *Eagle*, 428-29, *WW II Story*, 416, *Conspiracy*, 1310.

[1501] *Eagle*, 429, *Inferno*, 553, *Pacific*, 147-48, *Conspiracy*, 1311.

[1502] *Eagle*, 430, *WW II Story*, 416, *Conspiracy*, 1311-12.

[1503] *Eagle*, 431, *Inferno*, 553, *Pacific*, 148, *Conspiracy*, 1312-13.

[1504] *Eagle*, 433, *WW II Story*, 417, *Pacific*, 148, *Conspiracy*, 1314-15.

tecting its northern flank.[1505]

Starting at about 2330 on October 24, American battleships and destroyers, commanded by Admiral Oldendorf, attacked Nishimura's task force, destroying or seriously damaging almost all of the Japanese ships. Over 4,000 Japanese sailors died.[1506]

By October 25, Admiral Kurita had once again reversed course and was now sailing east through San Bernardino Strait north of Leyte Gulf. After clearing the Strait and moving south, the Japanese encountered five U.S. Navy escort carriers supporting MacArthur's troops ashore. The escort carriers, slow and lightly armed, were designed for antisubmarine duty and to support land operations, but not combat with battleships. The escort carriers launched their planes to attack the Japanese ships and then immediately steamed away from the Japanese threat. A hectic battle followed.[1507]

American planes and courageous small destroyers attacked Kurita's big ships while the Japanese blistered the escort carriers, which frantically requested protection from Admiral Halsey's departed Task Force 34. The escort carriers' commander, Rear Admiral Sprague, exclaimed, "That sonofabitch Halsey has left us bare-assed!" Just as Kurita's battleships were drawing within range of several escort carriers, Kurita decided to withdraw, fearing that other American carriers might be nearby and aware that Nishimura's task force had been clobbered. Sprague lost three escorts and a carrier.[1508]

To the north, Halsey, in the process of sinking all four decoy Japanese carriers, declined to immediately return to help the escort carriers. He was later criticized for leaving the Leyte Gulf ships unprotected against Kurita's task force. Admiral Nimitz sent a message, "Where is, repeat, where is Task Force 34, the world wonders," that embarrassed and angered Halsey.[1509]

In a move driven by desperation, the Japanese sent *kamikaze* planes to attack several escort carriers, sinking one and damaging two. Japan had been considering use of such suicide attacks since 1943, and was encouraged by the results.[1510]

The three day Battle of Leyte Gulf was the greatest naval confron-

---

[1505] *Eagle*, 434, *Conspiracy*, 1313-14.
[1506] *Eagle*, 434-35, *WW II Story*, 417-18, *Conspiracy*, 1314.
[1507] *Eagle*, 436-37, *Inferno*, 554, *Pacific*, 148, *Conspiracy*, 1316-18.
[1508] *Eagle*, 439, *Inferno*, 554-55, *Conspiracy*, 1318-20.
[1509] *Eagle*, 437-40, *WW II Story*, 419, 420, *Pacific*, 148.
[1510] *Eagle*, 440-41, *Inferno*, 555, *Conspiracy*, 1295-99, 1315-16, 1319, 1321-22.

tation in history and the last major naval action of World War II. The Japanese experienced a stunning defeat: three lost battleships, four sunk carriers, six lost cruisers, and more than a dozen sunk destroyers. The Japanese had over 11,000 killed to America's 2,803. Perhaps more damaging to Japan, the battle exposed the loss of skill and fighting spirit of the Japanese navy in late 1944.[1511]

The Land Campaign in the Philippines

When MacArthur landed on Leyte, Japan had some 20,000 troops there. By mid-November the Japanese ranks had swelled to 55,000, with 10,000 more men arriving on Leyte in early December. The Americans had about twice as many troops on Leyte as the Japanese.[1512]

Between mid-October and the end of December, the Japanese and Americans battled hard for control of Leyte under gruesome conditions. The Americans eventually prevailed, but at the cost of 15,500 casualties. Sixty-five thousand Japanese soldiers died in the Leyte fighting.[1513]

On December 15, 1944 (a day before the Battle of the Bulge began in Europe), MacArthur's troops, aided by navy ships, seized the Philippine island of Mindoro as a stepping stone to invading the big island of Luzon.[1514]

Admiral Halsey was providing naval support for MacArthur's invasion of Luzon when, on December 18, his ships, while trying to refuel at sea, were struck by a mighty typhoon. Three destroyers capsized, 790 sailors died and 156 planes were lost. Halsey was the subject of a court of inquiry that characterized his decision not to flee the oncoming typhoon as an error of judgment.[1515]

THE FINAL YEAR OF COMBAT IN THE PACIFIC (1945)

The Soviet Union Turns on Japan

During the Allied leaders' Yalta conference in January 1945, Stalin confirmed his willingness to attack the Japanese following Germany's defeat. In return, the British and Americans agreed that the Soviets

---

[1511] *Eagle*, 441, *Inferno*, 555, *Pacific*, 147-48, *Conspiracy*, 1321-22.

[1512] *Eagle*, 511-13, *WW II Story*, 420.

[1513] *Eagle*, 513-17, *Inferno*, 555, *WW II Story*, 420-24.

[1514] *Eagle*, 517-18.

[1515] *Admirals*, 406-12.

A CONCISE HISTORY OF THE SECOND WORLD WAR

could retake from Japan the lower half of Sakhalin Island, annex the Kurile Islands and restore some control over Manchuria. The Allies recognized that if Russia entered the war in Asia, Japan would be thwarted from sending more troops south to fend off an anticipated American invasion of the southern homeland island of Kyushu.[1516]

In April 1945, the Soviet Union informed Japan that it was terminating the neutrality pact the two nations had entered into four years earlier.[1517]

Japanese Abuse of Allied Prisoners

In 1944, Japan issued an order to its POW camp commandants to kill all of their POWs if the local military situation became desperate.[1518]

As Japan's defensive perimeter in the Pacific crumbled, it shipped Allied prisoners back to the home islands to serve as slave labor. Many died in transit from starvation, illness, lack of water and Allied attacks on unmarked Japanese transport vessels.[1519]

In the fall of 1944, Japanese ships containing Allied POWs (but with no special POW markings) were sunk by American submarines, resulting in over 4,000 Allied deaths. During the entire war, some 19,000 Allied POWs died at sea.[1520]

In February 1945, the Japanese on the island of Chichi Jima killed eight B-29 fliers and ate the flesh of four of them.[1521]

In the Palawan Massacre, the Japanese placed 150 American POWs in a Philippine air raid shelter, soaked them in gasoline and set them on fire. A few escaped to tell the story, but most were killed.[1522]

B-29 airmen captured in Japan were tortured, tried as war criminals and executed, beheaded, burned alive, stoned, or subjected live to lethal medical experiments.[1523]

The Philippine Campaign Continues

In early January 1945, MacArthur's troops — 175,000 of them — went ashore on the east coast of the Philippine island of Luzon and

---

[1516] *Eagle*, 553, *Masters*, 548, 555-56.
[1517] *Eagle*, 553.
[1518] *WW II Story*, 608, *Conspiracy*, 1327.
[1519] *WW II Story*, 595-601, *Conspiracy*, 1328.
[1520] *Eagle*, 400, *WW II Story*, 595.
[1521] *WW II Story*, 602.
[1522] *WW II Story*, 614, *Conspiracy*, 1327.
[1523] *WW II Story*, 602-06.

headed west for Manila and Clark Field.[1524]

While supporting the amphibious landing of American troops on Luzon, the U.S. Navy came under staggering *kamikaze* attacks. Japanese suicide pilots sank twenty-four ships and damaged sixty-seven others.[1525]

On January 28, U.S. Army Rangers infiltrated Japanese territory in the Philippines and freed 513 Allied POWs, many of whom were survivors of the Bataan Death March. The POWs told of other captives being held by the Japanese at the Santo Tomás internment camp in Manila. MacArthur promptly ordered part of his forces to hasten to Santo Tomás, and those captives were freed in early February.[1526]

By March 3, American troops had driven the Japanese out of Manila, but in the building-to-building battles some 100,000 civilians were killed. Also killed were 1,000 Americans and 16,000 Japanese.[1527]

After Manila was retaken, American forces in Luzon recaptured Bataan and the island of Corregidor.[1528]

MacArthur then ordered his Army troops to invade and take the southern Philippine islands of Palawan, Zamboanga, Panay, Mindoro and Cebu, all of which were in Allied hands by June 1945.[1529]

Spotty Japanese resistance in northern Luzon continued until the end of the war. Overall, the Japanese lost 400,000 men in Philippines fighting. The Americans lost 8,310 killed or missing, and 29,560 wounded.[1530]

Some critics argue that MacArthur's insistence on reclaiming the Philippines, while satisfying his ego, cost up to a half-million lives. Others contend that the Allies needed the bases in the Philippines in order to successfully invade the Japanese homelands.[1531]

As 1945 was unfolding, the forces commanded by Admiral Nimitz and General MacArthur were shrinking the defensive ring around the Japanese home islands.[1532]

Fire Bombing Japan

[1524] *Eagle*, 519-21, *Inferno*, 555.
[1525] *Eagle*, 520, *WW II Story*, 435.
[1526] *WW II Story*, 426-29.
[1527] *Eagle*, 524, *Inferno*, 556, *Conspiracy*, 1326.
[1528] *Eagle*, 525-26, *WW II Story*, 434-35.
[1529] *Eagle*, 527.
[1530] *Eagle*, 529, *WW II Story*, 435, *Ghosts*, 84.
[1531] *Inferno*, 556, *WW II Story*, 435.
[1532] *Eagle*, 478.

Early 1945 American high-altitude daylight bombing runs on Japanese cities using high-explosive bombs were relatively ineffective. This was largely because winds in the Siberian jet stream over Japan raced at up to 200 miles per hour, confounding the B-29s' Norden bombsights. In addition, the daytime planes were attacked by enemy fighters and flak. Thus, General Curtis LeMay decided to use another weapon — incendiary bombs.[1533]

On February 4, American B-29s flying at high altitude dropped incendiary bombs on Kobe, the sixth largest city in Japan, but with limited success.[1534]

On February 25, 1945, another high-altitude incendiary attack, this time on Tokyo, also achieved limited results. LeMay concluded that a low-altitude incendiary night attack would be more successful even if doing so exposed his American bombers to greater flak damage.[1535]

On March 9-10, 1945, 334 Marianas-based American B-29s, flying at night at low altitudes, firebombed Tokyo, killing or injuring about 130,000 people and destroying 267,000 buildings.[1536]

Prior to March 10, 1945, only about 1,300 Japanese had been killed in all Allied air raids on the home islands since the war began. The firebombing of Tokyo had an extraordinarily negative impact on the morale of Japan's civilians.[1537]

Beginning in March, American warplanes dropped thousands of mines in Japanese waters, augmenting the suffocating submarine blockade and making it even more difficult for Japanese ships to supply their homeland.[1538]

By June, the Americans had firebombed Tokyo, Nagoya, Kobe, Osaka, Yokohama and Kawasaki, destroying over forty percent of their urban areas and leaving millions of Japanese homeless.[1539]

The Marianas air bases were about 1,500 miles away from Tokyo. As a consequence, American pilots were required to fly very long and dangerous bombing missions. The Allies' need for runways closer to Japan was obvious.[1540]

[1533] *Eagle*, 503-04, *WW II Story*, 444-49, *Pacific*, 149-150, *Ghosts*, 97-98.
[1534] *Eagle*, 504.
[1535] *Eagle*, 504, *WW II Story*, 447-49.
[1536] *Engineers*, 324, 328, *Eagle*, 504-05, *Inferno*, 615-16, *WW II Story*, 449-50, *Pacific*, 150-51, *Conspiracy*, 1332, *Ghosts*, 114.
[1537] *WW II Story*, 456-61, *Ghosts*, 115.
[1538] *Inferno*, 616, *WW II Story*, 463-65.
[1539] *Eagle*, 505, *Inferno*, 616, *Conspiracy*, 95.
[1540] *Pacific*, 150-51.

Iwo Jima

Lava-covered Iwo Jima ("Sulfur Island") is a landmass roughly 4.5 miles long and 2.5 miles wide that juts out of the Pacific only 660 miles from Tokyo. It has no fresh water and is infested with insects. Anticipating an American attack, in July 1944 the Japanese evacuated all of the civilians and replaced them with 21,000 army and navy troops aiming weapons out of concrete bunkers and living in miles of connected tunnels.[1541]

The Allies' main reasons for wanting to take Iwo Jima were to halt attacks on Saipan's B-29s by Japanese planes flying from Iwo Jima, and because the island could serve as a base from which P-51s could escort those B-29s on their bombing runs to Japan. Since it had no deep water harbors, Iwo Jima was of little military value to the U.S. Navy.[1542]

Responsibility for the amphibious invasion of Iwo Jima was assigned to Admiral Spruance and his Fifth Fleet. Spruance had previously been in command at the Battle of Midway, the amphibious assaults on the Gilbert, Marshall and Mariana Islands, and the Battle of the Philippine Sea.[1543]

Shortly after the Joint Chiefs of Staff approved the Iwo Jima invasion plan in early October, 1944, new reconnaissance photos revealed significantly strengthened Japanese defenses. This raised questions about whether the cost of taking the island might exceed its strategic value. Partly because the Navy wanted to continue to attack the Japanese as its rival Army forces fought them in the Philippines, and partly because the Army Air Force wanted to demonstrate its military value through bombing missions against Japan, the invasion plan was not scrapped.[1544]

On February 16, 1945, after six months of Army Air Force bombing by B-24s, the Navy began three days of intense bombardment of Iwo Jima. Despite all of these explosives, many of the dug-in Japanese defensive facilities remained fully functional. The Marines requested more days of bombardment before invading, but the Navy declined because (a) it was preparing for the invasion of Okinawa which was scheduled to begin in just six weeks, (b) MacArthur refused to release for such bombing any of the six battleships and twenty-six destroyers

---

[1541] *Eagle*, 494-95, *Inferno*, 613, *WW II Story*, 530, 538, *Ghosts*, 4, 39-42, 103.

[1542] *WW II Story*, 530, *Pacific*, 151, *Ghosts*, 5, 27-31.

[1543] *Ghosts*, 7-8.

[1544] *Ghosts*, 34-37.

he was using in the Luzon invasion, and (c) other Navy battleships and cruisers were then occupied carrying out raids along the Japanese coast.[1545]

The talented and experienced General Kuribayashi commanded the Japanese forces on Iwo Jima. His plan was not to contest the American invasion on the beaches, but rather to inflict severe damage on the invading troops through both concealed guns aimed at the beaches and Japanese soldiers who would fight to heroic deaths.[1546]

On February 19, after several hours of additional naval bombardment, the first 30,000 U.S. Marines landed on the beaches of Iwo Jima. They were immediately pinned down by vicious Japanese artillery, mortar and machine gun fire. Eventually, some 82,000 Marines were put ashore.[1547]

On February 21, Japanese *kamikaze* attacks on Navy ships off of Iwo Jima sank the escort carrier *Bismarck*, severely damaged the light carrier *Saratoga*, and caused almost 1,800 Navy casualties.[1548]

After three days of lethal fighting, the Marines finally gained control of Mt. Suribachi, a 554 feet high peak at the southern end of the island. They raised an American flag, generating excited cheers from American troops below and the blowing of horns and whistles on nearby Navy ships. Several hours later, as a larger flag was raised on Suribachi, a photographer snapped the picture that became famous and served as the model for the Marine Memorial in Washington, D.C.[1549]

It took until the end of March 1945 for the Americans to knock out the Japanese on Iwo Jima. In the process, virtually all 21,000 Japanese troops were killed and the Americans suffered 6,821 dead and another 19,217 wounded. In addition, 2,648 Marines suffered "combat fatigue." This was the first Pacific island battle in which the Japanese inflicted a greater number of casualties than they suffered. The Iwo Jima losses had a sobering impact on the American public. Twenty-seven brave Marines and Navy corpsmen were awarded the Medal of Honor for their valiant service on rugged Iwo Jima.[1550]

Almost one-third of all the Marines who died in battle during World War II were killed on Iwo Jima. Admiral Nimitz said of the

---

[1545] *Eagle*, 498-99, *Pacific*, 155-56, *Ghosts*, 53-55.

[1546] *Ghosts*, 45-47.

[1547] *Eagle*, 499-500, *Inferno*, 613, *Pacific*, 157-165, *Ghosts*, 64.

[1548] *Ghosts*, 68.

[1549] *Eagle*, 501, *WW II Story*, 532, 543-45, *Pacific*, 170-72, *Ghosts*, 67-68, 130-36.

[1550] *Ghosts*, xvi, 82-85, 117, *Eagle*, 502-03, *Inferno*, 614, *WW II Story*, 531, 556, *Pacific*, 172-196, *Conspiracy*, 1323.

Marines who served there: "uncommon valor was a common virtue."[1551]

During the brutal fight for Iwo Jima, President Roosevelt rejected a proposal that the United States use poison gas to eliminate the dug-in Japanese who were killing so many Allied soldiers.[1552]

Despite having been an important justification for attacking Iwo Jima, the number of P-51s based there that subsequently accompanied B-29s on Japan bombing runs was relatively small, raising the question of whether the Iwo Jima invasion was worth the human cost to America.[1553]

Before the fighting on Iwo Jima ended, thirty-six B-29s made emergency landings on the island. During the remainder of the war, at least 2,251 American B-29 bombers (with crews of eleven) made landings on Iwo Jima, arguably saving the lives of up to 24,761 airmen. However, not all of the landings were made under emergency conditions.[1554]

The success of General Kuribayashi's fight-to-the-death strategy for defending Iwo Jima influenced the manner in which Japan planned to defend Okinawa, and likely would have strongly influenced the way in which Japan defended its homelands against an Allied invasion.[1555]

Success in Burma

In early spring 1945, British General Slim led a force of 530,000 Indian and British soldiers against 400,000 Japanese troops in northern Burma. His objective was to reopen the Burma Road.[1556]

The Burma Defense Army, composed of Burmese troops, had originally sided with the Japanese. However, in 1945, as the British moved toward Rangoon, the BDA switched allegiance and attacked local Japanese forces.[1557]

By May 1945, the war in Europe had ended and the British, aided by air superiority, had recaptured the Burmese capital of Rangoon and driven most of the Japanese out of that country.[1558]

[1551] *Ghosts*, xv, 126, 150.

[1552] *Conspiracy*, 1333, *Ghosts*, 119.

[1553] *Ghosts*, 98-99.

[1554] *Eagle*, 502, *WW II Story*, 468, *Ghosts*, 6, 93, 106-08.

[1555] *Ghosts*, 112-13.

[1556] *Inferno*, 611, *WW II Story*, 594.

[1557] *Inferno*, 612-13.

[1558] *Eagle*, 373-74, *Inferno*, 611, *WW II Story*, 594.

Okinawa

In their advance toward the enemy homeland, the Allies were determined to capture Okinawa, a sixty mile long island located near Formosa and about 350 miles southwest of Japan. Okinawa had been part of the Japanese empire since 1879. Its capture would provide the Allies with airbases and fleet anchorage during the anticipated invasion of the Japanese mainland, which would involve (a) landing up to 650,000 Americans on Kyushu ("Operation Olympic") in November 1945, and (b) a larger force invading the main island of Honshu and the city of Tokyo ("Operation Coronet") in March 1946.[1559]

On April 1, 1945 (Easter Sunday), the first American troops — some 50,000 out of a total force of about 180,000 Marines and Army soldiers — made an amphibious landing on Okinawa after days of heavy naval bombardment. Twelve hundred Navy ships supported the invasion force.[1560]

Rather than contest the landings on the beaches, the Japanese force of 100,000 elected to engage the Americans from buried and concealed defensive positions in the mountainous parts of Okinawa.[1561]

Using some 700 planes, the Japanese also launched repeated *kamikaze* and conventional air attacks on the huge Allied fleet supporting the Okinawa invasion. They caused considerable damage to ships, including the carriers *Bunker Hill* and *Enterprise*, and severe emotional strain on the sailors.[1562]

On April 6, 1945, the immense Japanese battleship *Yamato* sailed from the Inland Sea of Japan heading for a confrontation with the Americans at Okinawa. *Yamato's* objective was to attract Navy planes so that they would not be available to defend against *kamikaze* attacks on the American Okinawa fleet. American submarines spotted the huge Japanese ship and its escorts. The next day about 300 U.S. Navy carrier planes attacked and sank *Yamato*, a new light cruiser (*Yahagi*) and four destroyers, taking with them 3,600 Japanese lives.[1563]

Ernie Pyle, the famed American war journalist who had reported so well from Europe and the Pacific, was killed by enemy fire on April 18 on Ie Shima, a small island just off the shores of Okinawa.[1564]

[1559] *Eagle*, 532-33, 542, *Engineers*, 348, *Inferno*, 618, *WW II Story*, 607.

[1560] *Eagle*, 532, *Inferno*, 618, *WW II Story*, 558, 561, *Pacific*, 200-04.

[1561] *Eagle*, 533, *Inferno*, 618, *WW II Story*, 578, *Pacific*, 200.

[1562] *Eagle*, 535-38, *Inferno*, 619-22, *WW II Story*, 565-77, *Pacific*, 227-231, *Conspiracy*, 1335.

[1563] *Eagle*, 538, *WW II Story*, 567, *Pacific*, 226-27, *Conspiracy*, 1335.

[1564] *WW II Story*, 563-64, *Pacific*, 209.

The Okinawa battle was concentrated largely on the Shuri Line, a Japanese defensive position about five miles north of the southern tip of the island. In fifteen days of early fighting there, the Japanese lost almost 50,000 soldiers.[1565]

On June 4, another typhoon struck Halsey's task force supporting the Okinawa invasion. Again, he neglected to chart a course that would permit his ships to escape the storm. Many vessels suffered damage and six men died. Again, Halsey faced a court of inquiry and again he was deemed to have displayed a lack of sound judgment. But because of his popularity with the American public, suggestions that he be relieved of sea duty were rejected.[1566]

When the battle for Okinawa ended on June 21, after eighty-two days of combat, the Americans had scored another significant victory. However, 7,374 United States soldiers and 4,907 sailors had been killed, and 31,807 American soldiers and 4,874 sailors had been wounded, representing the worst American battle losses in the Pacific war. The Japanese sank thirty-six Allied ships, damaged 368 others and destroyed 763 American planes. In the conflict, Japan lost 70,000 troops and 80,000 Okinawans (mostly civilians).[1567]

On Okinawa, the defending Japanese force, cut off from support and subject to intense naval bombardment, had resolutely faced enemy air and ground attacks for more than 100 days. The conditions in the Japanese home islands would be more favorable to the Japanese, meaning that the Allies would face even more daunting challenges, including expected civilian opposition and suicides.[1568]

After Okinawa, the Allies felt great dread and anxiety over the huge number of lives that would be lost in the anticipated invasion of the Japanese home islands. Estimates of American casualties in just the forthcoming Kyushu invasion were 268,000 dead and wounded.[1569]

Planning to Invade a War-Weary Japan

The Allied invasion of Japan was scheduled to begin on Kyushu in November 1945, with MacArthur as supreme commander. In June, following Roosevelt's death on April 12, recently sworn in President

---

[1565] *WW II Story*, 577-586, *Pacific*, 216-19.

[1566] *Admirals*, 419-22.

[1567] *Eagle*, 540, *Masters*, 554, *Engineers*, 347-48, *Inferno*, 622, *WW II Story*, 576, 588-90, *Pacific*, 224, 237, *Conspiracy*, 1323.

[1568] *Eagle*, 543.

[1569] *Eagle*, 540, 543, *Inferno*, 622, *Pacific*, 233.

Truman approved those plans.[1570]

In 1944 and 1945, many Japanese elites favored peace. But the military high command, which had known since 1944 that the war could not be won, was determined to fight to the end in the hope of extracting peace terms more favorable than Roosevelt's "unconditional surrender." Especially important to them was preserving the role of the Emperor as the divine leader of Japan. In late June 1945, the Emperor intervened and asked that the government ministers pursue a diplomatic end to the war.[1571]

The Japanese desperately tried to persuade the Soviet Union to mediate the end of war on terms favorable to Japan, but with Japan near defeat the Soviets refused to help. American intelligence officers were aware of the failed efforts through intercepted Japanese communications.[1572]

On June 27, 1945, Stalin approved the final strategic plan under which the Soviet Union would attack Japan on August 11.[1573]

In mid-July 1945, Stalin met with the Chinese to obtain their agreement that the Red Army could march into China during the anticipated Soviet attack against Japanese forces there.[1574]

Potsdam and Discussion of the Atomic Bomb

President Truman, Stalin and Churchill and their military leaders met in Potsdam, Germany beginning on July 17, 1945. Stalin said that the Soviet Union would enter the war against Japan in mid-August 1945, and the parties discussed where to fix the location of the German/Polish border. Truman rejected Stalin's efforts to have the Soviet Union gain some post-war control over the Ruhr valley, Germany's industrial heartland. (Truman understood that for West Germany to restore its economy, coal from the Ruhr was needed to run railroads, which could be used to ship manufactured products to market and sold for currency).[1575]

On July 16, 1945, in the New Mexico desert, the United States successfully tested the first atomic bomb, the development of which

---

[1570] *Inferno*, 623, *Conspiracy*, 98, *Ghosts*, 120, *Slept*, 672.
[1571] *Eagle*, 547-48, *Inferno*, 626-27, *Conspiracy*, 72, 80-81, 99, *Ghosts*, 116.
[1572] *Eagle*, 548, *Conspiracy*, 97-102, 104, *Conspiracy*, 1335.
[1573] *Curse*, 167.
[1574] *Curse*, 158.
[1575] *Curse*, 158-61, 164, 295, *Pacific*, 236, *Crusade*, 442-43.

had cost some $600 million a year. That evening, Truman was informed (without details) of the test, the day before he first met Stalin.[1576]

When Stimson informed Eisenhower at Potsdam that the Americans had an atomic weapon, Ike argued against its use on Japan because he felt that the Japanese were already defeated and its use would shock world opinion and increase international tension.[1577]

On July 24, 1945, Truman told Stalin that the Americans "had a new weapon of unusual destructive force." Stalin replied that he "hoped we would make good use of it against the Japanese." From British and American spies working for the Soviets, Stalin had known for years of America's efforts to develop an atomic bomb. After speaking with Truman, Stalin privately pressed Soviet scientists to speed their efforts to develop an atomic weapon.[1578]

On July 26, 1945, Truman, Churchill and Chiang Kai-shek issued the Potsdam Declaration calling on Japan to surrender unconditionally or face "prompt and utter destruction." The Declaration did not specifically address whether the Emperor would still have a governmental role, promising only the establishment "in accordance with the freely expressed will of the Japanese people, of a peacefully inclined and responsible government."[1579]

The final Allied report of the Potsdam Conference stated that "We do not intend that the Japanese shall be enslaved as a race or destroyed as a nation, but stern justice shall be meted out to all war criminals, including those who have visited cruelties upon our prisoners."[1580]

The Japanese decided not to offer any immediate reply to the Potsdam Declaration, preferring instead to continue their efforts to persuade the Soviets to mediate the dispute. Two days after receiving the Declaration, Japanese Premier Suzuki claimed it was "of no great value" to the Japanese government, and newspaper reports said the Japanese cabinet had decided to treat the Declaration "with silent contempt." These statements led the Allies to conclude that Japan had rejected the terms of the Potsdam Declaration.[1581]

On July 26, the cruiser *Indianapolis* arrived at Tinian in the Maria-

[1576] *Curse*, 159, *Eagle*, 550, 552, *WW II Story*, 613, *Pacific*, 235-36, *Conspiracy*, 102-03.
[1577] *Ike*, 596, *Crusade*, 443.
[1578] *Curse*, 162-63, *Eagle*, 552-53, *Conspiracy*, 73, 104.
[1579] *Curse*, 165, *Eagle*, 546, *Inferno*, 626, *Conspiracy*, 104.
[1580] *Tears*, 328.
[1581] *Eagle*, 549, *WW II Story*, 616, *Conspiracy*, 104.

na Islands. In its hold were the firing mechanism and uranium bullet for the first bomb, "Little Boy." Four days later, a Japanese submarine sank the *Indianapolis*.[1582]

Dropping the Atomic Bomb

Following Japan's apparent rejection of the Potsdam Declaration, Truman and his advisors reluctantly decided to proceed with an atomic attack. Earlier, scientists had counseled the President that they could conceive of no way to demonstrate to the Japanese the extraordinary force of the bomb and achieve peace other than by direct military use.[1583]

An Army Air Force group, headed by Colonel Paul Tibbets, had for several months been making B-29 practice runs over Tokyo from Tinian.[1584]

The Americans were hardened in their decision to use the atomic weapon by the Japanese "sneak attack" on Pearl Harbor, Japanese atrocities in POW camps and against the Chinese, repeated *kamikaze* attacks, fight-to-the-death Japanese resistance in Iwo Jima and Okinawa, and the anticipated massive casualties that would be suffered while invading the Japanese home islands. Use of the atomic bomb was a continuation of the wartime killing of civilians that began years earlier when German submarines sank unarmed cruise ships and freighters, London was subjected to the *blitzkrieg*, the Allies bombed Dresden and other German cities, and Tokyo was fire-bombed.[1585]

The United States sought by using atomic weapons to avoid the tremendous loss of life that would occur if an invasion of Japan were necessary. The Japanese still had 2,500,000 combat troops in the home islands and 9,000 *kamikaze* planes. In addition, the United States was concerned that if the war did not soon end, Stalin would feed his desire to spread Communism by promptly taking control of Manchuria, parts of Japan and China.[1586]

On August 6, 1945, a United States B-29, the *Enola Gay*, dropped the first atomic bomb, weighing 9,000 pounds, on Hiroshima, the eighth largest city in Japan. Home to 245,000 residents, Hiroshima was the southern headquarters and supply depot for the Japanese army that

---

[1582] *WW II Story*, 616.

[1583] *Eagle*, 554, *WW II Story*, 610-12.

[1584] *Eagle*, 554.

[1585] *Eagle*, 555, *WW II Story*, 608-10, 615.

[1586] *Conspiracy*, 72-73, 77, 108.

would defend the island of Kyushu in the event of an Allied invasion. The bomb, called "Little Boy," had the power of 12,500 tons of conventional explosive. Almost 100,000 people died instantly and thousands of others died later of burns, shock or radiation.[1587]

Several hours after the Hiroshima bombing, President Truman announced the existence of the terrible new weapon and warned the Japanese that if they did not surrender, they could expect unprecedented ruin from the air. The Japanese government did not respond to Truman's statement.[1588]

Shortly after the Hiroshima attack, the Soviet Union declared war on Japan and Stalin advanced to August 9, 1945 the date of the planned Red Army attack on the Japanese.[1589]

In Moscow on August 8, 1945, the Japanese continued to seek from the Soviets a way to achieve peace without an unconditional surrender.[1590]

In the evening of August 8, another B-29 took off from Tinian. Several hours later it dropped on Nagasaki a 10,300 pound plutonium bomb, called "Fat Boy," having the explosive equivalence of 22,000 tons of TNT. At least 35,000 people were killed. Nagasaki was a major military port and home to major steel and torpedo plants.[1591]

The original target for "Fat Boy" was the city of Kokura, the center of Japan's steel industry. But an overcast sky and smoke from an earlier conventional bombing prevented the bombardier from seeing the aiming point, and so the plane was diverted to Nagasaki. The returning plane that dropped "Fat Boy" made an emergency landing on Okinawa with just seven gallons of fuel remaining.[1592]

The two atomic bombs killed about the same number of Japanese as the number of Chinese that Japanese soldiers killed during the Rape of Nanking.[1593]

The United States' inventory of atomic bombs fell to zero after Nagasaki, but America had the capacity to manufacture a new one every few weeks.[1594]

[1587] *Curse*, 167, *Eagle*, 555, *Inferno*, 628, *WW II Story*, 613, 618, *Pacific*, 236-38, *Conspiracy*, 64-66.

[1588] *Eagle*, 555, *WW II Story*, 625.

[1589] *Curse*, 167-69, *Eagle*, 555, *Conspiracy*, 67.

[1590] *Curse*, 167-68, *Conspiracy*, 107.

[1591] *Eagle*, 555, *Inferno*, 628, *WW II Story*, 613-626, 646, *Pacific*, 238, *Conspiracy*, 71.

[1592] *WW II Story*, 626-39, *Conspiracy*, 68-69.

[1593] *Conspiracy*, 71.

[1594] *Conspiracy*, 76.

Japan Surrenders

Even after Hiroshima and Nagasaki, the Japanese military did not want to surrender under the terms of the Potsdam Declaration. But late on August 9, 1945, the Emperor intervened to urge peace. On August 10, the Japanese, through Hirohito, offered to surrender on the condition that the Emperor's role as a sovereign ruler be preserved without prejudice.[1595]

After serious debate over whether to soften the unconditional surrender stance, on August 11 the Allies rejected the Japanese proposal. As a compromise, they proposed that "the authority of the Emperor ... shall be subject to the Supreme Commander of the Allied powers ...," and sent the proposal to the Swiss for delivery to the Japanese. The Allied response also made clear that Allied troops would remain in Japan until the objectives of the Potsdam Declaration had been achieved, including disarmament, a democratic form of government, reparations, and the prosecution of war criminals.[1596]

Between August 9 and 19, a Red Army force of 1,500,000 men overran Japanese troops in Manchuria, proceeded to Sakhalin Island and the Kurile Islands, and advanced into Korea, stopping at the 38th parallel. While the Soviets lost 12,000 dead, almost 80,000 Japanese died in that fighting.[1597]

On August 12, 1945, Japan executed eight captured U.S. airmen. Three days later, it executed eight more American airmen.[1598]

On August 14, 1945, the U.S. Army Air Force launched a 1,000 plane conventional bombing raid on Tokyo.[1599]

Also on August 14, 1945, after three days of debate and another Allied raid using conventional bombs, the Emperor told his ministers that he wanted to accept the Allies' latest terms and that he planned to announce the surrender to the nation in a radio broadcast that was designed to block the military from interfering with the surrender.[1600]

During the evening of August 14, Japanese army officers, intending to carry on the war, attempted a *coup d'état* in Tokyo that failed when senior officers declined to join the rebels. During the next few days,

---

[1595] *Curse*, 168, *Eagle*, 555-556, *Conspiracy*, 107-117.
[1596] *Eagle*, 556-57, *WW II Story*, 639, *Conspiracy*, 116-19.
[1597] *Curse*, 169-70, *Inferno*, 628.
[1598] *Curse*, 168.
[1599] *Curse*, 169, *Eagle*, 557, *WW II Story*, 639-40.
[1600] *Eagle*, 557, *WW II Story*, 639-40, *Conspiracy*, 1337.

several leaders of the Japanese government narrowly avoided assassination.[1601]

On August 14, Stalin signed a Sino-Soviet Treaty of Friendship and Mutual Assistance with the Kuomintang Chinese government led by Chiang Kai-shek, much to the annoyance of Mao Tse-tung, the leader of China's Communist Party.[1602]

Also on August 14 (United States time), Emperor Hirohito broadcast Japan's acceptance of the Allied surrender terms, noting that "the war situation has developed not necessarily to Japan's advantage."[1603]

On August 15, 1945, President Truman ordered all offensive military operations to end and issued General Order No. 1, which established how and to whom the Japanese were to surrender and specified that Korea would be divided at the 38th parallel.[1604]

Following Japan's announced surrender, President Truman appointed General MacArthur to serve as the military governor of the defeated nation. The challenge was how to deal with Japan going forward. Should it be reduced to nothing more than an agricultural state, or remade over years of occupation into a democratic society, or trusted (once demilitarized) to remake itself, or simply be stripped of its colonies and forced to find a way out of severe poverty? Japan had operated for more than a thousand years under the view that its emperor was a god-king. Could it be reformed without destroying the god-king concept? But could it be reformed without cooperation from the god-king? Ultimately, the United States decided that MacArthur should "exercise his authority through Japanese governmental machinery and agencies, including the Emperor."[1605]

Stalin pressed for the Soviet Union to have a role in the post-war occupation of Japan, but Truman refused.[1606]

On August 29, before the formal Japanese surrender, Admiral Halsey, having been informed of continuing Japanese mistreatment of POWs, sent a landing force into Tokyo Bay and liberated POWs being held there.[1607]

On August 31, General Wainwright arrived in Tokyo, four days after he was liberated from a POW camp in Manchuria by the invading

---

[1601] *Curse,* 169, *Eagle,* 557, *Conspiracy,* 135-145.

[1602] *Curse,* 172.

[1603] *Inferno,* 628-29, *Eagle,* 557, *Curse,* 169, *Conspiracy,* 145-48, 1339.

[1604] *Curse,* 170, 330, *Inferno,* 629.

[1605] *Conspiracy,* 161-170.

[1606] *Curse,* 170-72.

[1607] *WW II Story,* 642, *Conspiracy,* 172.

Red Army.[1608]

On September 2, 1945. Japanese government representatives signed the formal unconditional surrender documents aboard USS *Missouri* in the presence of General MacArthur, who had just been appointed Supreme Commander, Allied Powers in Japan. General Wainwright was in attendance.[1609]

World War II was finally at an end.

[1608] *WW II Story*, 644, *Conspiracy*, 177.
[1609] *Guns*, 631, *Curse*, 171, *Eagle*, 559, *WW II Story*, 644-46, *Conspiracy*, 177-78.

A CONCISE HISTORY OF THE SECOND WORLD WAR

Part 4

World War II's
Human and Economic Toll

ANY study of World War II warrants a review of the myriad ways in which the conflict impacted people — those who fought in the war, those who died, those who survived, and those not yet born. The effects, both mortal and economic, varied but were in every instance significant.

MILITARY AND CIVILIAN DEATHS

World Totals

World War II lasted six years and one day, entangled almost sixty nations, and caused the death of at least 60,000,000 people.[1610]

On average, 27,600 people perished on each of the war's deadly days.[1611]

National and Ethnic Totals

More than 26,000,000 (about fourteen percent) of the Soviet Union's 190,000,000 residents were killed during World War II. Of the dead, at least 16,000,000 were civilians and as many as 10,000,000 were in the military. In addition to the troops who were killed, some 2,000,000 Soviet civilians starved to death while in land their government controlled, and at least another 13,000,000 died from German weapons or while in regions occupied by Germany.[1612]

Between 1937 and 1945, the Japanese killed an estimated 15,000,000 Chinese through military action, starvation and disease, including plagues caused by Japanese biological warfare.[1613]

At least 5,000,000 residents of Southeast Asia perished during World War II from either starvation or attacks triggered by the Japa-

---

[1610] *Guns*, 631, *Curse*, 126, *Fateful Choices*, 290, *Inferno*, 152.
[1611] *Dawn*, 5, *Inferno*, xv.
[1612] *Guns*, 637, *Inferno*, 329, *Folly*, 10, *Curse*, 126.
[1613] *Inferno*, xv, 414-15, *WW II Story*, 640.

nese.[1614]

Overall, more than 2,000,000 Japanese died during World War II, including almost 400,000 killed by the Chinese between 1937 and 1945, 208,000 by the British, and 900,596 by the United States.[1615]

Approximately 5,500,000 Poles, about sixteen percent of the population, were killed during World War II.[1616]

In the 1939 German bombing of Warsaw, almost as many Poles were killed as the number of Germans who died in the Allied bombing of Dresden in 1945.[1617]

The Germans killed more Poles in the 1944 Warsaw uprising than the number of Japanese who were killed by atomic bombs the United States dropped on Hiroshima and Nagasaki.[1618]

The Soviets killed more than 4,500,000 German soldiers; the Americans and British another 500,000.[1619]

In the first five years of war, the German army lost 114,000 officers and 3,600,000 enlisted men.[1620]

Just on the Eastern Front, an average of 60,000 Axis soldiers died each month between June 1941 and May 1944.[1621]

The Allied bombing of Germany killed some 650,000 German civilians and injured another 800,000.[1622]

Many residents of the Soviet Union enlisted with the Germans and fought against Stalin's forces. Of those who did, 215,000 died wearing a German uniform.[1623]

The Germans killed between 5,290,000 and 6,000,000 Jews during World War II. Hitler's goal had been 11,000,000. About one-tenth of all those who died in World War II were Jews. Of the total number of Jews who died in World War II, only about three per cent, or 165,000, were Germans. Most of the Jews killed during World War II did not die in a concentration camp; they were shot dead.[1624]

As many as 12,000,000 people met their deaths in either Nazi con-

---

[1614] *Inferno*, 404.

[1615] *Inferno*, 415, *WW II Story*, 640.

[1616] *WW II Story*, 28-29, 640, *Iron Curtain*, 9, *Savage*, 14.

[1617] *Bloodlands*, 405.

[1618] *Bloodlands*, 406.

[1619] *Inferno*, 427.

[1620] *Guns*, 249.

[1621] *Inferno*, 156.

[1622] *WW II Story*, 481, *Air Masters*, 472.

[1623] *Inferno*, 153.

[1624] *Fateful Choices*, 432, *Inferno*, xvii, *WW II Story*, 520, *Bloodlands*, ix, 253, 382, 411, *Reich*, 965, 973, *Savage*, 16.

centration camps or the German slave labor system.[1625]

Between 1,500,000 and 2,000,000 Yugoslavs died in the war.[1626]

The United States suffered 409,399 military deaths during World War II, of whom 291,557 were killed in combat fighting Axis forces.[1627]

Great Britain lost as many as 397,700 killed in World War II.[1628]

Approximately 310,000 Italians were killed in the war.[1629]

French civilian and military deaths during the war totaled about 800,000, including some 70,000 civilians killed by Allied bombs.[1630]

Approximately six per cent of the Hungarian and Greek populations were killed during the war. Of the 410,000 Greeks who died, some 250,000 starved to death.[1631]

Some 210,000 were killed in the Netherlands during World War II, including 106,000 Jews.[1632]

Young Lives

Of all German boys born between 1915 and 1924, one-third were dead or missing by the end of World War II; two out of five who were born between 1920 and 1925 died.[1633]

In 1944, Germany began drafting boys no older than sixteen and men at least fifty years of age.[1634]

By February 1945, the Japanese had pressed into military service 1,250,000 boys between the ages of twelve and fourteen.[1635]

Casualty Rates

Of all military deaths the Allies suffered during World War II, sixty-five percent were from the Soviet Union, China bore twenty-three percent, Yugoslavia three percent, Britain and the United States two percent each, and France and Poland one percent each.[1636]

During the war, about eight percent of the German population died, compared with two percent for China, 3.44 percent for the

---

[1625] *WW II Story*, 520.
[1626] *WW II Story*, 640, *Iron Curtain*, 9.
[1627] *WW II Story*, 640, *Air Masters*, 472.
[1628] *Masters*, 580, *Iron Curtain*, 9.
[1629] *Savage*, 11.
[1630] *Inferno*, 514, *Folly*, 10.
[1631] *Iron Curtain*, 9, *Savage*, 13-14, 33.
[1632] *Savage*, 11.
[1633] *Guns*, 637, *Inferno*, 630.
[1634] *Guns*, 391, *Reich*, 1087, *Bulge*, 8.
[1635] *Burma*, 378.
[1636] *Inferno*, 316.

Netherlands, 6.67 percent for Yugoslavia, four percent for Greece, 1.35 percent for France, 3.78 percent for Japan, 0.94 percent for Britain and 0.32 percent for the United States.[1637]

The death rates in World War II for American military service members were as follows: Marines — 3.66 percent, Army — 2.5 percent, Navy — 1.5 percent.[1638]

Japanese military death rates in the war were 24.2 percent for soldiers and 19.7 percent for sailors.[1639]

German military death rates were: *Luftwaffe* (air force) — 17.35 per cent; *Wehrmacht* (regular armed forces) — 30.9 per cent; *Waffen SS* (Nazi armed forces) — 34.9 per cent.[1640]

Of 39,000 Germans who served on U-boats during the war, 27,491 were killed and another 5,000 taken prisoner.[1641]

While infantrymen accounted for just fourteen percent of the U.S. Army's overall forces abroad, they sustained seventy percent of the Army's casualties.[1642]

About twenty-two percent of U.S. submariners who made war patrols in World War II died in service — the highest casualty rate for any branch of the American military.[1643]

In World War II, 140,000 Allied airmen died. Of those, at least 13,000 were American airmen who were killed not in combat but in accidents. Fifty-six thousand, roughly half, of the Royal Air Force's heavy-bomber crew members died. In German bombing runs, 26,000 Americans died. Only one in four crews could expect to complete twenty-five missions.[1644]

Burials

Of the American servicemen killed during World War II, some 270,000 were initially buried overseas. Subsequently, sixty percent of those bodies were, at family direction, returned for burial in the United States.[1645]

[1637] *Inferno*, 316, *WW II Story*, 29.

[1638] *Inferno*, 316-17.

[1639] *Inferno*, 316.

[1640] *Inferno*, 316.

[1641] *WW II Story*, 177.

[1642] *Eagle*, 383, *Battle*, 508.

[1643] *Eagle*, 487, *Air Masters*, 471.

[1644] *Battle*, 497, *Inferno*, 457, 459, *Air Masters*, 7, 166, 246.

[1645] *Guns*, 638.

Mine Fields

Marshal Zhukov, who led the Red Army for much of the war, described how his army coped with enemy mine fields. If foot soldiers encountered a field in which personnel mines had been planted, they were ordered to cross the field as though there were no mines. The resulting loss of life was rationalized on the theory that as many would have been killed had the Germans manned that area with machine guns and artillery.[1646]

PSYCHIATRIC DAMAGE

The U. S. Army hospitalized approximately 929,000 men for "neuropsychiatric" reasons — battle fatigue — during World War II. More than 500,000 were discharged from service for psychiatric reasons.[1647]

In the Mediterranean theater of battle, over thirty percent of all nonfatal military casualties were psychiatric in nature.[1648]

The U.S. Army recognized that troops kept in battle too long suffer physical and mental exhaustion that leads to higher casualties, and that periodic periods of rest tend to restore the combat soldier's fighting ability. For Allied troops in Italy and northern Europe this was not always possible; some units faced as many as 500 days of combat.[1649]

Some stressed soldiers shot themselves or even deliberately contracted venereal disease in an effort to escape combat.[1650]

Almost every surviving American flier who overcame the likelihood of death and completed his tour of combat duty suffered at least one symptom of combat fatigue. In an effort to give some hope to crewmembers, the Army Air Force ruled that anyone who completed twenty-five missions would be sent home or given ground duty.[1651]

Over one third of German civilians who suffered through a major air raid experienced relatively permanent psychological effects.[1652]

[1646] *Crusade*, 467-68.

[1647] *Guns*, 340, *Dawn*, 405, *Battle*, 508.

[1648] *Air Masters*, 128.

[1649] *Crusade*, 454, *Air Masters*, 129.

[1650] *Crusade*, 455.

[1651] *Air Masters*, 125-27.

[1652] *Air Masters*, 476.

PHYSICAL DAMAGE

Some 17,000 American servicemen lost limbs in combat, while 100,000 Americans during the war suffered amputations in industrial accidents.[1653]

MILITARY MISCONDUCT

During World War II, about 21,000 U.S. Army soldiers deserted — defined as an unauthorized absence of two months or more.[1654]

On January 31, 1945, U.S. Army private Eddie D. Slovik was shot dead by an American firing squad for having deserted from duty in France. After capture, Slovik had been offered amnesty if he returned to the front, but he refused.[1655]

Almost 11,000 general courts martial were held for U.S. soldiers who committed serious crimes in Europe. General Eisenhower had to approve each sentence imposed by U.S. military courts.[1656]

During the war, 140 U.S. soldiers were court-martialed and executed for murder or rape.[1657]

Red Army soldiers faced severe punishment for disobeying orders. During World War II, Soviet military tribunals convicted a total of 994,000 Soviet troops, sentencing 158,000 to death, some 400,000 to prison, and at least 420,000 to serve in punitive military units (which frequently amounted to a death sentence).[1658]

Some 300,000 Soviet soldiers were shot dead by their own commanders without any hearing.[1659]

Germany executed at least 15,000 German soldiers during the war for desertion and cowardice.[1660]

Soviet troops rampaged against the defeated Germans. By late 1945, Red Army soldiers had sexually assaulted some 2,000,000 German women, some as young as eight and others as old as eighty-four. Many Germans committed suicide to escape Soviet revenge.[1661]

[1653] *Inferno*, xviii.
[1654] *Guns*, 528, *Battle*, 508.
[1655] *Guns*, 527-30, *Ike*, 670.
[1656] *Guns*, 528, *Supreme Commander*, 594.
[1657] *Dawn*, 463, *Generals' War*, 209.
[1658] *Curse*, 114, *Inferno*, 148.
[1659] *Inferno*, 148.
[1660] *Inferno*, 535.
[1661] *Guns*, 513, *Curse*, 113, *Inferno*, 599, 605-08, *WW II Story*, 527-28, *Bloodlands*, 316-18.

BLACKS

While at the outset of World War II there were fewer than 4,000 African-Americans in the United States military, over 1,000,000 joined before the war ended. Some 900,000 African-Americans served in the United States Army, predominately in black platoons commanded by white officers. Most were assigned to service units doing manual labor such as road building, stevedoring and laundering.[1662]

Although segregation persisted, the percentage of blacks working in American war industries rose from two in 1942 to eight in 1945.[1663]

Approximately 500,000 blacks from Africa and the Caribbean Islands served in the British military during the war, but at reduced pay.[1664]

WOMEN

Nineteen million women participated in America's workforce by the end of World War II, about 6,500,000 more than before 1942.[1665]

Over 80,000 American women served in the U.S. Navy, Marines and Coast Guard during World War II. Many thousands of others served in the Army. Women in the Army were first called WAACs (Women's Army Auxiliary Corps), then WACs (dropping the "Auxiliary"). Females in the Navy were named WAVES (Women Accepted for Volunteer Emergency Service).[1666]

During the first four years of the war, some 2,250,000 British women worked in their country's production of war materiel.[1667]

According to Nazi ideology, a woman's place was in the home. Thus, only 182,000 women labored in German war production during the first four years of World War II.[1668]

More than 800,000 Soviet women served in the Red Army, ninety-two of whom were designated Heroes of the Soviet Union and some of whom fought as snipers or pilots.[1669]

[1662] *Guns*, 554, *Eagle*, 386-87, *Ike*, 289-90.
[1663] *Inferno*, 390.
[1664] *Inferno*, 397-99.
[1665] *Guns*, 634, *Inferno*, 225, 344.
[1666] *Eagle*, 393-95.
[1667] *Reich*, 1087.
[1668] *Reich*, 1087.
[1669] *Inferno*, 345, *Folly*, 10.

After World War II ended, there were 20,000,000 more women in the Soviet Union than men.[1670]

During the war the Japanese forced about 100,000 Chinese females to serve as "comfort women" for its soldiers. The women were held captive and subjected to repeated rapes.[1671]

HUNGER AND HOMELESSNESS

Civilian hunger and food rationing were commonplace during World War II. For example, one British adult was due each week four ounces of lard or butter, twelve ounces of sugar, four ounces of bacon, two eggs, six ounces of meat, two ounces of tea and whatever home-grown fruits or vegetables were available. Conditions were better in the United States, but far worse in China, Italy, the Soviet Union, Japan and other combatant nations.[1672]

Stalin's rule was that Soviet soldiers received the most food; civilian workers less; and the old and "useless" got only starvation amounts. During the war, over 2,000,000 Soviets living in areas never occupied by the Germans died of hunger.[1673]

Germany's attacks left 25,000,000 people in the Soviet Union homeless.[1674]

The German air force dropped almost 50,000 tons of bombs on Britain, destroying over 200,000 homes and damaging an additional 4,500,000.[1675]

In Germany, the war destroyed one-half of that country's housing, leaving up to 20,000,000 homeless.[1676]

In Ukraine, 10,000,000 people were left homeless.[1677]

PRISONERS OF WAR AND FORCED LABOR

[1670] *Curse*, 127.

[1671] *Inferno*, 416-18.

[1672] *Inferno*, 338-42, *Ike*, 269.

[1673] *Inferno*, 175.

[1674] *Curse*, 127, *Bulge*, 12-13.

[1675] *Savage Continent: Europe in the Aftermath of World War II* ("*Savage*"), Keith Lowe, St. Martin's Press, New York (2012), 3.

[1676] *Inferno*, 631, *Air Masters*, 472, *Savage*, 5-6.

[1677] *Savage*, 6.

Between June 1941 and November 1942, some 5,150,000 Soviets were captured and became German POWs. In German prisoner-of-war camps, the death rate for Red Army soldiers exceeded fifty-seven per cent during the course of the war. A total of more than 3,000,000 Soviets held as POWs died from either starvation or being shot.[1678]

Soldiers of the Third Reich captured 235,473 British and American troops. Of them, 9,348, or four percent, died in captivity. Japanese soldiers captured 95,134 British, Australian, American, Canadian and New Zealand troops, of whom 27,256, or 28.65 percent, died in captivity.[1679]

During World War II, Germany forced up to 10,000,000 foreign workers and POWs, including women and children, to staff one-quarter of the country's work force performing industrial and farm labor. The workers received little food, clothing or medical care and lived in unsanitary conditions.[1680]

When Germany invaded the Soviet Union in June 1941, about 4,000,000 Soviet citizens were being held by Stalin in the *gulag*. The Soviets sent an additional 2,500,000 Soviet citizens to the *gulag* during the remainder of World War II.[1681]

For years after World War II ended, the Soviet Union forced over 1,600,000 Japanese prisoners of war to continue to perform labor for the Communist government.[1682]

At the end of the war, the Soviets also seized Germans, Poles and other eastern Europeans for forced labor. Some 600,000 Germans who were taken by the Soviets as POWs or laborers as the war ended died in captivity.[1683]

HOSTAGE EXECUTIONS

It was German policy to take 100 hostages for each German who was killed by locals in a conquered land. During the war the Germans executed almost 30,000 French, 8,000 Poles and 2,000 Dutch under this policy.[1684]

After two Czechs assassinated a Gestapo officer in May 1942, the

---

[1678] *Bloodlands*, 181, 184, *Reich*, 952-53.
[1679] *Conspiracy*, 1234, *Air Masters*, 389.
[1680] *Guns*, 391, *Bloodlands*, 244, *Reich*, 946-50, *Air Masters*, 466.
[1681] *Bloodlands*, 403.
[1682] *Curse*, 172.
[1683] *Bloodlands*, 318.
[1684] *Reich*, 956-57.

Germans executed over 1,300 Czechs, sent some 3,000 Jews to be exterminated, and eradicated the Czech town of Lidice and about 200 of its inhabitants.[1685]

In June 1944, German troops surrounded the French town of Oradour-sur-Glane, near Limoges, and executed 642 inhabitants, allegedly because explosives were found in the village.[1686]

As Japan's fate in the Pacific worsened, about 6,000 Japanese soldiers surrendered to Australian troops in British North Borneo. During a 150 mile march to an internment camp, surviving native tribesmen whose villages the Japanese had destroyed the previous year, were allowed to attack the unarmed Japanese prisoners, killing all but a few hundred.[1687]

BIOLOGICAL AND CHEMICAL WARFARE AND MEDICAL EXPERIMENTS

In China, Japanese Unit 731, inappropriately named the Kwantung Army Epidemic Protection and Water Supply Unit, used biological warfare to spread cholera, dysentery, plague and typhus germs by air and other means. The Japanese infected women in laboratories with syphilis, injected lethal viruses in civilians, and exploded anthrax near Chinese citizens who were tied to stakes. Japan planned to use biological warfare against Americans in the Saipan battle, but the ship transporting fleas infected with plague was sunk.[1688]

The Germans conducted a variety of medical experiments on prisoners, including high-altitude tests until breathing stopped, freezing until death, lethal doses of typhus and jaundice, sterilization, poison bullets and bone grafting. They also killed men and women to collect their skeletons, and even made lamp shades out of prisoner skin.[1689]

After the war ended, the Allies discovered and had to dispose of 211,000 tons of German poison gas weapons.[1690]

GERMAN PLUNDER

[1685] *Reich*, 991-93.
[1686] *Reich*, 993-94.
[1687] *Conspiracy*, 1344.
[1688] *Inferno*, 415.
[1689] *Reich*, 979-91.
[1690] *Guns*, 634.

The Nazi policy was that anything found in an invaded nation that might be useful to Germany "must be taken out ... and brought to Germany." According to post-war estimates, Germany plundered from the nations it invaded property worth 26,000,000,000 dollars.[1691]

According to a German war decree, the property of all Jews and Poles in Poland was confiscated without compensation. Over 20,000,000 acres of Polish land was seized and turned over to German settlers.[1692]

The Germans confiscated from France more than 10,000 valuable paintings, including those by Rembrandt, Rubens, Hals, Vermeer, Goya and Gainsborough.[1693]

From Jews who were exterminated in gas chambers, the Germans took all of their gold and jewelry, which the Germans later sold or stored.[1694]

TROOP LEVELS

A total of 16,112,566 Americans donned military uniforms during World War II.[1695]

In 1939, the Marine Corps had some 27,000 troops, about 800 of whom were officers. By March 1945, there were almost 500,000 Marines in uniform, a majority of whom had been drafted.[1696]

Between September 1, 1939 and September 2, 1945, the number of sailors and marines in the United States Navy grew from 383,150 to 3,405,525.[1697]

During World War II, 325,000 men enlisted in the Seabees, the American Construction Battalion founded on March 5, 1942. The Seabees built landing strips, ports, storage tanks, hospitals and other structures, and they fought the enemy. Around 200 were killed in combat and more than 2,000 Seabees were awarded Purple Hearts.[1698]

The Indian Army, which fought with the British, had 2,500,000 men, 87,000 of whom died during World War II.[1699]

[1691] *Reich*, 943-44.
[1692] *Reich*, 944.
[1693] *Reich*, 945-46.
[1694] *Reich*, 973-74.
[1695] *Guns*, 641.
[1696] *Ghosts*, 87-90.
[1697] *Admirals*, 458.
[1698] *Engineers*, 329-32.
[1699] *Masters*, 518, *Inferno*, 420.

During the war, the Soviet Union mobilized more troops than Germany, Britain and Italy combined.[1700]

Almost 150,000 Poles fought with the Allies during the war.[1701]

SUBMARINE WARFARE

During World War II, American forces sank over 2,000 Japanese merchant ships totaling 8,000,000 tons of shipping. Almost sixty percent of those Japanese shipping losses came at the hands of American submarines.[1702]

Japanese submarines sank only 184 ships during World War II.[1703]

German U-boats sank 2,775 Allied merchant ships and 175 Allied warships during World War II.[1704]

The Allies sank 754 of the 863 German submarines that participated in World War II.[1705]

UNITED STATES WAR PRODUCTION AND ECONOMIC AID

Roosevelt pledged in 1941 that America would serve as the "great arsenal of democracy" and it did so. During 1943 alone, the United States produced 86,000 planes, 45,000 tanks, 98,000 bazookas, 18,000 vessels, 648,000 trucks, 6,000,000 rifles and 26,000 mortars. During the entire war, only 139 private cars were manufactured in the United States while more than 300,000 combat planes were built.[1706]

In 1944, Germany produced 40,000 planes. The United States manufactured 96,000 planes that year.[1707]

By 1945, America had built two-thirds of all ships afloat and was producing more than half of all manufactured goods worldwide.[1708]

By the end of World War II, the United States had supplied its allies with 37,000 tanks, 800,000 trucks, almost 2,000,000 rifles, and 43,000 planes.[1709]

[1700] *Masters*, 536.
[1701] *Inferno*, 631.
[1702] *Engineers*, 335, *Ghosts*, 118.
[1703] *Engineers*, 340.
[1704] *WW II Story*, 177.
[1705] *WW II Story*, 177.
[1706] *Battle*, 450, *Sword*, 420.
[1707] *Air Masters*, 238.
[1708] *Guns*, 633.
[1709] *Dawn*, 7.

Between 1939 and 1945, the annual budget of the United States increased from $9 billion to $100 billion.[1710]

World War II cost American taxpayers $296,000,000,000 — about $4 trillion in 2012 dollars.[1711]

American Lend-Lease aid to the United Kingdom during World War II had a total value of $27,000,000,000. Before the Lend-Lease Act became law, the United States had sold $6,000,000,000 in goods to Britain.[1712]

Between September 1, 1939 and September 2, 1945, the United States Navy expanded from 790 ships to 6,768.[1713]

Between December 7, 1941 and Japan's surrender, the Allies consumed almost 7,000,000,000 barrels of oil, more than eighty-five percent of which America produced.[1714]

[1710] *Inferno*, 225.
[1711] *Guns*, 633.
[1712] *Masters*, 468.
[1713] *Admirals*, 458.
[1714] *Air Masters*, 328.

Part 5

Reflections on World War II

AFTER each war the victors set the peace terms, punish the losers and write the historical record. As Germany and Japan can attest, World War II was no exception. War also spawns intended and unintended consequences worthy of note. Finally, events that occurred during this massive conflict trigger ethical questions that challenge and provoke us even seventy-five years later.

CRIMINAL PROSECUTIONS

Legal Theories

Motivated by the excesses of World War I, beginning in 1928 sixty-three nations (including Japan and Germany) signed the Pact of Paris which condemned war as an implement of national policy except when used in self-defense. Many jurists believed that the Pact of Paris authorized holding governmental leaders of combatant nations individually responsible for war crimes.[1715]

In addition to the Pact of Paris, Japan's World War II Instrument of Surrender specifically acknowledged that the Allied nations had the right to prosecute individual Japanese war leaders for violations of international criminal law.[1716]

France

Following France's 1940 surrender to Germany, Marshal Pétain collaborated with Hitler and served as the first Premier of Vichy France. In 1945, a French jury convicted Pétain of treason to the Republic of France. He was sentenced to death, but because of his record of brave service in World War I, the sentence was commuted to imprisonment for life. He died in prison in 1951.[1717]

Pierre Laval, who served as the second Premier of Vichy France, was also convicted of treason by the French after the war. He was ex-

---

[1715] *Conspiracy*, xiii.
[1716] *Conspiracy*, xiii-iv.
[1717] *WW II Story*, 35.

ecuted.[1718]

Germany

When Allied forces advanced through Germany in early 1945, they captured many of Germany's most important government documents, which were therefore available later for use in war crimes trials.[1719]

On August 8, 1945, the Allies established the Nuremburg Military Tribunal in Nuremburg, Germany to try European war criminals.[1720]

From 1945 to 1948, United States military tribunals also tried 1,672 Germans who had acted during World War II as military officers, politicians, diplomats, industrialists, physicians and jurists.[1721]

Following trials in 1945-46 at the Nuremburg Military Tribunal, twenty-four senior Nazi defendants were convicted of war crimes. Ten of those criminals were executed by hanging.[1722]

Herman Göring survived the war, but was convicted of war crimes and sentenced to die by hanging on October 16, 1946. Two hours before his turn at the gallows, Göring committed suicide by taking potassium cyanide that had been smuggled into his cell.[1723]

The unrepentant Alfred Rosenberg, who headed the Nazi art looting organization and served as Hitler's main racial theorist, was convicted of war crimes and then hanged on October 16, 1946.[1724]

Ernst Kaltenbrunner, who led the Gestapo, was convicted of mass murders of civilians, establishing concentration camps, executing people based upon race, and other crimes, and was executed by hanging on October 16, 1946.[1725]

Other Germans who were convicted and sentenced to death included Ribbentrop, Keitel, Frank, Frick, Streicher, Seyss-Inquart, Sauckel and Jodl.[1726]

Albert Speer, who was Hitler's friend and personal architect, expressed remorse for his World War II actions. He was convicted of war crimes and crimes against humanity and sentenced to (and served)

[1718] *Reich*, 924.
[1719] *Conspiracy*, xli.
[1720] *Curse*, 178.
[1721] *Guns*, 635.
[1722] *Guns*, 635, *Reich*, 1143.
[1723] *Reich*, 1143, *Monuments Men*, 403.
[1724] *Monuments Men*, 42, 403, *Reich*, 1143.
[1725] *Monuments Men*, 403, *Reich*, 1143.
[1726] *Reich*, 1143.

twenty years in prison.[1727]

August Eigruber was convicted of war crimes committed at the Mauthausen concentration camp, including killing POWs. Just before he was hanged on May 28, 1947, he yelled out *Heil Hitler*.[1728]

Forty-three German soldiers convicted of killing dozens of American troops and Belgian citizens near Malmédy during the Battle of the Bulge were sentenced to death. Because of prosecutorial misdeeds, all of these death sentences were commuted.[1729]

Japan

More than two weeks elapsed between Japan's announced surrender on August 14, 1945 and the formal signing of surrender documents. During that time, the Japanese destroyed many important incriminating government documents and changed the names of numerous military personnel in an effort to thwart war crimes prosecutions.[1730]

After Japan's surrender, the War Crimes Office of the U.S. War Department prepared a list of twenty-five suspected senior Japanese war criminals. Evidence was gathered from many sources, including interviews of liberated American POWs about war crimes they had experienced. The first name on the resulting list of war criminals was that of General Hideki Tojo, Japan's war minister and prime minister for much of the war.[1731]

During discussions Tojo held with senior Japanese government officials before the formal Japanese surrender documents were signed, he agreed to accept responsibility for Japan's war actions in an effort to spare the Emperor from accountability.[1732]

On September 11, military policemen came to Tojo's Tokyo home to arrest him. He attempted suicide by shooting himself, but the bullet missed his heart. Tojo survived with the help of plasma from American soldiers.[1733]

On September 27, 1945, Emperor Hirohito visited General MacArthur at the American Embassy and offered to accept full responsibility for Japan's war conduct. MacArthur took this statement as an act of great courage and invited the Emperor to help him identify Jap-

---

[1727] *Monuments Men*, 403-04, *Reich*, 1143.

[1728] *Monuments Men*, 404.

[1729] *Guns*, 635.

[1730] *Conspiracy*, xli, 158-59.

[1731] *Tears*, 334, 343, *Conspiracy*, 181-83.

[1732] *Conspiracy*, 182.

[1733] *Conspiracy*, 182-83.

anese leaders who had given the Emperor sinister advice.[1734]

In late 1945, a military tribunal in Manila tried both General Ya-mashita, who commanded Japanese forces in the Philippines from 1944 until the war ended, and General Homma, who commanded the Japanese forces that had invaded the Philippines in 1941 and carried out the Bataan Death March. After unsuccessful appeals to the United States Supreme Court and to General MacArthur (to whom their wartime efforts had caused much embarrassment), Yamashita was hanged on February 23, 1946 and Homma was executed by firing squad on April 3, 1946.[1735]

Early in 1946, the International Military Tribunal for the Far East was set up in Tokyo to try other major Japanese war criminals. After a trial lasting two and one-half years, the Tribunal convicted twenty-five leaders of Japan (but not the Emperor) of war crimes committed by their subordinates. Seven were sentenced to death and eighteen to imprisonment.[1736]

In December 1948, the seven Japanese who were convicted of war crimes and sentenced to death (including Tojo and Admiral Shimada, head of the navy) were hanged.[1737]

General MacArthur, Washington representatives and the American war crimes prosecutor all took the position, despite the contrary view of other Allies, that there should be no prosecution of Emperor Hirohito. Disregarding many facts to the contrary, MacArthur insisted that there was no specific evidence of Hirohito's guilt and noted that Japan's surrender had been based on the understanding that the Emperor's position would be preserved.[1738]

Truman, Churchill, Atlee and Stalin concurred in the Allies' decision to grant Emperor Hirohito immunity from prosecution for war crimes during World War II, at least in part because Hirohito had called upon Japan to surrender in the face of opposition from some Japanese military leaders.[1739]

The Soviet Union

The Soviet Union tried some 55,000 Germans and Austrians for

[1734] *Conspiracy*, 192-93.
[1735] *Conspiracy*, 1343-55.
[1736] *Tears*, 353, *Conspiracy*, ix, 219, 237, 1355-60.
[1737] *Tears*, 343-385, *Conspiracy*, xi, 3, 184, 237, 1360-61.
[1738] *Conspiracy*, 218-234.
[1739] *Conspiracy*, xv.

war crimes and convicted 25,921.[1740]

Between 1946 and 1947, the Soviet Union sentenced almost 150,000 Red Army veterans to the *gulag* for having collaborated with the Germans.[1741]

Stalin died on March 5, 1953, without any criminal charges having been brought against him.[1742]

Norway

Quisling, the puppet Norwegian Prime Minister that Germany installed after its 1940 invasion, was convicted of treason in Norway and executed on October 24, 1945.[1743]

Belgium

While King Leopold III was not criminally prosecuted for his un-constitutional surrender to the Germans in May 1940, he remained in exile in Switzerland until July 1950. When he was finally recalled, there was so much citizen hostility toward him that he was forced to abdicate the throne in favor of his son.[1744]

Prosecution Totals

Overall, the Western Allies arrested some 200,000 suspected criminals following the war and charged more than 5,000 with significant war crimes.[1745]

Of about 5,000 Japanese who were arrested for acts of brutality, some 4,000 went to trial. Of those, about 800 were acquitted, 809 were put to death and some 2,400 were imprisoned for three or more years.[1746]

INTENDED AND UNINTENDED CONSEQUENCES

In Post-war Europe

Upon conclusion of the European conflict, control of defeated Germany was divided among four countries — the United States, Britain, France and the Soviet Union. (The City of Berlin, which lay en-

---

[1740] *Curse*, 178.
[1741] *Bloodlands*, 328.
[1742] *Bloodlands*, 368, *Ike*, 668, *Curse*, 378.
[1743] *Reich*, 709.
[1744] *Reich*, 730.
[1745] *Guns*, 635.
[1746] *Conspiracy*, 1345.

tirely within the Soviet section, was also divided into segments for purposes of control). In 1949, the portions initially under the control of the three western nations were consolidated and became the Federal Republic of Germany. Stalin rejected the reunification of all of Germany. The remaining portion in the east, ironically named the German Democratic Republic, remained controlled by Communists and the Soviet Union until 1990, when the reunification of a democratic Germany finally took place.[1747]

General Eisenhower was given command of the American occupation forces in post-war Germany. He assigned General Patton, as head of the Third Army, responsibility for the occupation of Bavaria. On September 22, 1945, Patton made comments to the press that seemed to equate Democrats and Republicans in America with Nazis. Faced with a public storm, Eisenhower felt compelled to relieve Patton of his duties as Third Army head and transferred him to the Fifteenth Army, which had no combat troops. This ended the decades-long friendship between Patton and Ike.[1748]

Following the German surrender in 1945, the 1938 merger of Austria into Germany was reversed and Austria once again became an independent nation.[1749]

Even though Poland was technically victorious in World War II, some forty-seven per cent of its prewar territory to the east was, at Stalin's urging and with the approvals of Churchill and Roosevelt, taken by the Soviet Union. Stalin then expelled over 1,500,000 Poles from the seized land.[1750]

Some of the land in the newly-configured Poland was taken from eastern Germany. Following the war's end, the Communist Polish government decided to "cleanse" the new Poland of Germans. In less than three years, about 7,600,000 Germans were forced to leave Poland and some 400,000 died.[1751]

In the end, Poland escaped Nazi tyranny only to fall prey to that of the Communist Soviet regime.[1752]

After the war ended, the Sudetenland was returned to Czechoslovakia and approximately 3,000,000 Germans living there were ex-

---

[1747] *Crusade*, 431, *Iron Curtain*, 66, 252.

[1748] *Ike*, 594-96, *Patton*, 287-88.

[1749] *Clark*, 249.

[1750] *Bloodlands*, 326-27, *Iron Curtain*, xxxii.

[1751] *Bloodlands*, 320-24, 331.

[1752] *Inferno*, 631.

pelled.[1753]

Despite his courageous leadership of Great Britain throughout most of World War II, in late July 1945, British voters elected a new government and ousted Winston Churchill as prime minister in favor of Clement Atlee, the leader of the Labour party.[1754]

Following Germany's defeat, Stalin took the position that the Soviet Union had been a victim of Germany and that ethnic Russians had suffered more deaths than anyone else in World War II. But this propaganda ignored Stalin's August 1939 alliance with Germany that encouraged Hitler's war-making and facilitated the Soviet Union's invasion and seizing that year of parts of Poland, Belarus and the Baltic states. Stalin's theory also ignored the fact that most of the people killed in Soviet territory after 1939 were not Russians, but Jews, Poles, Ukrainians and other natives of those seized lands.[1755]

While the fact that the Soviets spilled the most blood in World War II saved many Western Allied lives, the unanticipated price was that shortly thereafter some 90,000,000 eastern Europeans fell under Moscow's brutal control.[1756]

On March 5, 1946, Churchill, in a speech delivered in the United States, characterized the Soviet domination of Eastern Europe as taking place behind an "iron curtain." He was referring to the eight Eastern European nations over which the Soviet Union had taken control and imposed its Communist doctrine: Poland, Hungary, Czechoslovakia, eastern Germany, Romania, Bulgaria, Albania and Yugoslavia.[1757]

Stalin, confident that Communist candidates would prevail, had at Yalta promised to allow democratic elections in post-war Eastern Europe. However, when Communist candidates lost early elections in Germany, Austria and Hungary, the Soviets promptly made free and democratic elections a thing of the past.[1758]

Many Jews and others who had been held in concentration camps during the war had, for fear of further persecution, no desire to return to lands from which they had come. Others whose native country had been seized, including Estonians, Lithuanians, Latvians, Poles, Ukrainians, Romanians and Yugoslavs, also preferred to live in Western Eu-

---

[1753] *Bloodlands*, 314, 331.
[1754] *Conspiracy*, 117, *Crusade*, 446.
[1755] *Bloodlands*, 344-45.
[1756] *Inferno*, 631, 638.
[1757] *Curse*, 275, *Iron Curtain*, xix, xxiv.
[1758] *Iron Curtain*, xxxi, 255, *Bloodlands*, 321.

rope. The Western Allies adopted programs to deal with the concerns of these "displaced persons." When word spread that accommodations might be available, more people fled west from portions of Eastern Europe under Soviet control.[1759]

After the war ended, Stalin ordered the deportation to the *gulag* of about 200,000 Ukrainians, Lithuanians, Latvians and Estonians who had been living in territory seized by the Soviet Union.[1760]

By 1947, Stalin's claim for reparations due from Germany had reached the fanciful number of $128 billion. The Soviets simply took whatever they wanted from those in the territory they controlled. No compensation was paid. They dismantled more than 4,500 German factories and shipped them back to the Soviet Union. Often, the German workers at those factories were also taken against their will to the Soviet Union and required to perform forced labor there. Estimates are that from a third to a half of eastern Germany's industrial assets were removed between 1945 and 1947.[1761]

Stalin also made Hungary, Romania and Finland, as former German allies, pay reparations in oil, food, ships and equipment. The Soviets, under the specious theory that the property in Poland was once under German control, seized factories and other equipment from there, too.[1762]

Britain's post-war economy was so weak that its citizens were still on wartime rations in 1947. As a consequence, early that year Britain announced that it would end its aid to Greece and Turkey, increasing the risk that those notions would fall to Communism.[1763]

In a March 12, 1947 speech, President Truman reacted by noting that, in violation of the Yalta agreements, many Eastern European countries had recently "had totalitarian regimes forced upon them." He announced a United States policy that came to be called the Truman Doctrine: "to support free peoples who are resisting attempted subjugation by armed minorities or by outside pressures" through "economic and financial aid essential to economic stability and orderly political processes."[1764]

In June 1947, Secretary of State George Marshall, concerned about

---

[1759] *Crusade*, 439-41.
[1760] *Bloodlands*, 328-29.
[1761] *Curse*, 290, *Guns*, 516, *Iron Curtain*, 33-35.
[1762] *Iron Curtain*, 37-38.
[1763] *Curse*, 275.
[1764] *Curse*, 276-77, *Iron Curtain*, 219.

"hunger, poverty, desperation and chaos" in post-war Europe, said that if Europeans could develop an international, cooperative plan for recovery, the United States would be willing to provide economic support. His plan was open to participation by the Soviet Union and countries in Eastern Europe. Worried that participation would weaken the cause of Communism and require disclosure of unflattering Soviet economic data, Stalin rejected his nation's participation in the Marshall Plan, thereby spawning the Cold War.[1765]

Fourteen European countries agreed in 1947 to participate in the Marshall Plan, which the Secretary of State estimated would cost Americans between $15,100,000,000 and $17,800,000,000. On April 1, 1948, President Truman signed legislation funding the plan.[1766]

In response to the Truman Doctrine, Stalin established the Communist Information Bureau in 1947. Its purpose was to unify all significant Communist parties under Soviet control and to counter "the policy of the USA and Britain, aimed at strengthening imperialism."[1767]

In 1948, the United States began delivery of the first $4,000,000,000 in Marshall Plan aid to Western European countries. This helped resuscitate battered economies there. As the recipient nations fared better than those suffering under Soviet control, Stalin's prestige suffered.[1768]

In mid-1948, seeking to force the Western Allies out of Berlin, Stalin decided to set up a blockade there. Soviet occupation authorities refused to furnish electricity and blocked all Allied land routes to the city. For almost a year thereafter, the United States and Britain supplied the 2,000,000 people of Berlin by plane. Stalin then reluctantly relented. The Berlin Airlift further damaged Stalin's prestige and brought the Cold War into the open.[1769]

Another blow to Stalin's prestige came when Joseph Tito, the strong-willed and independent Communist leader of Yugoslavia, withdrew his country from the Soviet bloc in June 1948.[1770]

Initially, Stalin supported the 1948 establishment of the State of Israel, believing that it would become a socialist nation allied with the Soviet Union. But as Israel's ties to the United States grew, Stalin worried that Soviet Jews might divide their loyalties between Israel and the

---

[1765] *Curse*, 302-06, *Iron Curtain*, 219.
[1766] *Curse*, 306-07.
[1767] *Iron Curtain*, 220.
[1768] *Iron Curtain*, 253.
[1769] *Curse*, 323-26.
[1770] *Iron Curtain*, 254.

Soviet Union. Thus, beginning in the late 1940s, he expelled Jews from power positions in the Soviet Union.[1771]

In 1945, the Soviets took control of the German rocket-making facilities at Peenemünde, Germany and transported equipment and captured scientists back to the Soviet Union where they were used to develop missiles for Stalin, including the October 4, 1957 launch of "Sputnik."[1772]

In September 1949, the Soviet Union announced that it had successfully tested its first atomic bomb.[1773]

By 1949, the United States, Canada, Britain, France, Belgium, Luxembourg, the Netherlands, Portugal, Italy, Norway, Denmark and Iceland had ratified the North Atlantic Treaty and created NATO, through which the United States committed to defend those nations from Soviet aggression.[1774]

As the 1950s arrived, Stalin was no longer the all-powerful dictator of the Soviet Union. The Politburo once again played a meaningful role and Stalin made few public appearances. He died on March 5, 1953.[1775]

On June 17, 1953, hundreds of thousands of citizens of East Berlin engaged in strikes and protests against Stalinism. Their opposition was overcome only when the Communist government, backed by the Soviets, declared martial law.[1776]

In October 1956, Hungarian citizens revolted against the oppression of Communism. The Red Army quickly invaded Hungary and viciously struck down the uprising.[1777]

In 1961, Communists built a physical barrier — the Berlin Wall — in an effort to stem the flood of people fleeing west to escape the totalitarian regime in East Germany.[1778]

In 1989, protesters in East Germany tore down the Berlin Wall. During the twenty-eight years of its existence, tens of thousands of East Germans had been arrested trying to pass over the wall and hundreds of others had been shot seeking freedom.[1779]

[1771] *Bloodlands*, 345-51, *Curse*, 347-51.
[1772] *Ike*, 678-79, 699-700.
[1773] *Ike*, 617, *Curse*, 342.
[1774] *Curse*, 326, 344, *Iron Curtain*, 252.
[1775] *Bloodlands*, 368-69, *Curse*, 378.
[1776] *Curse*, 363.
[1777] *Curse*, 363.
[1778] *Iron Curtain*, xxv, *Curse*, 364.
[1779] *Iron Curtain*, xxxii, *Curse*, 364.

Faced with sustained resistance from the people living in its satellite countries, in 1991 the Soviet Union felt compelled to yield direct control over the Eastern European satellites and reverted to being the nation of Russia.[1780]

At no time between the Russian Revolution and 1989 had the Communist Soviet economy, regardless of how many of its people were sacrificed to promote it, matched capitalist western European prosperity levels. Indeed, even the economies of the defeated nations, Japan and Germany, fared better. In 1913, Japan was less prosperous than Russia. By 1989, Japan's per capita GDP was 2.5 times that of the Soviet Union. Post-war Western Europe (including Germany) was even further ahead of the Soviet Union economically.[1781]

In Post-War Asia

As Japan's defeat neared and its dream of a Far East rid of western colonialism faded, Japan turned many of its weapons over to native anti-colonialists in Southeast Asian countries. These weapons were later used to impede the British, French and Dutch post-war efforts to reestablish their spheres of influence in places like Viet Nam, Malaya and Indonesia. Ironically, the Asian war that Japan started led to the end of European colonialism in the Far East, but also the subjugation of Japan to Allied dictates.[1782]

General MacArthur, as Supreme Commander Allied Forces, served as the sole ruler of Japan for more than five years following its surrender, and throughout his term was quite popular with Japanese citizens.[1783]

After its surrender, Japan (with American encouragement) continued to use its Purple diplomatic code (which was beneficial to General MacArthur in carrying out his post-surrender duties) until November 1945 when a member of Congress revealed that the United States had broken the code. The Japanese were livid.[1784]

Among the reforms made to Japan's governance following its surrender were affording women the right to vote, demobilizing the army and navy, and dissolving the Japanese General Staff. In addition, the Emperor issued a statement on January 1, 1946, announcing that it was

---

[1780] *Bloodlands*, 371, *Curse*, 388.
[1781] *Curse*, 389.
[1782] *Conspiracy*, 1341-42, *Sword*, 74.
[1783] *Conspiracy*, 167, 188, *Ike*, 606.
[1784] *Judgment*, 223, 225, 248.

false to believe that "the Emperor is divine and that Japanese people are superior to other races and fated to rule the world."[1785]

On April 10, 1946, under pressure from the United States, Japanese voters approved a new national constitution, the language of which had been negotiated between MacArthur and Hirohito. Japan forever renounced war.[1786]

When the war ended, the Korean peninsula was divided at the 38th parallel. The United States helped set up an anti-Communist government in South Korea. In 1948, the Soviet Union set up a Communist government in North Korea, headed by Kim Il Sung, lighting a time bomb that exploded two years later as the Korean Conflict.[1787]

In October 1, 1949, the Chinese Communists under Mao Tse-tung won the long-fought Chinese civil war and established the Peoples Republic of China, thereby placing one fourth of the world's population under a Communist regime. Chiang Kai-shek and his Nationalists retreated to the island of Taiwan. The Japanese invasion of China in 1937 had ultimately and ironically benefitted the Chinese Communists.[1788]

With encouragement from Stalin, North Korea invaded South Korea on June 25, 1950. MacArthur served as commander of the American forces resisting the North Koreans and their ally, the Chinese. But in April 1951, after MacArthur advocated the use of atomic weapons in the Korean conflict and was insubordinate, President Truman fired him. On July 27, 1953, an armistice was signed that kept Korea divided at the 38th parallel.[1789]

The American occupation of Japan ended in 1952. Before then, the Emperor was forced to give most of his wealth, some $200-300 million, back to the Japanese people and his relatives were relegated to commoner status.[1790]

In May 1954, the French were defeated in their efforts to maintain Viet Nam as a colony.[1791]

By 1968, Japan had risen from total defeat to have a capitalist economy that was third strongest in the world. In June of that year,

---

[1785] *Conspiracy*, 196-97, 210-13.
[1786] *Conspiracy*, 213-18.
[1787] *Curse*, 170, 330, *Bloodlands*, 361.
[1788] *Curse*, 331, *Burma*, 452, *Bloodlands*, 360.
[1789] *Ike*, 622-24, 629-30, *Curse*, 332-42.
[1790] *Conspiracy*, 1369-71.
[1791] *Ike*, 682.

the United States returned control of Iwo Jima to the Japanese.[1792]

In the United States

In October 1945, General George Marshall retired as United States Army Chief of Staff, and was succeeded on December 3 by General Eisenhower, who reluctantly agreed to serve for two years until his Army retirement in 1947.[1793]

Shortly thereafter, President Truman appointed George Marshall to serve as Secretary of State. In that role, Marshall visited China and concluded that Chiang Kai-shek was corrupt and a poor leader. The United States ended aid to the Nationalist Chinese.[1794]

A Congressional committee investigated why the American military had been surprised by the attack on Pearl Harbor. The report of Congress, issued in July 1946, criticized the practice of the Army and Navy of maintaining separate intelligence agencies that did not always communicate fully with each other, and recommended that a unified intelligence agency be established. President Truman subsequently established the National Security Agency.[1795]

On September 17, 1947, the United States Air Force became an independent branch of America's military, having previously been a part of the Army.[1796]

Following the war, President Truman and the Army favored transferring Navy and Marine Corps airpower to a newly-created Air Force and limiting the size of the Marines to a just one regiment. The Marines opposed these efforts, citing their sacrifices and successes at Iwo Jima. Congress and the public supported the Marines, and the National Security Act of 1947 preserved the role of the Marines.[1797]

In 1948, Americans elected Harry Truman to serve a full term as President of the United States.[1798]

Eisenhower served as president of Columbia University from 1948 until January 1951, when, at President Truman's request, he returned to Europe to command all North Atlantic Treaty Organization

---

[1792] *Conspiracy*, 237-38, 1364, *Ghosts*, 194.

[1793] *Ike*, 600-01, 604.

[1794] *Burma*, 452, *Judgment*, 252, *Bloodlands*, 360.

[1795] *Judgment*, 291-93.

[1796] *Air Masters*, 519.

[1797] *Ghosts*, 157-88.

[1798] *Ike*, 615.

forces.[1799]

In January 1953, Eisenhower succeeded Truman as President of the United States. Ike was reelected in 1956 and served until 1961. Eisenhower died on March 28, 1969.[1800]

ETHICAL QUESTIONS

Rules of War

Are there any true and binding rules of war (establishing permissible and impermissible conduct) that govern all combatants?

If so, where do the rules come from? A deity? Treaties? Widely accepted ethical standards? The dictates of victors?

Who is bound by the rules of war? Nations? Religious groups? Insurgents? Individual leaders of such groups? Middle level administrators? Average soldiers and sailors? Even those who face death threats from superiors for not carrying out orders that violate rules of war?

How are violations of rules of war to be determined and punished? By the victors? By an international tribunal?

Civilian Deaths

In war, is it appropriate for a combatant, in pursuit of victory, to deliberately target an opponent's civilians?

If so, in what circumstances?

If not, is there any conduct that enemy civilians or their leader might engage in that would justify the civilians being targeted by an opposing combatant?

To satisfy its duty of providing security for its people, must a war combatant always include in its strategy the killing of enemy civilians if that strategy offers hope of a shortened contest?

Weapons

Are there some weapons that, because if their destructiveness, are never appropriate for use in war?

If so, what are they? Disease? Poison gas? Nuclear devices? Fire-bombing population centers? Surprise attacks? Starvation?

Concentration Camps

Would it be appropriate for a combatant to attempt to destroy

---

[1799] *Ike*, 612-16.
[1800] *Ike*, 615, 637-694, 723.

enemy concentration camps even if in the process substantial numbers of prisoners are killed?

Art and Antiquities

In carrying out its duty to protect its people, what responsibility does a combatant have to protect and preserve artworks and ancient treasures?

Is any duty to avoid destruction of art and antiquities affected by the fact that all or most of the pieces in question were created by or owned by the people who started the war?

Prisoners of War

Are there minimum standards for the ethical treatment of war prisoners, *e.g.*, survival, food, health care, security, punishment?

Slave Labor

Is it ever appropriate for a combatant during wartime to force captured civilians or military personnel to perform slave labor?

If so, under what circumstances would such slave labor be suitable?

If so, are there any minimum standards of treatment that must be applied to the slave laborers, *e.g.*, minimum number of calories per day, minimum health care, reasonable rules for punishment?

Invaded Territory

Does an invading combatant owe civilians in captured territory at least a subsistence amount of food, housing, security and health care?

The Conduct of Victors

Once war has ended are there any limits on what a prevailing combatant can do to the defeated combatant and its citizens? Punish its leaders? Install a new type of government? Ethnic cleansing? Strip the country of its resources? Reconfigure boundaries? Nationalize private property? Restrict egress? Nationalize artworks?

Sources

BOOKS

Ambrose, Stephen E., *The Supreme Commander*, Doubleday, Garden City, N.Y., 1970

Applebaum, Anne, *Iron Curtain: The Crushing of Eastern Europe 1944-1956*, Doubleday, New York, 2012

Atkinson, Rick, *An Army at Dawn: The War in North Africa, 1942-1943*, Henry Holt and Company, New York, 2002

Atkinson, Rick, *The Day of Battle: The War in Sicily and Italy*, 1943-1944, Henry Holt and Company, New York, 2007

Atkinson, Rick, *The Guns at Last Light: The War in Western Europe, 1944-1945*, Henry Holt and Company, New York, 2013

Bergamini, David, *Japan's Imperial Conspiracy: How Emperor Hirohito led Japan into War against the West*, William Morrow and Company, Inc., New York, 1971

Blumenson, Martin, *Mark Clark: The Last of the Great World War II Commanders*, Congdon & Weed, Inc., New York, 1984

Blumenson, Martin, *Patton: The Man Behind the Legend*, 1885-1945, William Morrow and Company, Inc., New York, 1985

Blumenson, Martin, *The Duel for France: 1944*, Da Capo Press, 1963

Borneman, Walter R., *The Admirals,* Little, Brown and Company, New York, 2012.

Bradley, Omar N., *A Soldier's Story*, Henry Holt and Company, Inc., New York, 1951

Burrell, Robert S., *The Ghosts of Iwo Jima*, Texas A&M University Press, College Station, 2006

Carley, Michael Jabara, *1939: The Alliance that Never Was and the Coming of World War II*, Ivan R. Dee, Chicago, 1999

Chalfont, Alun, *Montgomery of Alamein*, Atheneum, New York, 1976

Clausen, Henry C. and Bruce Lee, *Pearl Harbor: Final Judgment,* Crown Publishers, Inc., New York, 1992

Cole, Hugh, *The Ardennes: The Battle of the Bulge*, Konecky & Konecky, Old Sayrebrook, CT.

Edsel, Robert M., *The Monuments Men: Allied Heroes, Nazi Thieves, and the Greatest Treasure Hunt in History*, Center Street, New York, 2009

Eisenhower, Dwight D., *Crusade in Europe*, Doubleday & Company, Inc., Garden City, N.Y., 1948

Fromkin, David, *A Peace to End All Peace*, Henry Holt and Company, LLC,

New York, 1989

Gellately, Robert, *Stalin's Curse: Battling for Communism in War and Cold War*, Alfred A. Knopf, New York, 2013

Hastings, Max, *Inferno: The World at War, 1939-1945*, Alfred A. Knopf, New York, 2011

Hornfischer, James D., *Neptune's Inferno*, Bantom Books, New York, 2011

Irving, David, *The War Between the Generals: Inside the Allied High Command*, Congdon & Lattés, Inc., New York, 1981

Keith, Phil, *Stay the Rising Sun: The True Story of USS Lexington, Her Valiant Crew, and Changing the Course of World War II*, Zenith Press, Minneapolis, 2015

Kennedy, Paul, *Engineers of Victory: The Problem Solvers Who Turned the Tide in the Second World War*, Random House, New York, 2013

Kershaw, Ian, *Fateful Choices: Ten Decisions that Changed the World, 1940-1941*, Penguin Group (USA), Inc., New York, 2007

Korda, Michael, *IKE: An American Hero*, Harper Perennial, New York, 2008

Lowe, Keith, *Savage Continent: Europe in the Aftermath of World War II*, Keith Lowe, St. Martin's Press, New York, 2012

MacDonogh, Giles, *1938: Hitler's Gamble*, Basic Books, New York, 2009

McLynn, Frank, *The Burma Campaign: Disaster Into Triumph 1942-45*, Yale University Press, 2011

Miller, Donald L., *The Story of World War II*, Simon & Schuster, New York, 2001

Miller, Donald L., *Masters of the Air: America's Bomber Boys who Fought the Air War Against Nazi Germany*, Simon & Schuster, New York, 2006

Norman, Michael and Norman, Elizabeth M., *Tears in the Darkness: The Story of the Bataan Death March and its Aftermath*, Farrar, Strouse and Giroux, New York, 2009

Parshall, Jonathan and Tully, Anthony, *Shattered Sword: The Untold Story of the Battle of Midway*, Potomac Books, Washington, D.C., 2005

Pleshakov, Constantine, *Stalin's Folly*, Houghton Mifflin Company, New York, 2005

Prange, Gordon W., *At Dawn We Slept: The Untold Story of Pearl Harbor*, Penguin Books USA Inc., New York, 1982

Roberts, Andrew, *Masters and Commanders: How Four Titans Won the War in the West, 1941-1945*, Harper Collins Publishers, New York, 2009

Rosbottom, Ronald C., *When Paris Went Dark: The City of Light Under German Occupation, 1940-1944*, Little, Brown and Company, New York, 2014.

Shirer, William l., *The Rise and Fall of the Third Reich*, Simon and Schuster, New York, 1960

Snyder, Timothy, *Bloodlands: Europe between Hitler and Stalin*, Basic Books, New York, 2010

Spector, Ronald, *Eagle Against the Sun: The American War with Japan*, Vintage Books, New York, 1985

Toll, Ian W., *Pacific Crucible: War at Sea in the Pacific, 1941-1942*, W.W. Norton & Company, New York, 2012

Winik, Jay, *1944: FDR and the Year That Changed History*, Simon and Schuster, New York, 2015

Winterbotham, F. W., *The Ultra Secret*, Harper & Row, New York, 1974

Wright, Derrick, *Pacific Victory: Tarawa to Okinawa 1943-1945*, Sutton Publishing Limited, Gloucestershire, 2005

ARTICLES

Haskew, Michael E., *A Physician Predicted Roosevelt's Death in Office*, WWII History, Vol. 13, Number 3, Sovereign Media, McLean, Va., April 2014

A Concise History of the Second World War

Printed in Great Britain
by Amazon